Houghton
Mifflin
Harcourt

Algebra 2
Volume 1

TIMOTHY D. KANOLD

EDWARD B. BURGER

JULI K. DIXON

MATTHEW R. LARSON

STEVEN J. LEINWAND

© Houghton Mifflin Harcourt Publishing Company • Cover/TitlePage (Arches, Moab, UT) holbox/
Shutterstock; (Space Needle, WA) Bruntsch/Shutterstock; (Downtown, Chattanooga, TN) Sean Pavone/
Shutterstock.

Authors

Timothy D. Kanold, Ph.D., is an award-winning international educator, author, and consultant. He is a former superintendent and director of mathematics and science at Adlai E. Stevenson High School District 125 in Lincolnshire, Illinois. He is a past president of the National Council of Supervisors of Mathematics (NCSM) and the Council for the Presidential Awardees of Mathematics (CPAM). He  has served on several writing and leadership commissions for NCTM during the past decade. He presents motivational professional development seminars with a focus on developing professional learning communities (PLC's) to improve the teaching, assessing, and learning of students. He has recently authored nationally recognized articles, books, and textbooks for mathematics education and school leadership, including *What Every Principal Needs to Know about the Teaching and Learning of Mathematics*.

Edward B. Burger, Ph.D., is the President of Southwestern University, a former Francis Christopher Oakley Third Century Professor of Mathematics at Williams College, and a former vice provost at Baylor University. He has authored or coauthored more than sixty-five articles, books, and video series; delivered over five hundred addresses and workshops throughout the world; and made more than fifty radio and  television appearances. He is a Fellow of the American Mathematical Society as well as having earned many national honors, including the Robert Foster Cherry Award for Great Teaching in 2010. In 2012, Microsoft Education named him a "Global Hero in Education."

Juli K. Dixon, Ph.D., is a Professor of Mathematics Education at the University of Central Florida. She has taught mathematics in urban schools at the elementary, middle, secondary, and post-secondary levels. She is an active researcher and speaker with numerous publications and conference presentations. Key areas of focus are deepening teachers' content knowledge and communicating and justifying  mathematical ideas. She is a past chair of the NCTM Student Explorations in Mathematics Editorial Panel and member of the Board of Directors for the Association of Mathematics Teacher Educators.

Matthew R. Larson, Ph.D., is the K-12 mathematics curriculum specialist for the Lincoln Public Schools and served on the Board of Directors for the National Council of Teachers of Mathematics from 2010 to 2013. He is a past chair of NCTM's Research Committee and was a member of NCTM's Task Force on Linking Research and Practice. He is the author of several books on implementing the Common Core  Standards for Mathematics. He has taught mathematics at the secondary and college levels and held an appointment as an honorary visiting associate professor at Teachers College, Columbia University.

Steven J. Leinwand is a Principal Research Analyst at the American Institutes for Research (AIR) in Washington, D.C., and has over 30 years in leadership positions in mathematics education. He is past president of the National Council of Supervisors of Mathematics and served on the NCTM Board of Directors. He is the author of numerous articles, books, and textbooks  and has made countless presentations with topics including student achievement, reasoning, effective assessment, and successful implementation of standards.

Performance Task Consultant

Robert Kaplinsky
Teacher Specialist, Mathematics
Downey Unified School District
Downey, California

STEM Consultants
Science, Technology, Engineering, and Mathematics

Michael A. DiSpezio
Global Educator
North Falmouth, Massachusetts

Michael R. Heithaus
Executive Director, School of Environment, Arts, and Society
Professor, Department of Biological Sciences
Florida International University
North Miami, Florida

Reviewers

Mindy Eden
Richwoods High School
Peoria School District
Peoria, IL

Dustin Johnson
Badger High School Math Teacher
Department Chair
Lake Geneva-Genoa City Union High
School District
Lake Geneva, WI

Ashley D. McSwain
Murray High School
Murray City School District
Salt Lake City, UT

Rebecca Quinn
Doherty Memorial High School
Worcester Public Schools District
Worcester, MA

Ted Ryan
Madison LaFollette High School
Madison Metropolitan School District
Madison, WI

Tony Scoles
Fort Zumwalt School District
O'Fallon, MO

Cynthia L. Smith
Higley Unified School District
Gilbert, AZ

Phillip E. Spellane
Doherty Memorial High School
Worcester Public Schools District
Worcester, MA

Mona Toncheff
Math Content Specialist
Phoenix Union High School District
Phoenix, AZ

Functions

MODULE 1

Analyzing Functions

MODULE 2

Absolute Value Functions, Equations, and Inequalities

UNIT ★ 2

Volume 1

Quadratic Functions, Equations, and Relations

MODULE 3

Quadratic Equations

MODULE 4

Quadratic Relations and Systems of Equations

Polynomial Functions, Expressions, and Equations

UNIT 3

Volume 1

MODULE 5

Polynomial Functions

MODULE 6

Polynomials

MODULE 7

Polynomial Equations

Rational Functions, Expressions, and Equations

MODULE 8

Rational Functions

MODULE 9

Rational Expressions and Equations

UNIT 5

Radical Functions, Expressions, and Equations

Volume 1

MODULE 10

Radical Functions

MODULE 11

Radical Expressions and Equations

Images

Exponential and Logarithmic Functions and Equations

UNIT 6

Volume 2

MODULE 12 — Sequences and Series

MODULE 13 — Exponential Functions

MODULE 16

Logarithmic Properties and Exponential Equations

UNIT ★ 7

Volume 2

Trigonometric Functions

MODULE 17

Unit-Circle Definition of Trigonometric Functions

MODULE 18

Graphing Trigonometric Functions

Probability

MODULE 19

Introduction to Probability

MODULE 20

Conditional Probability and Independence of Events

Probability and Decision Making

Statistics

MODULE 22

Gathering and Displaying Data

MODULE 23

Data Distributions

Making Inferences from Data

Real-World Video 1161
Are You Ready? 1162

HMH Algebra 2
Online State Resources

Scan the QR code or visit:
my.hrw.com/nsmedia/osp/2015/ma/hs/tempaga
for correlations and other state-specific resources.

Succeeding with HMH Algebra 2

HMH Algebra 2 is built on the 5E instructional model–Engage, Explore, Explain, Elaborate, Evaluate–to develop strong conceptual understanding and mastery of key mathematics standards.

 **ENGAGE**

Preview the Lesson Performance Task in the Interactive Student Edition.

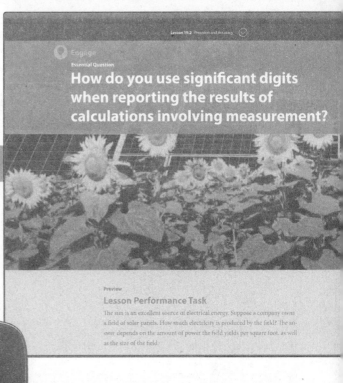

Lesson 19.2 Precision and Accuracy

Engage
Essential Question

How do you use significant digits when reporting the results of calculations involving measurement?

Preview

Lesson Performance Task

The sun is an excellent source of electrical energy. Suppose a company owns a field of solar panels. How much electricity is produced by the field? The answer depends on the amount of power the field yields per square foot, as well as the size of the field.

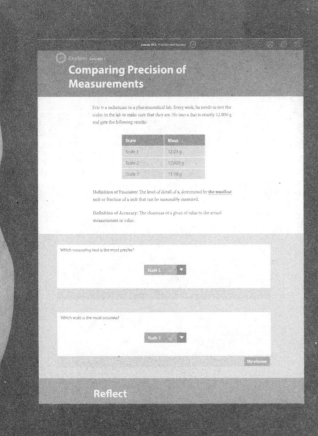

Explore Concept 1

Comparing Precision of Measurements

Eric is a technician in a pharmaceutical lab. Every week, he needs to test the scales in the lab to make sure that they are. He uses a that is exactly 12.000 g and gets the following results:

Scale	Mass
Scale 1	12.03 g
Scale 2	12.029 g
Scale 3	11.98 g

Definition of Precision: The level of detail of a, determined by **the smallest** unit or fraction of a unit that can be reasonably measured.

Definition of Accuracy: The closeness of a given value to the actual measurement or value.

Which measuring tool is the most precise?

[Scale 2 ▼]

Which scale is the most accurate?

[Scale 2 ▼]

My answer

Reflect

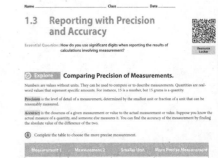

EXPLORE

Explore and interact with new concepts to develop a deeper understanding of mathematics in your book and the Interactive Student Edition.

Scan the QR code to access engaging videos, activities, and more in the Resource Locker for each lesson.

Name _____ Class _____ Date _____

1.3 Reporting with Precision and Accuracy

Essential Question: How do you use significant digits when reporting the results of calculations involving measurement?

Resource Locker

Explore Comparing Precision of Measurements.

Numbers are values without units. They can be used to compute or to describe measurements. Quantities are real-word values that represent specific amounts. For instance, 15 is a number, but 15 grams is a quantity.

Precision is the level of detail of a measurement, determined by the smallest unit or fraction of a unit that can be reasonably measured.

Accuracy is the closeness of a given measurement or value to the actual measurement or value. Suppose you know the actual measure of a quantity, and someone else measures it. You can find the accuracy of the measurement by finding the absolute value of the difference of the two.

(A) Complete the table to choose the more precise measurement.

Measurement 1	Measurement 2	Smaller Unit	More Precise Measurement
4 g	4.3 g		
5.71 oz	5.7 oz		
4.2 m	422 cm		
7 ft 2 in.	7.2 in.		

(B) Eric is a lab technician. Every week, he needs to test the scales in the lab to make sure that they are accurate. He uses a standard mass that is exactly 8.000 grams and gets the following results.

Scale	Mass
Scale 1	8.02 g
Scale 2	7.9 g

EXPLAIN

Learn concepts with step-by-step interactive examples. Every example is also supported by a Math On the Spot video tutorial.

Explain Concept 2

Determining Precision

As you have seen, measurements are given to a certain precision. Therefore, the value reported does not necessarily represent the actual value of the measurement. For example, a measurement of 5 centimeters, which is given to the nearest whole unit, can actually range from 0.5 units below the reported value, 4.5 centimeters, up to, but not including, 0.5 units above it, 5.5 centimeters. The actual length, L, is within a range of possible values: centimeters. Similarly, a length given to the nearest tenth can actually range from 0.05 units below the reported value up to, but not including, 0.05 units above it. So a length reported as 4.5 cm could actually be as low as 4.45 cm or as high as nearly 4.55 cm.

Your Turn Concept 2

| 1 | 2 | **3** | 4 | 5 | 6 | 7 | 8 | 9 | 10 | ▶ | 11-17 | Personal Math Trainer |

| Question 3 of 17 | View Step by Step | ▶ Video Tutor | Textbook | X² Animated Math |

Solve the quadratic equation by factoring.

$$7x + 44x = 7x - 10$$

$$x = \boxed{}, \boxed{}$$

Check

Save & Close   ? ⚠   Turn It In

Explain   Elaborate ▶

Check your understanding of new concepts and skills with Your Turn exercises in your book or online with Personal Math Trainer.

(C) Find the accuracy of each of the measurements in Step B.

Scale 1: Accuracy = |8.000 − _____| = _____

Scale 2: Accuracy = |8.000 − _____| = _____

Scale 3: Accuracy = |8.000 − _____| = _____

Complete each statement: the measurement for Scale _____, which is _____ grams,

is the most accurate because _____

Reflect

1. Discussion Given two measurements of the same quantity, is it possible that the more precise measurement is not the more accurate? Why do you think that is so?

_____

_____

Explain 1 Determining Precision of Calculated Measurements

As you have seen, measurements are reported to a certain precision. The reported value does not necessarily represent the actual value of the measurement. When you measure to the nearest unit, the actual length can be 0.5 unit less than the measured length or less than 0.5 unit greater than the measured length. So, a length reported as 4.5 centimeters could actually be anywhere between 4.45 centimeters and 4.55 centimeters, but not including 4.55 centimeters. It cannot include 4.55 centimeters because 4.55 centimeters reported to the nearest tenth would round up to 4.6 centimeters.

Example 1 Calculate the minimum and maximum possible areas. Round your answers to the nearest square centimeter.

(A) The length and width of a book cover are 28.3 centimeters and 21 centimeters, respectively.

Find the range of values for the actual length and width of the book cover.

Minimum length = (28.3 − 0.05) cm and maximum length = (28.3 + 0.05) cm, so 28.25 ≤ length < 28.35 cm.

Minimum width = (21 − 0.5) cm and maximum width = (21 + 0.5) cm, so 20.5 cm ≤ width < 21.5 cm.

Find the minimum and maximum areas.

Minimum area = minimum length · minimum width

= 28.25 cm · 20.5 cm ≈ 579 cm²

Maximum area = maximum length · maximum width

= 28.35 cm · 21.5 cm ≈ 610 cm²

So 579 cm² ≤ area < 610 cm².

© Houghton Mifflin Harcourt Publishing Company

ELABORATE

Show your understanding and reasoning with Reflect and Elaborate questions.

Elaborate

17. Given two measurements, is it possible that the more accurate measurement is not the more precise? Justify your answer.

_____

18. What is the relationship between the range of possible error in the measurements used in a calculation and the range of possible error in the calculated measurement?

_____

19. Essential Question Check-In How do you use significant digits to determine how to report a sum or product of two measurements?

_____

© Houghton Mifflin Harcourt Publishing Company · Image Credits: ©Michael Freeman/Corbis

Elaborate

Given two measurements, is it possible that the more precise measurement, may not be the more accurate?

[ ]

Formula   Send to Notebook

What is the relationship between the precision used in the length and width of the rectangle and the precision of the resulting area measurement?

[ ]

Formula   Send to Notebook

How are the significant digits related to the calculations using measurements?

© Houghton Mifflin Harcourt Publishing Company

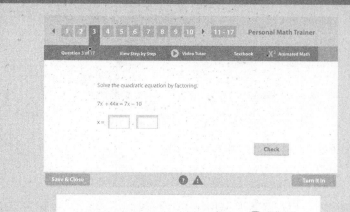

⭐ EVALUATE

Practice and apply skills and concepts with Evaluate exercises and a Lesson Performance Task in your book with plenty of workspace, or complete these exercises online with Personal Math Trainer.

⭐ Evaluate: Homework and Practice

1. The diagram represents the expression $x^3 + 4x + c$ with the constant term missing. Complete the square by filling in the bottom right corner with 1-tiles, and write the expression as a trinomial and in factored form.

- Online Homework
- Hints and Help
- Extra Practice

Complete the square to form a perfect square trinomial. Then factor the trinomial.

2. $m^2 + 10m +$ ☐   3. $g^2 - 20g +$ ☐

4. $y^2 + 2y +$ ☐

Lesson Performance Task

The quarterback of a football team is practicing throwing a 50-yard pass to a wide receiver. The quarterback can throw a pass with an initial vertical velocity of 40 feet per second and an initial height of 6 feet. He wants to throw the ball so it lands in the wide receiver's hands at a height of 6 feet at exactly the right time.

The wide receiver can run 40 yards in 4.4 seconds and begins running at top speed when the quarterback hikes the ball. How long should the quarterback wait between hiking the ball and throwing it?

Journal

Discuss the solution method you used with some of your classmates. Did your thinking change? Summarize anything you learned or shared below.

Formula

Self-Evaluation

This lesson covered the concepts below:

- Using Ratios and Proportions to Solve Problems
- Using Scale Drawings and Models to Solve Problems
- Using Dimensional Analysis to Convert Measurement
- Using Dimensional Analysis to Convert and Compare Rates
- Graphing a Proportional Relationship

⭐ LOOK BACK

Review what you have learned and prepare for high-stakes tests with a variety of resources, including Study Guide Reviews, Performance Tasks, and Assessment Readiness test preparation.

STUDY GUIDE REVIEW

19 Using Square Roots Solve Equations

Essential Question: How do you determine the best method for solving a quadratic equation or a system of equations?

Key Vocabulary
discriminant *(discriminante)* and behavior *(comportamiento asintótico)* quadratic formula *(fórmula cuadrática)*

KEY EXAMPLE *(Lesson 19.1)*

Solve $(x-3)^2 = 49$ using square roots.

$(x-3)^2 = 49$

$x - 3 = \pm\sqrt{49}$ Take the square root of both sides.

$x - 3 = \pm 7$ Use ± to show both square roots.

$x = \pm 7 + 3$

$x = 7 + 3$ and $x = -7 + 3$

$x = 10$ $x = -4$ Simplify each equation.

The solutions are −4 and 10.

KEY EXAMPLE *(Lesson 19.2)*

Solve $x^2 - 6x - 12 = 0$ by completing the square.

$x^2 - 6x - 12 = 0$

$x^2 - 6x = 12$ Add 12 to both sides.

$x^2 - 6x + 9 = 12 + 9$ Complete the square.

$(x-3)^2 = 21$ Factor left side.

$x - 3 = \pm\sqrt{21}$ Take square roots.

$x = 3 \pm \sqrt{21}$ Solve for x.

$x = 3 + \sqrt{21}$ or $x = 3 - \sqrt{21}$

KEY EXAMPLE *(Lesson 19.3)*

Solve $3x^2 - 5x - 4 = 0$ by using the quadratic formula.

$3x^2 - 5x - 4 = 0$

$a = 3, b = -5, c = -4$ Find a, b, c.

$x = \dfrac{-(-5) \pm \sqrt{(-5)^2 - 4(3)(-4)}}{2(3)}$ Use quadratic formula.

$\dfrac{5 \pm \sqrt{25 - (-48)}}{}$

MODULE PERFORMANCE TASK

Going Down?

Construct a ramp that is at least 4 feet long. The angle the ramp makes with the ground should be 30°. Working with a partner, release a ball from various points on the ramp. Measure the distance the ball rolls and the time (using a stopwatch) that it rolls. You should perform several trials for various distances.

The quadratic equation $d = \frac{1}{2}gt^2$ models the distance d (in feet) that the ball rolls in t seconds. Use your data and the equation to estimate the value of g. Create a report that explains your approach, organizes all of the collected data in tables, and shows your calculations. You can use a graphing calculator to fit your data to a quadratic regression line.

Use the space below to write down any questions you have or important information from your teacher.

Module 19   3   Study Guide Review

UNIT 1
Functions

Enlightened Images/Alamy

MATH IN CAREERS

Community Theater Owner
A community theater owner uses math to determine revenue, profit, and expenses related to operating the theater. Probability and statistical methods are useful for determining the types of performances that will appeal to the public and attract patrons. Community theater owners should also understand the geometry of stage sets, and algebraic formulas for stage lighting, including those used to calculate light beam spread, throw distance, angle, and overall length.

If you are interested in a career as a community theater owner, you should study these mathematical subjects:
- Algebra
- Geometry
- Trigonometry
- Business Math
- Probability
- Statistics

Research other careers that require determining revenue, profit, and expenses. Check out the career activity at the end of the unit to find out how **Community Theater Owners** use math.

Reading Start-Up

Vocabulary

Review Words

✔ coefficient *(coeficiente)*
✔ domain *(dominio)*
✔ function *(función)*
✔ inequality *(desigualdad)*
✔ interval *(intervalo)*
✔ quadratic function *(función ċuadrática)*
✔ range *(rango)*
✔ transformation *(transformación)*

Preview Words

conjunction *(conjunción)*
disjunction *(disyunción)*
even function *(función par)*
inverse function *(función inversa)*
odd function *(función impar)*
parameter *(parámetro)*

Visualize Vocabulary

Use the ✔ words to complete the graphic. You can put more than one word on each spoke of the information wheel.

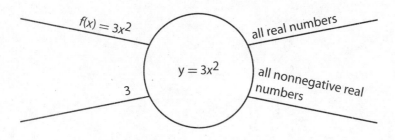

Understand Vocabulary

To become familiar with some of the vocabulary terms in the module, consider the following. You may refer to the module, the glossary, or a dictionary.

1. A _____ is a constant in the equation of a curve that yields a family of similar curves as it changes.

2. A function $f(x)$ such that $f(x) = f(-x)$ is an _____ .

3. A compound statement that uses the word *or* is a _____ .

Active Reading

Three-Panel Flip Chart Before beginning each lesson, create a three-panel flip chart to help you summarize important aspects of the lesson. As you study each lesson, record algebraic examples of functions on the first flap, their graphs on the second flap, and analyses of the functions on the third flap. Add to flip charts from previous lessons by extending the analyses of the functions when possible. For equations and inequalities, record an example on the first flap, a worked out solution on the second flap, and a graph on the third flap.

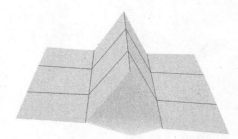

Analyzing Functions

Essential Question: How can you analyze functions to solve real-world problems?

REAL WORLD VIDEO
Pole vaulting is just one of many track-and-field events that feature a person or object flying through the air. The path of a pole vaulter or of a shot put can be modeled using a quadratic function.

MODULE PERFORMANCE TASK PREVIEW
How High Does a Pole Vaulter Go?

In pole vaulting, a person jumps over a horizontal bar with the assistance of a long fiberglass or carbon-fiber pole. The flexible pole makes it possible for vaulters to achieve much greater heights than jumping without a pole. The goal is to clear the bar without knocking it down. How can mathematics be used to compare the heights of a pole vaulter for two different vaults? Let's jump in and find out!

Are (YOU) Ready?

Complete these exercises to review skills you will need for this module.

• Online Homework
• Hints and Help
• Extra Practice

Algebraic Representations of Transformations

Example 1

Rotate $A(-6,3)$ 90° clockwise.
$(-6(-1), 3) = (6, 3)$ Multiply.
$A(-6, 3) \rightarrow A'(3, 6)$ Switch.

Translate $B(4,7)$ 5 units down.
$(4, 7-5) = (4, 2)$ Subtract.
$B(4, 7) \rightarrow B'(4,2)$

Find the location of A' given that A is $(1, 5)$.

1. Rotate 90° clockwise.

2. Translate 1 unit left.

3. Reflect across the x-axis.

Linear Functions

Example 2

Name the x- and y-intercepts for $y = -2x + 1$.

x-intercept: $0 = -2x + 1$, so $x = 0.5$.

y-intercept: $y = -2(0) + 1 = 1$

Find the x- and y-intercepts for each equation.

4. $y = 8x - 4$

5. $y = -x + 12$

6. $y = 1.2x + 4.8$

Properties of Translations, Reflections, and Rotations

Example 3

The point $P(1, -8)$ is reflected across the y-axis.
Name the quadrant that contains the image, P'.
$P(1, -8) \rightarrow P'(-1, -8)$, so P' is in Quadrant III.

Name the quadrant that contains the image of $R(7, 3)$ under the given transformation.

7. reflection across the x-axis

8. translation 8 units down

9. rotation 270° clockwise

Rate of Change and Slope

Example 4

Two points on a line are $(-3, 3)$ and $(4, 1)$. Find the slope.
$\dfrac{y_1 - y_2}{x_1 - x_2} = \dfrac{3 - 1}{-3 - 4} = -\dfrac{2}{7}$ The slope is $-\dfrac{2}{7}$.

Find the slope of the line that passes through the two points.

10. $(0, 5)$ and $(-9, -4)$

11. $(6, -2)$ and $(1, -1)$

12. $(-7, 3)$ and $(-4, -12)$

1.1 Domain, Range, and End Behavior

Essential Question: How can you determine the domain, range, and end behavior of a function?

Resource
Locker

🧭 Explore Representing an Interval on a Number Line

An **interval** is a part of a number line without any breaks. A *finite interval* has two endpoints, which may or may not be included in the interval. An *infinite interval* is unbounded at one or both ends.

Suppose an interval consists of all real numbers greater than or equal to 1. You can use the inequality $x \geq 1$ to represent the interval. You can also use *set notation* and *interval notation*, as shown in the table.

Description of Interval	Type of Interval	Inequality	Set Notation	Interval notation
All real numbers from a to b, including a and b	Finite	$a \leq x \leq b$	$\{x \mid a \leq x \leq b\}$	$[a, b]$
All real numbers greater than a	Infinite	$x > a$	$\{x \mid x > a\}$	$(a, +\infty)$
All real numbers less than or equal to a	Infinite	$x \leq a$	$\{x \mid x \leq a\}$	$(-\infty, a]$

For set notation, the vertical bar means "such that," so you read $\{x \mid x \geq 1\}$ as "the set of real numbers x such that x is greater than or equal to 1."

For interval notation, do the following:

- Use a square bracket to indicate that an interval includes an endpoint and a parenthesis to indicate that an interval doesn't include an endpoint.

- For an interval that is unbounded at its positive end, use the symbol for positive infinity, $+\infty$. For an interval that unbounded at its negative end, use the symbol for negative infinity, $-\infty$. Always use a parenthesis with positive or negative infinity.

So, you can write the interval $x \geq 1$ as $[1, +\infty)$.

(A) Complete the table by writing the finite interval shown on each number line as an inequality, using set notation, and using interval notation.

Finite Interval		
Inequality		
Set Notation		
Interval Notation		

Ⓑ Complete the table by writing the infinite interval shown on each number line as an inequality, using set notation, and using interval notation.

Infinite Interval	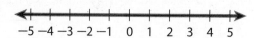	
Inequality		
Set Notation		
Interval Notation		

Reflect

1. Consider the interval shown on the number line.

$$\xleftarrow{\hspace{1cm}} \begin{array}{ccccccccccc} -5 & -4 & -3 & -2 & -1 & 0 & 1 & 2 & 3 & 4 & 5 \end{array} \xrightarrow{\hspace{1cm}}$$

    a. Represent the interval using interval notation. _____

    b. What numbers are in this interval? _____

2. What do the intervals [0, 5], [0, 5), and (0, 5) have in common? What makes them different?

_____

_____

_____

3. **Discussion** The symbol ∪ represents the *union* of two sets. What do you think the notation $(-\infty, 0) \cup (0, +\infty)$ represents?

_____

_____

_____

⚷ **Explain 1** **Identifying a Function's Domain, Range and End Behavior from its Graph**

Recall that the *domain* of a function f is the set of input values x, and the *range* is the set of output values $f(x)$. The **end behavior** of a function describes what happens to the $f(x)$-values as the x-values either increase without bound (approach positive infinity) or decrease without bound (approach negative infinity). For instance, consider the graph of a linear function shown. From the graph, you can make the following observations.

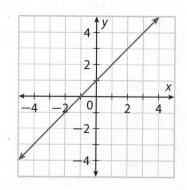

Statement of End Behavior	Symbolic Form of Statement
As the *x*-values increase without bound, the *f(x)*-values also increase without bound.	As $x \to +\infty$, $f(x) \to +\infty$.
As the *x*-values decrease without bound, the *f(x)*-values also decrease without bound.	As $x \to -\infty$, $f(x) \to -\infty$.

Example 1 Write the domain and the range of the function as an inequality, using set notation, and using interval notation. Also describe the end behavior of the function.

(A) The graph of the quadratic function $f(x) = x^2$ is shown.

Domain:

    Inequality: $-\infty < x < +\infty$

    Set notation: $\{x| -\infty < x < +\infty\}$

    Interval notation: $(-\infty, +\infty)$

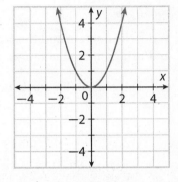

Range: End behavior:

    Inequality: $y \geq 0$ As $x \to +\infty$, $f(x) \to +\infty$.

    Set notation: $\{y|y \geq 0\}$ As $x \to -\infty$, $f(x) \to +\infty$.

    Interval notation: $[0, +\infty)$

(B) The graph of the exponential function $f(x) = 2^x$ is shown.

Domain:

    Inequality: _____

    Set notation: _____

    Interval notation: _____

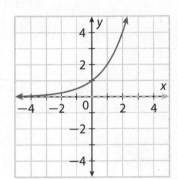

Range:

    Inequality: _____

    Set notation: _____

    Interval notation: _____

End behavior:

    As $x \to +\infty$, _____.

    As $x \to -\infty$, _____.

4. Why is the end behavior of a quadratic function different from the end behavior of a linear function?

    _____

    _____

5. In Part B, the $f(x)$-values decrease as the x-values decrease. So, why can't you say that $f(x) \rightarrow -\infty$ as $x \rightarrow -\infty$?

    _____

Your Turn

Write the domain and the range of the function as an inequality, using set notation, and using interval notation. Also describe the end behavior of the function.

6. The graph of the quadratic function $f(x) = -x^2$ is shown.

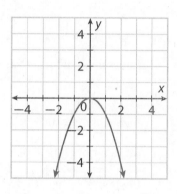

🔑 Explain 2   Graphing a Linear Function on a Restricted Domain

Unless otherwise stated, a function is assumed to have a domain consisting of all real numbers for which the function is defined. Many functions—such as linear, quadratic, and exponential functions—are defined all real numbers, so their domain, when written in interval notation, is $(-\infty, +\infty)$. Another way to write the set of real numbers is $\mathbb{R}$.

Sometimes a function may have a restricted domain. If the rule for a function and its restricted domain are given, you can draw its graph and then identify its range.

Example 2   **For the given function and domain, draw the graph and identify the range using the same notation as the given domain.**

Ⓐ $f(x) = \frac{3}{4}x + 2$ with domain $[-4, 4]$

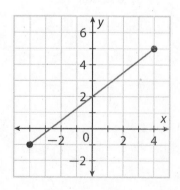

Since $f(x) = \frac{3}{4}x + 2$ is a linear function, the graph is a line segment with endpoints at $(-4, f(-4))$, or $(-4, -1)$, and $(4, f(4))$, or $(4, 5)$. The endpoints are included in the graph.

The range is $[-1, 5]$.

Ⓑ $f(x) = -x - 2$ with domain $\{x \mid x > -3\}$

Since $f(x) = -x - 2$ is a linear function, the graph is a ray with its endpoint at $(-3, f(-3))$,

or _____. The endpoint _____ included in the graph.

The range is _____.

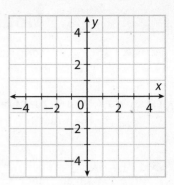

Reflect

7. In Part A, how does the graph change if the domain is $(-4, 4)$ instead of $[-4, 4]$?

_____

8. In Part B, what is the end behavior as x increases without bound? Why can't you talk about the end behavior as x decreases without bound?

_____

_____

Your Turn

For the given function and domain, draw the graph and identify the range using the same notation as the domain.

9. $f(x) = -\frac{1}{2}x + 2$ with domain $-6 \leq x < 2$ **10.** $f(x) = \frac{2}{3}x - 1$ with domain $(-\infty, 3]$

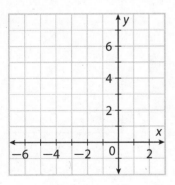

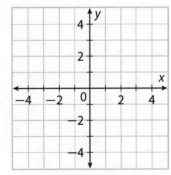

⊘ Explain 3 Modeling with a Linear Function

Recall that when a real-world situation involves a constant rate of change, a linear function is a reasonable model for the situation. The situation may require restricting the function's domain.

Example 3 Write a function that models the given situation. Determine a domain from the situation, graph the function using that domain, and identify the range.

(A) Joyce jogs at a rate of 1 mile every 10 minutes for a total of 40 minutes. (Use inequalities for the domain and range of the function that models this situation.)

Joyce's jogging rate is 0.1 mi/min. Her jogging distance d (in miles) at any time t (in minutes) is modeled by $d(t) = 0.1t$. Since she jogs for 40 minutes, the domain is restricted to the interval $0 \le t \le 40$.

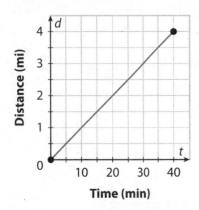

The range is $0 \le d \le 4$.

(B) A candle 6 inches high burns at a rate of 1 inch every 2 hours for 5 hours. (Use interval notation for the domain and range of the function that models this situation.)

The candle's burning rate is _____ in./h.
The candle's height h (in inches) at any time

t (in hours) is modeled by $h(t) =$ _____.
Since the candle burns for 5 hours, the domain is restricted to the

interval $\left[0, \boxed{} \right]$.

The range is _____.

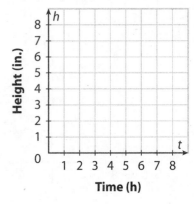

11. In Part A, suppose Joyce jogs for only 30 minutes.

    A. How does the domain change? _____

    B. How does the graph change? _____

    C. How does the range change? _____

Your Turn

12. While standing on a moving walkway at an airport, you are carried forward 25 feet every 15 seconds for 1 minute. Write a function that models this situation. Determine the domain from the situation, graph the function, and identify the range. Use set notation for the domain and range.

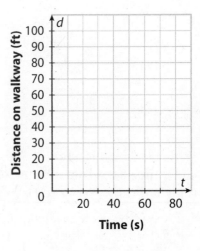

Elaborate

13. If a and b are real numbers such that $a < b$, use interval notation to write four different intervals having a and b as endpoints. Describe what numbers each interval includes.

_____

_____

_____

_____

14. What impact does restricting the domain of a linear function have on the graph of the function?

_____

_____

_____

15. **Essential Question Check-In** How does slope determine the end behavior of a linear function with an unrestricted domain?

_____

_____

_____

_____

_____

• Online Homework
• Hints and Help
• Extra Practice

1. Write the interval shown on the number line as an inequality, using set notation, and using interval notation.

2. Write the interval (5, 100] as an inequality and using set notation.

3. Write the interval $-25 \leq x < 30$ using set notation and interval notation.

4. Write the interval $\{x \mid -3 < x < 5\}$ as an inequality and using interval notation.

Write the domain and the range of the function as an inequality, using set notation, and using interval notation. Also describe the end behavior of the function or explain why there is no end behavior.

5. The graph of the quadratic function $f(x) = x^2 + 2$ is shown.

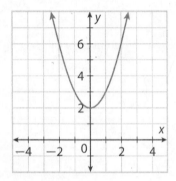

6. The graph of the exponential function $f(x) = 3^x$ is shown.

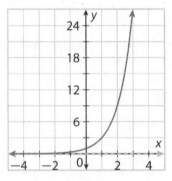

7. The graph of the linear function $g(x) = 2x - 2$ is shown.

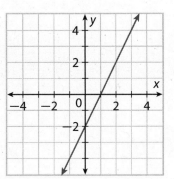

8. The graph of a function is shown.

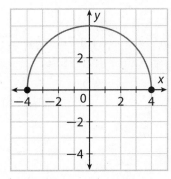

For the given function and domain, draw the graph and identify the range using the same notation as the given domain.

9. $f(x) = -x + 5$ with domain $[-3, 2]$

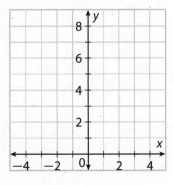

10. $f(x) = \frac{3}{2}x + 1$ with domain $\{x \mid x > -2\}$

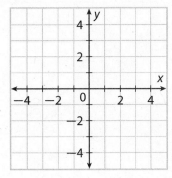

Write a function that models the given situation. Determine the domain from the situation, graph the function using that domain, and identify the range.

11. A bicyclist travels at a constant speed of 12 miles per hour for a total of 45 minutes. (Use set notation for the domain and range of the function that models this situation.)

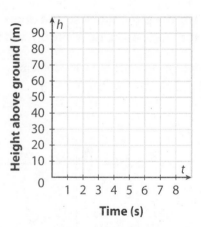

12. An elevator in a tall building starts at a floor of the building that is 90 meters above the ground. The elevator descends 2 meters every 0.5 second for 6 seconds. (Use an inequality for the domain and range of the function that models this situation.)

13. Explain the Error Cameron sells tickets at a movie theater. On Friday night, she worked from 4 p.m. to 10 p.m. and sold about 25 tickets every hour. Cameron says that the number of tickets, n, she has sold at any time t (in hours) can be modeled by the function $n(t) = 25t$, where the domain is $0 \leq t \leq 1$ and the range is $0 \leq n \leq 25$. Is Cameron's function, along with the domain and range, correct? Explain.

Alamy

14. Multi-Step The graph of the cubic function $f(x) = x^3$ is shown.

a. What are the domain, range, and end behavior of the function? (Write the domain and range as an inequality, using set notation, and using interval notation.)

b. How is the range of the function affected if the domain is restricted to $[-4, 4]$? (Write the range as an inequality, using set notation, and using interval notation.)

c. Graph the function with the restricted domain.

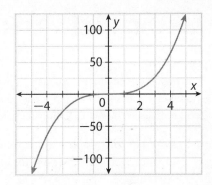

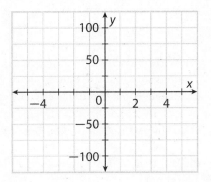

15. Represent Real-World Situations The John James Audubon Bridge is a cable-stayed bridge in Louisiana that opened in 2011. The height from the bridge deck to the top of the tower where a particular cable is anchored is about 500 feet, and the length of that cable is about 1200 feet. Draw the cable on a coordinate plane, letting the x-axis represent the bridge deck and the y-axis represent the tower. (Only use positive values of x and y.) Write a linear function whose graph models the cable. Identify the domain and range, writing each as an inequality, using set notation, and using interval notation.

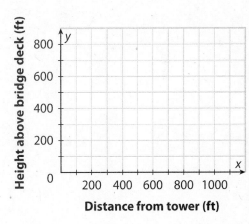

Lesson Performance Task

The fuel efficiency for a 2007 passenger car was 31.2 mi/gal. For the same model of car, the fuel efficiency increased to 35.6 mi/gal in 2012. The gas tank for this car holds 16 gallons of gas.

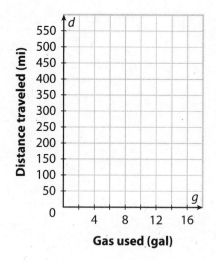

a. Write and graph a linear function that models the distance that each car can travel for a given amount of gas (up to one tankful).

b. Write the domain and range of each function using interval notation.

c. Write and simplify a function $f(g)$ that represents the *difference* in the distance that the 2012 car can travel and the distance that the 2007 car can travel on the same amount of gas. Interpret this function using the graphs of the functions from part a. Also find and interpret $f(16)$.

d. Write the domain and range of the difference function using set notation.

1.2 Characteristics of Function Graphs

Essential Question: What are some of the attributes of a function, and how are they related to the function's graph?

Resource Locker

🧭 Explore   Identifying Attributes of a Function from Its Graph

You can identify several attributes of a function by analyzing its graph. For instance, for the graph shown, you can see that the function's domain is $\{x|0 \leq x \leq 11\}$ and its range is $\{y| -1 \leq y \leq 1\}$. Use the graph to explore the function's other attributes.

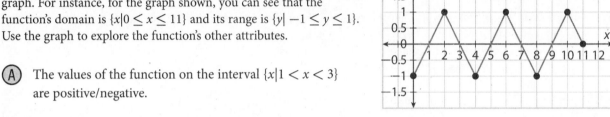

(A) The values of the function on the interval $\{x|1 < x < 3\}$ are positive/negative.

(B) The values of the function on the interval $\{x|8 < x < 9\}$ are positive/negative.

A function is **increasing** on an interval if $f(x_1) < f(x_2)$ when $x_1 < x_2$ for any x-values x_1 and x_2 from the interval. The graph of a function that is increasing on an interval rises from left to right on that interval. Similarly, a function is **decreasing** on an interval if $f(x_1) > f(x_2)$ when $x_1 < x_2$ for any x-values x_1 and x_2 from the interval. The graph of a function that is decreasing on an interval falls from left to right on that interval.

(C) The given function is increasing/decreasing on the interval $\{x|2 \leq x \leq 4\}$.

(D) The given function is increasing/decreasing on the interval $\{x|4 \leq x \leq 6\}$.

For the two points $(x_1, f(x_1))$ and $(x_2, f(x_2))$ on the graph of a function, the **average rate of change** of the function is the ratio of the change in the function values, $f(x_2) - f(x_1)$, to the change in the x-values, $x_2 - x_1$. For a linear function, the rate of change is constant and represents the slope of the function's graph.

(E) What is the given function's average rate of change on the interval $\{x|0 \leq x \leq 2\}$?

_____

A function may change from increasing to decreasing or from decreasing to increasing at *turning points*. The value of $f(x)$ at a point where a function changes from increasing to decreasing is a **maximum value**. A maximum value occurs at a point that appears higher than all nearby points on the graph of the function. Similarly, the value of $f(x)$ at a point where a function changes from decreasing to increasing is a **minimum value**. A minimum value occurs at a point that appears lower than all nearby points on the graph of the function. If the graph of a function has an endpoint, the value of $f(x)$ at that point is considered a maximum or minimum value of the function if the point is higher or lower, respectively, than all nearby points.

(F) At how many points does the given function change from increasing to decreasing? _____

Ⓖ What is the function's value at these points? _____

Ⓗ At how many points does the given function change from decreasing to increasing? _____

Ⓘ What is the function's value at these points? _____

A **zero** of a function is a value of x for which $f(x) = 0$. On a graph of the function, the zeros are the x-intercepts.

Ⓙ How many x-intercepts does the given function's graph have? _____

Ⓚ Identify the zeros of the function. _____

© Houghton Mifflin Harcourt Publishing Company

Reflect

1. **Discussion** Identify three different intervals that have the same average rate of change, and state what the rate of change is.

_____

_____

_____

2. **Discussion** If a function is increasing on an interval $\{x | a \le x \le b\}$, what can you say about its average rate of change on the interval? Explain.

_____

_____

_____

⊘ Explain 1 Sketching a Function's Graph from a Verbal Description

By understanding the attributes of a function, you can sketch a graph from a verbal description.

Example 1 Sketch a graph of the following verbal descriptions.

Ⓐ Lyme disease is a bacterial infection transmitted to humans by ticks. When an infected tick bites a human, the probability of transmission is a function of the time since the tick attached itself to the skin. During the first 24 hours, the probability is 0%. During the next three 24-hour periods, the rate of change in the probability is always positive, but it is much greater for the middle period than the other two periods. After 96 hours, the probability is almost 100%. Sketch a graph of the function for the probability of transmission.

Identify the axes and scales.

The x-axis will be time (in hours) and will run from 0 to at least 96. The y-axis will be the probability of infection (as a percent) from 0 to 100.

Probability of Transmission from Infected Tick

Identify key intervals.

The intervals are in increments of 24 hours: 0 to 24, 24 to 48, 48 to 72, 72 to 96, and 96 to 120.

Sketch the graph of the function.

Draw a horizontal segment at $y = 0$ for the first 24-hour interval. The function increases over the next three 24-hour intervals with the middle interval having the greatest increase (the steepest slope). After 96 hours, the graph is nearly horizontal at 100%.

(B) The incidence of a disease is the rate at which a disease occurs in a population. It is calculated by dividing the number of new cases of a disease in a given time period (typically a year) by the size of the population. **To avoid small decimal numbers, the rate is often expressed in terms of a large number of people rather than a single person.** For instance, the incidence of measles in the United States in 1974 was about 10 cases per 100,000 people.

From 1974 to 1980, there were drastic fluctuations in the incidence of measles in the United States. In 1975, there was a slight increase in incidence from 1974. The next two years saw a substantial increase in the incidence, which reached a maximum in 1977 of about 26 cases per 100,000 people. From 1977 to 1979, the incidence fell to about 5 cases per 100,000 people. The incidence fell much faster from 1977 to 1978 than from 1978 to 1979. Finally, from 1979 to 1980, the incidence stayed about the same. **Sketch a graph of the function for the incidence of measles.**

Incidence of Measles in the U.S.

Time (years since 1974)

Identify the axes and scales.

The x-axis will represent time given by years and will run from

0 to _____. The y-axis will

represent _____, measured in cases per 100,000 people, and will run from 0 to 30.

Identify key intervals.

The intervals are one-year increments from _____ to _____.

Sketch the graph of the function.

The first point on the graph is _____. The graph slightly rises/falls from $x = 0$ to $x = 1$.

From $x = 1$ to $x = 3$, the graph rises/falls to a maximum y-value of _____. The graph rises/falls steeply from $x = 3$ to $x = 4$ and then rises/falls less steeply from $x = 4$ to $x = 5$. The graph is horizontal from $x = 5$ to $x = 6$.

Reflect

3. In Part B, the graph is horizontal from 1979 to 1980. What can you say about the rate of change for the function on this interval?

_____

_____

4. A grocery store stocks shelves with 100 cartons of strawberries before the store opens. For the first 3 hours the store is open, the store sells 20 cartons per hour. Over the next 2 hours, no cartons of strawberries are sold. The store then restocks 10 cartons each hour for the next 2 hours. In the final hour that the store is open, 30 cartons are sold. Sketch a graph of the function.

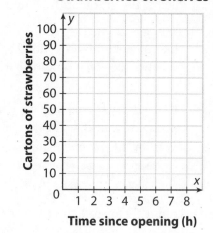

Strawberries on Shelves

Cartons of strawberries — Time since opening (h)

⚙ Explain 2 Modeling with a Linear Function

When given a set of paired data, you can use a scatter plot to see whether the data show a linear trend. If so, you can use a graphing calculator to perform linear regression and obtain a linear function that models the data. You should treat the least and greatest x-values of the data as the boundaries of the domain of the linear model.

When you perform linear regression, a graphing calculator will report the value of the *correlation coefficient r*. This variable can have a value from -1 to 1. It measures the direction and strength of the relationship between the variables x and y. If the value of r is negative, the y-values tend to decrease as the x-values increase. If the value of r is positive, the y-values tend to increase as the x-values increase. The more linear the relationship between x and y is, the closer the value of r is to -1 or 1 (or the closer the value of r^2 is to 1).

You can use the linear model to make predictions and decisions based on the data. Making a prediction within the domain of the linear model is called *interpolation*. Making a prediction outside the domain is called *extrapolation*.

Example 2 Perform a linear regression for the given situation and make predictions.

Ⓐ A photographer hiked through the Grand Canyon. Each day she stored photos on a memory card for her digital camera. When she returned from the trip, she deleted some photos from each memory card, saving only the best. The table shows the number of photos she kept from all those stored on each memory card. Use a graphing calculator to create a scatter plot of the data, find a linear regression model, and graph the model. Then use the model to predict the number of photos the photographer will keep if she takes 150 photos.

Grand Canyon Photos	
Photos Taken	**Photos Kept**
117	25
128	31
140	39
157	52
110	21
188	45
170	42

Step 1: Create a scatter plot of the data.

Let x represent the number of photos taken, and let y represent the number of photos kept. Use a viewing window that shows x-values from 100 to 200 and y-values from 0 to 60.

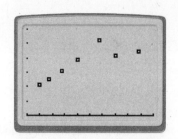

Notice that the trend in the data appears to be roughly linear, with y-values generally increasing as x-values increase.

Step 2: Perform linear regression. Write the linear model and its domain.

The linear regression model is $y = 0.33x - 11.33$. Its domain is $\{x \mid 110 \leq x \leq 188\}$.

Step 3: Graph the model along with the data to obtain a visual check on the goodness of fit.

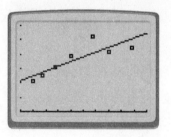

Notice that one of the data points is much farther from the line than the other data points are. The value of the correlation coefficient r would be closer to 1 without this data point.

Step 4: Predict the number of photos this photographer will keep if she takes 150 photos.

Evaluate the linear function when $x = 150$: $y = 0.33(150) - 11.33 \approx 38$. So, she will keep about 38 photos if she takes 150 photos.

B As a science project, Shelley is studying the relationship of car mileage (in miles per gallon) and speed (in miles per hour). The table shows the data Shelley gathered using her family's vehicle. Use a graphing calculator to create a scatter plot of the data, find a linear regression model, and graph the model. Then use the model to predict the gas mileage of the car at a speed of 20 miles per hour.

Speed (mi/h)	30	40	50	60	70
Mileage (mi/gal)	34.0	33.5	31.5	29.0	27.5

Step 1: Create a scatter plot of the data.

What do x and y represent?

_____

_____

What viewing window will you use?

_____

_____

What trend do you observe?

_____

_____

_____

Step 2: Perform linear regression. Write the linear model and its domain.

_____

_____

Step 3: Graph the model along with the data to obtain a visual check on the goodness of fit.

What can you say about the goodness of fit?

_____

_____

_____

Step 4: Predict the gas mileage of the car at a speed of 20 miles per hour.

_____

_____

_____

Reflect

5. Identify whether each prediction in Parts A and B is an interpolation or an extrapolation.

_____

_____

_____

Your Turn

6. Vern created a website for his school's sports teams. He has a hit counter on his site that lets him know how many people have visited the site. The table shows the number of hits the site received each day for the first two weeks. Use a graphing calculator to find the linear regression model. Then predict how many hits there will be on day 15.

Day	1	2	3	4	5	6	7	8	9	10	11	12	13	14
Hits	5	10	21	24	28	36	33	21	27	40	46	50	31	38

7. How are the attributes of increasing and decreasing related to average rate of change? How are the attributes of maximum and minimum values related to the attributes of increasing and decreasing?

_____

_____

_____

_____

_____

8. How can line segments be used to sketch graphs of functions that model real-world situations?

_____

_____

_____

_____

9. When making predictions based on a linear model, would you expect interpolated or extrapolated values to be more accurate? Justify your answer.

_____

_____

_____

_____

10. Essential Question Check-In What are some of the attributes of a function?

_____

_____

_____

_____

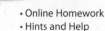
The graph shows a function that models the value V (in millions of dollars) of a stock portfolio as a function of time t (in months) over an 18-month period.

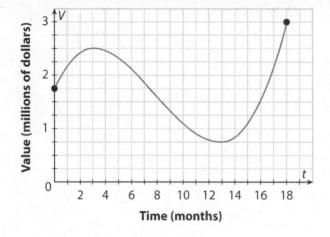

1. On what interval is the function decreasing?

   On what intervals is the function increasing?

2. Identify any maximum values and minimum values.

3. What are the function's domain and range?

The table of values gives the probability $P(n)$ for getting all 5's when rolling a number cube n times.

n	1	2	3	4	5
$P(n)$	$\dfrac{1}{6}$	$\dfrac{1}{36}$	$\dfrac{1}{216}$	$\dfrac{1}{1296}$	$\dfrac{1}{7776}$

4. Is $P(n)$ increasing or decreasing? Explain the significance of this.

5. What is the end behavior of $P(n)$? Explain the significance of this.

6. The table shows some values of a function. On which intervals is the function's average rate of change positive? Select all that apply.

x	0	1	2	3
f(x)	50	75	40	65

a. From $x = 0$ to $x = 1$ **c.** From $x = 0$ to $x = 3$ **e.** From $x = 1$ to $x = 3$

b. From $x = 0$ to $x = 2$ **d.** From $x = 1$ to $x = 2$ **f.** From $x = 2$ to $x = 3$

Use the graph of the function $f(x)$ to identify the function's specified attributes.

7. Find the function's average rate of change over each interval.

a. From $x = -3$ to $x = -2$ **b.** From $x = -2$ to $x = 1$

c. From $x = 0$ to $x = 1$ **d.** From $x = 1$ to $x = 2$

e. From $x = -1$ to $x = 0$ **f.** From $x = -1$ to $x = 2$

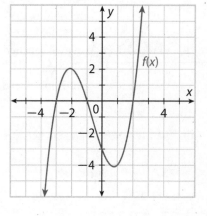

8. On what intervals are the function's values positive?

9. On what intervals are the function's values negative?

10. What are the zeros of the function?

11. The following describes the United States nuclear stockpile from 1944 to 1974. From 1944 to 1958, there was a gradual increase in the number of warheads from 0 to about 5000. From 1958 to 1966, there was a rapid increase in the number of warheads to a maximum of about 32,000. From 1966 to 1970, there was a decrease in the number of warheads to about 26,000. Finally, from 1970 to 1974, there was a small increase to about 28,000 warheads. Sketch a graph of the function.

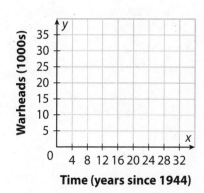

12. The following describes the unemployment rate in the United States from 2003 to 2013. In 2003, the unemployment rate was at 6.3%. The unemployment rate began to fall over the years and reached a minimum of about 4.4% in 2007. A recession that began in 2007 caused the unemployment rate to increase over a two-year period and reach a maximum of about 10% in 2009. The unemployment rate then decreased over the next four years to about 7.0% in 2013. Sketch a graph of the function.

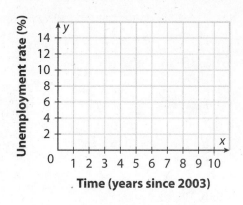

13. The following describes the incidence of mumps in the United States from 1984 to 2004. From 1984 to 1985, there was no change in the incidence of mumps, staying at about 1 case per 100,000 people. Then there was a spike in the incidence of mumps, which reached a peak of about 5.5 cases per 100,000 in 1987. Over the next year, there was a sharp decline in the incidence of mumps, to about 2 cases per 100,000 people in 1988. Then, from 1988 to 1989, there was a small increase to about 2.5 cases per 100,000 people. This was followed by a gradual decline, which reached a minimum of about 0.1 case per 100,000 in 1999. For the next five years, there was no change in the incidence of mumps. Sketch a graph of the function.

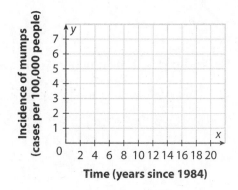

14. Aviation The table gives the lengths and wingspans of airplanes in an airline's fleet.

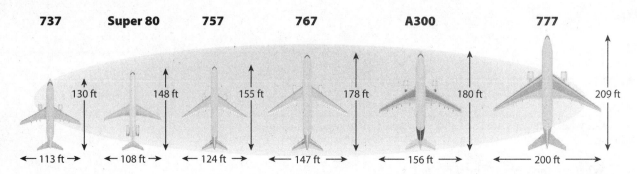

a. Make a scatter plot of the data with x representing length and y representing wingspan.

b. Sketch a line of fit.

c. Use the line of fit to predict the wingspan of an airplane with a length of 220 feet.

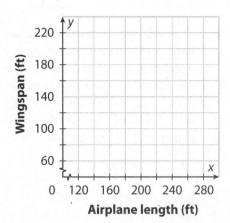

15. Golf The table shows the height (in feet) of a golf ball at various times (in seconds) after a golfer hits the ball into the air.

Time (s)	0	0.5	1	1.5	2	2.5	3	3.5	4
Height (ft)	0	28	48	60	64	60	48	28	0

a. Graph the data in the table. Then draw a smooth curve through the data points. (Because the golf ball is a projectile, its height h at time t can be modeled by a quadratic function whose graph is a parabola.)

b. What is the maximum height that the golf ball reaches?

c. On what interval is the golf ball's height increasing?

d. On what interval is the golf ball's height decreasing?

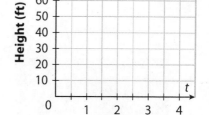

16. The model $a = 0.25t + 29$ represents the median age a of females in the United States as a function of time t (in years since 1970).

a. Predict the median age of females in 1995.

b. Predict the median age of females in 2015 to the nearest tenth.

17. Make a Prediction Anthropologists who study skeletal remains can predict a woman's height just from the length of her humerus, the bone between the elbow and the shoulder. The table gives data for humerus length and overall height for various women.

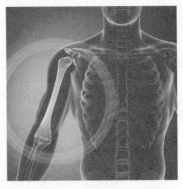

Humerus Length (cm)	35	27	30	33	25	39	27	31
Height (cm)	167	146	154	165	140	180	149	155

Using a graphing calculator, find the linear regression model and state its domain. Then predict a woman's height from a humerus that is 32 cm long, and tell whether the prediction is an interpolation or an extrapolation.

18. Make a Prediction Hummingbird wing beat rates are much higher than those in other birds. The table gives data about the mass and the frequency of wing beats for various species of hummingbirds.

Mass (g)	3.1	2.0	3.2	4.0	3.7	1.9	4.5
Frequency of Wing Beats (beats per second)	60	85	50	45	55	90	40

a. Using a graphing calculator, find the linear regression model and state its domain.

b. Predict the frequency of wing beats for a Giant Hummingbird with a mass of 19 grams.

c. Comment on the reasonableness of the prediction and what, if anything, is wrong with the model.

19. **Explain the Error** A student calculates a function's average rate of change on an interval and finds that it is 0. The student concludes that the function is constant on the interval. Explain the student's error, and give an example to support your explanation.

20. **Communicate Mathematical Ideas** Describe a way to obtain a linear model for a set of data without using a graphing calculator.

Lesson Performance Task

Since 1980 scientists have used data from satellite sensors to calculate a daily measure of Arctic sea ice extent. Sea ice extent is calculated as the sum of the areas of sea ice covering the ocean where the ice concentration is greater than 15%. The graph here shows seasonal variations in sea ice extent for 2012, 2013, and the average values for the 1980s.

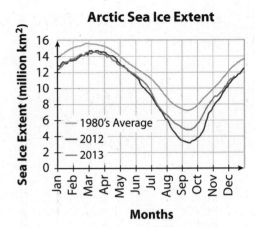

a. According to the graph, during which month does sea ice extent usually reach its maximum? During which month does the minimum extent generally occur? What can you infer about the reason for this pattern?

b. Sea ice extent reached its lowest level to date in 2012. About how much less was the minimum extent in 2012 compared with the average minimum for the 1980s? About what percentage of the 1980s average minimum was the 2012 minimum?

c. How does the maximum extent in 2012 compare with the average maximum for the 1980s? About what percentage of the 1980s average maximum was the 2012 maximum?

d. What do the patterns in the maximum and minimum values suggest about how climate change may be affecting sea ice extent?

e. How do the 2013 maximum and minimum values compare with those for 2012? What possible explanation can you suggest for the differences?

1.3 Transformations of Function Graphs

Essential Question: What are the ways you can transform the graph of the function f(x)?

Resource
Locker

⊘ Explore 1 Investigating Translations of Function Graphs

You can transform the graph of a function in various ways. You can translate the graph horizontally or vertically, you can stretch or compress the graph horizontally or vertically, and you can reflect the graph across the x-axis or the y-axis. How the graph of a given function is transformed is determined by the way certain numbers, called **parameters**, are introduced in the function.

The graph of $f(x)$ is shown. Use this graph for the exploration.

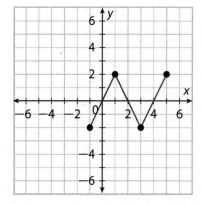

(A) First graph $g(x) = f(x) + k$ where k is the parameter. Let $k = 4$ so that $g(x) = f(x) + 4$. Complete the input-output table and then graph $g(x)$. In general, how is the graph of $g(x) = f(x) + k$ related to the graph of $f(x)$ when k is a positive number?

x	f(x)	f(x) + 4
−1	−2	2
1	2	6
3	−2	
5	2	

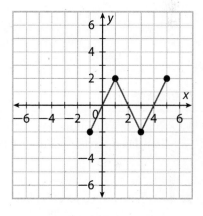

(B) Now try a negative value of k in $g(x) = f(x) + k$.
Let $k = -3$ so that $g(x) = f(x) - 3$. Complete the input-output table and then graph $g(x)$ on the same grid. In general, how is the graph of $g(x) = f(x) + k$ related to the graph of $f(x)$ when k is a negative number?

x	f(x)	f(x) − 3
−1	−2	−5
1	2	−1
3	−2	
5	2	

Ⓒ Now graph $g(x) = f(x - h)$ where h is the parameter. Let $h = 2$ so that $g(x) = f(x - 2)$. Complete the mapping diagram and then graph $g(x)$. (To complete the mapping diagram, you need to find the inputs for g that produce the inputs for f after you subtract 2. Work backward from the inputs for f to the missing inputs for g by adding 2.) In general, how is the graph of $g(x) = f(x - h)$ related to the graph of $f(x)$ when h is a positive number?

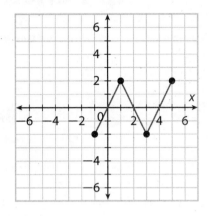

Input for g	Input for f	Output for f	Output for g
1	−1	−2	−2
3	1	2	2
☐	3	−2	−2
☐	5	2	2

_____

_____

Ⓓ **Make a Conjecture** How would you expect the graph of $g(x) = f(x - h)$ to be related to the graph of $f(x)$ when h is a negative number?

_____

_____

Reflect

1. Suppose a function $f(x)$ has a domain of $[x_1, x_2]$ and a range of $[y_1, y_2]$. When the graph of $f(x)$ is translated vertically k units where k is either positive or negative, how do the domain and range change?

_____

2. Suppose a function $f(x)$ has a domain of $[x_1, x_2]$ and a range of $[y_1, y_2]$. When the graph of $f(x)$ is translated horizontally h units where h is either positive or negative, how do the domain and range change?

_____

3. You can transform the graph of $f(x)$ to obtain the graph of $g(x) = f(x - h) + k$ by combining transformations. Predict what will happen by completing the table.

Sign of h	Sign of k	Transformations of the Graph of f(x)
+	+	Translate right h units and up k units.
+	−	
−	+	
−	−	

Investigating Stretches and Compressions of Function Graphs

In this activity, you will consider what happens when you multiply by a positive parameter inside or outside a function. Throughout, you will use the same function $f(x)$ that you used in the previous activity.

(A) First graph $g(x) = a \cdot f(x)$ where a is the parameter. Let $a = 2$ so that $g(x) = 2f(x)$. Complete the input-output table and then graph $g(x)$. In general, how is the graph of $g(x) = a \cdot f(x)$ related to the graph of $f(x)$ when a is greater than 1?

x	f(x)	2f(x)
−1	−2	−4
1	2	4
3	−2	
5	2	

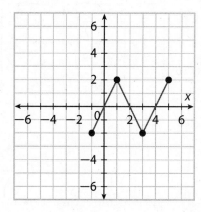

(B) Now try a value of a between 0 and 1 in $g(x) = a \cdot f(x)$. Let $a = \frac{1}{2}$ so that $g(x) = \frac{1}{2}f(x)$. Complete the input-output table and then graph $g(x)$. In general, how is the graph of $g(x) = a \cdot f(x)$ related to the graph of $f(x)$ when a is a number between 0 and 1?

x	f(x)	$\frac{1}{2}f(x)$
−1	−2	−1
1	2	1
3	−2	
5	2	

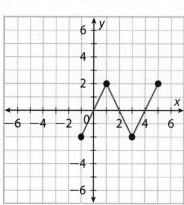

Ⓒ Now graph $g(x) = f\left(\frac{1}{b} \cdot x\right)$ where b is the parameter. Let $b = 2$ so that $g(x) = f\left(\frac{1}{2}x\right)$. Complete the mapping diagram and then graph $g(x)$. (To complete the mapping diagram, you need to find the inputs for g that produce the inputs for f after you multiply by $\frac{1}{2}$. Work backward from the inputs for f to the missing inputs for g by multiplying by 2.) In general, how is the graph of $g(x) = f\left(\frac{1}{b}x\right)$ related to the graph of $f(x)$ when b is a number greater than 1?

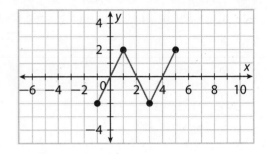

Ⓓ **Make a Conjecture** How would you expect the graph of $g(x) = f\left(\frac{1}{b} \cdot x\right)$ to be related to the graph of $f(x)$ when b is a number between 0 and 1?

Reflect

4. Suppose a function $f(x)$ has a domain of $[x_1, x_2]$ and a range of $[y_1, y_2]$. When the graph of $f(x)$ is stretched or compressed vertically by a factor of a, how do the domain and range change?

5. You can transform the graph of $f(x)$ to obtain the graph of $g(x) = a \cdot f(x-h) + k$ by combining transformations. Predict what will happen by completing the table.

Value of a	Transformations of the Graph of $f(x)$
$a > 1$	Stretch vertically by a factor of a, and translate h units horizontally and k units vertically.
$0 < a < 1$	

6. You can transform the graph of $f(x)$ to obtain the graph of $g(x) = f\left(\frac{1}{b}(x - h)\right) + k$ by combining transformations. Predict what will happen by completing the table.

Value of b	Transformations of the Graph of $f(x)$
$b > 1$	Stretch horizontally by a factor of b, and translate h units horizontally and k units vertically.
$0 < b < 1$	

⊘ Explore 3 **Investigating Reflections of Function Graphs**

When the parameter in a stretch or compression is negative, another transformation called a *reflection* is introduced. Examining reflections will also tell you whether a function is an *even function* or an *odd function*. An **even function** is one for which $f(-x) = f(x)$ for all x in the domain of the function, while an **odd function** is one for which $f(-x) = -f(x)$ for all x in the domain of the function. A function is not necessarily even or odd; it can be neither.

Ⓐ First graph $g(x) = a \cdot f(x)$ where $a = -1$. Complete the input-output table and then graph $g(x) = -f(x)$. In general, how is the graph of $g(x) = -f(x)$ related to the graph of $f(x)$?

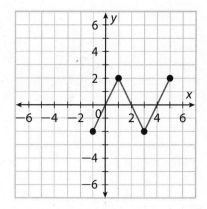

x	f(x)	−f(x)
−1	−2	2
1	2	−2
3	−2	
5	2	

Ⓑ Now graph $g(x) = f\left(\frac{1}{b} \cdot x\right)$ where $b = -1$. Complete the input-output table and then graph $g(x) = f(-x)$. In general, how is the graph of $g(x) = f(-x)$ related to the graph of $f(x)$?

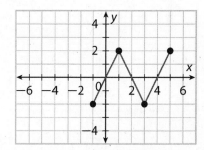

Input for g		Input for f	Output for f	Output for g
1	· (−1) →	−1	−2	−2
−1	→	1	2	2
☐	→	3	−2	−2
☐	→	5	2	2

Reflect

7. **Discussion** Suppose a function $f(x)$ has a domain of $\left[x_1, x_2\right]$ and a range of $\left[y_1, y_2\right]$. When the graph of $f(x)$ is reflected across the x-axis, how do the domain and range change?

8. For a function $f(x)$, suppose the graph of $f(-x)$, the reflection of the graph of $f(x)$ across the y-axis, is identical to the graph of $f(x)$. What does this tell you about $f(x)$? Explain.

9. Is the function whose graph you reflected across the axes in Steps A and B an even function, an odd function, or neither? Explain.

🔑 Explain 1 Transforming the Graph of the Parent Quadratic Function

You can use transformations of the graph of a basic function, called a *parent function*, to obtain the graph of a related function. To do so, focus on how the transformations affect reference points on the graph of the parent function.

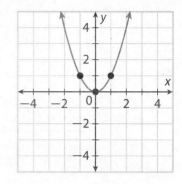

For instance, the parent quadratic function is $f(x) = x^2$. The graph of this function is a U-shaped curve called a *parabola* with a turning point, called a *vertex*, at (0, 0). The vertex is a useful reference point, as are the points $(-1, 1)$ and (1, 1).

Example 1 Describe how to transform the graph of $f(x) = x^2$ to obtain the graph of the related function $g(x)$. Then draw the graph of $g(x)$.

(A) $g(x) = -3f(x - 2) - 4$

Parameter and Its Value	Effect on the Parent Graph
$a = -3$	vertical stretch of the graph of $f(x)$ by a factor of 3 and a reflection across the x-axis
$b = 1$	Since $b = 1$, there is no horizontal stretch or compression.
$h = 2$	horizontal translation of the graph of $f(x)$ to the right 2 units
$k = -4$	vertical translation of the graph of $f(x)$ down 4 units

Applying these transformations to a point (x, y) on the parent graph results in the point $(x + 2, -3y - 4)$. The table shows what happens to the three reference points on the graph of $f(x)$.

Point on the Graph of $f(x)$	Corresponding Point on $g(x)$
$(-1, 1)$	$(-1 + 2, -3(1) - 4) = (1, -7)$
$(0, 0)$	$(0 + 2, -3(0) - 4) = (2, -4)$
$(1, 1)$	$(1 + 2, -3(1) - 4) = (3, -7)$

Use the transformed reference points to graph $g(x)$.

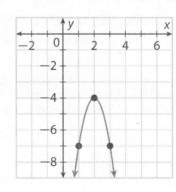

(B) $g(x) = f\left(\frac{1}{2}(x + 5)\right) + 2$

Parameter and Its Value	Effect on the Parent Graph
$a =$ ☐	Since $a = 1$, there is no vertical stretch, no vertical compression, and no reflection across the x-axis.
$b =$ ☐	The parent graph is stretched/compressed horizontally by a factor of _____. There is no reflection across the y-axis.
$h =$ ☐	The parent graph is translated _____ units horizontally/vertically.
$k =$ ☐	The parent graph is translated _____ units horizontally/vertically.

Applying these transformations to a point on the parent graph results in the point $(2x - 5, y + 2)$. The table shows what happens to the three reference points on the graph of $f(x)$.

Point on the Graph of $f(x)$	Corresponding Point on the Graph of $g(x)$
$(-1, 1)$	$(2(-1) - 5, 1 + 2) = (\ ☐\ ,\ ☐\ )$
$(0, 0)$	$(2(0) - 5, 0 + 2) = (\ ☐\ ,\ ☐\ )$
$(1, 1)$	$(2(1) - 5, 1 + 2) = (\ ☐\ ,\ ☐\ )$

Use the transformed reference points to graph $g(x)$.

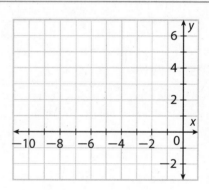

Reflect

10. Is the function $f(x) = x^2$ an even function, an odd function, or neither? Explain.

_____

_____

11. The graph of the parent quadratic function $f(x) = x^2$ has the vertical line $x = 0$ as its axis of symmetry. Identify the axis of symmetry for each of the graphs of $g(x)$ in Parts A and B. Which transformation(s) affect the location of the axis of symmetry?

_____

_____

12. Describe how to transform the graph of $f(x) = x^2$ to obtain the graph of the related function $g(x) = f\big(-4(x - 3)\big) + 1$. Then draw the graph of $g(x)$.

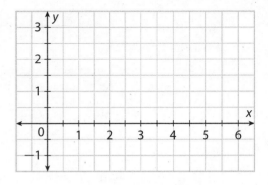

Explain 2 Modeling with a Quadratic Function

You can model real-world objects that have a parabolic shape using a quadratic function. In order to fit the function's graph to the shape of the object, you will need to determine the values of the parameters in the function $g(x) = a \cdot f\left(\frac{1}{b}(x - h)\right) + k$ where $f(x) = x^2$. Note that because $f(x)$ is simply a squaring function, it's possible to pull the parameter b outside the function and combine it with the parameter a. Doing so allows you to model real-objects using $g(x) = a \cdot f(x - h) + k$, which has only three parameters.

When modeling real-world objects, remember to restrict the domain of $g(x) = a \cdot f(x - h) + k$ to values of x that are based on the object's dimensions.

Example 2

An old stone bridge over a river uses a parabolic arch for support. In the illustration shown, the unit of measurement for both axes is feet, and the vertex of the arch is point C. Find a quadratic function that models the arch, and state the function's domain.

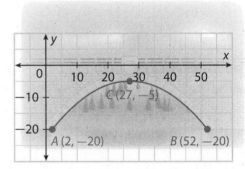

Analyze Information

Identify the important information.

- The shape of the arch is a _____.

- The vertex of the parabola is _____.

- Two other points on the parabola are _____ and _____.

Formulate a Plan

You want to find the values of the parameters a, h, and k in $g(x) = a \cdot f(x - h) + k$ where $f(x) = x^2$. You can use the coordinates of point _____ to find the values of h and k. Then you can use the coordinates of one of the other points to find the value of a.

Solve

The vertex of the graph of $g(x)$ is point C, and the vertex of the graph of $f(x)$ is the origin. Point C is the result of translating the origin 27 units to the right and 5 units down. This means that $h = 27$ and $k = -5$. Substituting these values into $g(x)$ gives $g(x) = a \cdot f(x - 27) - 5$. Now substitute the coordinates of point B into $g(x)$ and solve for a.

$g(x) = a \cdot f(x - 27) - 5$	Write the general function.
$g\left(\boxed{}\right) = a \cdot f(52 - 27) - 5$	Substitute 52 for x.
$-20 = a \cdot f(52 - 27) - 5$	Replace $g(52)$ with -20, the y-value of B.
$-20 = a \cdot f\left(\boxed{}\right) - 5$	Simplify.
$-20 = a(625) - 5$	Evaluate $f(25)$ for $f(x) = x^2$.
$a = \boxed{}$	Solve for a.

Substitute the value of a into $g(x)$.

$$g(x) = -\frac{3}{125} f(x - 27) - 5$$

The arch exists only between points A and B, so the domain of $g(x)$ is $\{x \mid 2 \leq x \leq 52\}$.

Justify and Evaluate

To justify the answer, verify that $g(2) = -20$.

$g(x) = -\frac{3}{125} f(x - 27) - 5$	Write the function.
$g\left(\boxed{}\right) = -\frac{3}{125} f\left(\boxed{} - 27\right) - 5$	Substitute 2 for x.
$= -\frac{3}{125} f\left(\boxed{}\right) - 5$	Subtract.
$= -\frac{3}{125} \cdot \left(\boxed{}\right) - 5$	Evaluate $f(-25)$.
$= -20$ ✓	Simplify.

13. The netting of an empty hammock hangs between its supports along a curve that can be modeled by a parabola. In the illustration shown, the unit of measurement for both axes is feet, and the vertex of the curve is point C. Find a quadratic function that models the hammock's netting, and state the function's domain.

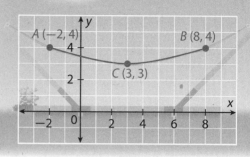

Elaborate

14. What is the general procedure to follow when graphing a function of the form $g(x) = a \cdot f(x - h) + k$ given the graph of $f(x)$?

_____

_____

_____

_____

15. What are the general steps to follow when determining the values of the parameters a, h, and k in $f(x) = a(x - h)^2 + k$ when modeling a parabolic real-world object?

_____

_____

_____

_____

_____

16. **Essential Question Check-In** How can the graph of a function $f(x)$ be transformed?

_____

_____

• Online Homework
• Hints and Help
• Extra Practice

Write $g(x)$ in terms of $f(x)$ after performing the given transformation of the graph of $f(x)$.

1. Translate the graph of $f(x)$ to the left 3 units.

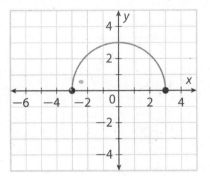

2. Translate the graph of $f(x)$ up 2 units.

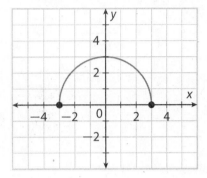

3. Translate the graph of $f(x)$ to the right 4 units.

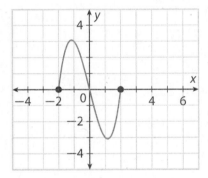

4. Translate the graph of $f(x)$ down 3 units.

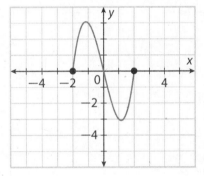

5. Stretch the graph of $f(x)$ horizontally by a factor of 3.

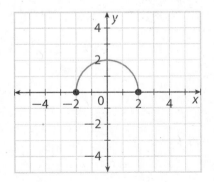

6. Stretch the graph of $f(x)$ vertically by a factor of 2.

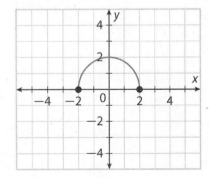

7. Compress the graph of $f(x)$ horizontally by a factor of $\frac{1}{3}$.

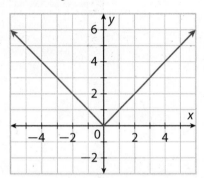

8. Compress the graph of $f(x)$ vertically by a factor of $\frac{1}{2}$.

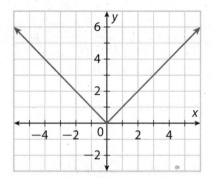

9. Reflect the graph of $f(x)$ across the y-axis.

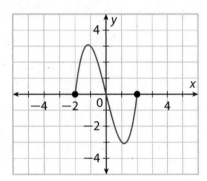

10. Reflect the graph of $f(x)$ across the x-axis.

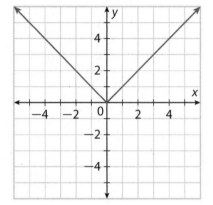

11. Reflect the graph of $f(x)$ across the y-axis.

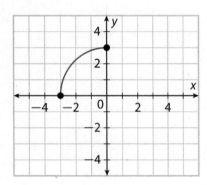

12. Reflect the graph of $f(x)$ across the x-axis.

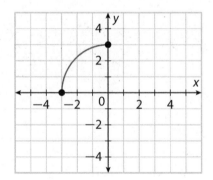

13. Determine if each function is an even function, an odd function, or neither.

a.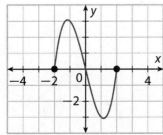

b.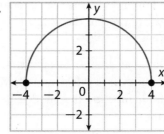

c.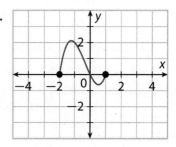

_____   _____   _____

14. Determine whether each quadratic function is an even function. Answer *yes* or *no*.

a. $f(x) = 5x^2$ _____

b. $f(x) = (x-2)^2$ _____

c. $f(x) = \left(\dfrac{x}{3}\right)^2$ _____

d. $f(x) = x^2 + 6$ _____

Describe how to transform the graph of $f(x) = x^2$ to obtain the graph of the related function $g(x)$. Then draw the graph of $g(x)$.

15. $g(x) = -\dfrac{f(x+4)}{3}$

16. $g(x) = f(2x) + 2$

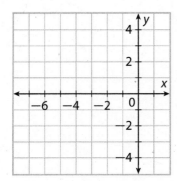

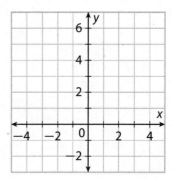

17. **Architecture** Flying buttresses were used in the construction of cathedrals and other large stone buildings before the advent of more modern construction materials to prevent the walls of large, high-ceilinged rooms from collapsing.

    The design of a flying buttress includes an arch. In the illustration shown, the unit of measurement for both axes is feet, and the vertex of the arch is point C. Find a quadratic function that models the arch, and state the function's domain.

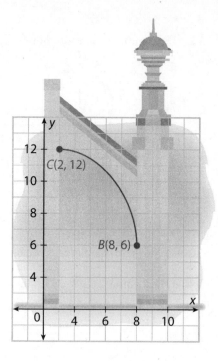

18. A red velvet rope hangs between two stanchions and forms a curve that can be modeled by a parabola. In the illustration shown, the unit of measurement for both axes is feet, and the vertex of the curve is point C. Find a quadratic function that models the rope, and state the function's domain.

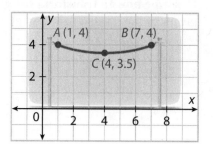

19. Multiple Representations The graph of the function

$g(x) = \left(\frac{1}{2}x + 2\right)^2$ is shown.

Use the graph to identify the transformations of the graph of $f(x) = x^2$ needed to produce the graph of $g(x)$. (If a stretch or compression is involved, give it in terms of a horizontal stretch or compression rather than a vertical one.) Use your list of

transformations to write $g(x)$ in the form $g(x) = f\left(\frac{1}{b}(x - h)\right) + k$. Then show why the new form of $g(x)$ is algebraically equivalent to the given form.

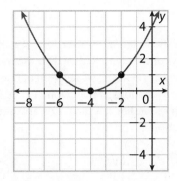

20. Represent Real-World Situations The graph of the ceiling function, $f(x) = \lceil x \rceil$, is shown. This function accepts any real number x as input and delivers the least integer greater than or equal to x as output. For instance, $f(1.3) = 2$ because 2 is the least integer greater than or equal to 1.3. The ceiling function is a type of *step function*, so named because its graph looks like a set of steps.

Write a function $g(x)$ whose graph is a transformation of the graph of $f(x)$ based on this situation: A parking garage charges $4 for the first hour or less and $2 for every additional hour or fraction of an hour. Then graph $g(x)$.

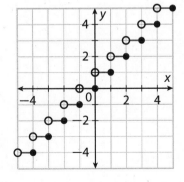

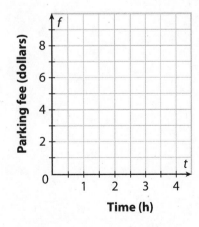

Time (h)

Lesson Performance Task

You are designing two versions of a chair, one without armrests and one with armrests. The diagrams show side views of the chair. Rather than use traditional straight legs for your chair, you decide to use parabolic legs. Given the function $f(x) = x^2$, write two functions, $g(x)$ and $h(x)$, whose graphs represent the legs of the two chairs and involve transformations of the graph of $f(x)$. For the chair without armrests, the graph of $g(x)$ must touch the bottom of the chair's seat. For the chair with armrests, the graph of $h(x)$ must touch the bottom of the armrest. After writing each function, graph it.

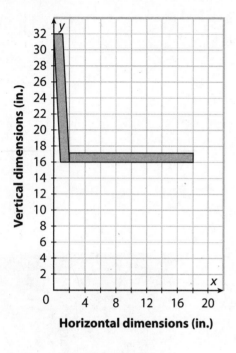

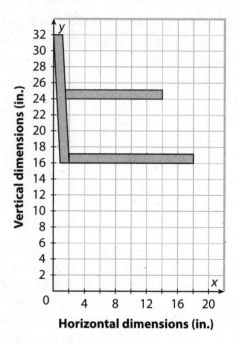

1.4 Inverses of Functions

Essential Question: What is an inverse function, and how do you know it's an inverse function?

⊘ Explore   Understanding Inverses of Functions

Recall that a *relation* is any pairing of the elements of one set (the domain) with the elements of a second set (the range). The elements of the domain are called inputs, while the elements of the range are called outputs. A function is a special type of relation that pairs every input with exactly one output. In a *one-to-one function*, no output is ever used more than once in the function's pairings. In a *many-to-one function*, at least one output is used more than once.

An **inverse relation** reverses the pairings of a relation. If a relation pairs an input x with an output y, then the inverse relation pairs an input y with an output x. The inverse of a function may or may not be another function. If the inverse of a function $f(x)$ is also a function, it is called the **inverse function** and is written $f^{-1}(x)$. If the inverse of a function is not a function, then it is simply an inverse relation.

Ⓐ The mapping diagrams show a function and its inverse. Complete the diagram for the inverse of the function.

Is the function one-to-one or many-to-one? Explain.

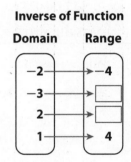

_____

_____

Is the inverse of the function also a function? Explain.

_____

_____

Ⓑ The mapping diagrams show a function and its inverse. Complete the diagram for the inverse of the function.

Is the function one-to-one or many-to-one? Explain.

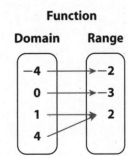
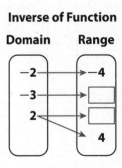

_____

_____

Is the inverse of the function also a function? Explain.

_____

_____

Ⓒ The graph of the original function in Step A is shown. Note that the graph also shows the dashed line $y = x$. Write the inverse of the function as a set of ordered pairs and graph them.

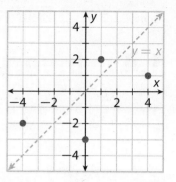

Function: $\{(-4, -2), (0, -3), (1, 2), (4, 1)\}$

Inverse of function:

$$\left\{\left(\square, \square\right), \left(\square, \square\right), \left(\square, \square\right), \left(\square, \square\right)\right\}$$

What do you observe about the graphs of the function and its inverse in relationship to the line $y = x$? Why does this make sense?

_____

_____

Ⓓ The **composition of two functions** $f(x)$ and $g(x)$, written $f(g(x))$ and read as "f of g of x," is a new function that uses the output of $g(x)$ as the input of $f(x)$. For example, consider the functions f and g with the following rules.

f: Add 1 to an input. g: Double an input.

Notice that $g(1) = 2(1) = 2$. So, $f(g(1)) = f(2) = 2 + 1 = 3$.

You can also find $g(f(x))$. Notice that $f(1) = 1 + 1 = 2$. So, $g(f(1)) = g(2) = 2(2) = 4$.

For these two functions, you can see that $f(g(1)) \neq g(f(1))$.

You can compose a function and its inverse. For instance, the mapping diagram shown illustrates $f^{-1}(f(x))$ where $f(x)$ is the original function from Step A and $f^{-1}(x)$ is its inverse. Notice that the range of $f(x)$ serves as the domain of $f^{-1}(x)$. Complete the diagram. What do you notice about the outputs of $f^{-1}(f(x))$? Explain why this makes sense.

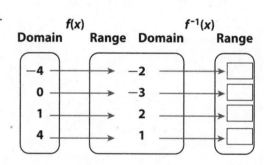

_____

_____

_____

_____

Reflect

1. What is the relationship between the domain and range of a relation and its inverse?

_____

_____

2. Discussion In Step D, you saw that for inverse functions, $f^{-1}(f(x)) = x$. What do you expect $f(f^{-1}(x))$ to equal? Explain.

_____

_____

Explain 1   Finding the Inverse of a Linear Function

Every linear function $f(x) = mx + b$ where $m \neq 0$ is a one-to-one function. So, its inverse is also a function. To find the inverse function, use the fact that inverse functions undo each other's pairings.

To find the inverse of a function $f(x)$:
1. Substitute y for $f(x)$.
2. Solve for x in terms of y.
3. Switch x and y (since the inverse switches inputs and outputs).
4. Replace y with $f^{-1}(x)$.

To check your work and verify that the functions are inverses, show that $f\big(f^{-1}(x)\big) = x$ and that $f^{-1}\big(f(x)\big) = x$.

Example 1   Find the inverse function $f^{-1}(x)$ for the given function $f(x)$. Use composition to verify that the functions are inverses. Then graph the function and its inverse.

(A) $f(x) = 3x + 4$

Replace $f(x)$ with y. $\qquad\qquad\qquad y = 3x + 4$

Solve for x. $\qquad\qquad\qquad\qquad\quad y - 4 = 3x$

$$\frac{y-4}{3} = x$$

Interchange x and y. $\qquad\qquad\quad y = \dfrac{x-4}{3}$

Replace y with $f^{-1}(x)$. $\qquad\quad f^{-1}(x) = \dfrac{x-4}{3}$

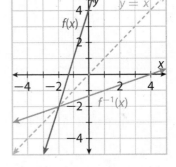

Check: Verify that $f^{-1}\big(f(x)\big) = x$ and $f\big(f^{-1}(x)\big) = x$.

$$f^{-1}\big(f(x)\big) = f^{-1}(3x+4) = \frac{(3x+4)-4}{3} = \frac{3x}{3} = x$$

$$f\big(f^{-1}(x)\big) = f\Big(\frac{x-4}{3}\Big) = 3\Big(\frac{x-4}{3}\Big) + 4 = (x-4) + 4 = x$$

(B) $f(x) = 2x - 2$

Replace $f(x)$ with y. $\qquad\qquad\qquad y = \boxed{}$

Solve for x. $\qquad\qquad y\ \boxed{} = 2x$

$$\frac{y+2}{2} = x$$

Interchange x and y. $\qquad\qquad\quad y = \boxed{}$

Replace y with $f^{-1}(x)$. $\qquad \boxed{} = \dfrac{x+2}{2}$

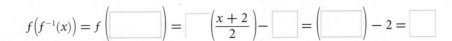

Check: Verify that $f^{-1}\big(f(x)\big) = x$ and $f\big(f^{-1}(x)\big) = x$.

$$f^{-1}\big(f(x)\big) = f^{-1}\left(\boxed{}\right) = \frac{(2x-2) + \boxed{}}{\boxed{}} = \frac{\boxed{}}{2} = \boxed{}$$

$$f\big(f^{-1}(x)\big) = f\left(\boxed{}\right) = \boxed{}\left(\frac{x+2}{2}\right) - \boxed{} = \left(\boxed{}\right) - 2 = \boxed{}$$

© Houghton Mifflin Harcourt Publishing Company

3. What is the significance of the point where the graph of a linear function and its inverse intersect?

_____

_____

4. The graph of a constant function $f(x) = c$ for any constant c is a horizontal line through the point $(0, c)$. Does a constant function have an inverse? Does it have an inverse function? Explain.

_____

_____

_____

Your Turn

Find the inverse function $f^{-1}(x)$ for the given function $f(x)$. Use composition to verify that the functions are inverses. Then graph the function and its inverse.

5. $f(x) = -2x + 3$

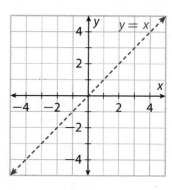

⚙ Explain 2 Modeling with the Inverse of a Linear Function

In a model for a real-world situation, the variables have specific real-world meanings. For example, the distance d (in miles) traveled in time t (in hours) at a constant speed of 60 miles per hour is $d = 60t$. Writing this in function notation as $d(t) = 60t$ emphasizes that this equation describes distance as a function of time.

You can find the inverse function for $d = 60t$ by solving for the independent variable t in terms of the dependent variable d. This gives the equation $t = \frac{d}{60}$. Writing this in function notation as $t(d) = \frac{d}{60}$ emphasizes that this equation describes time as a function of distance. Because the meanings of the variables can't be interchanged, you do not switch them at the end as you would switch x and y when working with purely mathematical functions. As you work with real-world models, you may have to restrict the domain and range.

Example 2 For the given function, state the domain of the inverse function using set notation. Then find an equation for the inverse function, and graph it. Interpret the meaning of the inverse function.

(A) The equation $C = 3.5g$ gives the cost C (in dollars) as a function of the number of gallons of gasoline g when the price is $3.50 per gallon.

The domain of the function $C = 3.5g$ is restricted to nonnegative numbers to make real-world sense, so the range of the function also consists of nonnegative numbers. This means that the

domain of the inverse function is $\{C \mid C \geq 0\}$

Solve the given equation for g to find the inverse function.

Write the equation. $\qquad$ $C = 3.5g$

Divide both sides by 3.5. $\qquad \dfrac{C}{3.5} = g$

So, the inverse function is $g = \dfrac{C}{3.5}$.

Graph the inverse function.

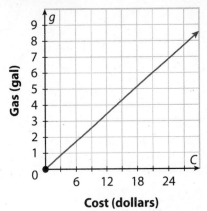

The inverse function gives the number of gallons of gasoline as a function of the cost (in dollars) when the price of gas is $3.50 per gallon.

(B) A car's gas tank, which can hold 14 gallons of gas, contains 4 gallons of gas when the driver stops at a gas station to fill the tank. The gas pump dispenses gas at a rate of 5 gallons per minute. The equation $g = 5t + 4$ gives the number of gallons of gasoline g in the tank as a function of the pumping time t (in minutes).

The range of the function $g = 5t + 4$ is the number of gallons

of gas in the tank, which varies from _____ gallons to _____

gallons. So, the domain of the inverse function

is $\left\{ g \;\middle|\; \boxed{} \leq g \leq \boxed{} \right\}$.

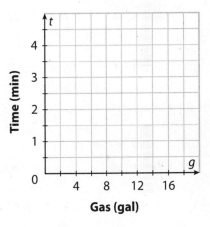

Solve the given equation for g to find the inverse function.

Write the equation. $\qquad g = \boxed{}\, t + \boxed{}$

Solve for t. $\qquad \dfrac{\boxed{}}{5} = t$

So, the inverse function is $t = \boxed{}$.

Graph the inverse function.

The inverse function gives _____ as a

function of _____ .

For the given function, determine the domain of the inverse function. Then find an equation for the inverse function, and graph it. Interpret the meaning of the inverse function.

6. A municipal swimming pool containing 600,000 gallons of water is drained. The amount of water w (in thousands of gallons) remaining in the pool at time t (in hours) after the draining begins is $w = 600 - 20t$.

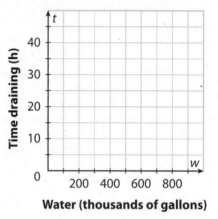

Water (thousands of gallons)

⊙ Elaborate

7. What must be true about a function for its inverse to be a function?

_____

8. A function rule indicates the operations to perform on an input to produce an output. What is the relationship between these operations and the operations indicated by the inverse function?

_____

_____

9. How can you use composition to verify that two functions $f(x)$ and $g(x)$ are inverse functions?

_____

_____

10. Describe a real-world situation modeled by a linear function for which it makes sense to find an inverse function. Give an example of how the inverse function might also be useful.

_____

_____

_____

11. **Essential Question Check-In** What is an inverse relation?

_____

_____

Evaluate: Homework and Practice

• Online Homework
• Hints and Help
• Extra Practice

The mapping diagrams show a function and its inverse. Complete the diagram for the inverse of the function. Then tell whether the inverse is a function, and explain your reasoning.

1.

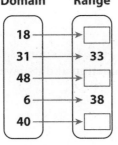

Function		Inverse of Function	
Domain	Range	Domain	Range
16	18	18	☐
33	31	31	33
12	48	48	☐
38	6	6	38
18	40	40	☐

2.

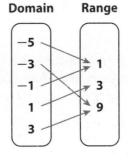

Function		Inverse of Function	
Domain	Range	Domain	Range
−5	1	1	☐
−3	3	3	−3
−1	9	9	1
1			☐
3			

Write the inverse of the given function as a set of ordered pairs and then graph the inverse on the coordinate plane.

3. Function:

$\{(-4, -3), (-2, -4), (0, -2), (1, 0), (2, 3)\}$

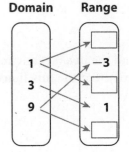

4. Function:

$\{(-3, -4), (-2, -3), (-1, 2), (1, 2), (2, 4), (3, 4)\}$

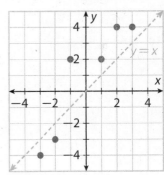

Find the inverse function $f^{-1}(x)$ for the given function $f(x)$.

5. $f(x) = 4x - 8$

6. $f(x) = \dfrac{x}{3}$

7. $f(x) = \dfrac{x+1}{6}$

8. $f(x) = -0.75x$

Find the inverse function $f^{-1}(x)$ for the given function $f(x)$. Use composition to verify that the functions are inverses. Then graph the function and its inverse.

9. $f(x) = -3x + 3$

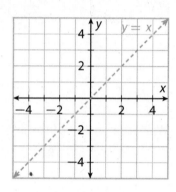

10. $f(x) = \dfrac{2}{5}x - 2$

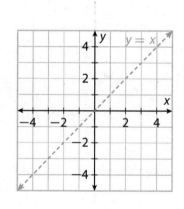

For the given function, determine the domain of the inverse function. Then find an equation for the inverse function, and graph it. Interpret the meaning of the inverse function.

11. **Geometry** The equation $A = \frac{1}{2}(20)h$ gives the area A (in square inches) of a triangle with a base of 20 inches as a function of its height h (in inches).

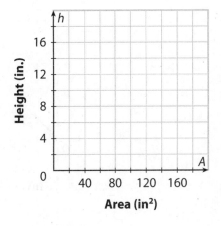

12. The label on a gallon of paint says that it will cover from 250 square feet to 450 square feet depending on the surface that is being painted. A painter has 12 gallons of paint on hand. The equation $A = 12c$ gives the area A (in square feet) that the 12 gallons of paint will cover if applied at a coverage rate c (in square feet per gallon).

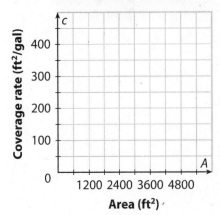

The graph of a function is given. Tell whether the function's inverse is a function, and explain your reasoning. If the inverse is not a function, tell how can you restrict the domain of the function so that its inverse is a function.

13.

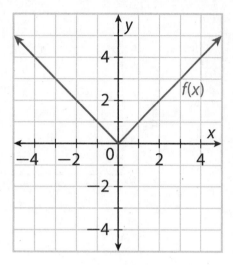

14.

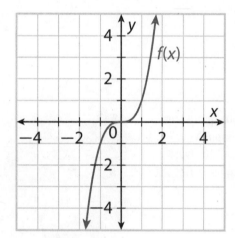

15. Multiple Response Identify the domain intervals over which the inverse of the graphed function is also a function. Select all that apply.

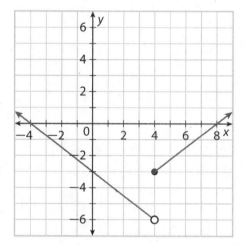

A. $[4, +\infty)$ D. $(-\infty, +\infty)$ G. $(4, 8)$

B. $(0, +\infty)$ E. $(-\infty, 4]$ H. $(8, +\infty)$

C. $[-4, +\infty)$ F. $(-\infty, 4)$ I. $(0, 8]$

16. Draw Conclusions Identify all linear functions that are their own inverse.

17. Make a Conjecture Among linear functions (excluding constant functions), quadratic functions, absolute value functions, and exponential functions, which types of function do you have to restrict the domain for the inverse to be a function? Explain.

18. Find the Error A student was asked to find the inverse of $f(x) = 2x + 1$. The student's work is shown. Explain why the student is incorrect and what the student should have done to get the correct answer.

> The function $f(x) = 2x + 1$ involves two operations: multiplying by 2 and adding 1. The inverse operations are dividing by 2 and subtracting 1. So, the inverse function is $f^{-1}(x) = \frac{x}{2} - 1$.

Lesson Performance Task

In an anatomy class, a student measures the femur of an adult male and finds the length of the femur to be 50.0 cm. The student is then asked to estimate the height of the male that the femur came from.

The table shows the femur lengths and heights of some adult males and females. Using a graphing calculator, perform linear regression on the data to obtain femur length as a function of height (one function for adult males, one for adult females). Then find the inverse of each function. Use the appropriate inverse function to find the height of the adult male and explain how the inverse functions would be helpful to a forensic scientist.

Femur Length (cm)	30	38	46	54	62
Male Height (cm)	138	153	168	183	198
Female Height (cm)	132	147	163	179	194

Analyzing Functions

Essential Question: How can you analyze functions to solve real-world problems?

Key Vocabulary

finite interval *(intervalo finito)*

infinite interval *(intervalo infinito)*

domain *(dominio)*

range *(rango)*

end behavior *(comportamiento final)*

KEY EXAMPLE (Lesson 1.1)

Write the domain and range of $f(x) = 3^x$ as an inequality, using set notation, and using interval notation. Then describe the end behavior of the function.

	Domain	Range
Inequality	$-\infty < x < +\infty$	$y > 0$
Set notation	$\{x \mid -\infty < x < +\infty\}$	$\{y \mid y > 0\}$
Interval notation	$(-\infty, +\infty)$	$(0, +\infty)$

End behavior: As $x \to +\infty$, $f(x) \to +\infty$, and as $x \to -\infty$, $f(x) \to 0$.

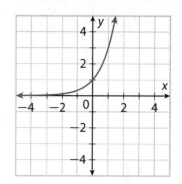

KEY EXAMPLE (Lesson 1.3)

Describe how to transform the graph of $f(x) = x^2$ to obtain the graph of the related function $g(x) = 2f(x - 1) + 3$.

Parameter	Effect on the Parent Graph
$a = 2$	vertical stretch of the graph of $f(x)$ by a factor of 2
$h = 1$	translation of the graph of $f(x)$ to the right 1 unit
$k = 3$	translation of the graph of $f(x)$ up 3 units

A point (x, y) on the graph of $f(x) = x^2$ becomes the point $(x + 1, 2y + 3)$.

KEY EXAMPLE (Lesson 1.4)

Find the inverse function $f^{-1}(x)$ for $f(x) = -2x + 3$.

$$y = -2x + 3$$ Replace $f(x)$ with y.

$$\frac{y - 3}{-2} = x$$ Solve for x.

$$y = \frac{x - 3}{-2}$$ Switch x and y.

$$f^{-1}(x) = \frac{x - 3}{-2}$$ Replace y with $f^{-1}(x)$.

EXERCISES

Write the domain and range of the function as an inequality, using set notation, and using interval notation. *(Lesson 1.1)*

1.

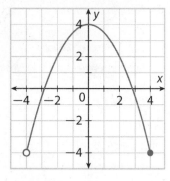

Domain:

Inequality:

Set notation:

Interval notation:

Range:

Inequality:

Set Notation:

Interval Notation:

2.

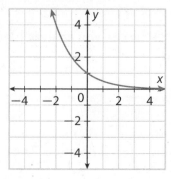

Domain:

Inequality:

Set notation:

Interval notation:

Range:

Inequality:

Set Notation:

Interval Notation:

Find the inverse function $f^{-1}(x)$ for the given function $f(x)$. *(Lesson 1.4)*

3. $f(x) = \dfrac{x + 3}{5}$

4. $f(x) = 2x + 6$

5. Explain how to transform the graph of the function $f(x) = x^2$ to obtain the graph of the related function $g(x) = -2f(x + 1) - 3$. *(Lesson 1.3)*

MODULE PERFORMANCE TASK

How High Does a Pole-Vaulter Go?

A pole-vaulter performs two vaults, which can be modeled using the functions $h_1(t) = 9.8t - 4.9t^2$ and $h_2(t) = 8.82t - 4.9t^2$ where h is the height in meters at time t in seconds. How do the two jumps compare graphically in terms of the vertices and intercepts, and what do these represent? Which was the higher jump? How do you know?

Use your own paper to complete the task. Be sure to write down all your data and assumptions. Then use graphs, numbers, words, or algebra to explain how you reached your conclusions.

(Ready) to Go On?

1.1–1.4 Analyzing Functions

• Online Homework
• Hints and Help
• Extra Practice

Write the domain and range of the function $g(x) = 3x^2 - 4$ as an inequality, using set notation, and using interval notation. Then, compare the function to $f(x) = x^2$ and describe the transformations. *(Lessons 1.1, 1.3)*

1.	Domain	Range	Transformations
Inequality			
Set notation			
Interval notation			

Find the inverse for each linear function. *(Lesson 1.4)*

2. $f(x) = -2x + 4$

3. $g(x) = \dfrac{x}{4} - 3$

4. $h(x) = \dfrac{3}{4}x + 1$

5. $j(x) = 5x - 6$

ESSENTIAL QUESTION

6. What are two ways the graphed function could be used to solve real-world problems? *(Lesson 1.2)*

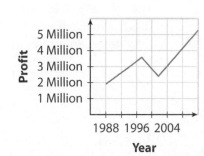

Assessment Readiness

1. Look at each equation. Does the graph of the equation have an end behavior that approaches infinity (∞) as $x \to -\infty$?
   Select Yes or No for A–C.

   A. $y = -2x - 5$ ◯ Yes ◯ No

   B. $y = 5(x + 2)^2 - 3$ ◯ Yes ◯ No

   C. $y = -3^x$ ◯ Yes ◯ No

2. Consider the function $g(x) = -f(x + 3) - 2$. Choose True or False for each statement.

   A. When compared to $f(x) = x^2$, $g(x)$ will have a vertical stretch of 3. ◯ True ◯ False

   B. When compared to $f(x) = x^2$, $g(x)$ will be reflected over the x-axis. ◯ True ◯ False

   C. When compared to $f(x) = x^2$, $g(x)$ will be translated left 3 units. ◯ True ◯ False

3. A bike rider starts at a fast pace and rides 40 miles in 2 hours. He gets tired, and slows down, traveling only 20 miles in the next 3 hours. He takes a rest for an hour, then rides back to where he started at a steady pace without stopping for 4 hours. Draw a graph to match the real world situation. Explain your choices.

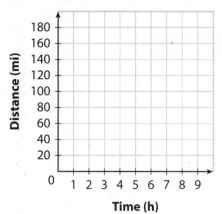

Distance from Starting Point

4. The function to convert Fahrenheit to Celsius is $°C = f(°F) = \frac{5(°F - 32)}{9}$. The inverse function will convert Celsius to Fahrenheit. What is the inverse function? Explain how determining this inverse is different than determining the previous inverses.

Absolute Value Functions, Equations, and Inequalities

Essential Question: How can you use absolute value functions to solve real-world problems?

REAL WORLD VIDEO
Gold jewelry is sold with a rating for purity. For instance, 18-karat gold is 75% pure by weight. The purity level has to meet tolerances that can be expressed using absolute value inequalities.

MODULE PERFORMANCE TASK PREVIEW
What Is the Purity of Gold?

Because gold is such a soft metal, it is usually mixed with another metal such as copper or silver. Pure gold is 24 karat, and 18 karat indicates a mixture of 18 parts gold and 6 parts of another metal or metals. Imagine someone wants to sell you a ring and claims it is 18 karat. How can you use math to be sure the gold is indeed 18 karat? Let's find out!

Are(YOU)Ready?

Complete these exercises to review skills you will need for this module.

One-Step Equations

Example 1   Solve $x - 6.8 = 2$ for x.

$$x - 6.8 + 6.8 = 2 + 6.8 \qquad \text{Add.}$$

$$x = 8.8 \qquad \text{Combine like terms.}$$

Solve each equation.

1. $r + 9 = 7$ _____

2. $\frac{w}{4} = -3$ _____

3. $10b = 14$ _____

Slope and Slope-Intercept Form

Example 2   Find the slope and y-intercept of $3x - y = 6$.

$$-3x + 3x - y = -3x + 6 \qquad \text{Write the equation in } y = mx + b \text{ form.}$$

$$-y(-1) = (-3x + 6)(-1)$$

$$y = 3x - 6 \qquad \text{The slope is 3 and the } y\text{-intercept is } -6.$$

Find the slope and y-intercept for each equation.

4. $y - 8 = 2x + 9$

5. $3y = 2(x - 3)$

6. $2y + 8x = 1$

_____

_____

_____

Linear Inequalities in Two Variables

Example 3   Graph $y < 2x - 3$.

Graph the y-intercept of $(0, -3)$.

Use the slope of 2 to plot a second point, and draw a dashed line connecting the points. Shade below the line.

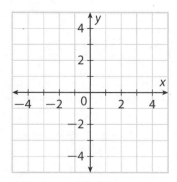

Graph and label each inequality on the coordinate plane.

7. $y \geq -x + 2$

8. $y < x - 1$

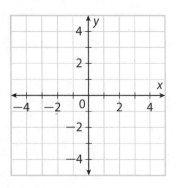

2.1   Graphing Absolute Value Functions

Essential Question: How can you identify the features of the graph of an absolute value function?

Explore 1   Graphing and Analyzing the Parent Absolute Value Function

Absolute value, written as $|x|$, represents the distance between x and 0 on a number line. As a distance, absolute value is always nonnegative. For every point on a number line (except at 0), there is another point on the opposite side of 0 that is the same distance from 0. For example, both 5 and −5 are five units away from 0. Thus, $|-5| = 5$ and $|5| = 5$.

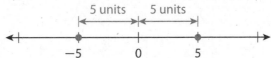

The absolute value function $|x|$, can be defined piecewise as $|x| = \begin{cases} x & x \geq 0 \\ -x & x < 0 \end{cases}$. When x is nonnegative, the function simply returns the number. When x is negative, the function returns the opposite of x.

(A)   Complete the input-output table for $f(x)$.

$f(x) = |x| = \begin{cases} x & x \geq 0 \\ -x & x < 0 \end{cases}$

x	f(x)
−8	
−4	
0	
4	
8	

(B)   Plot the points you found on the coordinate grid.
Use the points to complete the graph of the function.

(C)   Now, examine your graph of $f(x) = |x|$ and complete the following statements about the function.

$f(x) = |x|$ is symmetric about the _____ and therefore

is a(n) _____ function.

The domain of $f(x) = |x|$ is _____.

The range of $f(x) = |x|$ is _____.

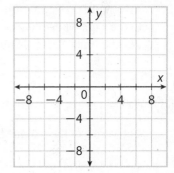

Reflect

1. Use the definition of the absolute value function to show that $f(x) = |x|$ is an even function.

_____

_____

_____

_____

_____

_____

✏️ Explain 1 Graphing Absolute Value Functions

You can apply general transformations to absolute value functions by changing parameters in the

equation $g(x) = a\left|\frac{1}{b}(x - h)\right| + k$.

Example 1 Given the function $g(x) = a\left|\frac{1}{b}(x - h)\right| + k$, find the vertex of the function. Use the vertex and two other points to help you graph $g(x)$.

(A) $g(x) = 4|x - 5| - 2$

The vertex of the parent absolute value function is at $(0, 0)$.

The vertex of $g(x)$ will be the point to which $(0, 0)$ is mapped by $g(x)$.

$g(x)$ involves a translation of $f(x)$ 5 units to the right and 2 units down.

The vertex of $g(x)$ will therefore be at $(5, -2)$.

Next, determine the location to which each of the points $(1, 1)$ and $(-1, 1)$ on $f(x)$ will be mapped.

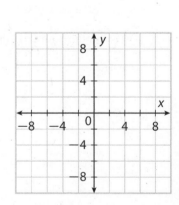

Since $a > 1$, then $g(x)$, in addition to being a translation, is also a vertical stretch of $f(x)$ by a factor of 4. The x-coordinate of each point will be shifted 5 units to the right while the y-coordinate will be stretched by a factor of 4 and then moved down 2 units. So, $(1, 1)$ moves to $(1 + 5, 4 \cdot |1| - 2) = (6, 2)$, and $(-1, 1)$ moves to $(-1 + 5, 4 \cdot |1| - 2) = (4, 2)$. Now plot the three points and graph $g(x)$.

(B) $g(x) = \left|-\frac{1}{2}(x + 3)\right| + 1$

The vertex of the parent absolute value function is at $(0, 0)$.

$g(x)$ is a translation of $f(x)$ _____ units to the _____

and _____ unit _____.

The vertex of $g(x)$ will therefore be at $\left(\boxed{}, \boxed{}\right)$.

Next, determine to where the points $(2, 2)$ and $(-2, 2)$ on $f(x)$ will

be mapped.

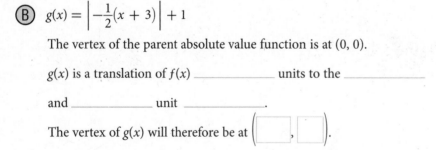

Since $|b| = 2$, $g(x)$ is also a _____ of $f(x)$ and since b is negative,

a _____ .

The x-coordinate will be reflected in the y-axis and _____ by a factor

of _____ , then moved _____ units to the _____ .

The y-coordinate will move _____ unit.

So, $(2, 2)$ becomes $\left(\boxed{}, \boxed{} \right) = \left(\boxed{}, \boxed{} \right)$, and $(-2, 2)$

becomes $\left(\boxed{}, \boxed{} \right)$. Now plot the three points and use them to sketch $g(x)$.

Your Turn

2. Given $g(x) = -\frac{1}{5}\left|(x + 6)\right| + 4$, find the vertex and two other points
    and use them to help you graph $g(x)$.

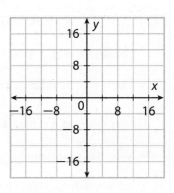

🔧 **Explain 2**   **Writing Absolute Value Functions from a Graph**

If an absolute value function in the form $g(x) = a\left|\frac{1}{b}(x - h)\right| + k$ has values other than 1 for
both a and b, you can rewrite that function so that the value of at least one of a or b is 1.

When a and b are positive: $a\left|\frac{1}{b}(x - h)\right| = \left|\frac{a}{b}(x - h)\right| = \frac{a}{b}\left|(x - h)\right|$.

When a is negative and b is positive, you can move the opposite of a inside the absolute value
expression. This leaves -1 outside the absolute value symbol: $-2\left|\frac{1}{b}\right| = -1(2)\left|\frac{1}{b}\right| = -1\left|\frac{2}{b}\right|$.

When b is negative, you can rewrite the equation without a negative sign, because of the
properties of absolute value: $a\left|\frac{1}{b}(x - h)\right| = a\left|\frac{1}{-b}(x - h)\right|$. This case has now been
reduced to one of the other two cases.

Example 2   **Given the graph of an absolute value function, write the**
function in the form $g(x) = a\left|\frac{1}{b}(x - h)\right| + k$.

(A) Let $a = 1$.

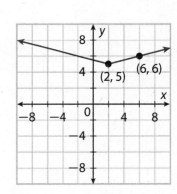

The vertex of $g(x)$ is at $(2, 5)$. This means that $h = 2$ and $k = 5$.
The value of a is given: $a = 1$.

Substitute these values into $g(x)$, giving $g(x) = \left|\frac{1}{b}(x - 2)\right| + 5$.

Choose a point on $g(x)$ like $(6, 6)$, Substitute these values into $g(x)$, and
solve for b.

Substitute. $\qquad 6 = \left|\dfrac{1}{b}(6-2)\right| + 5$

Simplify. $\qquad 6 = \left|\dfrac{1}{b}(4)\right| + 5$

Subtract 5 from each side. $\qquad 1 = \left|\dfrac{4}{b}\right|$

Rewrite the absolute value as two equations. $1 = \dfrac{4}{b}$ or $1 = -\dfrac{4}{b}$

Solve for b. $\qquad\qquad\qquad b = 4$ or $b = -4$

Based on the problem conditions, only consider $b = 4$. Substitute into $g(x)$ to find the equation for the graph.

$$g(x) = \left|\dfrac{1}{4}(x-2)\right| + 5$$

(B) Let $b = 1$.

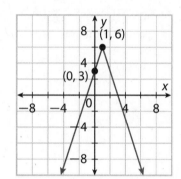

The vertex of $g(x)$ is at _____. This means that $h = \boxed{}$ and

$k = \boxed{}$ The value of b is given: $b = 1$.

Substitute these values into $g(x)$, giving $g(x) = a\left|x - \boxed{}\right| + \boxed{}$.

Now, choose a point on $g(x)$ with integer coordinates, $\left(0, \boxed{}\right)$.

Substitute these values into $g(x)$ and solve for a.

$$g(x) = a\left|x - \boxed{}\right| + \boxed{}$$

Substitute. $\qquad \boxed{} = a|0 - 1| + 6$

Simplify. $\qquad \boxed{} = a|-1| + 6$

Solve for a. $\qquad \boxed{} = a$

Therefore $g(x) = \boxed{}$.

Your Turn

3. Given the graph of an absolute value function, write the function in the form $g(x) = a\left|\dfrac{1}{b}(x - h)\right| + k$.

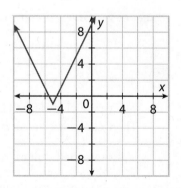

Explain 3   Modeling with Absolute Value Functions

Light travels in a straight line and can be modeled by a linear function. When light is reflected off a mirror, it travels in a straight line in a different direction. From physics, the angle at which the light ray comes in is equal to the angle at which it is reflected away: the angle of incidence is equal to the angle of reflection. You can use an absolute value function to model this situation.

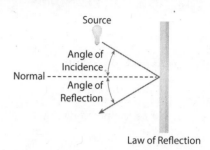

Law of Reflection

Example 3   **Solve the problem by modeling the situation with an absolute value function.**

At a science museum exhibit, a beam of light originates at a point 10 feet off the floor. It is reflected off a mirror on the floor that is 15 feet from the wall the light originates from. How high off the floor on the opposite wall does the light hit if the other wall is 8.5 feet from the mirror?

Analyze Information

Identify the important information.

- The model will be of the form $g(x) =$ _____.

- The vertex of $g(x)$ is   _____.

- Another point on $g(x)$ is   _____.

- The opposite wall is _____ feet from the first wall.

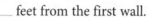

Formulate a Plan

Let the base of the first wall be the origin. You want to find the value of $g(x)$ at $x =$ [   ], which will give the height of the beam on the opposite wall. To do so, find the value of the parameters in the transformation of the parent function.

In this situation, let $b = 1$. The vertex of $g(x)$ will give you the values of _____. Use a second point to solve for a. Evaluate $g\left(\;\boxed{}\;\right)$.

Solve

The vertex of $g(x)$ is at $\left(\;\boxed{}\;, 0\right)$. Substitute, giving $g(x) = a\left|x - \boxed{}\right| + \boxed{}$.

Evaluate $g(x)$ at _____ and solve for a.

Substitute. $10 = a\left|\;\boxed{} - 15\;\right| + \boxed{}$

Simplify. $\boxed{} = a\left|\;\boxed{}\;\right|$

Simplify. $10 = \boxed{}\, a$

Solve for a. $a = \boxed{}$

Therefore $g(x) =$ _____. Find $g\left(\;\boxed{}\;\right)$. $g(23.5) = \boxed{}$

The answer of _____ makes sense because the function is symmetric with

respect to the line _____. The distance from this line to the second wall is

a little more than _____ the distance from the line to the beam's origin.

Since the beam originates at a height of _____, it should hit the second wall

at a height of a little over _____.

Your Turn

4. Two students are passing a ball back and forth, allowing it to bounce once between them. If one student bounce-passes the ball from a height of 1.4 m and it bounces 3 m away from the student, where should the second student stand to catch the ball at a height of 1.2 m? Assume the path of the ball is linear over this short distance.

Elaborate

5. In the general form of the absolute value function, what does each parameter represent?

_____

_____

6. Discussion Explain why the vertex of $f(x) = |x|$ remains the same when $f(x)$ is stretched or compressed but not when it is translated.

_____

_____

_____

7. Essential Question Check-In What are the features of the graph of an absolute value function?

_____

• Online Homework
• Hints and Help
• Extra Practice

Predict what the graph of each given function will look like. Verify your prediction using a graphing calculator. Then sketch the graph of the function.

1. $g(x) = 5|x - 3|$

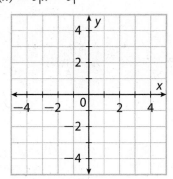

2. $g(x) = -4|x + 2| + 5$

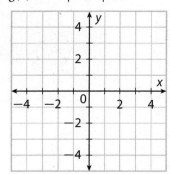

3. $g(x) = \left|\dfrac{7}{5}(x - 6)\right| + 4$

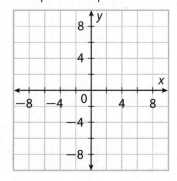

4. $g(x) = \left|\dfrac{3}{7}(x - 4)\right| + 2$

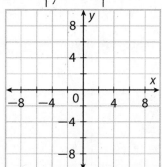

5. $g(x) = \dfrac{7}{4}\left|(x - 2)\right| - 3$

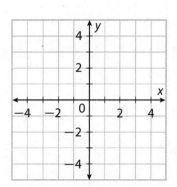

Graph the given function and identify the domain and range.

6. $g(x) = |x|$

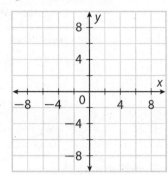

7. $g(x) = \frac{4}{3}|(x-5)| + 7$

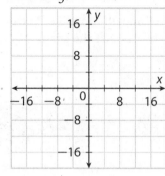

8. $g(x) = -\frac{7}{6}|(x-2)|$

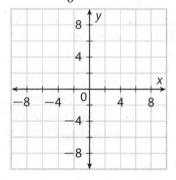

9. $g(x) = \left|\frac{3}{4}(x-2)\right| - 7$

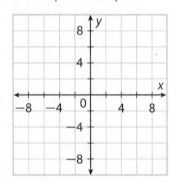

10. $g(x) = \left|\frac{5}{7}(x-4)\right|$

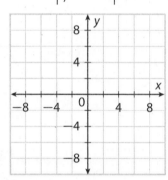

11. $g(x) = \left|-\frac{7}{3}(x+5)\right| - 4$

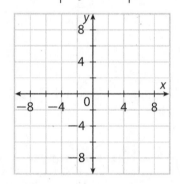

Write the absolute value function in standard form for the given graph. Use a or b as directed, $b > 0$.

12. Let $a = 1$.

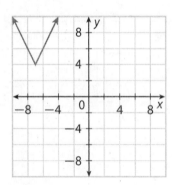

13. Let $b = 1$.

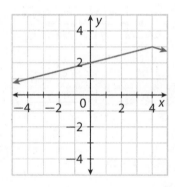

14. A rainstorm begins as a drizzle, builds up to a heavy rain, and then drops back to a drizzle. The rate r (in inches per hour) at which it rains is given by the function $r = -0.5|t - 1| + 0.5$, where t is the time (in hours). Graph the function. Determine for how long it rains and when it rains the hardest.

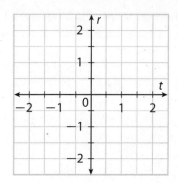

15. While playing pool, a player tries to shoot the eight ball into the corner pocket as shown. Imagine that a coordinate plane is placed over the pool table. The eight ball is at $\left(5, \frac{5}{4}\right)$ and the pocket they are aiming for is at $(10, 5)$. The player is going to bank the ball off the side at $(6, 0)$.

a. Write an equation for the path of the ball.

b. Did the player make the shot? How do you know?

16. Sam is sitting in a boat on a lake. She can get burned by the sunlight that hits her directly and by sunlight that reflects off the water. Sunlight reflects off the water at the point (2, 0) and hits Sam at the point (3.5, 3). Write and graph the function that shows the path of the sunlight.

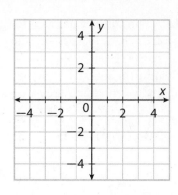

17. The Transamerica Pyramid is an office building in San Francisco. It stands 853 feet tall and is 145 feet wide at its base. Imagine that a coordinate plane is placed over a side of the building. In the coordinate plane, each unit represents one foot. Write an absolute value function whose graph is the V-shaped outline of the sides of the building, ignoring the "shoulders" of the building.

18. Match each graph with its function.

_____ $y = |x + 6| - 4$ _____ $y = |x - 6| - 4$ _____ $y = |x - 6| + 4$

A
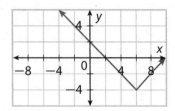

B
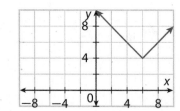

C
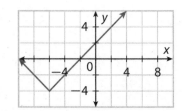

19. Explain the Error Explain why the graph shown is not the graph of $y = |x + 3| + 2$. What is the correct equation shown in the graph?

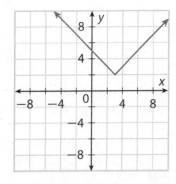

20. Multi-Step A golf player is trying to make a hole-in-one on the miniature golf green shown. Imagine that a coordinate plane is placed over the golf green. The golf ball is at (2.5, 2) and the hole is at (9.5, 2). The player is going to bank the ball off the side wall of the green at (6, 8).

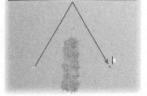

a. Write an equation for the path of the ball.

b. Use the equation in part a to determine if the player makes the shot.

Lesson Performance Task

Suppose a musical piece calls for an orchestra to start at *fortissimo* (about 90 decibels), decrease steadily in loudness to *pianissimo* (about 50 decibels) in four measures, and then increase steadily back to *fortissimo* in another four measures.

    a. Write a function to represent the sound level *s* in decibels as a function of the number of measures *m*.

    b. After how many measures should the orchestra be at the loudness of *mezzo forte* (about 70 decibels)?

    c. Describe what the graph of this function would look like.

2.2 Solving Absolute Value Equations

Essential Question: How can you solve an absolute value equation?

Resource Locker

⊘ Explore   Solving Absolute Value Equations Graphically

Absolute value equations differ from linear equations in that they may have two solutions. This is indicated with a **disjunction**, a mathematical statement created by a connecting two other statements with the word "or." To see why there can be two solutions, you can solve an absolute value equation using graphs.

(A)   Solve the equation $2|x - 5| - 4 = 2$.

Plot the function $f(x) = 2|x - 5| - 4$ on the grid. Then plot the function $g(x) = 2$ as a horizontal line on the same grid, and mark the points where the graphs intersect.

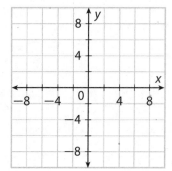

(B)   Write the solution to this equation as a disjunction:

$x =$ _____ or $x =$ _____

Reflect

1. Why might you expect most absolute value equations to have two solutions? Why not three or four?

_____

_____

_____

2. Is it possible for an absolute value equation to have no solutions? one solution? If so, what would each look like graphically?

_____

_____

_____

🔑 Explain 1 Solving Absolute Value Equations Algebraically

To solve absolute value equations algebraically, first isolate the absolute value expression on one side of the equation the same way you would isolate a variable. Then use the rule:

If $|x| = a$ (where a is a positive number), then $x = a$ OR $x = -a$.

Notice the use of a **disjunction** here in the rule for values of x. You cannot know from the original equation whether the expression inside the absolute value bars is positive or negative, so you must work through both possibilities to finish isolating x.

Example 1 Solve each absolute value equation algebraically. Graph the solutions on a number line.

(A) $|3x| + 2 = 8$

Subtract 2 from both sides. $|3x| = 6$

Rewrite as two equations. $3x = 6$ or $3x = -6$

Solve for x. $x = 2$ or $x = -2$

(B) $3|4x - 5| - 2 = 19$

Add 2 to both sides. $3|4x - 5| = \boxed{}$

Divide both sides by 3. $|4x - 5| = \boxed{}$

Rewrite as two equations. $4x - 5 = \boxed{}$ or $4x - 5 = \boxed{}$

Add 5 to all four sides. $4x = \boxed{}$ or $4x = \boxed{}$

Solve for x. $x = \boxed{}$ or $x = -\dfrac{\boxed{}}{\boxed{}}$

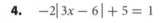

Your Turn

Solve each absolute value equation algebraically. Graph the solutions on a number line.

3. $\frac{1}{2}|x + 2| = 10$

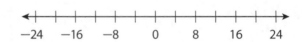

4. $-2|3x - 6| + 5 = 1$

 **Absolute Value Equations with Fewer than Two Solutions**

You have seen that absolute value equations have two solutions when the isolated absolute value expression is equal to a positive number. When the absolute value is equal to zero, there is a single solution because zero is its own opposite. When the absolute value expression is equal to a negative number, there is no solution because absolute value is never negative.

Example 2 Isolate the absolute value expression in each equation to determine if the equation can be solved. If so, finish the solution. If not, write "no solution."

(A) $-5|x + 1| + 2 = 12$

Subtract 2 from both sides.	$-5|x + 1| = 10$
Divide both sides by -5.	$|x + 1| = -2$
Absolute values are never negative.	No Solution

(B) $\frac{3}{5}|2x - 4| - 3 = -3$

Add 3 to both sides.	$\frac{3}{5}|2x - 4| = \boxed{}$
Multiply both sides by $\frac{5}{3}$.	$|2x - 4| = \boxed{}$
Rewrite as one equation.	$2x - 4 = \boxed{}$
Add 4 to both sides.	$2x = \boxed{}$
Divide both sides by 2.	$x = \boxed{}$

Your Turn

Isolate the absolute value expression in each equation to determine if the equation can be solved. If so, finish the solution. If not, write "no solution."

5. $3\left|\frac{1}{2}x + 5\right| + 7 = 5$

6. $9\left|\frac{4}{3}x - 2\right| + 7 = 7$

7. Why is important to solve both equations in the disjunction arising from an absolute value equation? Why not just pick one and solve it, knowing the solution for the variable will work when plugged backed into the equation?

_____

_____

_____

_____

_____

8. **Discussion** Discuss how the range of the absolute value function differs from the range of a linear function. Graphically, how does this explain why a linear equation always has exactly one solution while an absolute value equation can have one, two, or no solutions?

_____

_____

_____

_____

_____

_____

9. **Essential Question Check-In** Describe, in your own words, the basic steps to solving absolute value equations and how many solutions to expect.

_____

_____

_____

_____

_____

_____

_____

Solve the following absolute value equations by graphing.

1. $|x - 3| + 2 = 5$

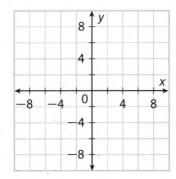

2. $2|x + 1| + 5 = 9$

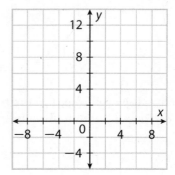

3. $-2|x + 5| + 4 = 2$

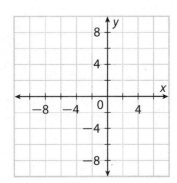

4. $\left|\frac{3}{2}(x - 2)\right| + 3 = 2$

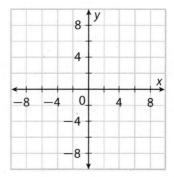

Solve each absolute value equation algebraically. Graph the solutions on a number line.

5. $|2x| = 3$

6. $\left|\frac{1}{3}x + 4\right| = 3$

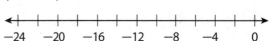

7. $3|2x - 3| + 2 = 3$

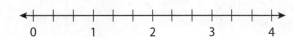

8. $-8|-x - 6| + 10 = 2$

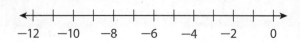

Isolate the absolute value expressions in the following equations to determine if they can be solved. If so, find and graph the solution(s). If not, write "no solution".

9. $\frac{1}{4}|x + 2| + 7 = 5$

10. $-3|x - 3| + 3 = 6$

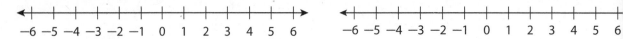

11. $2\big(|x + 4| + 3\big) = 6$

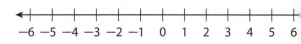

12. $5|2x + 4| - 3 = -3$

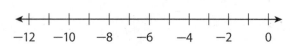

Solve the absolute value equations.

13. $|3x - 4| + 2 = 1$

14. $7\left|\frac{1}{2}x + 3\frac{1}{2}\right| - 2 = 5$

15. $\left|2(x+5)-3\right|+2=6$

<-+--+--+--+--+--+--+--+--+--+--+--+--+-->
  -6   -5   -4   -3   -2   -1   0

16. $-5\left|-3x+2\right|-2=-2$

<-+--+--+--+--+--+--+--+--+--+--+--+--+-->
   -2   -1   0   1   2

17. The bottom of a river makes a V-shape that can be modeled with the absolute value function, $d(h)=\frac{1}{5}\left|h-240\right|-48$, where d is the depth of the river bottom (in feet) and h is the horizontal distance to the left-hand shore (in feet).

A ship risks running aground if the bottom of its keel (its lowest point under the water) reaches down to the river bottom. Suppose you are the harbormaster and you want to place buoys where the river bottom is 30 feet below the surface. How far from the left-hand shore should you place the buoys?

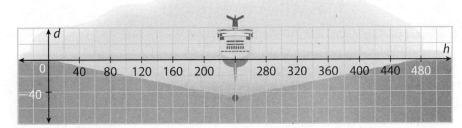

18. A flock of geese is approaching a photographer, flying in formation. The photographer starts taking photographs when the lead goose is 300 feet horizontally from her, and continues taking photographs until it is 100 feet past. The flock is flying at a steady 30 feet per second. Write and solve an equation to find the times after the photographing begins that the lead goose is at a horizontal distance of 75 feet from the photographer.

19. Geometry Find the points where a circle centered at (3, 0) with a radius of 5 crosses the x-axis. Use an absolute value equation and the fact that all points on a circle are the same distance (the radius) from the center.

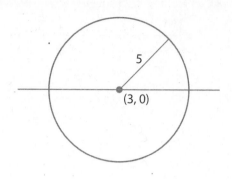

5

(3, 0)

20. Select the value or values of x that satisfy the equation $-\frac{1}{2}|3x - 3| + 2 = 1$.

A. $x = \frac{5}{3}$　　　　　　　B. $x = -\frac{5}{3}$

C. $x = \frac{1}{3}$　　　　　　　D. $x = -\frac{1}{3}$

E. $x = 3$　　　　　　　F. $x = -3$

G. $x = 1$　　　　　　　H. $x = -1$

21. Terry is trying to place a satellite dish on the roof of his house at the recommended height of 30 feet. His house is 32 feet wide, and the height of the roof can be described by the function $h(x) = -\frac{3}{2}|x - 16| + 24$, where x is the distance along the width of the house. Where should Terry place the dish?

22. Explain the Error While attempting to solve the equation $-3|x - 4| - 4 = 3$, a student came up with the following results. Explain the error and find the correct solution:

$$-3|x - 4| - 4 = 3$$

$$-3|x - 4| = 7$$

$$|x - 4| = -\frac{7}{3}$$

$$x - 4 = -\frac{7}{3} \quad \text{or} \quad x - 4 = \frac{7}{3}$$

$$x = \frac{5}{3} \quad \text{or} \quad x = \frac{19}{3}$$

23. Communicate Mathematical Ideas Solve this absolute value equation and explain what algebraic properties make it possible to do so.

$$3|x - 2| = 5|x - 2| - 7$$

24. Justify Your Reasoning This absolute value equation has nested absolute values. Use your knowledge of solving absolute value equations to solve this equation. Justify the number of possible solutions.

$$\left| |2x + 5| - 3 \right| = 10$$

25. Check for Reasonableness For what type of real-world quantities would the negative answer for an absolute value equation not make sense?

Lesson Performance Task

A snowball comes apart as a child throws it north, resulting in two halves traveling away
from the child. The child is standing 12 feet south and 6 feet east of the school door, along an
east-west wall. One fragment flies off to the northeast, moving 2 feet east for every
5 feet north of travel, and the other moves 2 feet west for every 5 feet north of travel.
Write an absolute value function that describes the northward position, $n(e)$, of both fragments
as a function of how far east of the school door they are. How far apart are
the fragments when they strike the wall?

2.3 Solving Absolute Value Inequalities

Essential Question: What are two ways to solve an absolute value inequality?

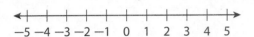 **Explore** **Visualizing the Solution Set of an Absolute Value Inequality**

You know that when solving an absolute value equation, it's possible to get two solutions. Here, you will explore what happens when you solve absolute value inequalities.

Ⓐ Determine whether each of the integers from −5 to 5 is a solution of the inequality $|x| + 2 < 5$. Write *yes* or *no* for each number in the table. If a number is a solution, plot it on the number line.

Number	Solution?
$x = -5$	
$x = -4$	
$x = -3$	
$x = -2$	
$x = -1$	
$x = 0$	
$x = 1$	
$x = 2$	
$x = 3$	
$x = 4$	
$x = 5$	

```
←+—+—+—+—+—+—+—+—+—+—+→
 −5 −4 −3 −2 −1  0  1  2  3  4  5
```

Ⓑ Determine whether each of the integers from −5 to 5 is a solution of the inequality $|x| + 2 > 5$. Write *yes* or *no* for each number in the table. If a number is a solution, plot it on the number line.

Number	Solution?
$x = -5$	
$x = -4$	
$x = -3$	
$x = -2$	
$x = -1$	
$x = 0$	
$x = 1$	
$x = 2$	
$x = 3$	
$x = 4$	
$x = 5$	

```
←+—+—+—+—+—+—+—+—+—+—+→
 −5 −4 −3 −2 −1  0  1  2  3  4  5
```

Ⓒ State the solutions of the equation $|x| + 2 = 5$ and relate them to the solutions you found for the inequalities in Steps A and B.

_____

_____

Ⓓ If x is any real number and not just an integer, graph the solutions of $|x| + 2 < 5$ and $|x| + 2 > 5$.

Graph of all real solutions of $|x| + 2 < 5$:

Graph of all real solutions of $|x| + 2 > 5$:

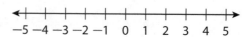

Reflect

1. It's possible to describe the solutions of $|x| + 2 < 5$ and $|x| + 2 > 5$ using inequalities that don't involve absolute value. For instance, you can write the solutions of $|x| + 2 < 5$ as $x > -3$ and $x < 3$. Notice that the word *and* is used because x must be both greater than -3 and less than 3. How would you write the solutions of $|x| + 2 > 5$? Explain.

_____

_____

2. Describe the solutions of $|x| + 2 \leq 5$ and $|x| + 2 \geq 5$ using inequalities that don't involve absolute value.

_____

_____

🔑 Explain 1 — Solving Absolute Value Inequalities Graphically

You can use a graph to solve an absolute value inequality of the form $f(x) > g(x)$ or $f(x) < g(x)$, where $f(x)$ is an absolute value function and $g(x)$ is a constant function. Graph each function separately on the same coordinate plane and determine the intervals on the x-axis where one graph lies above or below the other. For $f(x) > g(x)$, you want to find the x-values for which the graph $f(x)$ is above the graph of $g(x)$. For $f(x) < g(x)$, you want to find the x-values for which the graph of $f(x)$ is below the graph of $g(x)$.

Example 1 Solve the inequality graphically.

Ⓐ $|x + 3| + 1 > 4$

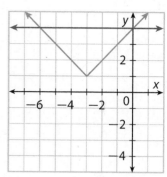

The inequality is of the form $f(x) > g(x)$, so determine the intervals on the x-axis where the graph of $f(x) = |x + 3| + 1$ lies above the graph of $g(x) = 4$.

The graph of $f(x) = |x + 3| + 1$ lies above the graph of $g(x) = 4$ to the left of $x = -6$ and to the right of $x = 0$, so the solution of $|x + 3| + 1 > 4$ is $x < -6$ or $x > 0$.

© Houghton Mifflin Harcourt Publishing Company

Ⓑ $|x - 2| - 3 < 1$

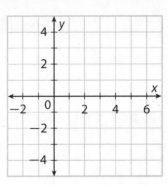

The inequality is of the form $f(x) < g(x)$, so determine the intervals

on the x-axis where the graph of $f(x) = |x - 2| - 3$ lies _____
the graph of $g(x) = 1$.

The graph of $f(x) = |x - 2| - 3$ lies _____ the graph of

$g(x) = 1$ between $x =$ [____] and $x =$ [____], so the solution of

$|x - 2| - 3 < 1$ is $x >$ [____] and $x <$ [____].

Reflect

3. Suppose the inequality in Part A is $|x + 3| + 1 \geq 4$ instead of $|x + 3| + 1 > 4$. How does the solution change?

   _____

4. In Part B, what is another way to write the solution $x > -2$ and $x < 6$?

   _____

5. **Discussion** Suppose the graph of an absolute value function $f(x)$ lies entirely above the graph of the constant function $g(x)$. What is the solution of the inequality $f(x) > g(x)$? What is the solution of the inequality $f(x) < g(x)$?

   _____

   _____

   _____

   _____

Your Turn

6. Solve $|x + 1| - 4 \leq -2$ graphically.

⚙ Explain 2 Solving Absolute Value Inequalities Algebraically

To solve an absolute value inequality algebraically, start by isolating the absolute value expression. When the absolute value expression is by itself on one side of the inequality, apply one of the following rules to finish solving the inequality for the variable.

Solving Absolute Value Inequalities Algebraically
1. If $|x| > a$ where a is a positive number, then $x < -a$ or $x > a$.
2. If $|x| < a$ where a is a positive number, then $-a < x < a$.

Example 2 Solve the inequality algebraically. Graph the solution on a number line.

Ⓐ $|4 - x| + 15 > 21$

$|4 - x| > 6$

$4 - x < -6$ or $4 - x > 6$

$-x < -10$ or $-x > 2$

$x > 10$ or $x < -2$

The solution is $x > 10$ or $x < -2$.

$-6\ -4\ -2\quad 0\quad 2\quad 4\quad 6\quad 8\quad 10\ 12\ 14$

Ⓑ $|x + 4| - 10 \le -2$

$|x + 4| \le \boxed{}$

$x + 4 \ge \boxed{}$ and $x + 4 \le \boxed{}$

$x \ge \boxed{}$ and $x \le \boxed{}$

The solution is $x \ge \boxed{}$ and $x \le \boxed{}$,

or $\boxed{} \le x \le \boxed{}$.

$-12\qquad -8\qquad -4\qquad 0\qquad 4$

Reflect

7. In Part A, suppose the inequality were $|4 - x| + 15 > 14$ instead of $|4 - x| + 15 > 21$. How would the solution change? Explain.

_____

_____

_____

_____

8. In Part B, suppose the inequality were $|x + 4| - 10 \le -11$ instead of $|x + 4| - 10 \le -2$. How would the solution change? Explain.

_____

_____

_____

_____

Solve the inequality algebraically. Graph the solution on a number line.

9. $3|x - 7| \geq 9$ **10.** $|2x + 3| < 5$

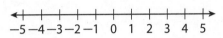

🔑 Explain 3   Solving a Real-World Problem with Absolute Value Inequalities

Absolute value inequalities are often used to model real-world situations involving a margin of error or *tolerance*. Tolerance is the allowable amount of variation in a quantity.

Example 3

A machine at a lumber mill cuts boards that are 3.25 meters long. It is acceptable for the length to differ from this value by at most 0.02 meters. Write and solve an absolute value inequality to find the range of acceptable lengths.

🧩 Analyze Information

Identify the important information.

- The boards being cut are ☐ meters long.
- The length can differ by at most 0.02 meters.

🧩 Formulate a Plan

Let the length of a board be ℓ. Since the sign of the difference between ℓ and 3.25 doesn't matter, take the absolute value of the difference. Since the absolute value of the difference can be at most 0.02, the inequality that models the situation is

$$\left| \ell - \boxed{} \right| \leq \boxed{}.$$

🧩 Solve

$$|\ell - 3.25| \leq 0.02$$

$$\ell - 3.25 \geq -0.02 \text{ and } \ell - 3.25 \leq 0.02$$

$$\ell \geq \boxed{} \text{ and } \qquad \ell \leq \boxed{}$$

So, the range of acceptable lengths is $\boxed{} \leq \ell \leq \boxed{}.$

Justify and Evaluate

The bounds of the range are positive and close to [ ], so this is a reasonable answer.

The answer is correct since [ ] $+ 0.02 = 3.25$ and [ ] $- 0.02 = 3.25$.

Your Turn

11. A box of cereal is supposed to weigh 13.8 oz, but it's acceptable for the weight to vary as much as 0.1 oz. Write and solve an absolute value inequality to find the range of acceptable weights.

Elaborate

12. Describe the values of x that satisfy the inequalities $|x| < a$ and $|x| > a$ where a is a positive constant.

_____

_____

_____

13. How do you algebraically solve an absolute value inequality?

_____

_____

_____

14. Explain why the solution of $|x| > a$ is all real numbers if a is a negative number.

_____

_____

15. **Essential Question Check-In** How do you solve an absolute value inequality graphically?

_____

_____

_____

⭐ Evaluate: Homework and Practice

• Online Homework
• Hints and Help
• Extra Practice

1. Determine whether each of the integers from -5 to 5 is a solution of the inequality $|x - 1| + 3 \geq 5$. If a number is a solution, plot it on the number line.

2. Determine whether each of the integers from -5 to 5 is a solution of the inequality $|x + 1| - 2 \leq 1$. If a number is a solution, plot it on the number line.

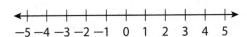

Solve each inequality graphically.

3. $2|x| \leq 6$

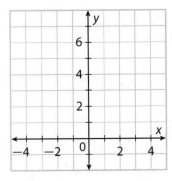

4. $|x - 3| - 2 > -1$

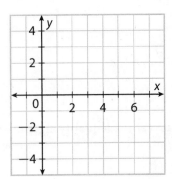

5. $\frac{1}{2}|x| + 2 < 3$

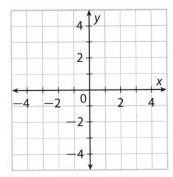

6. $|x + 2| - 4 \geq -2$

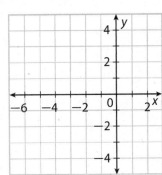

Match each graph with the corresponding absolute value inequality. Then give the solution of the inequality.

A. $2|x| + 1 > 3$ **B.** $2|x + 1| < 3$ **C.** $2|x| - 1 > 3$ **D.** $2|x - 1| < 3$

7.

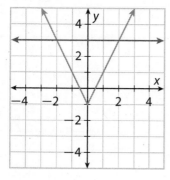

8.

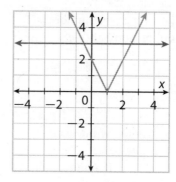

9.

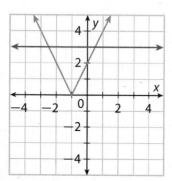

10.

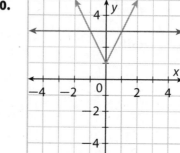

Solve each absolute value inequality algebraically. Graph the solution on a number line.

11. $2\left|x - \dfrac{7}{2}\right| + 3 > 4$

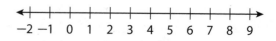

12. $|2x + 1| - 4 < 5$

13. $3|x + 4| + 2 \geq 5$

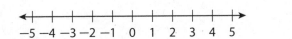

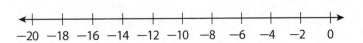

14. $|x + 11| - 8 \leq -3$

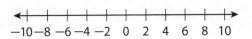

15. $-5|x - 3| - 5 < 15$

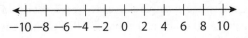

16. $8|x + 4| + 10 < 2$

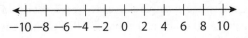

Solve each problem using an absolute value inequality.

17. The thermostat for a house is set to 68 °F, but the actual temperature may vary by as much as 2 °F. What is the range of possible temperatures?

18. The balance of Jason's checking account is $320. The balance varies by as much as $80 each week. What are the possible balances of Jason's account?

19. On average, a squirrel lives to be 6.5 years old. The lifespan of a squirrel may vary by as much as 1.5 years. What is the range of ages that a squirrel lives?

20. You are playing a history quiz game where you must give the years of historical events. In order to score any points at all for a question about the year in which a man first stepped on the moon, your answer must be no more than 3 years away from the correct answer, 1969. What is the range of answers that allow you to score points?

21. The speed limit on a road is 30 miles per hour. Drivers on this road typically vary their speed around the limit by as much as 5 miles per hour. What is the range of typical speeds on this road?

22. Represent Real-World Problems A poll of likely voters shows that the incumbent will get 51% of the vote in an upcoming election. Based on the number of voters polled, the results of the poll could be off by as much as 3 percentage points. What does this mean for the incumbent?

23. Explain the Error A student solved the inequality $|x - 1| - 3 > 1$ graphically. Identify and correct the student's error.

I graphed the functions $f(x) = |x - 1| - 3$ and $g(x) = 1$. Because the graph of $g(x)$ lies above the graph of $f(x)$ between $x = -3$ and $x = 5$, the solution of the inequality is $-3 < x < 5$.

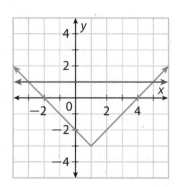

24. Multi-Step Recall that a literal equation or inequality is one in which the constants have been replaced by letters.

    a. Solve $\left| ax + b \right| > c$ for x. Write the solution in terms of a, b, and c. Assume that $a > 0$ and $c \geq 0$.

    b. Use the solution of the literal inequality to find the solution of $\left| 10x + 21 \right| > 14$.

    c. In Part a, explain how the restrictions $a > 0$ and $c \geq 0$ affect finding the solutions of the inequality.

Lesson Performance Task

The distance between the Sun and each planet in our solar system varies because the planets travel in elliptical orbits around the Sun. Here is a table of the average distance and the variation in the distance for the five innermost planets in our solar system.

	Average Distance	Variation
Mercury	36.0 million miles	7.39 million miles
Venus	67.2 million miles	0.43 million miles
Earth	93.0 million miles	1.55 million miles
Mars	142 million miles	13.2 million miles
Jupiter	484 million miles	23.2 million miles

a. Write and solve an inequality to represent the range of distances that can occur between the Sun and each planet.

b. Calculate the percentage variation (variation divided by average distance) in the orbit of each of the planets. Based on these percentages, which planet has the most elliptical orbit?

Absolute Value Functions, Equations, and Inequalities

Essential Question: How can you use absolute value functions to solve real-world problems?

KEY EXAMPLE *(Lesson 2.1)*

Given the function $g(x) = \left| \frac{1}{3}(x + 6) \right| - 1$, predict what the graph will look like compared to the parent function, $f(x) = |x|$.

The graph of $g(x)$ will be the graph of $f(x)$ translated down 1 unit and left 6 units. There will also be a horizontal stretch of $f(x)$ by a factor of 3.

KEY EXAMPLE *(Lesson 2.2)*

Solve $6|2x + 3| + 1 = 25$ algebraically.

$6|2x + 3| = 24$	Subtract 1 from both sides.
$|2x + 3| = 4$	Divide both sides by 6.
$2x + 3 = 4$ or $2x + 3 = -4$	Rewrite as two equations.
$2x = 1$ or $2x = -7$	Subtract 3 from both sides.
$x = \frac{1}{2}$ or $x = -\frac{7}{2}$	Solve for x.
So, $x = \frac{1}{2}$ or $-\frac{7}{2}$.	

KEY EXAMPLE *(Lesson 2.3)*

Solve $|x + 2| - 4 < 4$ algebraically, then graph the solution on a number line.

$$|x + 2| - 4 < 4$$

$|x + 2| < 8$	Add 4 to both sides.
$x + 2 < 8$ and $x + 2 > -8$	Rewrite as two inequalities.
$x < 6$ and $x > -10$	Subtract 2 from both sides.

The solution is $x < 6$ and $x > -10$.

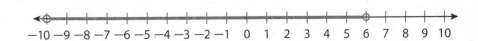

EXERCISES

Solve. *(Lessons 2.2, 2.3)*

1. $-10|x + 2| = -70$

2. $|3x + 7| = 27$

3. $\frac{1}{7}|8 + x| \le 5$

4. $|x - 2| - 5 > 10$

5. Explain how the graph of $g(x) = \left|\frac{3}{7}(x - 4)\right| + 2$ compares to the graph of $h(x) = \frac{3}{7}(x - 4) + 2$. *(Lesson 2.1)*

6. Leroy wants to place a chimney on his roof. It is recommended that the chimney be set at a height of at least 25 feet. The height of the roof is described by the function $r(x) = -\frac{4}{3}|x - 10| + 35$, where x is the width of the roof. Where should Leroy place the chimney if the house is 40 feet wide? *(Lesson 2.3)*

MODULE PERFORMANCE TASK

What Is the Purity of Gold?

The purity of gold in jewelry is measured in "karats," with 24-karat gold the highest purity (100% pure gold). You have three gold rings labeled 10 karat, 14 karat, and 18 karat, and would like to know if the rings are correctly labeled. The table shows the results of an analysis of the rings.

Ring Label	Actual Percentage of Gold
10-karat	40.6%
14-karat	59.5%
18-karat	71.2%

In the United States, jewelry manufacturers are legally allowed a half karat tolerance. Determine which of the rings, if any, have an actual percentage of gold that falls outside this tolerance.

Use your own paper to list any additional information you will need and then complete the task. Be sure to write down all your data and assumptions. Then use graphs, numbers, words, or algebra to explain how you reached your conclusion.

2.1–2.3 Absolute Value Functions, Equations, and Inequalities

Personal Math Trainer

• Online Homework
• Hints and Help
• Extra Practice

Solve. *(Lesson 2.2)*

1. $|-2x - 3| = 6$

2. $\frac{1}{4}|-4 - 3x| = 2$

3. $|3x + 8| = 2$

4. $4|x + 7| + 3 = 59$

Solve each inequality using the method indicated. *(Lesson 2.3)*

5. $|5x + 2| \leq 13$ (algebraically)

6. $|x - 2| + 1 \leq 5$ (graphically)

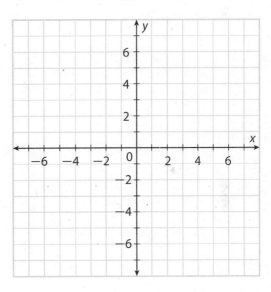

ESSENTIAL QUESTION

7. Write a real world situation that could be modeled by $|x - 14| = 3$.

Assessment Readiness

1. Look at each inequality. Will the graph of the inequality be reflected over the x-axis when compared to $f(x) = |x|$? Select Yes or No for A–C.

   A. $g(x) = 3|x - 4|$ ◯ Yes   ◯ No

   B. $h(x) = -\frac{1}{2}|x|$ ◯ Yes   ◯ No

   C. $j(x) = |x + 3| - 2$ ◯ Yes   ◯ No

2. Consider the absolute value equation $\frac{2}{3}|x - 4| + 2 = 5$. Choose True or False for each statement.

   A. Solving $\frac{2}{3}|x - 4| + 2 = 5$ gives the same   ◯ True   ◯ False
   x-values as solving $\left|\frac{2}{3}(x - 4)\right| + 2 = 5$.

   B. To solve the equation for x, the first   ◯ True   ◯ False
   step is to add 4 to both sides.

   C. Before the step to rewrite as two equations, ◯ True   ◯ False
   the equation looks like: $|x - 4| = 3$.

3. Describe the domain, range, and vertex of the function $f(x) = 3|x - 4| + 2$. Explain your answers.

4. Laurie wants to put a portable cellular phone mini-tower on her roof. The tower cannot be placed higher than 30 feet. The slant of her roof can be represented by the equation $r(x) = -\frac{1}{4}|x| + 60$. If her house is 40 feet wide, where could she place the tower? Explain.

Assessment Readiness

- Online Homework
- Hints and Help
- Extra Practice

1. Consider the function $f(x) = 2(x-1)^2 + 5$. Choose True or False for each statement.

   A. The range is $y \geq 5$. ○ True ○ False

   B. The range is $y \geq 7$. ○ True ○ False

   C. The domain is $-\infty < x < \infty$. ○ True ○ False

2. Consider the function $g(x) = -3f(x+1) - 1$. Choose True or False for each statement.

   A. When compared to $f(x) = 2x$, $g(x)$ will be reflected over the x-axis. ○ True ○ False

   B. When compared to $f(x) = 2x$, $g(x)$ will have a vertical stretch of 3. ○ True ○ False

   C. When compared to $f(x) = 2x$, $g(x)$ will be translated right 1 unit and up 1 unit. ○ True ○ False

3. Consider the equation $f(x) = \frac{1}{2}x - 5$. Is the given equation the inverse of $f(x)$? Select Yes or No for A–C.

   A. $f^{-1}(x) = 2x - 10$ ○ Yes ○ No

   B. $f^{-1}(x) = -\frac{1}{2}x + 5$ ○ Yes ○ No

   C. $f^{-1}(x) = 2x + 10$ ○ Yes ○ No

4. Consider the equation $3|x - 2| + 6 = 12$. Choose True or False for each statement.

   A. The equation can be solved using the Pythagorean Theorem. ○ True ○ False

   B. The solutions of the equation are $x = 4$ and $x = 0$. ○ True ○ False

   C. The first step to solving the equation could be subtracting 6 from both sides of the equation. ○ True ○ False

5. Look at each function. Will the graph of the function be stretched or compressed in the horizontal direction when compared to $f(x) = |x|$? Select Yes or No for A–C.

   A. $g(x) = 2|x + 1| - 4$ ○ Yes ○ No

   B. $h(x) = |x - 2| - 1$ ○ Yes ○ No

   C. $j(x) = \left|\frac{1}{2}x - 7\right| + 2$ ○ Yes ○ No

6. A triathlete is training for her next race and starts by swimming 2 miles in 1 hour. She rests for 1 hour and then rides her bike 100 miles in 5 hours. She rests another hour and runs 20 miles in 5 hours. Draw a graph showing the distance she travels over time. Explain your choice.

7. The maximum number of oranges in a box of volume one cubic foot can be modeled by the inequality $|x - 17| \leq 5$, depending on the size of the oranges. Solve the inequality to find the greatest and least numbers of oranges that could be in a box. Explain your answer.

8. How does the end behavior of $f(x) = (x - 2)^2 + 3$ differ from that of $g(x) = -(3x + 7)^2 - 8$ as $x \rightarrow -\infty$? Explain your answer.

Performance Tasks

★ **9.** The revenue from an amusement park ride is given by the admission price of $3 times the number of riders. As part of a promotion, the first 10 riders ride for free.

  A. What kind of transformation describes the change in the revenue based on the promotion?

  B. Write a function rule for this transformation.

★★10. An automotive mechanic charges $50 to diagnose the problem in a vehicle and $65 per hour for labor to fix it.

A. If the mechanic increases his diagnostic fee to $60, what kind of transformation is this to the graph of the total repair bill?

B. If the mechanic increases his labor rate to $75 per hour, what kind of transformation is this to the graph of the total repair bill?

C. If it took 3 hours to repair your car, which of the two rate increases would have a greater effect on your total bill?

★★11. Diving Scuba divers must know that the deeper the dive, the greater the water pressure in pounds per square inch (psi) for fresh water diving, as shown in the table.

Depth (feet)	Pressure (psi)
34	29.4
68	44.1
102	58.8

A. Write the pressure as a function of depth, and identify a reasonable domain and range for this function.

B. Find the inverse of the function from part **A**. What does the inverse function represent?

C. The point $(25.9, 25.9)$ is an approximate solution to both the function from part **A** and its inverse. What does this point mean in the context of the problem?

Community Theater Owner A community theater currently sells 200 season tickets at $50 each. In order to increase its season-ticket revenue, the theater surveys its season-ticket holders to see if they would be willing to pay more. The survey finds that for every $5 increase in the price of a season ticket, the theater would lose 10 season-ticket holders. What action, if any, should the theater owner take to increase revenue?

a. Let n be the number of $5 price increases in the cost of a season ticket. Write an expression for the cost of a season ticket after n price increases, and an expression for the number of season-ticket holders after n price increases.

b. Use the expressions from part **a** to create a revenue function, $R(n)$, from the survey information.

c. Determine a constraint on the value of n. That is, write and solve an inequality that represents an upper bound on the value of n, then state a reasonable domain for the revenue function.

d. Graph the revenue function. Be sure to label the axes with the quantities they represent and indicate the axis scales by showing numbers for some grid lines.

e. Write a brief paragraph describing what actions the theater owner should take to maximize revenue. Include what happens to the number of season-ticket holders as well as the season-ticket prices.

UNIT 2

Quadratic Functions, Equations, and Relations

MATH IN CAREERS

Toy Manufacturer A toy manufacturer uses math to calculate the cost of manufacturing, including labor and materials, as well as to predict sales, determine profits, and keep track of orders and inventory. Toy manufacturers study market trends and use statistics to understand the economics of supply and demand for their products. They may also apply three-dimensional modeling to determine the amount of materials needed for toy construction.

If you are interested in a career as a toy manufacturer, you should study these mathematical subjects:
- Algebra
- Geometry
- Trigonometry
- Business Math
- Technical Math

Research other careers that require understanding how to predict sales of goods. Check out the career activity at the end of the unit to find out how **Toy Manufacturers** use math.

Reading Start-Up

Visualize Vocabulary

Use the ✔ words to complete the graphic. Place one word in each of the four sections of the frame.

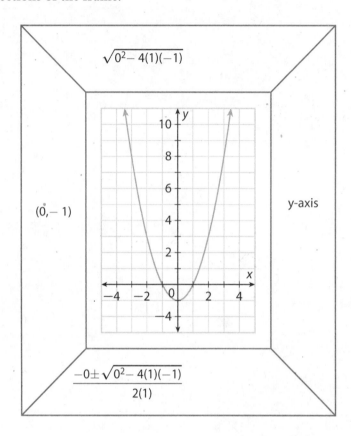

$$\sqrt{0^2 - 4(1)(-1)}$$

$(0, -1)$

y-axis

$$\frac{-0 \pm \sqrt{0^2 - 4(1)(-1)}}{2(1)}$$

Understand Vocabulary

To become familiar with some of the vocabulary terms in the module, consider the following. You may refer to the module, the glossary, or a dictionary.

1. Every point on a parabola is equidistant from a fixed line, called the
   _____, and a fixed point, called the _____.

2. A _____ is any number that can be written as $a + bi$,
   where a and b are real numbers and $i = \sqrt{-1}$.

3. A _____ is a rectangular array of numbers.

Active Reading

Four-Corner Fold Before beginning each lesson, create a four-corner fold to help you organize the characteristics of key concepts. As you study each lesson, define new terms, including an example and a graph or diagram where applicable.

Quadratic Equations

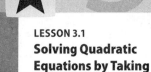

Essential Question: How can you use quadratic equations to solve real-world problems?

REAL WORLD VIDEO
Safe drivers are aware of stopping distances and carefully judge how fast they can travel based on road conditions. Stopping distance is one of many everyday functions that can be modeled with quadratic equations.

MODULE PERFORMANCE TASK PREVIEW
Can You Stop in Time?

When a driver applies the brakes, the car continues to travel for a certain distance until coming to a stop. The stopping distance for a vehicle depends on many factors, including the initial speed of the car and road conditions. How far will a car travel after the brakes are applied? Let's hit the road and find out!

Are(YOU)Ready?

Complete these exercises to review skills you will need for this module.

• Online Homework
• Hints and Help
• Extra Practice

One-Step Inequalities

Example 1   Solve $-2x \leq 9$ for x.
$x \geq -4.5$

Divide both sides by -2. Because you are dividing by a negative number, flip the inequality symbol.

Solve each inequality.

1. $n - 12 > 9$

2. $-3p < -27$

3. $\dfrac{k}{4} \geq -1$

_____

_____

_____

Exponents

Example 2   Simplify $\dfrac{3a^5b^2}{9a^2b}$.

$$\dfrac{3a^5b^2}{9a^2b} = \dfrac{3^1 a^5 b^2}{3^2 a^2 b^1} = \dfrac{a^{5-2} b^{2-1}}{3^{2-1}} = \dfrac{a^3 b}{3}$$

Subtract exponents when dividing.

Simplify each expression.

4. $\dfrac{16p^2}{2p^4}$

5. $5vw^5 \cdot 2v^4$

6. $\dfrac{3x^7 y}{6x^4 y^2}$

_____

_____

_____

Solving Quadratic Equations by Factoring

Example 3   Factor to solve $x^2 + 2x - 15 = 0$ for x.

Pairs of factors of -15 are:
1 and -15
3 and -5
5 and -3
15 and -1

The pair with the sum of the middle term, 2, is 5 and -3.

$(x + 5)(x - 3) = 0$

Either $x + 5 = 0$ or $x - 3 = 0$, so the solutions are -5 and 3.

Factor to solve each equation.

7. $x^2 - 7x + 6 = 0$

8. $x^2 - 18x + 81 = 0$

9. $x^2 - 16 = 0$

_____

_____

_____

3.1 Solving Quadratic Equations by Taking Square Roots

Resource Locker

Essential Question: What is an imaginary number, and how is it useful in solving quadratic equations?

⊘ Explore   Investigating Ways of Solving Simple Quadratic Equations

There are many ways to solve a quadratic equation. Here, you will use three methods to solve the equation $x^2 = 16$: by graphing, by factoring, and by taking square roots.

Ⓐ Solve $x^2 = 16$ by graphing.

First treat each side of the equation as a function, and graph the two functions, which in this case are $f(x) = x^2$ and $g(x) = 16$, on the same coordinate plane.

Then identify the x-coordinates of the points where the two graphs intersect.

$x = \boxed{}$ or $x = \boxed{}$

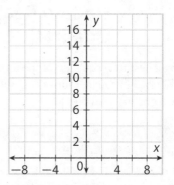

Ⓑ Solve $x^2 = 16$ by factoring.

This method involves rewriting the equation so that 0 is on one side in order to use the *zero-product property*, which says that the product of two numbers is 0 if and only if at least one of the numbers is 0.

Write the equation. $x^2 = 16$

Subtract 16 from both sides. $x^2 - \boxed{} = 0$

Factor the difference of two squares. $\left(x + \boxed{}\right)(x - 4) = 0$

Apply the zero-product property. $x + \boxed{} = 0$ or $x - 4 = 0$

Solve for x. $x = \boxed{}$ or $x = 4$

Ⓒ Solve $x^2 = 16$ by taking square roots.

A real number x is a *square root* of a nonnegative real number a provided $x^2 = a$. A square root is written using the radical symbol $\sqrt{}$. Every positive real number a has both a positive square root, written $\sqrt{a}$, and a negative square root, written $-\sqrt{a}$. For instance, the square roots of 9 are $\pm\sqrt{9}$ (read "plus or minus the square root of 9"), or ± 3. The number 0 has only itself as its square root: $\pm\sqrt{0} = 0$.

Write the equation. $x^2 = 16$

Use the definition of square root. $x = \pm\sqrt{16}$

Simplify the square roots. $x = \boxed{}$

1. Which of the three methods would you use to solve $x^2 = 5$? Explain, and then use the method to find the solutions.

   _____

   _____

   _____

2. Can the equation $x^2 = -9$ be solved by any of the three methods? Explain.

   _____

   _____

   _____

   _____

⊘ Explain 1 Finding Real Solutions of Simple Quadratic Equations

When solving a quadratic equation of the form $ax^2 + c = 0$ by taking square roots, you may need to use the following properties of square roots to simplify the solutions. (In a later lesson, these properties are stated in a more general form and then proved.)

Property Name	Words	Symbols	Numbers
Product property of square roots	The square root of a product equals the product of the square roots of the factors.	$\sqrt{ab} = \sqrt{a} \cdot \sqrt{b}$ where $a \geq 0$ and $b \geq 0$	$\sqrt{12} = \sqrt{4 \cdot 3}$ $= \sqrt{4} \cdot \sqrt{3}$ $= 2\sqrt{3}$
Quotient property of square roots	The square root of a fraction equals the quotient of the square roots of the numerator and the denominator.	$\sqrt{\dfrac{a}{b}} = \dfrac{\sqrt{a}}{\sqrt{b}}$ where $a \geq 0$ and $b > 0$	$\sqrt{\dfrac{5}{9}} = \dfrac{\sqrt{5}}{\sqrt{9}}$ $= \dfrac{\sqrt{5}}{3}$

Using the quotient property of square roots may require an additional step of *rationalizing the denominator* if the denominator is not a rational number. For instance, the quotient property allows you to write $\sqrt{\dfrac{2}{7}}$ as $\dfrac{\sqrt{2}}{\sqrt{7}}$, but $\sqrt{7}$ is not a rational number. To rationalize the denominator, multiply $\dfrac{\sqrt{2}}{\sqrt{7}}$ by $\dfrac{\sqrt{7}}{\sqrt{7}}$ (a form of 1) and get this result: $\dfrac{\sqrt{2}}{\sqrt{7}} \cdot \dfrac{\sqrt{7}}{\sqrt{7}} = \dfrac{\sqrt{14}}{\sqrt{49}} = \dfrac{\sqrt{14}}{7}$.

Example 1 Solve the quadratic equation by taking square roots.

(A) $2x^2 - 16 = 0$

Add 16 to both sides.	$2x^2 = 16$
Divide both sides by 2.	$x^2 = 8$
Use the definition of square root.	$x = \pm\sqrt{8}$
Use the product property.	$x = \pm\sqrt{4} \cdot \sqrt{2}$
Simplify.	$x = \pm 2\sqrt{2}$

(B) $-5x^2 + 9 = 0$

Subtract 9 from both sides.	$-5x^2 = \boxed{}$
Divide both sides by $\boxed{}$.	$x^2 = \boxed{}$
Use the definition of square root.	$x = \pm\sqrt{\boxed{}}$
Use the quotient property.	$x = \pm\boxed{}$
Simplify the numerator.	$x = \pm\boxed{}$
Rationalize the denominator.	$x = \pm\boxed{}$

Your Turn

Solve the quadratic equation by taking square roots.

3. $x^2 - 24 = 0$

4. $-4x^2 + 13 = 0$

 Explain 2 ## Solving a Real-World Problem Using a Simple Quadratic Equation

Two commonly used quadratic models for falling objects near Earth's surface are the following:

- Distance fallen (in feet) at time t (in seconds): $d(t) = 16t^2$

- Height (in feet) at time t (in seconds): $h(t) = h_0 - 16t^2$ where h_0 is the object's initial height (in feet)

For both models, time is measured from the instant that the object begins to fall. A negative value of t would represent a time before the object began falling, so negative values of t are excluded from the domains of these functions. This means that for any equation of the form $d(t) = c$ or $h(t) = c$ where c is a constant, a negative solution should be rejected.

Example 2 Write and solve an equation to answer the question. Give the exact answer and, if it's irrational, a decimal approximation (to the nearest tenth of a second).

(A) If you drop a water balloon, how long does it take to fall 4 feet?

Using the model $d(t) = 16t^2$, solve the equation $d(t) = 4$.

Write the equation.	$16t^2 = 4$
Divide both sides by 16.	$t^2 = \dfrac{1}{4}$
Use the definition of square root.	$t = \pm\sqrt{\dfrac{1}{4}}$
Use the quotient property.	$t = \pm\dfrac{1}{2}$

Reject the negative value of t. The water balloon falls 4 feet in $\frac{1}{2}$ second.

(B) The rooftop of a 5-story building is 50 feet above the ground. How long does it take the water balloon dropped from the rooftop to pass by a third-story window at 24 feet?

Using the model $h(t) = h_0 - 16t^2$, solve the equation $h(t) = 24$. (When you reach the step at which you divide both sides by -16, leave 16 in the denominator rather than simplifying the fraction because you'll get a rational denominator when you later use the quotient property.)

Write the equation.	$\boxed{} - 16t^2 = \boxed{}$
Subtract 50 from both sides.	$-16t^2 = \boxed{}$
Divide both sides by -16.	$t^2 = \boxed{}$
Use the definition of square root.	$t = \pm\sqrt{\boxed{}}$
Use the quotient property to simplify.	$t = \pm\boxed{}$

Reject the negative value of t. The water balloon passes by the third-story window

in $\boxed{} \approx \boxed{}$ seconds.

Reflect

5. **Discussion** Explain how the model $h(t) = h_0 - 16t^2$ is built from the model $d(t) = 16t^2$.

_____

_____

_____

Write and solve an equation to answer the question. Give the exact answer and, if it's irrational, a decimal approximation (to the nearest tenth of a second).

6. How long does it take the water balloon described in Part B to hit the ground?

7. On the moon, the distance d (in feet) that an object falls in time t (in seconds) is modeled by the function $d(t) = \frac{8}{3}t^2$. Suppose an astronaut on the moon drops a tool. How long does it take the tool to fall 4 feet?

⚙ Explain 3   Defining Imaginary Numbers

You know that the quadratic equation $x^2 = 1$ has two real solutions, the equation $x^2 = 0$ has one real solution, and the equation $x^2 = -1$ has no real solutions. By creating a new type of number called *imaginary numbers*, mathematicians allowed for solutions of equations like $x^2 = -1$.

Imaginary numbers are the square roots of negative numbers. These numbers can all be written in the form bi where b is a nonzero real number and i, called the **imaginary unit**, represents $\sqrt{-1}$. Some examples of imaginary numbers are the following:

- $2i$
- $-5i$
- $-\dfrac{i}{3}$ or $-\dfrac{1}{3}i$
- $i\sqrt{2}$ (Write the i in front of the radical symbol for clarity.)
- $\dfrac{i\sqrt{3}}{2}$ or $\dfrac{\sqrt{3}}{2}i$

Given that $i = \sqrt{-1}$, you can conclude that $i^2 = -1$. This means that the square of any imaginary number is a negative real number. When squaring an imaginary number, use the power of a product property of exponents: $(ab)^m = a^m \cdot b^m$.

Example 3 Find the square of the imaginary number.

(A) $5i$

$$(5i)^2 = 5^2 \cdot i^2$$
$$= 25(-1)$$
$$= -25$$

(B) $-i\sqrt{2}$

$$(-i\sqrt{2})^2 = \boxed{}^2 \cdot i^2$$
$$= \boxed{}\,(-1)$$
$$= \boxed{}$$

Reflect

8. By definition, i is a square root of -1. Does -1 have another square root? Explain.

Your Turn

Find the square of the imaginary number.

9. $-2i$

10. $\dfrac{\sqrt{3}}{3}i$

🔑 Explain 4 Finding Imaginary Solutions of Simple Quadratic Equations

Using imaginary numbers and the property below, you can solve simple quadratic equations that do not have real solutions.

Square Root of a Negative Number Property
For a positive real number r, $\sqrt{-r} = i\sqrt{r}$. For example, $\sqrt{-6} = i\sqrt{6}$.

Note that this property effectively extends the Product Property of Square Roots to cases where one of the radicands is negative. The property cannot be extended to cases where both radicands are negative because then $i^2 = \sqrt{-1} \cdot \sqrt{-1} = \sqrt{(-1)(-1)} = \sqrt{1} = 1$, which contradicts the fact that $i^2 = -1$.

Example 4 Solve the quadratic equation by taking square roots. Allow for imaginary solutions.

(A) $x^2 + 12 = 0$

Write the equation. $\qquad\qquad x^2 + 12 = 0$

Subtract 12 from both sides. $\qquad\qquad x^2 = -12$

Use the definition of square root. $\qquad\qquad x = \pm\sqrt{-12}$

Use the fact that for $r > 0$, $\sqrt{-r} = i\sqrt{r}$. $\qquad\qquad x = \pm i\sqrt{12}$

Use the product property of square roots. $\qquad\qquad x = \pm i\sqrt{(4)(3)} = \pm 2i\sqrt{3}$

(B) $4x^2 + 11 = 6$

Write the equation. $4x^2 + 11 = 6$

Subtract 11 from both sides. $\boxed{} x^2 = \boxed{}$

Divide both sides by $\boxed{}$. $x^2 = \boxed{}$

Use the definition of square root. $x = \pm\sqrt{\boxed{}}$

Use the fact that for $r > 0$, $\sqrt{-r} = i\sqrt{r}$. $x = \pm i\sqrt{\boxed{}}$

Use the quotient property of square roots. $x = \pm \boxed{}$

Your Turn

Solve the quadratic equation by taking square roots. Allow for imaginary solutions.

11. $\frac{1}{4}x^2 + 9 = 0$ **12.** $-5x^2 + 3 = 10$

💬 **Elaborate**

13. The quadratic equations $4x^2 + 32 = 0$ and $4x^2 - 32 = 0$ differ only by the sign of the constant term. Without actually solving the equations, what can you say about the relationship between their solutions?

_____

_____

14. What kind of a number is the square of an imaginary number?

_____

_____

15. Why do you reject negative values of t when solving equations based on the models for a falling object near Earth's surface, $d(t) = 16t^2$ for distance fallen and $h(t) = h_0 - 16t^2$ for height during a fall?

_____

_____

16. **Essential Question Check-In** Describe how to find the square roots of a negative number.

_____

_____

1. Solve the equation $x^2 - 2 = 7$ using the indicated method.

   a. Solve by graphing.

   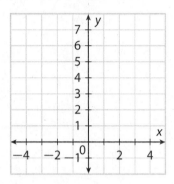

   b. Solve by factoring.

   c. Solve by taking square roots.

2. Solve the equation $2x^2 + 3 = 5$ using the indicated method.

   a. Solve by graphing.

   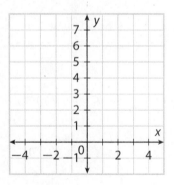

   b. Solve by factoring.

   c. Solve by taking square roots.

Solve the quadratic equation by taking square roots.

3. $4x^2 = 24$

4. $-\dfrac{x^2}{5} + 15 = 0$

5. $2(5 - 5x^2) = 5$

6. $3x^2 - 8 = 12$

Write and solve an equation to answer the question. Give the exact answer and, if it's irrational, a decimal approximation (to the nearest tenth of a second).

7. A squirrel in a tree drops an acorn. How long does it take the acorn to fall 20 feet?

8. A person washing the windows of an office building drops a squeegee from a height of 60 feet. How long does it take the squeegee to pass by another window washer working at a height of 20 feet?

Geometry Determine the lengths of the sides of the rectangle using the given area. Give answers both exactly and approximately (to the nearest tenth).

9. The area of the rectangle is 45 cm².

10. The area of the rectangle is 54 cm².

Find the square of the imaginary number.

11. $3i$

12. $i\sqrt{5}$

13. $-i\dfrac{\sqrt{2}}{2}$

Determine whether the quadratic equation has real solutions or imaginary solutions by solving the equation.

14. $15x^2 - 10 = 0$

15. $\dfrac{1}{2}x^2 + 12 = 4$

16. $5(2x^2 - 3) = 4(x^2 - 10)$

Solve the quadratic equation by taking square roots. Allow for imaginary solutions.

17. $x^2 = -81$

18. $x^2 + 64 = 0$

19. $5x^2 - 4 = -8$

20. $7x^2 + 10 = 0$

Geometry Determine the length of the sides of each square using the given information. Give answers both exactly and approximately (to the nearest tenth).

21. The area of the larger square is 42 cm^2 more than the area of the smaller square.

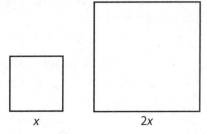

x $2x$

22. If the area of the larger square is decreased by 28 cm^2, the result is half of the area of the smaller square.

23. Determine whether each of the following numbers is real or imaginary.

a. i

    ☐ Real   ☐ Imaginary

b. A square root of 5

    ☐ Real   ☐ Imaginary

c. $(2i)^2$

    ☐ Real   ☐ Imaginary

d. $(-5)^2$

    ☐ Real   ☐ Imaginary

e. $\sqrt{-3}$

    ☐ Real   ☐ Imaginary

f. $-\sqrt{10}$

    ☐ Real   ☐ Imaginary

H.O.T. Focus on Higher Order Thinking

24. Critical Thinking When a batter hits a baseball, you can model the ball's height using a quadratic function that accounts for the ball's initial vertical velocity. However, once the ball reaches its maximum height, its vertical velocity is momentarily 0 feet per second, and you can use the model $h(t) = h_0 - 16t^2$ to find the ball's height h (in feet) at time t (in seconds) as it falls to the ground.

a. Suppose a fly ball reaches a maximum height of 67 feet and an outfielder catches the ball 3 feet above the ground. How long after the ball begins to descend does the outfielder catch the ball?

b. Can you determine (without writing or solving any equations) the total time the ball was in the air? Explain your reasoning and state any assumptions you make.

25. Represent Real-World Situations The aspect ratio of an image on a screen is the ratio of image width to image height. An HDTV screen shows images with an aspect ratio of 16:9. If the area of an HDTV screen is 864 in², what are the dimensions of the screen?

26. Explain the Error Russell wants to calculate the amount of time it takes for a load of dirt to fall from a crane's clamshell bucket at a height of 16 feet to the bottom of a hole that is 32 feet deep. He sets up the following equation and tries to solve it.

$$16 - 16t^2 = 32$$
$$-16t^2 = 16$$
$$t^2 = -1$$
$$t = \pm\sqrt{-1}$$
$$t = \pm i$$

Does Russell's answer make sense? If not, find and correct Russell's error.

Lesson Performance Task

A suspension bridge uses two thick cables, one on each side of the road, to hold up the road. The cables are suspended between two towers and have a parabolic shape. Smaller vertical cables connect the parabolic cables to the road. The table gives the lengths of the first few vertical cables starting with the shortest one.

Displacement from the Shortest Vertical Cable (m)	Height of Vertical Cable (m)
0	3
1	3.05
2	3.2
3	3.45

Find a quadratic function that describes the height (in meters) of a parabolic cable above the road as a function of the horizontal displacement (in meters) from the cable's lowest point. Use the function to predict the distance between the towers if the parabolic cable reaches a maximum height of 48 m above the road at each tower.

3.2 Complex Numbers

Essential Question: What is a complex number, and how can you add, subtract, and multiply complex numbers?

Resource
Locker

⊘ Explore   Exploring Operations Involving Complex Numbers

In this lesson, you'll learn to perform operations with *complex numbers*, which have a form similar to linear binomials such as $3 + 4x$ and $2 - x$.

(A) Add the binomials $3 + 4x$ and $2 - x$.

Group like terms. $(3 + 4x) + (2 - x) = \left(3 + \boxed{}\right) + \left(4x + \boxed{}\right)$

Combine like terms. $= \left(\boxed{} + \boxed{}\right)$

(B) Subtract $2 - x$ from $3 + 4x$.

Rewrite as addition. $(3 + 4x) - (2 - x) = (3 + 4x) + \left(-2 + \boxed{}\right)$

Group like terms. $= \left(3 + \boxed{}\right) + \left(4x + \boxed{}\right)$

Combine like terms. $= \left(\boxed{} + \boxed{}\right)$

(C) Multiply the binomials $3 + 4x$ and $2 - x$.

Use FOIL. $(3 + 4x)(2 - x) = 6 + (-3x) + \boxed{} + \boxed{}$

Combine like terms. $= 6 + \boxed{} + \boxed{}$

Reflect

1. In Step A, you found that $(3 + 4x) + (2 - x) = 5 + 3x$. Suppose $x = i$ (the imaginary unit).

    What equation do you get? _____

2. In Step B, you found that $(3 + 4x) + (2 - x) = 1 + 5x$. Suppose $x = i$ (the imaginary unit).

    What equation do you get? _____

3. In Step C, you found that $(3 + 4x)(2 - x) = 6 + 5x - 4x^2$. Suppose $x = i$ (the imaginary unit). What equation do you get? How can you further simplify the right side of this equation?

    _____

    _____

Defining Complex Numbers

A **complex number** is any number that can be written in the form $a + bi$, where a and b are real numbers and $i = \sqrt{-1}$. For a complex number $a + bi$ a is called the *real part* of the number, and b is called the *imaginary part*. (Note that "imaginary part" refers to the real multiplier of i; it does not refer to the imaginary number bi.) The Venn diagram shows some examples of complex numbers.

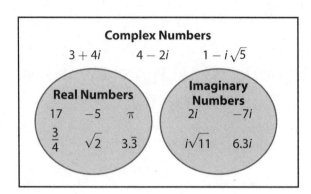

Notice that the set of real numbers is a subset of the set of complex numbers. That's because a real number a can be written in the form $a + 0i$ (whose imaginary part is 0). Likewise, the set of imaginary numbers is also a subset of the set of complex numbers, because an imaginary number bi (where $b \neq 0$) can be written in the form $0 + bi$ (whose real part is 0).

Example 1   Identify the real and imaginary parts of the given number. Then tell which of the following sets the number belongs to: real numbers, imaginary numbers, and complex numbers.

Ⓐ $9 + 5i$

The real part of $9 + 5i$ is 9, and the imaginary part is 5. Because both the real and imaginary parts of $9 + 5i$ are nonzero, the number belongs only to the set of complex numbers.

Ⓑ $-7i$

The real part of $-7i$ is ____, and the imaginary part is ____. Because the real/imaginary part is 0,

the number belongs to these sets: _____

Your Turn

Identify the real and imaginary parts of the given number. Then tell which of the following sets the number belongs to: real numbers, imaginary numbers, and complex numbers.

4.   11

5. $-1 + i$

⊙ Explain 2 Adding and Subtracting Complex Numbers

To add or subtract complex numbers, add or subtract the real parts and the imaginary parts separately.

Example 2 Add or subtract the complex numbers.

Ⓐ $(-7 + 2i) + (5 - 11i)$

Group like terms. $\qquad (-7 + 2i) + (5 - 11i) = (-7 + 5) + (2i + (-11i))$

Combine like terms. $\qquad\qquad\qquad\qquad\qquad = -2 + (-9i)$

Write addition as subtraction. $\qquad\qquad\qquad\quad = -2 - 9i$

Ⓑ $(18 + 27i) - (2 + 3i)$

Group like terms. $\qquad (18 + 27i) - (2 + 3i) = \left(18 - \boxed{}\right) + \left(\boxed{} - 3i\right)$

Combine like terms. $\qquad\qquad\qquad\qquad\qquad = \boxed{} + \boxed{} \, i$

Reflect

6. Is the sum $\left(a + bi\right) + \left(a - bi\right)$ where a and b are real numbers, a real number or an imaginary number? Explain.

_____

_____

_____

Your Turn

Add or subtract the complex numbers.

7. $\left(17 - 6i\right) - \left(9 + 10i\right)$

8. $\left(16 + 17i\right) + \left(-8 - 12i\right)$

⊙ Explain 3 Multiplying Complex Numbers

To multiply two complex numbers, use the distributive property to multiply each part of one number by each part of the other. Use the fact that $i^2 = -1$ to simplify the result.

Example 3 Multiply the complex numbers.

Ⓐ $(4 + 9i)(6 - 2i)$

Use the distributive property. $(4 + 9i)(6 - 2i) = 24 - 8i + 54i - 18i^2$

Substitute -1 for i^2. $= 24 - 8i + 54i - 18(-1)$

Combine like terms. $= 42 + 46i$

Ⓑ $(-3 + 12i)(7 + 4i)$

Use the distributive property. $(-3 + 12i)(7 + 4i) = \boxed{} - 12i + \boxed{} + 48i^2$

Substitute -1 for i^2. $= \boxed{} - 12i + \boxed{} + 48(-1)$

Combine like terms. $= \boxed{} + \boxed{}\, i$

Reflect

9. Is the product of $(a + bi)(a - bi)$, where a and b are real numbers, a real number or an imaginary number? Explain.

Your Turn

Multiply the complex numbers.

10. $(6 - 5i)(3 - 10i)$

11. $(8 + 15i)(11 + i)$

Explain 4 Solving a Real-World Problem Using Complex Numbers

Electrical engineers use complex numbers when analyzing electric circuits. An electric circuit can contain three types of components: resistors, inductors, and capacitors. As shown in the table, each type of component has a different symbol in a circuit diagram, and each is represented by a different type of complex number based on the phase angle of the current passing through it.

Circuit Component	Symbol in Circuit Diagram	Phase Angle	Representation as a Complex Number
Resistor	—⩗⩗⩗—	$0°$	A real number a
Inductor	—⦙⦙⦙⦙—	$90°$	An imaginary number bi where $b > 0$
Capacitor	—⊣⊢—	$-90°$	An imaginary number bi where $b < 0$

A diagram of an alternating current (AC) electric circuit is shown along with the *impedance* (measured in ohms, Ω) of each component in the circuit. An AC power source, which is shown on the left in the diagram and labeled 120 V (for volts), causes electrons to flow through the circuit. Impedance is a measure of each component's opposition to the electron flow.

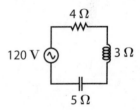

Example 4 **Use the diagram of the electric circuit to answer the following questions.**

(A) The total impedance in the circuit is the sum of the impedances for the individual components. What is the total impedance for the given circuit?

Write the impedance for each component as a complex number.

- Impedance for the resistor: 4
- Impedance for the inductor: $3i$
- Impedance for the capacitor: $-5i$

Then find the sum of the impedances.

Total impedance $= 4 + 3i + (-5i) = 4 - 2i$

(B) Ohm's law for AC electric circuits says that the voltage V (measured in volts) is the product of the current I (measured in amps) and the impedance Z (measured in ohms): $V = I \cdot Z$. For the given circuit, the current I is $24 + 12i$ amps. What is the voltage V for each component in the circuit?

Use Ohm's law, $V = I \cdot Z$, to find the voltage for each component. Remember that Z is the impedance from Part A.

Voltage for the resistor $= I \cdot Z = (24 + 12i)\left(\boxed{}\right) = 96 + \boxed{}\,i$

Voltage for the inductor $= I \cdot Z = (24 + 12i)\left(\boxed{}\right) = -36 + \boxed{}\,i$

Voltage for the capacitor $= I \cdot Z = (24 + 12i)\left(\boxed{}\right) = \boxed{} - 120i$

Reflect

12. Find the sum of the voltages for the three components in Part B. What do you notice?

Your Turn

13. Suppose the circuit analyzed in Example 4 has a second resistor with an impedance of 2 Ω added to it. Find the total impedance. Given that the circuit now has a current of $18 + 6i$ amps, also find the voltage for each component in the circuit.

💬 Elaborate

14. What kind of number is the sum, difference, or product of two complex numbers?

_____

15. When is the sum of two complex numbers a real number? When is the sum of two complex numbers an imaginary number?

_____

_____

_____

16. Discussion What are the similarities and differences between multiplying two complex numbers and multiplying two binomial linear expressions in the same variable?

_____

_____

_____

_____

17. Essential Question Check-In How do you add and subtract complex numbers?

_____

 # Evaluate: Homework and Practice

• Online Homework
• Hints and Help
• Extra Practice

1. Find the sum of the binomials $3 + 2x$ and $4 - 5x$. Explain how you can use the result to find the sum of the complex numbers $3 + 2i$ and $4 - 5i$.

2. Find the product of the binomials $1 - 3x$ and $2 + x$. Explain how you can use the result to find the product of the complex numbers $1 - 3i$ and $2 + i$.

Identify the real and imaginary parts of the given number. Then tell which of the following sets the number belongs to: real numbers, imaginary numbers, and complex numbers.

3. $5 + i$

4. $7 - 6i$

5. 25

6. $i\sqrt{21}$

Add.

7. $(3 + 4i) + (7 + 11i)$

8. $(2 + 3i) + (6 - 5i)$

9. $(-1 - i) + (-10 + 3i)$

10. $(-9 - 7i) + (6 + 5i)$

Subtract.

11. $(2 + 3i) - (7 + 6i)$

12. $(4 + 5i) - (14 - i)$

13. $(-8 - 3i) - (-9 - 5i)$

14. $(5 + 2i) - (5 - 2i)$

Multiply.

15. $(2 + 3i)(3 + 5i)$

16. $(7 + i)(6 - 9i)$

17. $(-4 + 11i)(-5 - 8i)$

18. $(4 - i)(4 + i)$

Use the diagram of the electric circuit and the given current to find the total impedance for the circuit and the voltage for each component.

19.

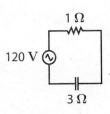

1 Ω

120 V

3 Ω

The circuit has a current of $12 + 36i$ amps.

20.

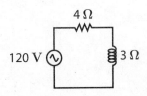

4 Ω

120 V

3 Ω

The circuit has a current of $19.2 - 14.4i$ amps.

21.

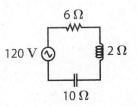

6 Ω

120 V

2 Ω

10 Ω

The circuit has a current of $7.2 + 9.6i$ amps.

22.

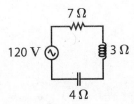

7 Ω

120 V

3 Ω

4 Ω

The circuit has a current of $16.8 + 2.4i$ amps.

23. Match each product on the right with the corresponding expression on the left.

A. $(3 - 5i)(3 + 5i)$ _____ $-16 + 30i$

B. $(3 + 5i)(3 + 5i)$ _____ -34

C. $(-3 - 5i)(3 + 5i)$ _____ 34

D. $(3 - 5i)(-3 - 5i)$ _____ $16 - 30i$

H.O.T. Focus on Higher Order Thinking

24. Explain the Error While attempting to multiply the expression $(2 - 3i)(3 + 2i)$, a student made a mistake. Explain and correct the error.

$$(2 - 3i)(3 + 2i) = 6 - 9i + 4i - 6i^2$$

$$= 6 - 9(-1) + 4(-1) - 6(1)$$

$$= 6 + 9 - 4 - 6$$

$$= 5$$

25. Critical Thinking Show that $\sqrt{3} + i\sqrt{3}$ and $-\sqrt{3} - i\sqrt{3}$ are the square roots of $6i$.

26. Justify Reasoning What type of number is the product of two complex numbers that differ only in the sign of their imaginary parts? Prove your conjecture.

Lesson Performance Task

Just as real numbers can be graphed on a real number line, complex numbers can be graphed on a complex *plane*, which has a horizontal real axis and a vertical imaginary axis. When a set that involves complex numbers is graphed on a complex plane, the result can be an elaborate self-similar figure called a *fractal*. Such a set is called a Julia set.

Consider Julia sets having the quadratic recursive rule $f(n + 1) = (f(n))^2 + c$ for some complex number $f(0)$ and some complex constant c. For a given value of c, a complex number $f(0)$ either belongs or doesn't belong to the "filled-in" Julia set corresponding to c depending on what happens with the sequence of numbers generated by the recursive rule.

a. Letting $c = i$, generate the first few numbers in the sequence defined by $f(0) = 1$ and $f(n + 1) = (f(n))^2 + i$. Record your results in the table.

n	$f(n)$	$f(n + 1) = (f(n))^2 + i$
0	$f(0) = 1$	$f(1) = (f(0))^2 + i = (1)^2 + i = 1 + i$
1	$f(1) = 1 + i$	$f(2) = (f(1))^2 + i = (1 + i)^2 + i = \boxed{}$
2	$f(2) = \boxed{}$	$f(3) = (f(2))^2 + i = (\boxed{})^2 + i = \boxed{}$
3	$f(3) = \boxed{}$	$f(4) = (f(3))^2 + i = (\boxed{})^2 + i = \boxed{}$

b. The *magnitude* of a complex number $a + bi$ is the real number $\sqrt{a^2 + b^2}$. In the complex plane, the magnitude of a complex number is the number's distance from the origin. If the magnitudes of the numbers in the sequence generated by a Julia set's recursive rule, where $f(0)$ is the starting value, remain bounded, then $f(0)$ belongs to the "filled-in" Julia set. If the magnitudes increase without bound, then $f(0)$ doesn't belong to the "filled-in" Julia set. Based on your completed table for $f(0) = 1$, would you say that the number belongs to the "filled-in" Julia set corresponding to $c = i$? Explain.

c. Would you say that $f(0) = i$ belongs to the "filled-in" Julia set corresponding to $c = i$? Explain.

3.3 Finding Complex Solutions of Quadratic Equations

Essential Question: How can you find the complex solutions of any quadratic equation?

Explore   Investigating Real Solutions of Quadratic Equations

(A) Complete the table.

$ax^2 + bx + c = 0$	$ax^2 + bx = -c$	$f(x) = ax^2 + bx$	$g(x) = -c$
$2x^2 + 4x + 1 = 0$			
$2x^2 + 4x + 2 = 0$			
$2x^2 + 4x + 3 = 0$			

(B) The graph of $f(x) = 2x^2 + 4x$ is shown. Graph each $g(x)$. Complete the table.

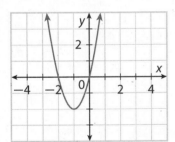

Equation	Number of Real Solutions
$2x^2 + 4x + 1 = 0$	
$2x^2 + 4x + 2 = 0$	
$2x^2 + 4x + 3 = 0$	

(C) Repeat Steps A and B when $f(x) = -2x^2 + 4x$.

$ax^2 + bx + c = 0$	$ax^2 + bx = -c$	$f(x) = ax^2 + bx$	$g(x) = -c$
$-2x^2 + 4x - 1 = 0$			
$-2x^2 + 4x - 2 = 0$			
$-2x^2 + 4x - 3 = 0$			

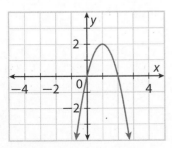

Equation	Number of Real Solutions
$-2x^2 + 4x - 1 = 0$	
$-2x^2 + 4x - 2 = 0$	
$-2x^2 + 4x - 3 = 0$	

Reflect

1. Look back at Steps A and B. Notice that the minimum value of $f(x)$ in Steps A and B is -2. Complete the table by identifying how many real solutions the equation $f(x) = g(x)$ has for the given values of $g(x)$.

Value of $g(x)$	Number of Real Solutions of $f(x) = g(x)$
$g(x) = -2$	
$g(x) > -2$	
$g(x) < -2$	

2. Look back at Step C. Notice that the maximum value of $f(x)$ in Step C is 2. Complete the table by identifying how many real solutions the equation $f(x) = g(x)$ has for the given values of $g(x)$.

Value of $g(x)$	Number of Real Solutions of $f(x) = g(x)$
$g(x) = 2$	
$g(x) > 2$	
$g(x) < 2$	

3. You can generalize Reflect 1: For $f(x) = ax^2 + bx$ where $a > 0$, $f(x) = g(x)$ where $g(x) = -c$ has real solutions when $g(x)$ is greater than or equal to the minimum value of $f(x)$. The minimum value of $f(x)$ is

$$f\left(-\frac{b}{2a}\right) = a\left(-\frac{b}{2a}\right)^2 + b\left(-\frac{b}{2a}\right) = a\left(\frac{b^2}{4a^2}\right) - \frac{b^2}{2a} = \frac{b^2}{4a} - \frac{b^2}{2a} = \frac{b^2}{4a} - \frac{2b^2}{4a} = -\frac{b^2}{4a}.$$

So, $f(x) = g(x)$ has real solutions when $g(x) \geq -\frac{b^2}{4a}$.

Substitute $-c$ for $g(x)$. $-c \geq -\frac{b^2}{4a}$

Add $\frac{b^2}{4a}$ to both sides. $\frac{b^2}{4a} - c \geq 0$

Multiply both sides by $4a$, which is positive. $b^2 - 4ac \geq 0$

In other words, the equation $ax^2 + bx + c = 0$ where $a > 0$ has real solutions when $b^2 - 4ac \geq 0$.

Generalize the results of Reflect 2 in a similar way. What do you notice?

Explain 1 **Finding Complex Solutions by Completing the Square**

Recall that completing the square for the expression $x^2 + bx$ requires adding $\left(\frac{b}{2}\right)^2$ to it, resulting in the perfect square trinomial $x^2 + bx + \left(\frac{b}{2}\right)^2$, which you can factor as $\left(x + \frac{b}{2}\right)^2$. Don't forget that when $x^2 + bx$ appears on one side of an equation, adding $\left(\frac{b}{2}\right)^2$ to it requires adding $\left(\frac{b}{2}\right)^2$ to the other side as well.

Example 1 Solve the equation by completing the square. State whether the solutions are real or non-real.

Ⓐ $3x^2 + 9x - 6 = 0$

1. Write the equation in the form $x^2 + bx = c$.

$$3x^2 + 9x - 6 = 0$$

$$3x^2 + 9x = 6$$

$$x^2 + 3x = 2$$

2. Identify b and $\left(\frac{b}{2}\right)^2$.

$$b = 3$$

$$\left(\frac{b}{2}\right)^2 = \left(\frac{3}{2}\right)^2 = \frac{9}{4}$$

3. Add $\left(\frac{b}{2}\right)^2$ to both sides of the equation.

$$x^2 + 3x + \frac{9}{4} = 2 + \frac{9}{4}$$

4. Solve for x.

$$\left(x + \frac{3}{2}\right)^2 = 2 + \frac{9}{4}$$

$$\left(x + \frac{3}{2}\right)^2 = \frac{17}{4}$$

$$x + \frac{3}{2} = \pm\sqrt{\frac{17}{4}}$$

$$x + \frac{3}{2} = \pm\frac{\sqrt{17}}{2}$$

$$x = -\frac{3}{2} \pm \frac{\sqrt{17}}{2}$$

$$x = \frac{-3 \pm \sqrt{17}}{2}$$

There are two real solutions: $\dfrac{-3 + \sqrt{17}}{2}$ and $\dfrac{-3 - \sqrt{17}}{2}$.

Ⓑ $x^2 - 2x + 7 = 0$

1. Write the equation in the form $x^2 + bx = c$.

2. Identify b and $\left(\frac{b}{2}\right)^2$.

$$b = \boxed{}$$

$$\left(\frac{b}{2}\right)^2 = \left(\frac{\boxed{}}{2}\right)^2 = \boxed{}$$

3. Add $\left(\frac{b}{2}\right)^2$ to both sides.

$$x^2 - 2x + \boxed{} = -7 + \boxed{}$$

4. Solve for x.

$$x^2 + 2x\,\boxed{} = -7 + \boxed{}$$

$$\left(x - \boxed{}\right)^2 = \boxed{}$$

$$x - \boxed{} = \pm\sqrt{\boxed{}}$$

$$x = 1 \pm \sqrt{\boxed{}}$$

There are two real/non-real solutions: _____ and _____.

4. How many complex solutions do the equations in Parts A and B have? Explain.

_____

_____

Your Turn

Solve the equation by completing the square. State whether the solutions are real or non-real.

5. $x^2 + 8x + 17 = 0$

6. $x^2 + 10x - 7 = 0$

⚙ Explain 2 Identifying Whether Solutions Are Real or Non-real

By completing the square for the general quadratic equation $ax^2 + bx + c = 0$, you can obtain the *quadratic formula*, $x = \frac{-b \pm \sqrt{b^2 - 4ac}}{2a}$, which gives the solutions of the general quadratic equation. In the quadratic formula, the expression under the radical sign, $b^2 - 4ac$, is called the *discriminant*, and its value determines whether the solutions of the quadratic equation are real or non-real.

Value of Discriminant	Number and Type of Solutions
$b^2 - 4ac > 0$	Two real solutions
$b^2 - 4ac = 0$	One real solution
$b^2 - 4ac < 0$	Two non-real solutions

Example 2   Answer the question by writing an equation and determining whether the solutions of the equation are real or non-real.

(A)   A ball is thrown in the air with an initial vertical velocity of 14 m/s from an initial height of 2 m. The ball's height h (in meters) at time t (in seconds) can be modeled by the quadratic function $h(t) = -4.9t^2 + 14t + 2$. Does the ball reach a height of 12 m?

Set $h(t)$ equal to 12. $-4.9t^2 + 14t + 2 = 12$

Subtract 12 from both sides. $-4.9t^2 + 14t + 10 = 0$

Find the value of the discriminant. $14^2 - 4(-4.9)(-10) = 196 - 196 = 0$

Because the discriminant is zero, the equation has one real solution, so the ball does reach a height of 12 m.

Ⓑ A person wants to create a vegetable garden and keep the rabbits out by enclosing it with 100 feet of fencing. The area of the garden is given by the function $A(w) = w(50 - w)$ where w is the width (in feet) of the garden. Can the garden have an area of 700 ft²?

Set $A(w)$ equal to 700.

$$w(50 - w) = \boxed{}$$

Multiply on the left side.

$$50w - w^2 = \boxed{}$$

Subtract 700 from both sides.

$$-w^2 + 50w - \boxed{} = 0$$

Find the value of the discriminant.

Because the discriminant is [positive/zero/negative], the equation has [two real/one real/two non-real] solutions, so the garden [can/cannot] have an area of 700 ft².

Your Turn

Answer the question by writing an equation and determining if the solutions are real or non-real.

7. A hobbyist is making a toy sailboat. For the triangular sail, she wants the height h (in inches) to be twice the length of the base b (in inches). Can the area of the sail be 10 in²?

🔧 **Explain 3** **Finding Complex Solutions Using the Quadratic Formula**

When using the quadratic formula to solve a quadratic equation, be sure the equation is in the form $ax^2 + bx + c = 0$.

Example 3 Solve the equation using the quadratic formula. Check a solution by substitution.

Ⓐ $-5x^2 - 2x - 8 = 0$

Write the quadratic formula.

$$x = \frac{-b \pm \sqrt{b^2 - 4ac}}{2a}$$

Substitute values.

$$= \frac{-(-2) \pm \sqrt{(-2)^2 - 4(-5)(-8)}}{2(-5)}$$

Simplify.

$$= \frac{2 \pm \sqrt{-156}}{-10} = \frac{1 \pm i\sqrt{39}}{-5}$$

So, the two solutions are $-\dfrac{1}{5} - \dfrac{i\sqrt{39}}{5}$ and $-\dfrac{1}{5} + \dfrac{i\sqrt{39}}{5}$.

Check by substituting one of the values.

Substitute. $\qquad -5\left(-\dfrac{1}{5} - \dfrac{i\sqrt{39}}{5}\right)^2 - 2\left(-\dfrac{1}{5} - \dfrac{i\sqrt{39}}{5}\right) - 8 \overset{?}{=} 0$

Square. $\qquad -5\left(\dfrac{1}{25} + \dfrac{2i\sqrt{39}}{25} - \dfrac{39}{25}\right) - 2\left(-\dfrac{1}{5} - \dfrac{i\sqrt{39}}{5}\right) - 8 \overset{?}{=} 0$

Distribute. $\qquad -\dfrac{1}{5} - \dfrac{2i\sqrt{39}}{5} + \dfrac{39}{5} + \dfrac{2}{5} + \dfrac{2i\sqrt{39}}{5} - 8 \overset{?}{=} 0$

Simplify. $\qquad\qquad\qquad\qquad\qquad\qquad \dfrac{40}{5} - 8 \overset{?}{=} 0$

$\qquad\qquad\qquad\qquad\qquad\qquad\qquad\qquad 0 = 0$

Ⓑ $\quad 7x^2 + 2x + 3 = -1$

Write the equation with 0 on one side. $\qquad 7x^2 + 2x + \boxed{} = 0$

Write the quadratic formula. $\quad x = \dfrac{-b \pm \sqrt{b^2 - 4ac}}{2a}$

Substitute values. $\quad = \dfrac{-\boxed{} \pm \sqrt{\left(\boxed{}\right)^2 - 4\left(\boxed{}\right)\left(\boxed{}\right)}}{2\left(\boxed{}\right)}$

Simplify. $\quad = \dfrac{-\boxed{} \pm \sqrt{-\boxed{}}}{14}$

$\qquad\qquad = \dfrac{-\boxed{} \pm \boxed{}\,i\sqrt{\boxed{}}}{14} = \dfrac{-\boxed{} \pm \boxed{}\,i\sqrt{\boxed{}}}{7}$

So, the two solutions are _____ and _____.

Check by substituting one of the values.

Substitute.

Square.

Distribute.

Simplify.

Solve the equation using the quadratic formula. Check a solution by substitution.

8. $6x^2 - 5x - 4 = 0$

9. $x^2 + 8x + 12 = 2x$

Elaborate

10. Discussion Suppose that the quadratic equation $ax^2 + bx + c = 0$ has $p + qi$ where $q \neq 0$ as one of its solutions. What must the other solution be? How do you know?

_____

_____

_____

_____

11. Discussion You know that the graph of the quadratic function $f(x) = ax^2 + bx + c$ has the vertical line $x = -\frac{b}{2a}$ as its axis of symmetry. If the graph of $f(x)$ crosses the x-axis, where do the x-intercepts occur relative to the axis of symmetry? Explain.

_____

_____

_____

_____

_____

12. Essential Question Check-In Why is using the quadratic formula to solve a quadratic equation easier than completing the square?

_____

_____

_____

_____

★ Evaluate: Homework and Practice

• Online Homework
• Hints and Help
• Extra Practice

1. The graph of $f(x) = x^2 + 6x$ is shown. Use the graph to determine how many real solutions the following equations have: $x^2 + 6x + 6 = 0$, $x^2 + 6x + 9 = 0$, and $x^2 + 6x + 12 = 0$. Explain.

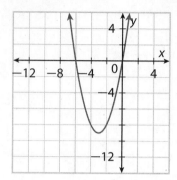

2. The graph of $f(x) = -\frac{1}{2}x^2 + 3x$ is shown. Use the graph to determine how many real solutions the following equations have: $-\frac{1}{2}x^2 + 3x - 3 = 0$, $-\frac{1}{2}x^2 + 3x - \frac{9}{2} = 0$, and $-\frac{1}{2}x^2 + 3x - 6 = 0$. Explain.

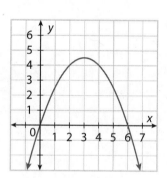

Solve the equation by completing the square. State whether the solutions are real or non-real.

3. $x^2 + 4x + 1 = 0$

4. $x^2 + 2x + 8 = 0$

5. $x^2 - 5x = -20$

6. $5x^2 - 6x = 8$

7. $7x^2 + 13x = 5$

8. $-x^2 - 6x - 11 = 0$

Without solving the equation, state the number of solutions and whether they are real or non-real.

9. $-16x^2 + 4x + 13 = 0$

10. $7x^2 - 11x + 10 = 0$

11. $-x^2 - \frac{2}{5}x = 1$

12. $4x^2 + 9 = 12x$

Answer the question by writing an equation and determining whether the solutions of the equation are real or non-real.

13. A gardener has 140 feet of fencing to put around a rectangular vegetable garden. The function $A(w) = 70w - w^2$ gives the garden's area A (in square feet) for any width w (in feet). Does the gardener have enough fencing for the area of the garden to be 1300 ft²?

14. A golf ball is hit with an initial vertical velocity of 64 ft/s. The function $h(t) = -16t^2 + 64t$ models the height h (in feet) of the golf ball at time t (in seconds). Does the golf ball reach a height of 60 ft?

15. As a decoration for a school dance, the student council creates a parabolic arch with balloons attached to it for students to walk through as they enter the dance. The shape of the arch is modeled by the equation $y = x(5 - x)$, where x and y are measured in feet and where the origin is at one end of the arch. Can a student who is 6 feet 6 inches tall walk through the arch without ducking?

16. A small theater company currently has 200 subscribers who each pay $120 for a season ticket. The revenue from season-ticket subscriptions is $24,000. Market research indicates that for each $10 increase in the cost of a season ticket, the theater company will lose 10 subscribers. A model for the projected revenue R (in dollars) from season-ticket subscriptions is $R(p) = (120 + 10p)(200 - 10p)$, where p is the number of $10 price increases. According to this model, is it possible for the theater company to generate $25,600 in revenue by increasing the price of a season ticket?

Solve the equation using the quadratic formula. Check a solution by substitution.

17. $x^2 - 8x + 27 = 0$

18. $x^2 - 30x + 50 = 0$

19. $x + 3 = x^2$ **20.** $2x^2 + 7 = 4x$

21. Place an X in the appropriate column of the table to classify each equation by the number and type of its solutions.

Equation	Two Real Solutions	One Real Solution	Two Non-Real Solutions
$x^2 - 3x + 1 = 0$			
$x^2 - 2x + 1 = 0$			
$x^2 - x + 1 = 0$			
$x^2 + 1 = 0$			
$x^2 + x + 1 = 0$			
$x^2 + 2x + 1 = 0$			
$x^2 + 3x + 1 = 0$			

22. Explain the Error A student used the method of completing the square to solve the equation $-x^2 + 2x - 3 = 0$. Describe and correct the error.

$$-x^2 + 2x - 3 = 0$$

$$-x^2 + 2x = 3$$

$$-x^2 + 2x + 1 = 3 + 1$$

$$(x + 1)^2 = 4$$

$$x + 1 = \pm\sqrt{4}$$

$$x + 1 = \pm 2$$

$$x = -1 \pm 2$$

So, the two solutions are $-1 + 2 = 1$ and $-1 - 2 = -3$.

23. Make a Conjecture Describe the values of c for which the equation $x^2 + 8x + c = 0$ has two real solutions, one real solution, and two non-real solutions.

24. Analyze Relationships When you rewrite $y = ax^2 + bx + c$ in vertex form by completing the square, you obtain these coordinates for the vertex: $\left(-\dfrac{b}{2a}, c - \dfrac{b^2}{4a}\right)$. Suppose the vertex of the graph of $y = ax^2 + bx + c$ is located on the x-axis. Explain how the coordinates of the vertex and the quadratic formula are in agreement in this situation.

Lesson Performance Task

Matt and his friends are enjoying an afternoon at a baseball game. A batter hits a towering home run, and Matt shouts, "Wow, that must have been 110 feet high!" The ball was 4 feet off the ground when the batter hit it, and the ball came off the bat traveling vertically at 80 feet per second.

a. Model the ball's height h (in feet) at time t (in seconds) using the projectile motion model $h(t) = -16t^2 + v_0 t + h_0$ where v_0 is the projectile's initial vertical velocity (in feet per second) and h_0 is the projectile's initial height (in feet). Use the model to write an equation based on Matt's claim, and then determine whether Matt's claim is correct.

b. Did the ball reach a height of 100 feet? Explain.

c. Let h_{max} be the ball's maximum height. By setting the projectile motion model equal to h_{max}, show how you can find h_{max} using the discriminant of the quadratic formula.

d. Find the time at which the ball reached its maximum height.

Quadratic Equations

Essential Question: How can you use quadratic equations to solve real-world problems?

Key Vocabulary

complex number
  (número complejo)
imaginary number
  (número imaginario)
imaginary unit
  (unidad imaginaria)
pure imaginary number
  (número imaginario puro)

KEY EXAMPLE   *(Lessons 3.1, 3.2)*

Take square roots to solve the quadratic equations.

$3x^2 - 27 = 9$

$3x^2 = 36$ Add 27 to both sides.

$x^2 = 12$ Divide both sides by 3.

$x = \pm\sqrt{12}$ Square root

$x = \pm\sqrt{4} \cdot \sqrt{3}$ Product Property

$x = \pm 2\sqrt{3}$ Simplify.

$x^2 + 20 = 0$

$x^2 = -20$ Subtract 20 on both sides.

$x = \pm\sqrt{-20}$ Square root

$x = \pm\sqrt{(-1)(5)(4)}$ Product Property

$x = \pm 2i\sqrt{5}$ Simplify.

KEY EXAMPLE   *(Lesson 3.3)*

Solve $2x^2 + 4x - 8 = 0$ by completing the square.

$2x^2 + 4x = 8$ Write the equation in the form $x^2 + bx = c$.

$x^2 + 2x = 4$ Divide both sides by 2.

$x^2 + 2x + 1 = 4 + 1$ Add $\left(\frac{b}{2}\right)^2$ to both sides of the equation.

$(x + 1)^2 = 5$ Solve for x.

$x + 1 = \pm\sqrt{5}$

$x = -1 \pm\sqrt{5}$

EXERCISES

Solve using the method stated. *(Lessons 3.1, 3.3)*

1. $x^2 - 16 = 0$ (square root)

2. $2x^2 - 10 = 0$ (square root)

3. $3x^2 - 6x - 12 = 0$ (completing the square)

4. $x^2 + 6x + 10 = 0$ (completing the square)

5. $x^2 - 4x + 4 = 0$ (factoring)

6. $x^2 - x - 30 = 0$ (factoring)

7. Explain when a quadratic equation can be solved using factoring. *(Lessons 3.1, 3.3)*

8. Can any quadratic equation be solved by completing the square? Explain. *(Lessons 3.1, 3.3)*

MODULE PERFORMANCE TASK

Can You Stop in Time?

A driver sees a tree fall across the road 125 feet in front of the car. The driver is barely able to stop the car before hitting the tree. Below what speed in miles per hour must the car have been traveling when the driver saw the tree fall?

The equation for braking distance is $d = \dfrac{s^2}{2\mu g}$, where d is braking distance, s is speed of the car, μ is the coefficient of friction between the tires and the road, and g is the acceleration due to gravity, 32.2 ft/s^2.

Start by listing on your own paper the information you will need and the steps you will take to solve the problem. Then complete the task, using numbers, words, or algebra to explain how you reached your conclusion.

(Ready) to Go On?

3.1–3.3 Quadratic Equations

Solve the equations by taking square roots, completing the square, factoring, or using the quadratic formula. *(Lessons 3.1, 3.2, 3.3)*

1. $2x^2 - 16 = 0$

2. $2x^2 - 6x - 20 = 0$

3. $2x^2 + 2x - 2 = 0$

4. $x^2 + x = 30$

5. $x^2 - 5x = 24$

6. $-4x^2 + 8 = 24$

7. $x^2 + 30 = 24$

8. $x^2 + 4x + 3 = 0$

ESSENTIAL QUESTION

9. Write a real world situation that could be modeled by the equation $7m \cdot 5m = 875$. *(Lesson 3.1)*

Assessment Readiness

1. Which of the following equations, when graphed, has two x-intercepts?

   A. $x^2 + 16 = 0$ ◯ Yes   ◯ No

   B. $2x^2 - 20 = 10$ ◯ Yes   ◯ No

   C. $-3x^2 - 6 = 0$ ◯ Yes   ◯ No

2. Consider the equation $4x^2 + 4x - 16 = 0$. Choose True or False for each statement.

   A. To solve this equation using complete   ◯ True   ◯ False

   the square, $\left(\frac{b}{2}\right)^2 = \left(\frac{4}{2}\right)^2 = 4$.

   B. If solving this equation using factoring,   ◯ True   ◯ False

   then $(x + 4)(x - 4) = 0$

   C. After completing the square,   ◯ True   ◯ False

   $x = -\frac{1}{2} \pm \frac{\sqrt{17}}{2}$.

3. Consider the equation $ax^2 + bx = 25$. For what values of a and b would you solve this equation by taking a square root? For what values of a would the square root result in an imaginary number? Explain your answers.

4. Consider the equation $f(x) = ax^2 + bx + c$. For what values of a would the quadratic function open upward? For what values of a would the quadratic function open downward? What would happen to the function if the value of a were 0? Explain.

Quadratic Relations and Systems of Equations

Essential Question: How can you use systems of equations to solve real-world problems?

REAL WORLD VIDEO
Video game designers need a solid understanding of algebra, including systems of quadratic equations, in order to program realistic interactions within the game environment.

MODULE PERFORMANCE TASK PREVIEW

How Can You Hit a Moving Target with a Laser Beam?

Video games can be a lot of fun. They can also help players to develop and hone skills such as following instructions, using logic in problem solving, hand-eye coordination, and fine motor and spatial abilities. Video game designers often use mathematics to program realistic interactions in the video world. How can math be used to aim a laser beam to hit a virtual clay disk flying through the air? Set your sights on the target and let's get started!

Are YOU Ready?

Complete these exercises to review skills you will need for this module.

Graphing Linear Nonproportional Relationships

Example 1   Graph $y = -2x - 3$.

x	0	-2	-3
y	-3	1	3

Make a table of values. Plot the points and draw a line through them.

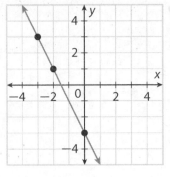

Graph each equation.

1. $y = -x + 5$

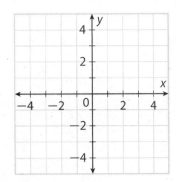

2. $y = 3x - 2$

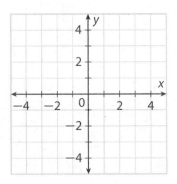

Multi-Step Equations

Example 2   Solve $4(x - 2) = 12$ for x.

$4x - 8 = 12$ Distribute.

$4x = 20$ Add 8 to both sides.

$x = 5$ Divide by 4.

Solve each equation.

3. $5 - 3x = 7(x - 1)$ _____

4. $3x + 2(x - 1) = 28$ _____

5. $2(6 - 5x) = 5x + 9$ _____

Solving Systems of Two Linear Equations

Example 3   Solve the system $\begin{cases} y = 2x + 8 \\ 3x + 2y = 2 \end{cases}$.

$3x + 2(2x + 8) = 2$ Substitute.

$x = -2$ Solve for x.

$y = 2(-2) + 8 = 4$ Solve for y.

The solution is $(-2, 4)$.

Solve each system.

6. $\begin{cases} y = 10 - 3x \\ 5x - y = 6 \end{cases}$ _____

7. $\begin{cases} 2x - 3y = 4 \\ -x + 2y = 3 \end{cases}$ _____

8. $\begin{cases} 5x - 2y = 4 \\ 3x + 2y = -12 \end{cases}$ _____

4.1 Circles

Resource
Locker

Essential Question: What is the standard form for the equation of a circle, and what does the standard form tell you about the circle?

⊘ Explore   Deriving the Standard-Form Equation of a Circle

Recall that a circle is the set of points in a plane that are a fixed distance, called the radius, from a given point, called the center.

(A) The coordinate plane shows a circle with center $C(h, k)$ and radius r. $P(x, y)$ is an arbitrary point on the circle but is not directly above or below or to the left or right of C. $A(x, k)$ is a point with the same x-coordinate as P and the same y-coordinate as C. Explain why $\triangle CAP$ is a right triangle.

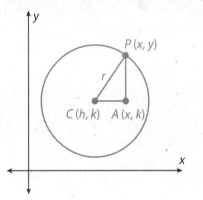

_____

_____

_____

_____

_____

(B) Identify the lengths of the sides of $\triangle CAP$. Remember that point P is arbitrary, so you cannot rely upon the diagram to know whether the x-coordinate of P is greater than or less than h or whether the y-coordinate of P is greater than or less than k, so you must use absolute value for the lengths of the legs of $\triangle CAP$. Also, remember that the length of the hypotenuse of $\triangle CAP$ is just the radius of the circle.

The length of segment AC is $\boxed{}$.

The length of segment AP is $\boxed{}$.

The length of segment CP is _____.

(C) Apply the Pythagorean Theorem to $\triangle CAP$ to obtain an equation of the circle.

$$\left(x - \boxed{}\right)^2 + \left(y - \boxed{}\right)^2 = \boxed{}^2$$

1. **Discussion** Why isn't absolute value used in the equation of the circle?

_____

_____

2. **Discussion** Why does the equation of the circle also apply to the cases in which P has the same x-coordinate as C or the same y-coordinate as C so that $\triangle CAP$ doesn't exist?

_____

_____

_____

_____

_____

⚒ Explain 1 Writing the Equation of a Circle

The standard-form equation of a circle with center $C(h, k)$ and radius r is $(x - h)^2 + (y - k)^2 = r^2$. If you solve this equation for r, you obtain the equation $r = \sqrt{(x - h)^2 + (y - k)^2}$, which gives you a means for finding the radius of a circle when the center and a point $P(x, y)$ on the circle are known.

Example 1 Write the equation of the circle.

(A) The circle with center $C(-3, 2)$ and radius $r = 4$

Substitute -3 for h, 2 for k, and 4 for r into the general equation and simplify.

$$\left(x - (-3)\right)^2 + \left(y - 2\right)^2 = 4^2$$

$$(x + 3)^2 + (y - 2)^2 = 16$$

(B) The circle with center $C(-4, -3)$ and containing the point $P(2, 5)$

Step 1 Find the radius.

$$r = CP$$

$$= \sqrt{\left(\boxed{} - (-4)\right)^2 + \left(\boxed{} - (-3)\right)^2}$$

$$= \sqrt{\left(\boxed{}\right)^2 + \left(\boxed{}\right)^2}$$

$$= \sqrt{\boxed{} + \boxed{}}$$

$$= \sqrt{\boxed{}} = \boxed{}$$

Step 2 Write the equation of the circle.

$$\left(x - (-4)\right)^2 + \left(y - (-3)\right)^2 = \boxed{}$$

$$(x + 4)^2 + (y + 3)^2 = \boxed{}$$

Write the equation of the circle.

3. The circle with center $C(1, -4)$ and radius $r = 2$

4. The circle with center $C(-2, 5)$ and containing the point $P(-2, -1)$

Explain 2 Rewriting an Equation of a Circle to Graph the Circle

Expanding the standard-form equation $(x - h)^2 + (y - k)^2 = r^2$ results in a general second-degree equation in two variables having the form $x^2 + y^2 + cx + dy + e = 0$. In order to graph such an equation or an even more general equation of the form $ax^2 + ay^2 + cx + dy + e = 0$. you must complete the square on both x and y to put the equation in standard form and identify the circle's center and radius.

Example 2 Graph the circle after writing the equation in standard form.

(A) $x^2 + y^2 - 10x + 6y + 30 = 0$

Write the equation. $\qquad x^2 + y^2 - 10x + 6y + 30 = 0$

Prepare to complete the square on x and y. $\left(x^2 - 10x + \blacksquare\right) + \left(y^2 + 6y + \blacksquare\right) = -30 + \blacksquare + \blacksquare$

Complete both squares. $\left(x^2 - 10x + 25\right) + \left(y^2 + 6y + 9\right) = -30 + 25 + 9$

Factor and simplify. $\qquad (x - 5)^2 + (y + 3)^2 = 4$

The center of the circle is $C(5, -3)$, and the radius is $r = \sqrt{4} = 2$.

Graph the circle.

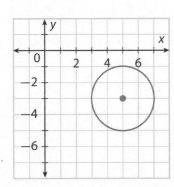

(B) $4x^2 + 4y^2 + 8x - 16y + 11 = 0$

Write the equation. $\qquad$ $4x^2 + 4y^2 + 8x - 16y + 11 = 0$

Factor 4 from the x terms and the y terms. $\qquad$ $4(x^2 + 2x) + 4(y^2 - 4y) + 11 = 0$

Prepare to complete the square on x and y. $\qquad$ $4\left(x^2 + 2x + \blacksquare\right) + 4\left(y^2 - 4y + \blacksquare\right) = -11 + 4\left(\blacksquare\right) + 4\left(\blacksquare\right)$

Complete both squares. $\qquad$ $4\left(x^2 + 2x + \boxed{}\right) + 4\left(y^2 - 4y + \boxed{}\right) = -11 + 4\left(\boxed{}\right) + 4\left(\boxed{}\right)$

Factor and simplify. $\qquad$ $4\left(x + \boxed{}\right)^2 + 4\left(y - \boxed{}\right)^2 = \boxed{}$

Divide both sides by 4. $\qquad$ $\left(x + \boxed{}\right)^2 + \left(y - \boxed{}\right)^2 = \boxed{}$

The center is $C\left(\boxed{}, \boxed{}\right)$, and the radius is $r = \sqrt{\boxed{}} = \boxed{}$.

Graph the circle.

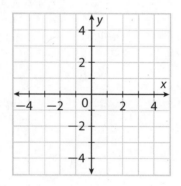

Your Turn

Graph the circle after writing the equation in standard form.

5. $x^2 + y^2 + 4x + 6y + 4 = 0$

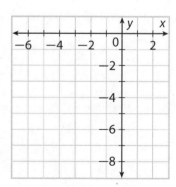

6. $9x^2 + 9y^2 - 54x - 72y + 209 = 0$

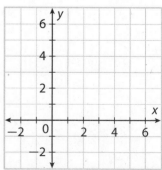

✏ Explain 3 Solving a Real-World Problem Involving a Circle

A circle in a coordinate plane divides the plane into two regions: points inside the circle and points outside the circle. Points inside the circle satisfy the inequality $(x - h)^2 + (y - k)^2 < r^2$, while points outside the circle satisfy the inequality $(x - h)^2 + (y - k)^2 > r^2$.

Example 3 **Write an inequality representing the given situation, and draw a circle to solve the problem.**

(A) The table lists the locations of the homes of five friends along with the locations of their favorite pizza restaurant and the school they attend. The friends are deciding where to have a pizza party based on the fact that the restaurant offers free delivery to locations within a 3-mile radius of the restaurant. At which homes should the friends hold their pizza party to get free delivery?

Place	Location
Alonzo's home	A(3, 2)
Barbara's home	B(2, 4)
Constance's home	C(−2, 3)
Dion's home	D(0, −1)
Eli's home	E(1, −4)
Pizza restaurant	(−1, 1)
School	(1, −2)

Write the equation of the circle with center (−1, 1) and radius 3.

$$\left(x - (-1)\right)^2 + (y - 1)^2 = 3^2, \text{ or } (x + 1)^2 + (y - 1)^2 = 9$$

The inequality $(x + 1)^2 + (y - 1)^2 < 9$ represents the situation. Plot the points from the table and graph the circle.

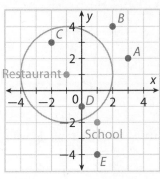

The points inside the circle satisfy the inequality. So, the friends should hold their pizza party at either Constance's home or Dion's home to get free delivery.

(B) In order for a student to ride the bus to school, the student must live more than 2 miles from the school. Which of the five friends are eligible to ride the bus?

Write the equation of the circle with center $\left(\boxed{}, \boxed{}\right)$ and radius ___.

$$\left(x - \boxed{}\right)^2 + \left(y - \boxed{}\right)^2 = \boxed{}^2$$

$$\left(x - \boxed{}\right)^2 + \left(y + \boxed{}\right)^2 = \boxed{}$$

The inequality $\left(x - \boxed{}\right)^2 + \left(y + \boxed{}\right)^2 > \boxed{}$ represents the situation. Use the coordinate grid in Part A to graph the circle.

The points _____ the circle satisfy the inequality. So, _____ are eligible to ride the bus.

7. For Part B, how do you know that point *E* isn't outside the circle?

_____

_____

_____

Write an inequality representing the given situation, and draw a circle to solve the problem.

8. Sasha delivers newspapers to subscribers that live within a 4-block radius of her house. Sasha's house is located at point $(0, -1)$. Points *A*, *B*, *C*, *D*, and *E* represent the houses of some of the subscribers to the newspaper. To which houses does Sasha deliver newspapers?

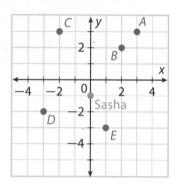

💬 Elaborate

9. Describe the process for deriving the equation of a circle given the coordinates of its center and its radius.

_____

_____

_____

_____

10. What must you do with the equation $ax^2 + ay^2 + cx + dy + e = 0$ in order to graph it?

_____

_____

_____

11. What do the inequalities $(x - h)^2 + (y - k)^2 < r^2$ and $(x - h)^2 + (y - k)^2 > r^2$ represent?

_____

_____

_____

12. **Essential Question Check-In** What information must you know or determine in order to write an equation of a circle in standard form?

_____

_____

_____

Write the equation of the circle.

1. The circle with $C(4, -11)$ and radius $r = 16$

2. The circle with $C(-7, -1)$ and radius $r = 13$

3. The circle with center $C(-8, 2)$ and containing the point $P(-1, 6)$

4. The circle with center $C(5, 9)$ and containing the point $P(4, 8)$

In Exercises 5–12, graph the circle after writing the equation in standard form.

5. $x^2 + y^2 - 2x - 8y + 13 = 0$

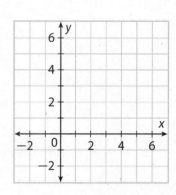

Graph the circle after writing the equation in standard form.

6. $x^2 + y^2 + 6x - 10y + 25 = 0$

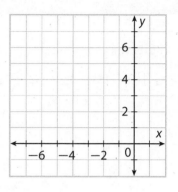

7. $x^2 + y^2 + 4x + 12y + 39 = 0$

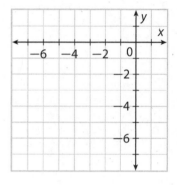

8. $x^2 + y^2 - 8x + 4y + 16 = 0$

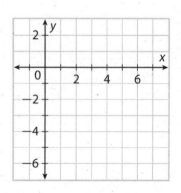

9. $8x^2 + 8y^2 - 16x - 32y - 88 = 0$

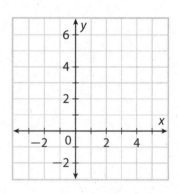

10. $2x^2 + 2y^2 + 20x + 12y + 50 = 0$

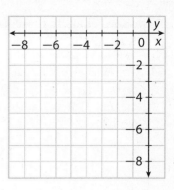

11. $12x^2 + 12y^2 - 96x - 24y + 201 = 0$

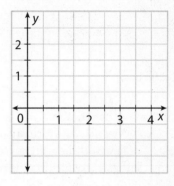

12. $16x^2 + 16y^2 + 64x - 96y + 199 = 0$

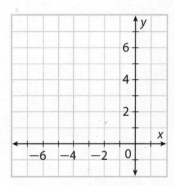

In Exercises 13–20, write an inequality representing the problem, and draw a circle to solve the problem.

13. A router for a wireless network on a floor of an office building has a range of 35 feet. The router is located at the point (30, 30). The lettered points in the coordinate diagram represent computers in the office. Which computers will be able to connect to the network through the router?

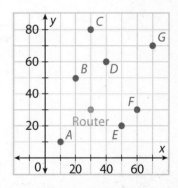

Write an inequality representing the problem, and draw a circle to solve the problem.

14. The epicenter of an earthquake is located at the point $(20, -30)$. The earthquake is felt up to 40 miles away. The labeled points in the coordinate diagram represent towns near the epicenter. In which towns is the earthquake felt?

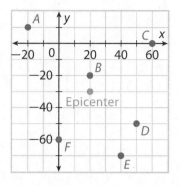

15. Aida's cat has disappeared somewhere in her apartment. The last time she saw the cat, it was located at the point $(30, 40)$. Aida knows all of the cat's hiding places, which are indicated by the lettered points in the coordinate diagram. If she searches for the cat no farther than 25 feet from where she last saw it, which hiding places will she check?

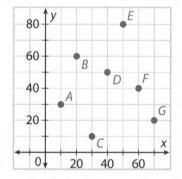

16. A rock concert is held in a large state park. The concert stage is located at the point $(-2, 2)$, and the music can be heard as far as 4 miles away. The lettered points in the coordinate diagram represent campsites within the park. At which campsites can the music be heard?

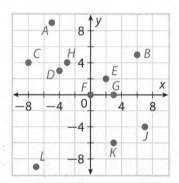

17. Business When Claire started her in-home computer service and support business, she decided not to accept clients located more than 10 miles from her home. Claire's home is located at the point (5, 0), and the lettered points in the coordinate diagram represent the homes of her prospective clients. Which prospective clients will Claire not accept?

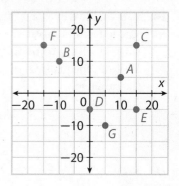

18. Aviation An airport's radar system detects airplanes that are in flight as far as 60 miles from the airport. The airport is located at $(-20, 40)$. The lettered points in the coordinate diagram represent the locations of airplanes currently in flight. Which airplanes does the airport's radar system detect?

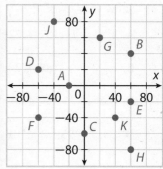

19. Due to a radiation leak at a nuclear power plant, the towns up to a distance of 30 miles from the plant are to be evacuated. The nuclear power plant is located at the point $(-10, -10)$. The lettered points in the coordinate diagram represent the towns in the area. Which towns are in the evacuation zone?

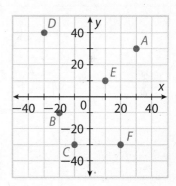

20. Bats that live in a cave at point $(-10, 0)$ have a feeding range of 40 miles. The lettered points in the coordinate diagram represent towns near the cave. In which towns are bats from the cave not likely to be observed? Write an inequality representing the problem, and draw a circle to solve the problem.

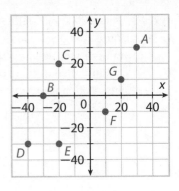

21. Match the equations to the center and radius of the circle each represents. Show your work.

A. $x^2 + y^2 + 18x + 22y - 23 = 0$ _____ $C(9, -11); r = 13$

B. $x^2 + y^2 - 18x + 22y + 33 = 0$ _____ $C(9, 11); r = 15$

C. $25x^2 + 25y^2 - 450x - 550y - 575 = 0$ _____ $C(-9, -11); r = 15$

D. $25x^2 + 25y^2 + 450x - 550y + 825 = 0$ _____ $C(-9, 11); r = 13$

22. Multi-Step A garden sprinkler waters the plants in a garden within a 12-foot spray radius. The sprinkler is located at the point $(5, -10)$. The lettered points in the coordinate diagram represent the plants. Use the diagram for parts a–c.

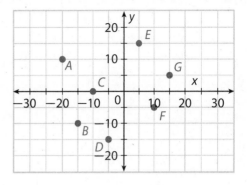

a. Write an inequality that represents the region that does not get water from the sprinkler. Then draw a circle and use it to identify the plants that do not get water from the sprinkler.

b. Suppose a second sprinkler with the same spray radius is placed at the point $(10, 10)$. Write a system of inequalities that represents the region that does not get water from either sprinkler. Then draw a second circle and use it to identify the plants that do not get water from either sprinkler.

c. Where would you place a third sprinkler with the same spray radius so all the plants get water from a sprinkler? Write a system of inequalities that represents the region that does not get water from any of the sprinklers. Then draw a third circle to show that every plant receives water from a sprinkler.

23. **Represent Real-World Situations** The orbit of the planet Venus is nearly circular. An astronomer develops a model for the orbit in which the Sun has coordinates $S(0, 0)$, the circular orbit of Venus passes through $V(41, 53)$, and each unit of the coordinate plane represents 1 million miles. Write an equation for the orbit of Venus. How far is Venus from the sun?

24. **Draw Conclusions** The *unit circle* is defined as the circle with radius 1 centered at the origin. A *Pythagorean triple* is an ordered triple of three positive integers, (a, b, c), that satisfy the relationship $a^2 + b^2 = c^2$. An example of a Pythagorean triple is $(3, 4, 5)$. In parts a–d, you will draw conclusions about Pythagorean triples.

a. Write the equation of the unit circle.

b. Use the Pythagorean triple $(3, 4, 5)$ and the symmetry of a circle to identify the coordinates of two points on the part of the unit circle that lies in Quadrant I. Explain your reasoning.

c. Use your answer from part b and the symmetry of a circle to identify the coordinates of six other points on the unit circle. This time, the points should be in Quadrants II, III, and IV.

d. Find a different Pythagorean triple and use it to identify the coordinates of eight points on the unit circle.

25. Make a Conjecture In a two-dimensional plane, coordinates are given by ordered pairs of the form (x, y). You can generalize coordinates to three-dimensional space by using ordered triples of the form (x, y, z) where the coordinate z is used to indicate displacement above or below the xy-plane. Generalize the standard-form equation of a circle to find the general equation of a sphere. Explain your reasoning.

Lesson Performance Task

A highway that runs straight east and west passes 6 miles south of a radio tower. The broadcast range of the station is 10 miles.

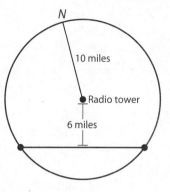

a. Determine the distance along the highway that a car will be within range of the radio station's signal.

b. Given that the car is traveling at a constant speed of 60 miles per hour, determine the amount of time the car is within range of the signal.

4.2 Parabolas

Essential Question: How is the distance formula connected with deriving equations for both vertical and horizontal parabolas?

Resource Locker

⊘ Explore   Deriving the Standard-Form Equation of a Parabola

A **parabola** is defined as a set of points equidistant from a line (called the **directrix**) and a point (called the **focus**). The focus will always lie on the axis of symmetry, and the directrix will always be perpendicular to the axis of symmetry. This definition can be used to derive the equation for a horizontal parabola opening to the right with its vertex at the origin using the distance formula. (The derivations of parabolas opening in other directions will be covered later.)

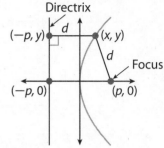

(A) The coordinates for the focus are given by

[   ] .

(B) Write down the expression for the distance from a point (x, y) to the coordinates of the focus:

$$d = \sqrt{\left(\boxed{} - \boxed{}\right)^2 + \left(\boxed{} - \boxed{}\right)^2}$$

(C) The distance from a point to a line is measured by drawing a perpendicular line segment from the point to the line. Find the point where a horizontal line from (x, y) intersects the directrix (defined by the line $x = -p$ for a parabola with its vertex on the origin).

[   ]

(D) Write down the expression for the distance from a point, (x, y) to the point from Step C:

$$d = \sqrt{\left(\boxed{} - \boxed{}\right)^2 + \left(\boxed{} - \boxed{}\right)^2}$$

(E) Setting the two distances the same and simplifying gives.

$$\sqrt{(x - p)^2 + y^2} = \sqrt{(x + p)^2}$$

To continue solving the problem, square both sides of the equation and expand the squared binomials.

$$\boxed{} x^2 + \boxed{} \cdot xp + \boxed{} p^2 + y^2 = \boxed{} x^2 + \boxed{} xp + \boxed{} p^2$$

(F) Collect terms.

$$\boxed{} x^2 + \boxed{} px + \boxed{} p^2 + y^2 = 0$$

(G) Finally, simplify and arrange the equation into the **standard form for a horizontal parabola** (with vertex at (0, 0)):

$$y^2 = \boxed{}$$

1. Why was the directrix placed on the line $x = -p$?

_____

_____

_____

_____

2. **Discussion** How can the result be generalized to arrive at the standard form for a horizontal parabola with a vertex at (h, k):

$(y - k)^2 = 4p(x - h)$?

_____

_____

_____

⊘ Explain 1 Writing the Equation of a Parabola with Vertex at $(0, 0)$

The equation for a horizontal parabola with vertex at $(0, 0)$ is written in the standard form as $y^2 = 4px$. It has a vertical directrix along the line $x = -p$, a horizontal axis of symmetry along the line $y = 0$, and a focus at the point $(p, 0)$. The parabola opens toward the focus, whether it is on the right or left of the origin $(p > 0$ or $p < 0)$. Vertical parabolas are similar, but with horizontal directrices and vertical axes of symmetry:

Parabolas with Vertices at the Origin		
	Vertical	**Horizontal**
Equation in standard form	$x^2 = 4py$	$y^2 = 4px$
$p > 0$	Opens upward	Opens rightward
$p < 0$	Opens downward	Opens leftward
Focus	$(0, p)$	$(p, 0)$
Directrix	$y = -p$	$x = -p$
Axis of Symmetry	$x = 0$	$y = 0$

Example 1 Find the equation of the parabola from the description of the focus and directrix. Then make a sketch showing the parabola, the focus, and the directrix.

(A) Focus $(-8, 0)$, directrix $x = 8$

A vertical directrix means a horizontal parabola.

Confirm that the vertex is at $(0, 0)$:

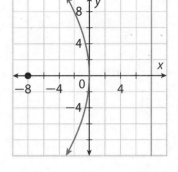

   a. The y-coordinate of the vertex is the same as the focus: 0.

   b. The x-coordinate is halfway between the focus (-8) and the directrix $(+8)$: 0.

   c. The vertex is at $(0, 0)$.

Use the equation for a horizontal parabola, $y^2 = 4px$, and replace p with the x coordinate of the focus: $y^2 = 4(-8)x$

Simplify: $y^2 = -32x$

Plot the focus and directrix and sketch the parabola.

(B) Focus $(0, -2)$, directrix $y = 2$

A [vertical/horizontal] directrix means a [vertical/horizontal] parabola.

Confirm that the vertex is at $(0, 0)$:

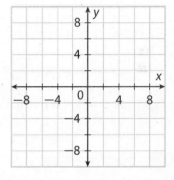

   a. The x-coordinate of the vertex is the same as the focus: 0.

   b. The y-coordinate is halfway between the focus, ☐ and the directrix, ☐ : 0

   c. The vertex is at $(0, 0)$.

Use the equation for a vertical parabola, ☐ , and replace p with the y-coordinate of the focus: $x^2 = 4 \cdot$ ☐ $\cdot y$

Simplify: $x^2 =$ ☐

Plot the focus, the directrix, and the parabola.

Your Turn

Find the equation of the parabola from the description of the focus and directrix. Then make a sketch showing the parabola, the focus, and the directrix.

3. Focus $(2, 0)$, directrix $x = -2$

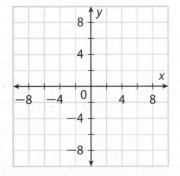

4. Focus $\left(0, -\frac{1}{2}\right)$, directrix $y = \frac{1}{2}$

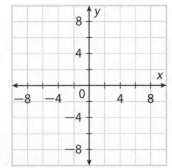

Writing the Equation of a Parabola with Vertex at (h, k)

The standard equation for a parabola with a vertex (h, k) can be found by translating from $(0, 0)$ to (h, k): substitute $(x - h)$ for x and $(y - k)$ for y. This also translates the focus and directrix each by the same amount.

Parabolas with Vertex (h, k)		
	Vertical	**Horizontal**
Equation in standard form	$(x - h)^2 = 4p(y - k)$	$(y - k)^2 = 4p(x - h)$
$p > 0$	Opens upward	Opens rightward
$p < 0$	Opens downward	Opens leftward
Focus	$(h, k + p)$	$(h + p, k)$
Directrix	$y = k - p$	$x = h - p$
Axis of Symmetry	$x = h$	$y = k$

p is found halfway from the directrix to the focus:

- For vertical parabolas: $p = \dfrac{(y \text{ value of focus}) - (y \text{ value of directrix})}{2}$

- For horizontal parabolas: $p = \dfrac{(x \text{ value of focus}) - (x \text{ value of directrix})}{2}$

The vertex can be found from the focus by relating the coordinates of the focus to h, k, and p.

Example 2   **Find the equation of the parabola from the description of the focus and directrix. Then make a sketch showing the parabola, the focus, and the directrix.**

Ⓐ   Focus $(3, 2)$, directrix $y = 0$

A horizontal directrix means a vertical parabola.

$p = \dfrac{(y \text{ value of focus}) - (y \text{ value of directrix})}{2} = \dfrac{2 - 0}{2} = 1$

$h = $ the x-coordinate of the focus $= 3$

Solve for k: The y-value of the focus is $k + p$, so
$k + p = 2$

$k + 1 = 2$

$\quad k = 1$

Write the equation: $(x - 3)^2 = 4(y - 1)$

Plot the focus, the directrix, and the parabola.

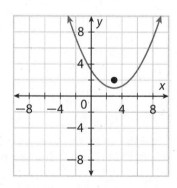

Ⓑ Focus $(-1, -1)$, directrix $x = 5$

A vertical directrix means a _____ parabola.

$p = \dfrac{(x \text{ value of focus}) - (x \text{ value of directrix})}{2} = \dfrac{\boxed{} - \boxed{}}{2} = \boxed{}$

$k =$ the y-coordinate of the focus $= \boxed{}$

Solve for h: The x-value of the focus is $h + p$, so

$h + p = \boxed{}$

$h + (-3) = \boxed{}$

$h = \boxed{}$

Write the equation: $(y + 1)^2 = \boxed{} \left(x - \boxed{}\right)$

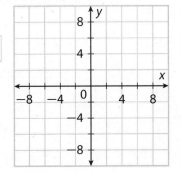

Find the equation of the parabola from the description of the focus and directrix. Then make a sketch showing the parabola, the focus, and the directrix.

5. Focus $(5, -1)$, directrix $x = -3$

6. Focus $(-2, 0)$, directrix $y = 4$

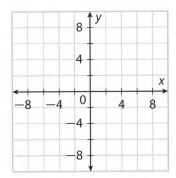

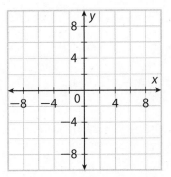

⚙ Explain 3 Rewriting the Equation of a Parabola to Graph the Parabola

A **second-degree equation in two variables** is an equation constructed by adding terms in two variables with powers no higher than 2. The general form looks like this:

$$ax^2 + by^2 + cx + dy + e = 0$$

Expanding the standard form of a parabola and grouping like terms results in a second-degree equation with either $a = 0$ or $b = 0$, depending on whether the parabola is vertical or horizontal. To graph an equation in this form requires the opposite conversion, accomplished by completing the square of the squared variable.

Example 3 Convert the equation to the standard form of a parabola and graph the parabola, the focus, and the directrix.

(A) $x^2 - 4x - 4y + 12 = 0$

Isolate the x terms and complete the square on x.

Isolate the x terms.	$x^2 - 4x = 4y - 12$
Add $\left(\dfrac{-4}{2}\right)^2$ to both sides.	$x^2 - 4x + 4 = 4y - 8$
Factor the perfect square trinomial on the left side.	$(x - 2)^2 = 4y - 8$
Factor out 4 from the right side.	$(x - 2)^2 = 4(y - 2)$

This is the standard form for a vertical parabola. Now find p, h, and k from the standard form $(x - h)^2 = 4p(y - k)$ in order to graph the parabola, focus, and directrix.

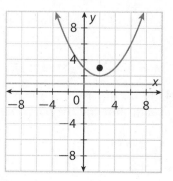

$4p = 4$, so $p = 1$.   Vertex $= (h, k) = (2, 2)$.

$h = 2$, $k = 2$.   Focus $= (h, k + p) = (2, 2 + 1) = (2, 3)$.

                             Directrix: $y = k - p = 2 - 1$, or $y = 1$.

(B) $y^2 + 2x + 8y + 18 = 0$

Isolate the ☐ terms.	$y^2 + 8y = -2x - 18$
Add $\left(\dfrac{\boxed{}}{2}\right)^2$ to both sides.	$y^2 + 8y + \boxed{} = -2x - \boxed{}$
Factor the perfect square trinomial.	$\left(y + \boxed{}\right)^2 = -2x - \boxed{}$
Factor out ☐ on the right.	$\left(y + \boxed{}\right)^2 = \boxed{}\left(x + \boxed{}\right)$

Identify the features of the graph using the standard form of a horizontal parabola, $(y - k)^2 = 4p(x - h)$:

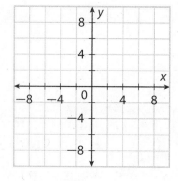

$4p = \boxed{}$, so $p = \boxed{}$.

$h = \boxed{}$, $k = \boxed{}$

Vertex $= (h, k) = \left(\boxed{}, \boxed{}\right)$

Focus $= (h + p, k) = \left(\boxed{}, \boxed{}\right)$

Directrix: $x = h - p$ or $x = \boxed{}$

Your Turn

Convert the equation to the standard form of a parabola and graph the parabola, the focus, and the directrix.

7. $y^2 - 12x - 4y + 64 = 0$

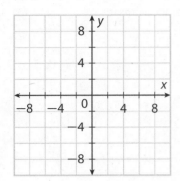

8. $x^2 + 8x - 16y - 48 = 0$

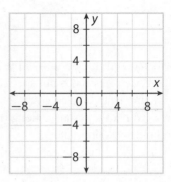

🔑 Explain 4 Solving a Real-World Problem

Parabolic shapes occur in a variety of applications in science and engineering that take advantage of the concentrating property of reflections from the parabolic surface at the focus.

(A) Parabolic microphones are so-named because they use a parabolic dish to bounce sound waves toward a microphone placed at the focus of the parabola in order to increase sensitivity. The dish shown has a cross section dictated by the equation $x = 32y^2$ where x and y are in inches. How far from the center of the dish should the microphone be placed?

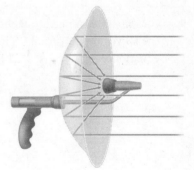

The cross section matches the standard form of a horizontal parabola with $h = 0, k = 0, p = 8$.

Therefore the vertex, which is the center of the dish, is at $(0, 0)$ and the focus is at $(8, 0)$, 8 inches away.

Ⓑ A reflective telescope uses a parabolic mirror to focus light rays before creating an image with the eyepiece. If the focal length (the distance from the bottom of the mirror's bowl to the focus) is 140 mm and the mirror has a 70 mm diameter (width), what is the depth of the bowl of the mirror?

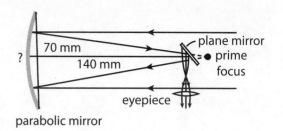

70 mm

140 mm

?

plane mirror

prime focus

eyepiece

parabolic mirror

The distance from the bottom of the mirror's bowl to the focus is p. The vertex location is not specified (or needed), so use $(0, 0)$ for simplicity. The equation for the mirror is a horizontal parabola (with x the distance along the telescope and y the position out from the center).

$$\left(y - \boxed{}\right)^2 = 4p\left(x - \boxed{}\right)$$

$$y^2 = \boxed{}\,x$$

Since the diameter of the bowl of the mirror is 70 mm, the points at the rim of the mirror have y-values of 35 mm and -35 mm. The x-value of either point will be the same as the x-value of the point directly above the bottom of the bowl, which equals the depth of the bowl. Since the points on the rim lie on the parabola, use the equation of the parabola to solve for the x-value of either edge of the mirror.

$$\boxed{}^2 = \boxed{}\,x$$

$$x \approx \boxed{} \text{ mm}$$

The bowl is approximately 2.19 mm deep.

Your Turn

9. A football team needs one more field goal to win the game. The goalpost that the ball must clear is 10 feet (~3.3 yd) off the ground. The path of the football after it is kicked for a 35-yard field goal is given by the equation $y - 11 = -0.0125\,(x - 20)^2$, in yards. Does the team win?

10. Examine the graphs in this lesson and determine a relationship between the separation of the focus and the vertex, and the shape of the parabola. Demonstrate this by finding the relationship between p for a vertical parabola with vertex of $(0, 0)$ and a, the coefficient of the quadratic parent function $y = ax^2$.

_____

_____

_____

_____

11. Essential Question Check-In How can you use the distance formula to derive an equation relating x and y from the definition of a parabola based on focus and directrix?

_____

_____

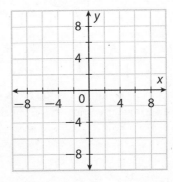

☆ Evaluate: Homework and Practice

- Online Homework
- Hints and Help
- Extra Practice

Find the equation of the parabola with vertex at $(0, 0)$ from the description of the focus and directrix and plot the parabola, the focus, and the directrix.

1. Focus at $(3, 0)$, directrix: $x = -3$

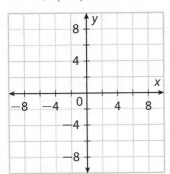

2. Focus at $(0, -5)$, directrix: $y = 5$

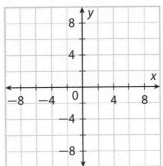

3. Focus at $(-1, 0)$, directrix: $x = 1$

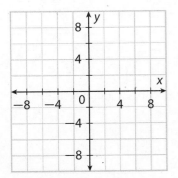

4. Focus at $(0, 2)$, directrix: $y = -2$

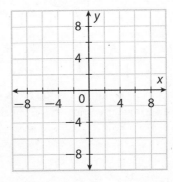

Find the equation of the parabola with the given information.

5. Vertex: $(-3, 6)$; Directrix: $x = -1.75$

6. Vertex: $(6, 20)$; Focus: $(6, 11)$

Find the equation of the parabola with vertex at (h, k) from the description of the focus and directrix and plot the parabola, the focus, and the directrix.

7. Focus at $(5, 3)$, directrix: $y = 7$

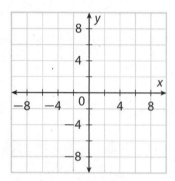

8. Focus at $(-3, 3)$, directrix: $x = 3$

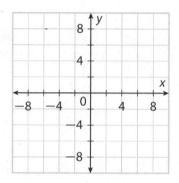

Convert the equation to the standard form of a parabola and graph the parabola, the focus, and the directrix.

9. $y^2 - 20x - 6y - 51 = 0$

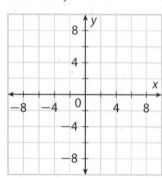

10. $x^2 - 14x - 12y + 73 = 0$

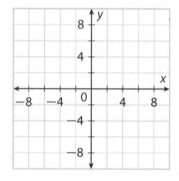

11. Communications The equation for the cross section of a parabolic satellite television dish is $y = \frac{1}{50}x^2$, measured in inches. How far is the focus from the vertex of the cross section?

12. Engineering The equation for the cross section of a spotlight is $y + 5 = \frac{1}{12}x^2$, measured in inches. The bulb is located at the focus. How far is the bulb from the vertex of the cross section?

13. When a ball is thrown into the air, the path that the ball travels is modeled by the parabola $y - 7 = -0.0175(x - 20)^2$, measured in feet. What is the maximum height the ball reaches? How far does the ball travel before it hits the ground?

14. A cable for a suspension bridge is modeled by $y - 55 = 0.0025x^2$, where x is the horizontal distance, in feet, from the support tower and y is the height, in feet, above the bridge. How far is the lowest point of the cable above the bridge?

15. Match each equation to its graph.

_____ $y + 1 = \frac{1}{16}(x - 2)^2$ _____ $y - 1 = \frac{1}{16}(x + 2)^2$ _____ $x + 1 = -\frac{1}{16}(y - 2)^2$

A.
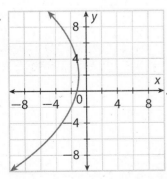

B.
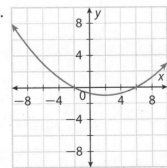

C.
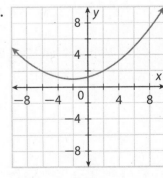

Shutterstock

Derive the equation of the parabolas with the given information.

16. An upward-opening parabola with a focus at $(0, p)$ and a directrix $y = -p$.

17. A leftward-opening parabola with a focus at $(-p, 0)$ and directrix $x = p$.

18. Multi-Step A tennis player hits a tennis ball just as it hits one end line of the court. The path of the ball is modeled by the equation $y - 4 = -\frac{4}{1521}(x - 39)^2$ where $x = 0$ is at the end line. The tennis net is 3 feet high, and the total length of the court is 78 feet.

   a. How far is the net located from the player?

   b. Explain why the ball will go over the net.

   c. Will the ball land "in," that is, inside the court or on the opposite endline?

19. Critical Thinking The latus rectum of a parabola is the line segment perpendicular to the axis of symmetry through the focus, with endpoints on the parabola. Find the length of the latus rectum of a parabola. Justify your answer. Hint: Set the coordinate system such that the vertex is at the origin and the parabola opens rightward with the focus at $(p, 0)$.

20. Explain the Error Lois is finding the focus and directrix of the parabola $y - 8 = -\frac{1}{2}(x + 2)^2$. Her work is shown. Explain what Lois did wrong, and then find the correct answer.

$h = -2, k = 8$

$4p = -\frac{1}{2}$, so $p = -\frac{1}{8}$, or $p = -0.125$

$\text{Focus} = (h, k + p) = (-2, 7.875)$

Directrix: $y = k - p$, or $y = 8.125$

Lesson Performance Task

Parabolic microphones are used for field audio during sports events. The microphones are manufactured such that the equation of their cross section is $x = \frac{1}{34}y^2$, in inches. The feedhorn part of the microphone is located at the focus.

a. How far is the feedhorn from the edge of the parabolic surface of the microphone?

b. What is the diameter of the microphone? Explain your reasoning.

c. If the diameter is increased by 5 inches, what is the new equation of the cross section of the microphone?

4.3 Solving Linear-Quadratic Systems

Essential Question: How can you solve a system composed of a linear equation in two variables and a quadratic equation in two variables?

Resource
Locker

⊘ Explore   Investigating Intersections of Lines and Graphs of Quadratic Equations

There are many real-world situations that can be modeled by linear or quadratic functions. What happens when the two situations overlap? Examine graphs of linear functions and quadratic functions and determine the ways they can intersect.

Ⓐ Examine the two graphs below to consider the ways a line could intersect the parabola.

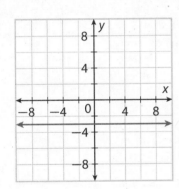   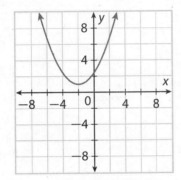

Ⓑ Sketch three graphs of a line and a parabola: one showing intersection in one point, one showing intersection in two points, and one not showing intersection.

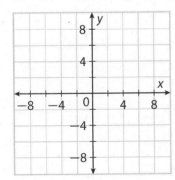   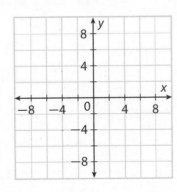   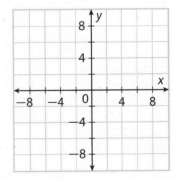

Ⓒ So a constant linear function and a quadratic function can intersect at _____ points.

1. If a line intersects a circle at one point, what is the relationship between the line and the radius of the circle at that point?

2. **Discussion** Does a line have to be horizontal to intersect a parabola at exactly one point?

✏ Explain 1 Solving Linear-Quadratic Systems Graphically

Graph each equation by hand and find the set of points where the two graphs intersect.

Example 1 Solve the given linear-quadratic system graphically.

(A) $\begin{cases} 2x - y = 3 \\ y + 6 = 2(x + 1)^2 \end{cases}$

Plot the line and the parabola.

Solve each equation for y.

$2x - y = 3$
$\quad y = 2x - 3$
$y + 6 = 2(x + 1)^2$
$\quad y = 2(x + 1)^2 - 6$

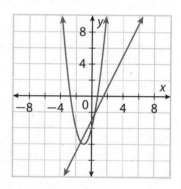

Find the approximate points of intersection: Estimating from the graph, the intersection points appear to be near $(-1.5, -5.5)$ and $(0.5, -2.5)$.

The exact solutions (which can be found algebraically) are $\left(\frac{-1 - \sqrt{3}}{2}, -\sqrt{3} - 4\right)$ and $\left(\frac{-1 + \sqrt{3}}{2}, \sqrt{3} - 4\right)$, or about $(-1.37, -5.73)$ and $(0.37, -2.27)$.

(B) $\begin{cases} 3x + y = 4.5 \\ y = \frac{1}{2}(x - 3)^2 \end{cases}$

Plot the line and the parabola on the axes provided.

Solve each equation for y.

$3x + y = 4.5$

$y = $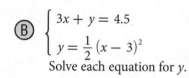

$y = $ [ ]

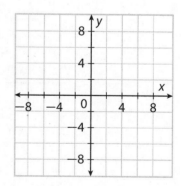

Find the approximate point(s) of intersection: _____ .

Note that checking these coordinates in the original system shows that this is an exact solution.

Solve the given linear-quadratic system graphically.

3. $\begin{cases} y + 3x = 0 \\ y - 6 = -3x^2 \end{cases}$

4. $\begin{cases} y + 1 = \frac{1}{2}(x - 3)^2 \\ x - y = 6 \end{cases}$

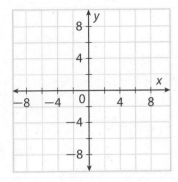

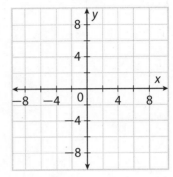

⚙ Explain 2 Solving Linear-Quadratic Systems Algebraically

Use algebra to find the solution. Use substitution or elimination.

Example 2 Solve the given linear-quadratic system algebraically.

Ⓐ $\begin{cases} 3x - y = 7 \\ y + 4 = 2(x + 5)^2 \end{cases}$

Solve this system using elimination.
First line up the terms.

$7 + y = 3x$
$4 + y = 2(x + 5)^2$

Subtract the second equation from
the first to eliminate the y variable.

$7 + y = 3x$
$\underline{-\left(4 + y = 2(x + 5^2)\right)}$
$3 = 3x - 2(x + 5)^2$

Solve the resulting equation for x
using the quadratic formula.

$3 = 3x - 2(x + 5)^2$

$3 = 3x - 2(x^2 + 10x + 25)$

$3 = 3x - 2x^2 - 20x - 50$

$0 = -2x^2 - 17x - 53$

$2x^2 + 17x + 53 = 0$

$x = \dfrac{-17 \pm \sqrt{17^2 - 4 \cdot 2 \cdot 53}}{2 \cdot 2}$

$= \dfrac{-17 \pm \sqrt{289 - 424}}{4}$

There is no real number equivalent to $\sqrt{-135}$, so the system
has no solution.

$= \dfrac{-17 \pm \sqrt{-135}}{4}$

$$\text{(B)} \quad \begin{cases} y = \dfrac{1}{4}(x-3)^2 \\ 3x - 2y = 13 \end{cases}$$

Solve the system by substitution. The first equation is already solved for y. Substitute the expression $\frac{1}{4}(x-3)^2$ for y in the second equation.

$$3x - 2\left(\frac{1}{4}(x-3)^2\right) = 13$$

Now, solve for x.

$$13 = 3x - 2\left(\frac{1}{4}(x-3)^2\right)$$

$$13 = 3x - \boxed{}\,(x-3)^2$$

$$13 = 3x - \frac{1}{2}\left(\boxed{}\right)$$

$$13 = 3x - \frac{1}{2}x^2 + 3x - \frac{9}{2}$$

$$13 = -\frac{1}{2}x^2 + \boxed{} - \frac{9}{2}$$

$$0 = -\frac{1}{2}x^2 + 6x - \frac{35}{2}$$

$$0 = x^2 \boxed{}$$

$$0 = \left(x\,\boxed{}\right)\left(x\,\boxed{}\right)$$

$$x = \left(\boxed{}\right) \text{ or } x = \left(\boxed{}\right)$$

So the line and the parabola intersect at two points. Use the x-coordinates of the intersections to find the points.

Solve $3x - 2y = 13$ for y.

$$3x - 2y = 13$$

$$-2y = 13 - 3x$$

$$y = \boxed{}$$

Find y when $x = 5$ and when $x = 7$.

$$y = -\frac{13 - 3 \cdot 5}{2} \qquad\qquad y = -\frac{13 - 3 \cdot 7}{2}$$

$$= -\frac{13 - 15}{2} \qquad\qquad\quad = -\frac{13 - 21}{2}$$

$$= -\frac{-2}{2} \qquad\qquad\qquad = -\frac{-8}{2}$$

$$= 1 \qquad\qquad\qquad\qquad = 4$$

So the solutions to the system are _____.

Reflect

5. How can you check algebraic solutions for reasonableness?

_____

_____

Solve the given linear-quadratic system algebraically.

6. $\begin{cases} x - 6 = -\frac{1}{6}y^2 \\ 2x + y = 6 \end{cases}$

7. $\begin{cases} x - y = 7 \\ x^2 - y = 7 \end{cases}$

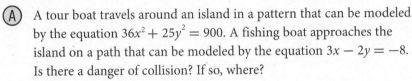 Solving Real-World Problems

You can use the techniques from the previous examples to solve real-world problems.

Example 3 Solve each problem.

(A) A tour boat travels around an island in a pattern that can be modeled by the equation $36x^2 + 25y^2 = 900$. A fishing boat approaches the island on a path that can be modeled by the equation $3x - 2y = -8$. Is there a danger of collision? If so, where?

Write the system of equations.

$\begin{cases} 36x^2 + 25y^2 = 900 \\ 3x - 2y = -8 \end{cases}$

Solve the second equation for x.

$$3x - 2y = -8$$
$$3x = 2y - 8$$
$$x = \frac{2y - 8}{3}$$

Substitute for x in the first equation.

$$36x^2 + 25y^2 = 900$$

$$36\left(\frac{2y - 8}{3}\right)^2 + 25y^2 = 900$$

$$36\left(\frac{4y^2 - 32y + 64}{9}\right) + 25y^2 = 900$$

$$4\left(4y^2 - 32y + 64\right) + 25y^2 = 900$$

$$16y^2 - 128y + 256 + 25y^2 = 900$$

$$41y^2 - 128y - 644 = 0$$

Solve using the quadratic equation.

$$y = \frac{128 \pm \sqrt{128^2 - 4(41)(-644)}}{2(41)}$$

$$= \frac{128 \pm \sqrt{122{,}000}}{82}$$

$$\approx -2.70 \text{ or } 5.82$$

Collisions can occur when $y \approx -2.70$ or $y \approx 5.82$.

To find the x-values, substitute the y-values into $x = \frac{2y - 8}{3}$.

$$x = \frac{2(-2.70) - 8}{3} \qquad\qquad x = \frac{2(5.82) - 8}{3}$$

$$= \frac{-5.40 - 8}{3} \qquad\qquad\quad = \frac{11.64 - 8}{3}$$

$$= \frac{-13.40}{3} \qquad\qquad\qquad = \frac{3.64}{3}$$

$$\approx -4.47 \qquad\qquad\qquad\quad \approx 1.21$$

So the boats could collide at approximately $(-4.47, -2.70)$ or $(1.21, 5.82)$.

(B) The range of the signal from a radio station is bounded by a circle described by the equation $x^2 + y^2 = 2025$. A stretch of highway near the station is modeled by the equation $y - 15 = \frac{1}{20}x$. At which points, if any, does a car on the highway enter and exit the broadcast range of the station?

Write the system of equations.

$$\begin{cases} x^2 + y^2 = 2025 \\ y - 15 = \frac{1}{20}x \end{cases}$$

Solve the second equation for y.

$$y - 15 = \frac{1}{20}x$$

$$y = \boxed{}$$

Substitute for x in the first equation.

$$x^2 + y^2 = 2025$$

$$x^2 + \left(\boxed{}\right)^2 = 2025$$

$$x^2 + \boxed{} = 2025$$

$$\boxed{}x^2 + \frac{3}{2}x + 225 = 2025$$

$$\frac{401}{400}x^2 + \frac{3}{2}x - \boxed{} = 0$$

$$401x^2 + 600x - 720000 = 0$$

Solve using the quadratic formula.

$$y = \frac{-600 \pm \sqrt{600^2 - 4(401)(-720000)}}{2(401)}$$

$$= \frac{600 \pm \sqrt{1,155,240,000}}{802}$$

$$\approx \boxed{} \text{ or } \boxed{} \text{ (rounded to the nearest hundredth)}$$

To find the y-values, substitute the x-values into $y = \frac{1}{20}x + 15$.

The car will be within the radio station's broadcast area between _____.

8. An asteroid is traveling toward Earth on a path that can be modeled by the equation $y = \frac{1}{28}x - 7$. It approaches a satellite in orbit on a path that can be modeled by the equation $\frac{x^2}{49} + \frac{y^2}{51} = 1$. What are the approximate coordinates of the points where the satellite and asteroid might collide?

9. The owners of a circus are planning a new act. They want to have a trapeze artist catch another acrobat in mid-air as the second performer comes into the main tent on a zip-line. If the path of the trapeze can be modeled by the parabola $y = \frac{1}{4}x^2 + 16$ and the path of the zip-line can be modeled by $y = 2x + 12$, at what point can the trapeze artist grab the second acrobat?

Elaborate

10. A parabola opens to the left. Identify an infinite set of parallel lines that will intersect the parabola only once.

_____

11. If a parabola can intersect a line from the set of lines $\left\{ x = a \middle| a \in R \right\}$ in 0, 1, or 2 points, what do you know about the parabola?

_____

12. **Essential Question Check-In** How can you solve a system composed of a linear equation in two variables and a quadratic equation in two variables?

_____

_____

1. How many points of intersection are on the graph?

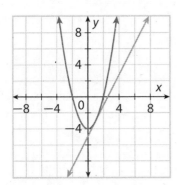

2. How many points of intersection are there on the graph

of $\begin{cases} y = x^2 + 3x - 2 \\ y - x = 4 \end{cases}$?

Solve each given linear-quadratic system graphically. If necessary, round to the nearest integer.

3. $\begin{cases} y = -(x-2)^2 + 4 \\ y = -5 \end{cases}$

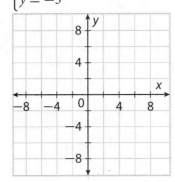

4. $\begin{cases} y - 3 = (x-1)^2 \\ 2x + y = 5 \end{cases}$

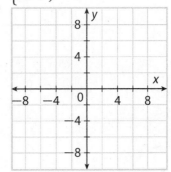

5. $\begin{cases} x = y^2 - 5 \\ -x + 2y = 12 \end{cases}$

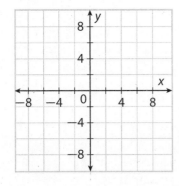

6. $\begin{cases} x - 4 = (y+1)^2 \\ 3x - y = 17 \end{cases}$

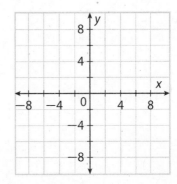

7. $\begin{cases} (y-4)^2 + x^2 = -12x - 20 \\ x = y \end{cases}$

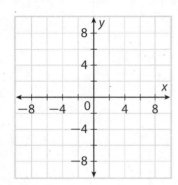

8. $\begin{cases} 5 - y = x^2 + x \\ y + 1 = \dfrac{3}{4}x \end{cases}$

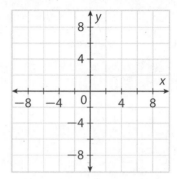

Solve each linear-quadratic system algebraically.

9. $\begin{cases} 6x + y = -16 \\ y + 7 = x^2 \end{cases}$

10. $\begin{cases} y - 5 = (x-2)^2 \\ x + 2y = 6 \end{cases}$

11. $\begin{cases} y^2 - 26 = -x^2 \\ x - y = 6 \end{cases}$

12. $\begin{cases} y - 3 = x^2 - 2x \\ 2x + y = 1 \end{cases}$

13. $\begin{cases} y = x^2 + 1 \\ y - 1 = x \end{cases}$

14. $\begin{cases} y = x^2 + 2x + 7 \\ y - 7 = x \end{cases}$

15. Jason is driving his car on a highway at a constant rate of 60 miles per hour when he passes his friend Alan whose car is parked on the side of the road. Alan has been waiting for Jason to pass so that he can follow him to a nearby campground. To catch up to Jason's passing car, Alan accelerates at a constant rate. The distance d, in miles, that Alan's car travels as a function of time t, in hours, since Jason's car has passed is given by $d = 3600t^2$. Find how long it takes Alan's car to catch up with Jason's car.

16. The flight of a cannonball toward a hill is described by the parabola $y = 2 + 0.12x - 0.002x^2$.

The hill slopes upward along a path given by $y = 0.15x$.

Where on the hill does the cannonball land?

17. Amy throws a quarter from the top of a building at the same time that a balloon is released from the ground. The equation describing the height y above ground of the quarter in feet is $y = 64 - 2x^2$, where x is the time in seconds. The equation describing the elevation of the balloon in feet is $y = 6x + 8$, where x is the time in seconds. After how many seconds will the balloon and quarter pass each other? Check your solution for reasonableness.

18. The range of an ambulance service is a circular region bounded by the equation $x^2 + y^2 = 400$. A straight road within the service area is represented by $y = 3x + 20$. Find the length of the road, in miles, that lies within the range of the ambulance service (round your answer to the nearest hundredth).

Recall that the distance formula is
$$d = \sqrt{(x_2 - x_1)^2 + (y_2 - y_1)^2}.$$

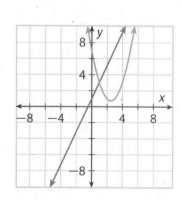

19. Match the equations with their solutions.

_____ $\begin{cases} y = x - 2 \\ -x^2 + y = 4x - 2 \end{cases}$ **A.** $(4, 3)\ (-4, -3)$

_____ $\begin{cases} y = (x - 2)^2 \\ y = -5x - 8 \end{cases}$ **B.** $(0, -2)\ (5, 3)$

_____ $\begin{cases} 4y = 3x \\ x^2 + y^2 = 25 \end{cases}$ **C.** $(2, 0)$

_____ $\begin{cases} y = (x - 2)^2 \\ y = 0 \end{cases}$ **D.** No solution

20. A student solved the system $\begin{cases} y - 7 = x^2 - 5x \\ y - 2x = 1 \end{cases}$ graphically and determined the only solution to be $(1, 3)$. Was this a reasonable answer? How do you know?

21. **Explain the Error** A student was asked to come up with a system of equations, one linear and one quadratic, that has two solutions. The student gave $\begin{cases} y^2 = -(x+1)^2 + 9 \\ y = x^2 - 4x + 3 \end{cases}$ as the answer. What did the student do wrong?

22. **Analyze Relationships** The graph shows a quadratic function and a linear function $y = d$. If the linear function were changed to $y = d + 3$, how many solutions would the new system have? If the linear function were changed to $y = d - 5$, how many solutions would the new system have? Give reasons for your answers.

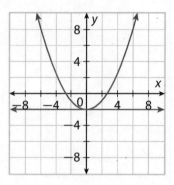

23. **Make a Conjecture** Given $y = 100x^2$ and $y = 0.0001x^2$, what can you say about any line that goes through the vertex of each but is not horizontal or vertical?

24. **Communicate Mathematical Ideas** Explain why a system of a linear equation and a quadratic equation cannot have an infinite number of solutions.

Lesson Performance Task

Suppose an aerial freestyle skier goes off a ramp with her path represented by the equation $y = -0.024(x - 25)^2 + 40$ where $x = 0$ represents the end of the ramp. If the surface of the mountain is represented by the linear equation $y = -0.5x + 25$, find the horizontal distance in feet the skier lands from the end of the ramp.

4.4 Solving Linear Systems in Three Variables

Essential Question: How can you find the solution(s) of a system of three linear equations in three variables?

Resource
Locker

 Explore **Recognizing Ways that Planes Can Intersect**

Recall that a linear equation in two variables defines a line. Consider a *linear equation in three variables*. An example is shown.

$$5 = 3x + 2y + 6z$$

A **linear equation in three variables** has three distinct variables, each of which is either first degree or has a coefficient of zero.

Just as the two numbers that satisfy a linear equation in two variables are called an ordered pair, the three numbers that satisfy a linear equation in three variables are called an **ordered triple** and are written (x, y, z).

The set of all ordered pairs satisfying a linear equation in two variables forms a line. Likewise the set of all ordered triples satisfying a linear equation in three variables forms a plane.

Three linear equations in three variables, considered together, form a system of three linear equations in three variables. The solutions of a system like this depend on the ways three planes can intersect.

(A) The diagrams show some ways three planes can intersect. How many points lie on all 3

planes? _____

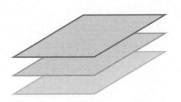 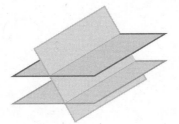 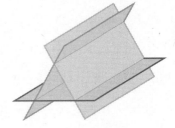

(B) The diagram shows three intersecting planes.

How many points lie on all 3 planes? _____

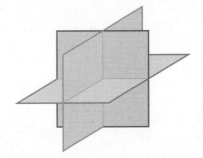

Ⓒ The diagram shows planes intersecting in a different way.

Describe the intersection. _____

How many points lie in all 3 planes? _____

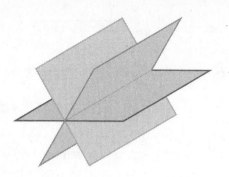

Reflect

1. Discussion Give an example of three planes that intersect at exactly one point.

_____

_____

⚙ **Explain 1** **Solving a System of Three Linear Equations Using Substitution**

A system of three linear equations is solved in the same manner as a system of two linear equations. It just has more steps.

Example 1 Solve the system using substitution.

Ⓐ $\begin{cases} -2x + y + 3z = 20 & \boxed{1} \\ -3x + 2y + z = 21 & \boxed{2} \\ 3x - 2y + 3z = -9 & \boxed{3} \end{cases}$

Choose an equation and variable to start with. The easiest equations to solve are those that have a variable with a coefficient of 1. Solve for y.

$$-2x + y + 3z = 20$$

$$y = 2x - 3z + 20$$

Now substitute for y in equations $\boxed{2}$ and $\boxed{3}$ and simplify.

$21 = -3x + 2(2x - 3z + 20) + z$	$-9 = 3x - 2(2x - 3z + 20) + 3z$
$21 = -3x + 4x - 6z + 40 + z$	$-9 = 3x - 4x + 6z - 40 + 3z$
$21 = x - 5z + 40$	$-9 = -x + 9z - 40$
$-19 = x - 5z \qquad \boxed{4}$	$31 = -x + 9z \qquad \boxed{5}$

This results in the following linear system in two variables:

$$\begin{cases} -19 = x - 5z & \boxed{4} \\ 31 = -x + 9z & \boxed{5} \end{cases}$$

Solve equation [4] for x.

$x = 5z - 19$

Substitute into equation [5] and solve for z. Then use the value for z to find the values of x.

$31 = -(5z - 19) + 9z$ $31 = -x + 9(3)$

$31 = 4z + 19$ $31 = -x + 27$

$3 = z$ $-4 = x$

Finally, solve the equation for y when $x = -4$ and $z = 3$.

$y = 2x - 3z + 20$

$y = 2(-4) - 3(3) + 20$

$y = 3$

Therefore, the solution to the system of three linear equations is the ordered triple $(-4, 3, 3)$.

(B) There is a unique vertical parabola passing through any three noncollinear points in the coordinate plane provided that no two of the points have the same x-coordinate. Find the vertical parabola that passes through the points $(2, 1)$, $(-1, 4)$, and $(-2, 3)$.

The general form of a vertical parabola is the quadratic equation $y = ax^2 + bx + c$. In order to find the equation of the parabola, we must identify the values of a, b, and c. Since each point lies on the parabola, substituting the coordinates of each point into the general equation produces a different equation.

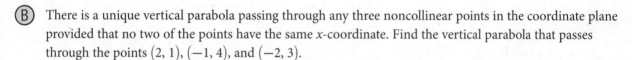

$$\begin{cases} 1 = a(2)^2 + b(2) + c \\ 4 = a(-1)^2 + b(-1) + c \\ \boxed{} = a\left(\boxed{}\right)^2 + b\left(\boxed{}\right) + c \end{cases} \Rightarrow \begin{cases} 1 = 4a + 2b + c & \boxed{1} \\ 4 = a - b + c & \boxed{2} \\ 3 = 4a - 2b + c & \boxed{3} \end{cases}$$

Choose an equation in which it is relatively easy to isolate a variable. Solve equation [2] for c.

$c = 4 - a + \boxed{}$ [2]

Now substitute for c in equations [1] and [3].

$1 = 4a + 2b + \left(\boxed{} \right)$ $3 = 4a - 2b + \left(\boxed{} \right)$

$1 = \boxed{} + 3b + 4$ $3 = 3a - \boxed{} + 4$

$\boxed{} = 3a + 3b$ [4] $\boxed{} = 3a - b$ [5]

This results in the following linear system in two variables:

$$\begin{cases} 3a + 3b = -3 & [4] \\ 3a - b = -1 & [5] \end{cases}$$

Solve equation [5] for b.

$b = 3a + \boxed{}$

Substitute into equation [4] and solve for a. Then use the value for a to find the values of b.

$$3a + 3\left(\boxed{}\right) = -3 \qquad\qquad 3\left(-\frac{1}{2}\right) + 3b = -3$$

$$3a + 9a + \boxed{} = -3 \qquad\qquad \boxed{} + 3b = -3$$

$$12a = \boxed{} \qquad\qquad\qquad 3b = \boxed{}$$

$$a = \boxed{} \qquad\qquad\qquad b = \boxed{}$$

Then use the values a and b to solve for c.

$$c = 4 - a + b = 4 - \left(-\frac{1}{2}\right) + \left(-\frac{1}{2}\right) = 4$$

So the equation of the parabola connecting $(2, 1)$, $(-1, 4)$, and $(-2, 3)$ is

$$y = \boxed{}x^2 - \boxed{}x + \boxed{}.$$

Your Turn

2. $$\begin{cases} x + 2y + z = 8 \\ 2x + y - z = 4 \\ x + y + 3z = 7 \end{cases}$$

3. $$\begin{cases} 2x - y - 3z = 1 \\ 4x + 3y + 2z = -4 \\ -3x + 2y + 5z = -3 \end{cases}$$

Explain 2   **Solving a System of Three Linear Equations Using Elimination**

You can also solve systems of three linear equations using elimination.

Example 2

 A.
$$\begin{cases} -2x + y + 3z = 20 & \boxed{1} \\ -3x + 2y + z = 21 & \boxed{2} \\ 3x - 2y + 3z = -9 & \boxed{3} \end{cases}$$

Begin by looking for variables with coefficients that are either the same or additive inverses of each other. When subtracted or added, these pairs will eliminate that variable. Subtract equation $\boxed{3}$ from equation $\boxed{1}$ to eliminate the z variable.

$$\boxed{1} \qquad -2x + y + 3z = 20$$
$$\boxed{3} \qquad \underline{3x - 2y + 3z = -9}$$
$$\qquad\qquad -5x + 3y + 0 = 29 \quad \boxed{4}$$

Next multiply $\boxed{2}$ by -3 and add it to $\boxed{1}$ to eliminate the same variable.

$$\boxed{1} \qquad -2x + y + 3z = 20 \qquad\qquad -2x + y + 3z = 20$$
$$\boxed{2} \quad \underline{-3(-3x + 2y + z = 21)} \quad \Rightarrow \quad \underline{9x - 6y - 3z = -63}$$
$$\qquad\qquad\qquad\qquad\qquad\qquad\qquad 7x - 5y + 0 = -43 \quad \boxed{5}$$

This results in the system of two linear equations below.

$$\begin{cases} -5x + 3y = 29 & \boxed{4} \\ 7x - 5y = -43 & \boxed{5} \end{cases}$$

To solve this system, multiply $\boxed{4}$ by 5 and add the result to the product of $\boxed{5}$ and 3.

$$\boxed{4} \qquad 5(-5x + 3y = 29) \qquad\qquad -25x + 15y = 145$$
$$\boxed{5} \qquad \underline{3(7x - 5y = -43)} \quad \Rightarrow \quad \underline{21x - 15y = -129}$$
$$\qquad\qquad\qquad\qquad\qquad\qquad\qquad -4x + 0 = 16$$
$$\qquad\qquad\qquad\qquad\qquad\qquad\qquad\qquad -4x = 16$$
$$\qquad\qquad\qquad\qquad\qquad\qquad\qquad\qquad\qquad x = -4$$

Substitute to solve for y and z.

$$-5x + 3y = 29 \quad [4] \qquad\qquad -3x + 2y + z = 21 \quad [2]$$
$$-5(-4) + 3y = 29 \qquad\qquad -3(-4) + 2(3) + z = 21$$
$$\qquad\qquad y = 3 \qquad\qquad\qquad\qquad\qquad z = 3$$

The solution to the system is the ordered triple $(-4, 3, 3)$.

Ⓑ $\begin{cases} x + 2y + 3z = 9 \quad \boxed{1} \\ x + 3y + 2z = 5 \quad \boxed{2} \\ x + 4y - z = -5 \quad \boxed{3} \end{cases}$

Begin by subtracting equation $\boxed{2}$ from equation $\boxed{1}$ to eliminate _____.

$\boxed{1} \qquad x + 2y + 3z = 9$

$\boxed{2} \qquad \underline{x + 3y + 2z = 5}$

$\qquad\qquad 0x - y + z = 4 \quad \boxed{4}$

Now subtract equation $\boxed{3}$ from equation $\boxed{1}$ to eliminate _____.

$\boxed{1} \qquad x + 2y + 3z = 9$

$\boxed{3} \qquad \underline{x + 4y - z = -5}$

$\qquad\qquad 0x - 2y + 4z = 14 \quad \boxed{5}$

This results in a system of two linear equations:

$\begin{cases} \rule{3cm}{0.4pt} \quad \boxed{4} \\ \rule{3cm}{0.4pt} \quad \boxed{5} \end{cases}$

To solve this system, multiply equation $\boxed{5}$ by _____ and add it to equation $\boxed{4}$.

$\boxed{4} \qquad\qquad -y + z = 4 \qquad\qquad\qquad -y + z = 4$

$\boxed{5} \qquad \underline{-\frac{1}{2}\left(-2y + 4z = 14\right)} \quad \Rightarrow \quad \underline{y - 2z = -7}$

$\qquad\qquad\qquad\qquad\qquad\qquad\qquad\qquad\quad 0y - z = -3$

$\qquad\qquad\qquad\qquad\qquad\qquad\qquad\qquad\qquad\quad z = 3$

Substitute to solve for y and x.

$-y + z = 4 \qquad [4] \qquad\qquad x + 2y + 3z = 9 \qquad [1]$

$-y + 3 = 4 \qquad\qquad\qquad\quad x + 2(-1) + 3(3) = 9$

$\qquad y = -1 \qquad\qquad\qquad\qquad\qquad x = 2$

The solution to the system is the ordered triple _____.

4.
$$\begin{cases} x + 2y + z = 8 \\ 2x + y - z = 4 \\ x + y + 3z = 7 \end{cases}$$

1
2
3

5.
$$\begin{cases} 2x - y - 3z = 1 \\ 4x + 3y + 2z = -4 \\ -3x + 2y + 5z = -3 \end{cases}$$

1
2
3

⚙ Explain 3 Solving a System of Three Linear Equations Using Matrices

You can represent systems of three linear equations in a *matrix*. A **matrix** is a rectangular array of numbers enclosed in brackets. Matrices are referred to by size: an *m*-by-*n* matrix has *m* rows and *n* columns.

A system of three linear equations can be written in a 3-by-4 matrix by first rearranging the equations so all of the variables are to the left of the equals sign and the constant term is to the right. Each row now corresponds to an equation. Enter the coefficients of the variables in the equation as the first three numbers in the row. Enter the constant that was on the right side of the equation as the fourth number.

The system $\begin{cases} 2x + y + 3z = 20 \\ 5x + 2y + z = 21 \\ 3x - 2y + 7z = 9 \end{cases}$ is expressed as $\begin{bmatrix} 2 & 1 & 3 & 20 \\ 5 & 2 & 1 & 21 \\ 3 & -2 & 7 & -9 \end{bmatrix}$ in matrix form.

Gaussian Elimination is a formalized process of using matrices to eliminate two of the variables in each equation in the system. This results in an easy way to find the solution set. The process involves using *elementary row operations* to generate equivalent matrices that lead to a solution.

The **elementary row operations** are

(1) Multiplying a row by a constant – When performing row multiplication, the product of the original value and the constant replaces each value in the row.

(2) Adding two rows – In row addition, each value in the second row mentioned in the addition is replaced by the sum of the values in the equivalent column of the two rows being added. These operations can also be performed together.

The elimination can be continued past this point to a matrix in which the solutions can be simply read directly out of the matrix. You can use a graphing calculator to perform these operations. The commands are shown in the table.

Command	Meaning	Syntax
*row(	replace each value in the row indicated with the product of the current value and the given number	*row(value,matrix,row)
row+(	replace rowB with the sum of rowA and the current rowB	row+(matrix,rowA,rowB)
*row+(	replace rowB with the product of the given value and rowA added to the current value of rowB	*row+(value,matrix,rowA,rowB)

Example 3 Solve the system of three linear equations using matrices.

$$\begin{cases} -2x + y + 3z = 20 \\ -3x + 2y + z = 21 \\ 3x - 2y + 3z = -9 \end{cases}$$

Input the system as a 3-by-4 matrix. Multiply the first row by –0.5. Enter the command into your calculator. Press enter to view the result.

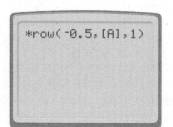

To reuse the resulting matrix, store it into Matrix B. Add 3 times row 1 to row 2. Press enter to view the result. Remember to store the result into a new matrix.

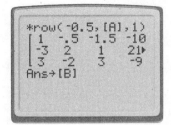

```
*row(-0.5,[A],1)
[1    -.5  -1.5  -10 ]
[-3    2    1     21▸]
[3    -2    3     -9 ]
Ans→[B]
```

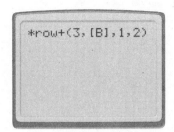

```
*row+(3,[B],1,2)
```

```
*row+(3,[B],1,2)
[1   -.5  -1.5  -10 ]
[0   .5   -3.5  -9 ▸]
[3   -2    3     -9 ]
```

Multiply row 2 by 2.

Add −3 times row 1 to row 3.

Add 0.5 times row 2 to row 3.

```
*row(2,[C],2)
[1   -.5  -1.5  -10 ]
[0    1    -7   -18▸]
[3   -2    3    -9  ]
```

```
*row+(-3,[D],1,▸
[1   -.5  -1.5  -10 ]
[0    1    -7   -18▸]
[0   -.5  7.5   21  ]
```

```
*row+(0.5,[E],2▸
[1   -.5  -1.5  -10 ]
[0    1    -7   -18▸]
[0    0    4     12 ]
```

Multiply row 3 by 0.25.

Add 7 times row 3 to row 2.

Add 1.5 times row 3 to row 1.

```
*row(0.25,[F],3)
[1   -.5  -1.5  -10 ]
[0    1    -7   -18▸]
[0    0    1     3  ]
```

```
*row+(7,[G],3,2)
[1   -.5  -1.5  -10 ]
[0    1    0     3 ▸]
[0    0    1     3  ]
```

```
*row+(1.5,[H],3▸
[1   -.5  0   -5.5 ]
[0    1   0    3   ]
[0    0   1    3   ]
```

Add 0.5 times row 2 to row 1.

```
*row+(0.5,[I],2▸
[1   0   0   -4 ]
[0   1   0    3 ]
[0   0   1    3 ]
```

The first row tells us that $x = -4$, the second row tells us that $y = 3$, and the third row tells us that $z = 3$. So the solution is the ordered triple $(-4, 3, 3)$.

Ⓑ $\begin{cases} x + 2y + 3z = 9 \\ x + 3y + 2z = 5 \\ x + 4y - z = -5 \end{cases}$

Write as a matrix.

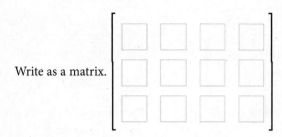

Perform row operations.

$-r1 + r2$

$$\begin{bmatrix} 1 & 2 & 3 & 9 \\ 0 & 1 & -1 & -4 \\ 1 & 4 & -1 & -5 \end{bmatrix}$$

$-r1 + r3$

$$\begin{bmatrix} 1 & 2 & 3 & 9 \\ 0 & 1 & -1 & -4 \\ 0 & 2 & -4 & -14 \end{bmatrix}$$

$-2r2 + r3$

$$\begin{bmatrix} 1 & 2 & 3 & 9 \\ 0 & 1 & -1 & -4 \\ 0 & 0 & -2 & -6 \end{bmatrix}$$

$-0.5r3$

$$\begin{bmatrix} 1 & 2 & 3 & 9 \\ 0 & 1 & -1 & -4 \\ \square & \square & \square & \square \end{bmatrix}$$

$r3 + r2$

$$\begin{bmatrix} 1 & 2 & 3 & 9 \\ 0 & 1 & 0 & -1 \\ 0 & 0 & 1 & 3 \end{bmatrix}$$

$-3r3 + r1$

$$\begin{bmatrix} \square & \square & \square & \square \\ 0 & 1 & 0 & -1 \\ 0 & 0 & 1 & 3 \end{bmatrix}$$

$-2r2 + r1$

$$\begin{bmatrix} 1 & 0 & 0 & 2 \\ 0 & 1 & 0 & -1 \\ 0 & 0 & 1 & 3 \end{bmatrix}$$

The solution is the ordered triple _____.

Your Turn

6. $\begin{cases} x + 2y + z = 8 \\ 2x + y - z = 4 \\ x + y + 3z = 7 \end{cases}$

Example 4

Ⓐ A child has $6.17 in change in her piggy bank. The change consists of 113 coins in a mix of pennies, nickels, and quarters. If there are 8 times as many nickels as pennies, how many of each coin does the child have? Solve using substitution.

Begin by setting up a system of equations, and use p for the number of pennies, n for the number of nickels, and q for the number of quarters. Use the relationships in the problem statement to write the equations.

The total number of coins is the sum of the number of each coin. So, the first equation is $p + n + q = 113$.

The total value of the coins is $6.17 or 617 cents (converting the value to cents will allow all coefficients to be integers). The second equation will be $p + 5n + 25q = 617$.

The third relationship given is that there are eight times as many nickels as pennies or, $n = 8p$. This gives the following system of equations:

$$\begin{cases} p + n + q = 113 & \boxed{1} \\ p + 5n + 25q = 617 & \boxed{2} \\ n = 8p & \boxed{3} \end{cases}$$

Equation $\boxed{3}$ is already solved for n. Substitute for n in equations $\boxed{1}$ and $\boxed{2}$ and simplify.

$p + (8p) + q = 113$ $\qquad\qquad\qquad$ $p + 5(8p) + 25q = 617$

$\qquad 9p + q = 113 \quad \boxed{4}$ $\qquad\qquad\qquad$ $p + 40p + 25q = 617$

$\qquad\qquad\qquad\qquad\qquad\qquad\qquad\qquad$ $41p + 25q = 617 \quad \boxed{5}$

This results in the following linear system in two variables:

Solve equation $\boxed{4}$ for q.

$$\begin{cases} 9p + q = 113 & \boxed{4} \\ 41p + 25q = 617 & \boxed{5} \end{cases}$$

$9p + q = 113$

$q = 113 - 9p$

Substitute for q in equation $\boxed{5}$ and solve for p. $\qquad$ Use $p = 12$ to find q and n.

$41p + 25(113 - 9p) = 617$ $\qquad\qquad$ $q = 113 - 9p$ $\qquad\qquad$ $n = 8p$

$41p + 2825 - 225p = 617$ $\qquad\qquad$ $q = 113 - 9(12)$ $\qquad\qquad$ $n = 8(12)$

$\qquad\qquad 12 = p$ $\qquad\qquad\qquad\qquad\qquad$ $q = 5$ $\qquad\qquad\qquad\qquad$ $n = 96$

The child's piggy bank contains 12 pennies, 96 nickels, and 5 quarters.

A student is shopping for clothes. The student needs to buy an equal number of shirts and ties. He also needs to buy four times as many shirts as pants. Shirts cost $35, ties cost $25, and pants cost $40. If the student spends $560, how many shirts, pants, and ties did he get?

Begin by setting up a system of equations, using s for the number of shirts, t for the number of ties, and p for the number pairs of pants. Use the relationships in the problem statement to write the equations.

The number of shirts is equal to the number of ties. So, the first equation is $s = t$.

The number of shirts is equal to 4 times the number of pairs of pants, so a second equation is $s =$ ☐ .

The total the student spent is the sum of the cost of the shirts, the ties, and the pairs of pants.

$35s + 25t + 40p =$ ☐

The system of equations is below.

$$\begin{cases} s = t \\ s = 4p \\ 35s + 25t + 40p = 560 \end{cases}$$

1
2
3

Equation [1] is already solved for t. Solve equation [2] for p.

$4p = s$

$p =$ ☐

Substitute for p and t in equation [3] and solve for s.

$35s + 25(s) + 40\left(\dfrac{1}{4}s\right) = 560$

$35s + 25s + 10s = 560$

☐$s = 560$

$s =$ ☐

Evaluate the equation solved for p above at $s = 8$ to find p.

$p = \dfrac{1}{4}s$

$p = \dfrac{1}{4}(8) = 2$

Recall that $s = t$, so $t = 8$.

The student bought ☐ shirts, ☐ ties, and ☐ pairs of pants.

7. Louie Dampier is the leading scorer in the history of the American Basketball Association (ABA). His 13,726 points were scored on two-point baskets, three-point baskets, and one-point free throws. In his ABA career, Dampier made 2144 more two-point baskets than free throws and 1558 more free throws than three-point baskets. How many three-point baskets, two-point baskets, and free throws did Dampier make?

Elaborate

8. If you are given a system of linear equations in three variables, but the system only has two equations, what happens when you try to solve it?

_____

_____

_____

9. Discussion Why does a system need to have at least as many equations as unknowns to have a unique solution?

_____

_____

_____

10. Essential Question Check-In How can you find the solution to a system of three linear equations in three variables?

_____

_____

_____

_____

Solve the system using substitution.

1. $\begin{cases} 4x + y - 2z = -6 \quad \boxed{1} \\[2mm] 2x - 3y + 3z = 9 \quad \boxed{2} \\[2mm] x - 2y = 0 \quad \boxed{3} \end{cases}$

2. $\begin{cases} x + 5y + 3z = 4 \quad \boxed{1} \\[2mm] 4y - z = 3 \quad \boxed{2} \\[2mm] 6x - 2y + 4z = 0 \quad \boxed{3} \end{cases}$

Solve the system using elimination.

3. $\begin{cases} 4x + y - 2z = -6 \quad \boxed{1} \\[2mm] 2x - 3y + 3z = 9 \quad \boxed{2} \\[2mm] x - 2y = 0 \quad \boxed{3} \end{cases}$

4. $\begin{cases} x + 5y + 3z = 4 & \boxed{1} \\ 4y - z = 3 & \boxed{2} \\ 6x - 2y + 4z = 0 & \boxed{3} \end{cases}$

5. $\begin{cases} 2x - y + 3z = -12 & \boxed{1} \\ -x + 2y - 3z = 15 & \boxed{2} \\ y + 5z = -6 & \boxed{3} \end{cases}$

Solve the system of three linear equations using matrices.

6.
$$\begin{cases} 4x + y - 2z = -6 \quad \boxed{1} \\ 2x - 3y + 3z = 9 \quad \boxed{2} \\ x - 2y = 0 \quad \boxed{3} \end{cases}$$

7.
$$\begin{cases} x + 5y + 3z = 4 \quad \boxed{1} \\ 4y - z = 3 \quad \boxed{2} \\ 6x - 2y + 4z = 0 \quad \boxed{3} \end{cases}$$

Solve the system of linear equations using your method of choice.

8.
$$\begin{cases} 2x - y + 3z = 5 & \boxed{1} \\ -6x + 3y - 9z = -15 & \boxed{2} \\ 4x - 2y + 6z = 10 & \boxed{3} \end{cases}$$

9.
$$\begin{cases} 3x + 4y - z = -7 & \boxed{1} \\ x - 5y + 2z = 19 & \boxed{2} \\ 5x + y - 2z = 5 & \boxed{3} \end{cases}$$

10. Find the equation of the vertical parabola passing through the points $(3, 7)$, $(30, -11)$, and $(0, -1)$.

11. Geometry In triangle XYZ, the measure of angle X is eight times the sum of the measures of angles Y and Z. The measure of angle Y is three times the measure of angle Z. What are the measures of the angles?

12. The combined age of three relatives is 120 years. James is three times the age of Dan, and Paul is two times the sum of the ages of James and Dan. How old is each person?

13. Economics At a stock exchange there were a total of 10,000 shares sold in one day. Stock A had four times as many shares sold as Stock B. The number of shares sold for Stock C was equal to the sum of the numbers of shares sold for Stock A and Stock B. How many shares of each stock were sold?

14. Communicate Mathematical Ideas Explain how you know when a system has infinitely many solutions or when it has no solutions.

15. Explain the Error When given this system of equations, a student was asked to solve using matrices. Find and correct the student's error.

$$\begin{cases} 5x + 7y + 9x = 0 \\ x - y + z = -3 \\ 8x + y = 12 \end{cases}$$

$$\begin{bmatrix} 5 & 7 & 9 \\ 1 & -1 & 1 \\ 8 & 1 & 0 \end{bmatrix}$$

16. Critical Thinking Explain why the following system of equations cannot be solved.

$$\begin{cases} 7x + y + 6z = 1 \\ -x - 4y + 8z = 9 \end{cases}$$

Lesson Performance Task

A company that manufactures inline skates needs to order three parts—part A, part B, and part C. For one shipping order the company needs to buy a total of 6000 parts. There are four times as many B parts as C parts. The total number of A parts is one-fifth the sum of the B and C parts. On previous orders, the costs had been \$0.25 for part A, \$0.50 for part B, and \$0.75 for part C, resulting in a cost of \$3000 for all the parts in one order. When filling out an order for new parts, the company sees that it now costs \$0.60 for part A, \$0.40 for part B, and \$0.60 for part C. Will the company be able to buy the same quantity of parts at the same price as before with the new prices?

Key Vocabulary

directrix *(directriz)*

focus of a parabola *(foco de una parábola)*

linear equation in three variables *(ecuación lineal en tres variables)*

matrix *(matriz)*

ordered triple *(tripleta ordenada)*

KEY EXAMPLE (Lesson 4.1)

Write the equation of a circle that has a center at (−3, 5) and a radius of 9.

$(x - h)^2 + (y - k)^2 = r^2$	The standard form of the equation of a circle
$h = -3$	x-coordinate of center
$k = 5$	y-coordinate of center
$r = 9$	radius
$(x - (-3))^2 + (y - 5)^2 = 9^2$	Substitute.
$(x + 3)^2 + (y - 5)^2 = 81$	Simplify.

KEY EXAMPLE (Lesson 4.3)

Solve the system using elimination.

$$\begin{cases} 5x + y = 10 \\ y + 2 = 3(x + 4)^2 \end{cases}$$

$y - 10 = -5x$ First, line up the terms.

$y + 2 = 3(x + 4)^2$

$\cancel{y} - 10 = -5x$ Subtract the second equation from the first.

$\underline{\cancel{-y} + (-2) = -3(x + 4)^2}$

$-12 = 5x - 3(x + 4)^2$

$-12 = 5x - 3(x + 4)^2$

$-12 = 5x - 3x^2 - 24x - 48$

$0 = -3x^2 - 19x - 36$ Solve the resulting equation for x.

$x = \dfrac{19 \pm \sqrt{(-19)^2 - 4(-3)(-36)}}{2(-3)}$

$x = \dfrac{19 \pm i\sqrt{71}}{-6}$

There is no real number equivalent, so the system has no solution.

Radius: 6   Radius: 1.5

Find the center and radius of the given circle. *(Lessons 4.1)*

3. $(x - 5)^2 + (y - 8)^2 = 144$ **4.** $x^2 + (y + 6)^2 = 50$

Find the solution to the system of equations using graphing or elimination. *(Lessons 4.2, 4.3, 4.4)*

5. $\begin{cases} 4x + 3y = 1 \\ y = x^2 - x - 1 \end{cases}$ **6.** $\begin{cases} x - 3y = 2 \\ y = x^2 + 2x - 34 \end{cases}$

7. $\begin{cases} 3x + 5y - 2z = -7 \\ -2x + 7y + 6z = -3 \\ 8x + 3y - 10z = -11 \end{cases}$ **8.** $\begin{cases} 3x + 24y + 9z = 9 \\ x - 8y - 3z = 37 \\ 2x - 16y - 6z = 75 \end{cases}$

MODULE PERFORMANCE TASK

How Can You Hit a Moving Target with a Laser Beam?

A video game designer is creating a game similar to skeet shooting, where a player will use a laser beam to hit a virtual clay disk launched into the air. The disk is launched from the ground and, if nothing blows it up, it reaches a maximum height of 30 meters and returns to the ground 60 meters away. The laser is fired from a height of 5 meters above the ground. Where should the designer point the laser to hit the disk at its maximum height?

Use your own paper to complete the task. Be sure to write down all your data and assumptions. Then use graphs, numbers, words, or algebra to explain how you reached your conclusion.

Find the equation of the circle with the given characteristics. *(Lessons 4.1)*

1. Center: $(0, -2)$

Radius: 1

2. Center: $(-4, 4.5)$

Radius: 16

Find the center and radius of the given circle. *(Lesson 4.1)*

3. $x^2 + y^2 = 25$

4. $(x - 18)^2 + (y + 18)^2 = 70$

Solve the system of equations using any method. *(Lessons 4.3, 4.4)*

5. $\begin{cases} y + 12 = 4x \\ y - 20 = x^2 - 8x \end{cases}$

6. $\begin{cases} y = x + 2 \\ 2y - 12 = 2x^2 - 8x \end{cases}$

7. $\begin{cases} x + y + z = 9 \\ x - 8y - z = -27 \\ 2x - y + z = 6 \end{cases}$

8. $\begin{cases} -3x - 12y - 3z = 0 \\ x + 4y + z = 10 \\ -2x - 8y - 2z = -34 \end{cases}$

ESSENTIAL QUESTION

9. Describe a real world situation that might involve three linear equations in three variables. *(Lesson 4.4)*

1. Look at each focus and directrix. Is the resulting parabola horizontal? Select Yes or No for A–C.

   A. Focus $(-5, 0)$, Directrix $x = 5$ ○ Yes   ○ No

   B. Focus $(4, 0)$, Directrix $x = -4$ ○ Yes   ○ No

   C. Focus $(0, -3)$, Directrix $y = 3$ ○ Yes   ○ No

2. Consider the system of equations $\begin{cases} y = x^2 + 6x + 10 \\ y + 6 = 2x \end{cases}$. Choose Yes or No for each statement.

   A. Another way to write this system is   ○ Yes   ○ No

   $$\begin{cases} y = x^2 + 6x + 10 \\ y = 2x - 6 \end{cases}$$

   B. The only way to solve this system is by graphing.   ○ Yes   ○ No

   C. There is only one solution to the system, $(-4, 2)$.   ○ Yes   ○ No

3. Explain how a system of three equations in three variables can have infinitely many solutions.

4. Robin solved a quadratic equation using the process shown. Describe and correct her mistake.

   $$0 = \frac{x^2}{4} - 2x + 7$$

   $$x = \frac{-(-2) \pm \sqrt{(-2)^2 - 4\left(\frac{1}{4}\right)(7)}}{2(1/4)}$$

   $$= \frac{2 \pm \sqrt{-4 - 7}}{\frac{1}{2}}$$

   $$= 4 \pm 2\sqrt{-11}$$

   $$= 4 \pm 2i\sqrt{11}$$

- Online Homework
- Hints and Help
- Extra Practice

1. Consider the function $f(x) = 3(x - 7)^2 + 2$. Choose True or False for each statement.

   A. The axis of symmetry for $f(x)$ is $x = 7$.   ○ True   ○ False

   B. The range is $\{ y \mid y \in \Re \}$.   ○ True   ○ False

   C. The vertex of $f(x)$ is $(7, -2)$.   ○ True   ○ False

2. Look at each quadratic equation. Does the equation have real roots? Select Yes or No for A–C.

   A. $x^2 - 25 = 0$ ○ Yes   ○ No

   B. $-\frac{1}{2}x^2 - 3 = 0$ ○ Yes   ○ No

   C. $3x^2 - 4 = 2$ ○ Yes   ○ No

3. Consider the equation $3x^2 - 12x + 15 = 0$. Choose True or False for each statement.

   A. If solving this equation using factoring, then $(x - 5)(x + 1) = 0$.   ○ True   ○ False

   B. After completing the square, $x = -2 \pm \sqrt{11}$.   ○ True   ○ False

   C. To solve this equation using complete the square, $\left(\frac{b}{2}\right)^2 = \left(\frac{-4}{2}\right)^2 = 4$.   ○ True   ○ False

4. Consider the system of equations $\begin{cases} y = 2x^2 - 3x + 5 \\ y - 3 = x \end{cases}$. Choose True or False for each statement.

   A. The only way to solve this equation is by elimination.   ○ True   ○ False

   B. Another way to write this system is $\begin{cases} y = 2x^2 - 3x + 5 \\ y = x + 3 \end{cases}$ ○ True   ○ False

   C. There are three possible solutions to the system.   ○ True   ○ False

5. Look at each focus and directrix. Is the resulting parabola vertical? Select Yes or No for A–C.

   A. Focus $(6, -3)$, Directrix $x = 2$ ○ Yes   ○ No

   B. Focus $(-4, -2)$, Directrix $y = -3$ ○ Yes   ○ No

   C. Focus $(0, 1)$, Directrix $y = 2$ ○ Yes   ○ No

6. Marcia shoots an arrow that hits a bull's-eye 80 feet away. The release point and bull's-eye are at the same height. Before hitting the bull's-eye, the arrow reaches a maximum height of 4 feet above its release point. If the bull's-eye is considered to be at (80, 0), what function (in standard form) could represent the path of the arrow if x is the horizontal distance from Marcia and y represents the height of the arrow in relation to its release point? How high is the arrow above its release point after traveling 20 feet horizontally? Explain.

7. Consider the equation $-4x^2 + x = 3$. What method should be used to most easily solve the equation if you have a choice between taking the square root, completing the square, using the quadratic formula, or factoring? Explain your reasoning, and then solve the equation.

8. Ronald says $f(x) = 0.5x + 1.5$ is the inverse of $g(x) = -1.5x + 4$. Is Ronald's answer correct? Explain why or why not.

Performance Tasks

★ **9.** Keille is building a rectangular pen for a pet rabbit. She can buy wire fencing in a roll of 40 ft or a roll of 80 ft. The graph shows the area of pens she can build with each type of roll.

   A. Describe the function for an 80 ft roll of fencing as a transformation of the function for a 40 ft roll of fencing.

   B. Is the largest pen Keille can build with an 80 ft roll of fencing twice as large as the largest pen she can build with a 40 ft roll of fencing? Explain.

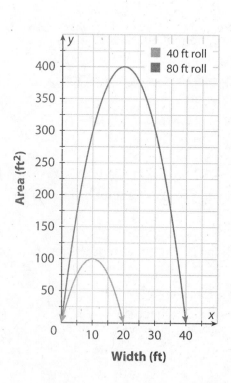

★10. The spittlebug is the world's highest-jumping animal relative to its body length of about 6 millimeters. The height h of a spittlebug's jump in millimeters can be modeled by the function $h(t) = -4000t^2 + 3000t$, where t is the time in seconds.

   A. What is the maximum height that the spittlebug will reach?

   B. What is the ratio of a spittlebug's maximum jumping height to its body length? In the best human jumpers, this ratio is about 1.38 to 1. Compare the ratio for spittlebugs with the ratio for the best human jumpers.

★★11. The light produced by high-pressure sodium vapor streetlamps for different energy usages is shown in the table.

High-Pressure Sodium Vapor Streetlamps					
Energy Use (watts)	35	50	70	100	150
Light Output (lumens)	2250	4000	5800	9500	16,000

   A. Find a quadratic model for the light output with respect to energy use.

   B. Find a linear model for the light output with respect to energy use.

   C. Apply each model to estimate the light output in lumens of a 200-watt bulb.

   D. Which model gives the better estimate? Explain.

Toy Manufacturer A company is marketing a new toy. The function $s(p) = -50p^2 + 3000p$ models how the total sales s of the toy, in dollars, depends on the price p of the toy, in dollars.

a. Complete the square to write the function in vertex form.

b. Graph the function. Be sure to label the axes with the quantities they represent and indicate the axis scales by showing numbers for some grid lines.

c. What is the vertex of the graph? What does the vertex represent in this situation?

d. The model predicts that total sales will be $40,000 when the toy price is $20. At what other price does the model predict that the total sales will be $40,000? Use the symmetry of the graph to support your answer.

e. According to the model, at what nonzero price should the manufacturer expect to sell no toys? How can you determine this price using the graph?

Polynomial Functions, Expressions, and Equations

MATH IN CAREERS

Statistician Statisticians use math to describe patterns and relationships. Statisticians design surveys and collect data, and rely on mathematical modeling and computational methods to analyze their findings. They use these findings and analyses to help solve problems in various fields, such as business, engineering, the sciences, and government.

If you are interested in a career as a statistician, you should study these mathematical subjects:

- Algebra
- Geometry
- Calculus
- Differential Equations
- Probability
- Statistics

Research other careers that require understanding and analyzing data. Check out the career activity at the end of the unit to find out how Statisticians use math.

Reading Start-Up

Vocabulary

Review Words
- ✔ coefficient *(coeficiente)*
- ✔ factor *(factor)*
- ✔ parameter *(parámetro)*
- ✔ real number *(número real)*
- ✔ term *(término)*
- ✔ transformation *(transformación)*

Preview Words
binomial *(binomio)*
cubic function *(función cúbica)*
monomial *(monomio)*
polynomial *(polinomio)*
root *(raíz)*
trinomial *(trinomio)*

Visualize Vocabulary

Use the review words to complete the chart.

	a number or expression that divides a product exactly.
	a rational or irrational number
	a number, variable, product, or quotient in an expression
	one of the constants in a function or equation that may be changed
	a change in the size, position, or shape of a figure or graph
	a numerical factor in a term of an algebraic expression

Understand Vocabulary

To become familiar with some of the vocabulary terms in the module, consider the following. You may refer to the module, the glossary, or a dictionary.

1. A polynomial with two terms is a _____.

2. A polynomial function of degree 3 is a _____.

3. A _____ of a polynomial is a zero of the function associated with that polynomial.

Active Reading

Key-Term Fold Before beginning the unit, create a key-term fold to help you organize what you learn. Write a vocabulary term on each tab of the key-term fold. Under each tab, write the definition of the term and an example.

Polynomial Functions

Essential Question: How can polynomial functions help to solve real-world problems?

REAL WORLD VIDEO
Engineers who design roller coasters use mathematics, including polynomial functions, to model the shape of the track.

MODULE PERFORMANCE TASK PREVIEW

What's the Function of a Roller Coaster?

Nothing compares with riding a roller coaster. The thrill of a steep drop, the breathtaking speed, and the wind in your face make the ride unforgettable. How can a polynomial function model the path of a roller coaster? Hang on to your seat and let's find out!

Are (YOU) Ready?

Complete these exercises to review skills you will need for this module.

Classifying Polynomials

Example 1 Classify the polynomial $2x^4 + x^3 - 1$ by its degree and number of terms.

Because the greatest exponent is 4, this is a quartic polynomial.

Because the polynomial has three terms, it is a trinomial.

The polynomial $2x^4 + x^3 - 1$ is a quartic trinomial.

- Online Homework
- Hints and Help
- Extra Practice

Classify the polynomial by its degree and number of terms.

1. $3x^3$

2. $9x - 3y + 7$

3. $x^2 - 4$

4. $x^5 + x^4$

5. $5x^3 - 7y^2 + 2$

6. x

Transforming Cubic Functions

Example 2 The graph of $f(x) = 0.5(x - 3)^3 + 2$ is transformed 4 units right and 5 units down. Write the new function.

The inflection point is $(3, 2)$. Its location after the transformation is $(3 + 4, 2 - 5)$, or $(7, -3)$.

After the transformation, the function is $f'(x) = 0.5(x - 7)^3 - 3$.

Write the new function after the given transformation.

7. $g(x) = 0.25(x - 6)^3 - 1$
10 units left, 7 units down

8. $h(x) = (x + 9)^3 - 5$
6 units right, 4 units up

9. $f(x) = -0.5(x + 8)^3 + 12$
1 unit left, 3 units up

10. $f(x) = x^3$
3 units right, 2 units up

11. $g(x) = 5(x + 1)^3 - 4$
1 unit right, 4 units up

12. $h(x) = (x - 5)^3 + 5$
0.5 unit right, 1.5 units down

Name _____ Class _____ Date _____

5.1 Graphing Cubic Functions

Essential Question: How are the graphs of $f(x) = a(x - h)^3 + k$ and $f(x) = \left(\frac{1}{b}(x - h)\right)^3 + k$ related to the graph of $f(x) = x^3$?

Resource Locker

⊘ Explore 1 Graphing and Analyzing $f(x) = x^3$

You know that a quadratic function has the standard form $f(x) = ax^2 + bx + c$ where a, b, and c are real numbers and $a \neq 0$. Similarly, *a* **cubic function** has the standard form $f(x) = ax^3 + bx^2 + cx + d$ where a, b, c and d are all real numbers and a $\neq$ 0. You can use the basic cubic function, $f(x) = x^3$, as the parent function for a family of cubic functions related through transformations of the graph of $f(x) = x^3$.

(A) Complete the table, graph the ordered pairs, and then draw a smooth curve through the plotted points to obtain the graph of $f(x) = x^3$.

x	$y = x^3$
-2	
-1	
0	
1	
2	

(B) Use the graph to analyze the function and complete the table.

Attributes of $f(x) = x^3$	
Domain	$\mathbb{R}$
Range	
End behavior	As $x \to +\infty$, $f(x) \to$ ⬚ .
	As $x \to -\infty$, $f(x) \to$ ⬚ .
Zeros of the function	$x = 0$
Where the function has positive values	$x > 0$
Where the function has negative values	
Where the function is increasing	
Where the function is decreasing	The function never decreases.
Is the function even $\left(f(-x) = f(x)\right)$ odd	

1. How would you characterize the rate of change of the function on the intervals $[-1, 0]$ and $[0, 1]$ compared with the rate of change on the intervals $[-2, -1]$ and $[1, 2]$? Explain.

_____

_____

_____

_____

2. A graph is said to be *symmetric about the origin* (and the origin is called the graph's *point of symmetry*) if for every point (x, y) on the graph, the point $(-x, -y)$ is also on the graph. Is the graph of $f(x) = x^3$ symmetric about the origin? Explain.

_____

_____

3. The graph of $g(x) = (-x)^3$ is a reflection of the graph of $f(x) = x^3$ across the y-axis, while the graph of $h(x) = -x^3$ is a reflection of the graph of $f(x) = x^3$ across the x-axis. If you graph $g(x)$ and $h(x)$ on a graphing calculator, what do you notice? Explain why this happens.

_____

_____

_____

⊘ Explain 1   Graphing Combined Transformations of $f(x) = x^3$

When graphing transformations of $f(x) = x^3$, it helps to consider the effect of the transformations on the three reference points on the graph of $f(x)$: $(-1, -1)$, $(0, 0)$, and $(1,1)$. The table lists the three points and the corresponding points on the graph of $g(x) = a\left(\frac{1}{b}(x - h)\right)^3 + k$. Notice that the point $(0, 0)$, which is the point of symmetry for the graph of $f(x)$, is affected only by the parameters h and k. The other two reference points are affected by all four parameters.

$f(x) = x^3$		$g(x) = a\left(\frac{1}{b}(x - h)\right)^3 + k$	
x	y	x	y
-1	-1	$-b + h$	$-a + k$
0	0	h	k
1	1	$b + h$	$a + k$

Example 1 Identify the transformations of the graph of $f(x) = x^3$ that produce the graph of the given function $g(x)$. Then graph $g(x)$ on the same coordinate plane as the graph of $f(x)$ by applying the transformations to the reference points $(-1, -1)$, $(0, 0)$, and $(1, 1)$.

Ⓐ $g(x) = 2(x - 1)^3 - 1$

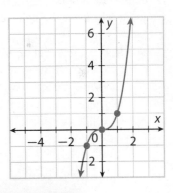

The transformations of the graph of $f(x)$ that produce the graph of $g(x)$ are:

- a vertical stretch by a factor of 2
- a translation of 1 unit to the right and 1 unit down

Note that the translation of 1 unit to the right affects only the x-coordinates of points on the graph of $f(x)$, while the vertical stretch by a factor of 2 and the translation of 1 unit down affect only the y-coordinates.

$f(x) = x^3$		$g(x) = 2(x - 1)^3 - 1$	
X	y	X	y
−1	−1	−1 + 1 = 0	2(−1) − 1 = −3
0	0	0 + 1 = 1	2(0) − 1 = −1
1	1	1 + 1 = 2	2(1) − 1 = 1

Ⓑ $g(x) = \left(2(x + 3)\right)^3 + 4$

The transformations of the graph of $f(x)$ that produce the graph of $g(x)$ are:

- a horizontal compression by a factor of $\frac{1}{2}$
- a translation of 3 units to the left and 4 units up

Note that the horizontal compression by a factor of $\frac{1}{2}$ and the translation of 3 units to the left affect only the x-coordinates of points on the graph of $f(x)$, while the translation of 4 units up affects only the y-coordinates.

$f(x) = x^3$		$g(x) = \left(2(x + 3)\right)^3 + 4$	
X	y	X	y
−1	−1	□(−1) + □ = □	−1 + □ = □
0	0	□(0) + □ = □	0 + □ = □
1	1	□(1) + □ = □	1 + □ = □

Your Turn

Identify the transformations of the graph of $f(x) = x^3$ that produce the graph of the given function $g(x)$. Then graph $g(x)$ on the same coordinate plane as the graph of $f(x)$ by applying the transformations to the reference points $(-1, -1)$, $(0, 0)$, and $(1, 1)$.

4. $g(x) = -\frac{1}{2}(x - 3)^3$

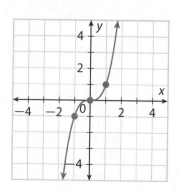

Explain 2   Writing Equations for Combined Transformations of $f(x) = x^3$

Given the graph of the transformed function $g(x) = a\left(\frac{1}{b}(x - h)\right)^3 + k$, you can determine the values of the parameters by using the same reference points that you used to graph $g(x)$ in the previous example.

Example 2   A general equation for a cubic function $g(x)$ is given along with the function's graph. Write a specific equation by identifying the values of the parameters from the reference points shown on the graph.

(A) $g(x) = a(x - h)^3 + k$

Identify the values of h and k from the point of symmetry.

$(h, k) = (2, 1)$, so $h = 2$ and $k = 1$.

Identify the value of a from either of the other two reference points.

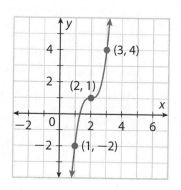

The rightmost reference point has general coordinates $(h + 1, a + k)$. Substituting 2 for h and 1 for k and setting the general coordinates equal to the actual coordinates gives this result:

$(h + 1, a + k) = (3, a + 1) = (3, 4)$, so $a = 3$.

Write the function using the values of the parameters: $g(x) = 3(x - 2)^3 + 1$

Ⓑ $g(x) = \left(\frac{1}{b}(x - h)\right)^3 + k$

Identify the values of h and k from the point of symmetry.

$(h, k) = \left(-4, \boxed{}\right)$, so $h = -4$ and $k = \boxed{}$.

Identify the value of b from either of the other two reference points.

The rightmost reference point has general coordinates

$(b + h, 1 + k)$. Substituting -4 for h and _____ for k and setting the general coordinates equal to the actual coordinates gives this result:

$\left(b + h, 1 + \boxed{}\right) = \left(b - 4, \boxed{}\right) = (-3.5, 2)$, so $b = \boxed{}$.

Write the function using the values of the parameters, and then simplify.

$g(x) = \left(\dfrac{1}{\boxed{}}\left(x - \boxed{}\right)\right)^3 + \boxed{}$

or

$g(x) = \left(\boxed{}\left(x + \boxed{}\right)\right)^3 + \boxed{}$

Your Turn

A general equation for a cubic function $g(x)$ is given along with the function's graph. Write a specific equation by identifying the values of the parameters from the reference points shown on the graph.

5. $g(x) = a(x - h)^3 + k$

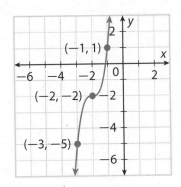

6. $g(x) = \left(\frac{1}{b}(x - h)\right)^3 + k$

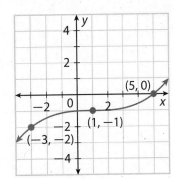

⊘ Explain 3   Modeling with a Transformation of $f(x) = x^3$

You may be able to model a real-world situation that involves volume with a cubic function. Sometimes mass may also be involved in the problem. Mass and volume are related through *density*, which is defined as an object's mass per unit volume. If an object has mass m and volume V, then its density d is $d = \frac{m}{V}$. You can rewrite the formula as $m = dV$ to express mass in terms of density and volume.

Example 3   Use a cubic function to model the situation, and graph the function using calculated values of the function. Then use the graph to obtain the indicated estimate.

(A) Estimate the length of an edge of a child's alphabet block (a cube) that has a mass of 23 g and is made from oak with a density of 0.72 g/cm³.

Let ℓ represent the length (in centimeters) of an edge of the block. Since the block is a cube, the volume V (in cubic centimeters) is $V(\ell) = \ell^3$. The mass m (in grams) of the block is $m(\ell) = 0.72 \cdot V(\ell) = 0.72\ell^3$. Make a table of values for this function.

Length (cm)	Mass (g)
0	0
1	0.72
2	5.76
3	19.44
4	46.08

Draw the graph of the mass function, recognizing that the graph is a vertical compression of the graph of the parent cubic function by a factor of 0.72. Then draw the horizontal line $m = 23$ and estimate the value of ℓ where the graphs intersect.

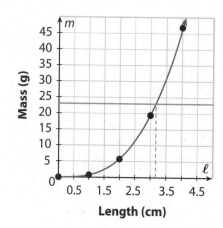

The graphs intersect where $\ell \approx 3.2$, so the edge length of the child's block is about 3.2 cm.

B Estimate the radius of a steel ball bearing with a mass of 75 grams and a density of 7.82 g/cm³.

Let r represent the radius (in centimeters) of the ball bearing.
The volume V (in cubic centimeters) of the ball bearing is

$V(r) = \boxed{} r^3$. The mass m (in grams) of the ball

bearing is $m(r) = 7.82 \cdot V(r) = \boxed{} r^3$.

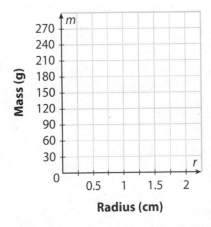

Radius (cm)	Mass (g)
0	
0.5	
1	
1.5	
2	

Draw the graph of the mass function, recognizing that the graph is a vertical _____

of the graph of the parent cubic function by a factor of _____. Then draw the

horizontal line $m = \boxed{}$ and estimate the value of r where the graphs intersect.

The graphs intersect where $r \approx \boxed{}$, so the radius of the steel ball bearing is about

_____ cm.

Reflect

7. **Discussion** Why is it important to plot multiple points on the graph of the volume function.

_____

_____

_____

_____

Use a cubic function to model the situation, and graph the function using calculated values of the function. Then use the graph to obtain the indicated estimate.

8. Polystyrene beads fill a cube-shaped box with an effective density of 0.00076 kg/cm^3 (which accounts for the space between the beads). The filled box weighs 6 kilograms while the empty box had weighed 1.5 kilograms. Estimate the inner edge length of the box.

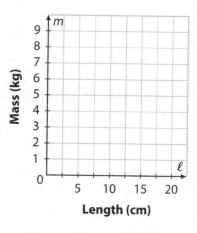

Elaborate

9. Identify which transformations (stretches or compressions, reflections, and translations) of $f(x) = x^3$ change the following attributes of the function.

    a. End behavior

    _____

    _____

    b. Location of the point of symmetry

    _____

    _____

    c. Symmetry about a point

    _____

10. **Essential Question Check-In** Describe the transformations you must perform on the graph of $f(x) = x^3$ to obtain the graph of $g(x) = a(x - h)^3 + k$.

    _____

    _____

    _____

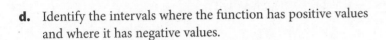

⭐ Evaluate: Homework and Practice

• Online Homework
• Hints and Help
• Extra Practice

1. Graph the parent cubic function $f(x) = x^3$ and use the graph to answer each question.

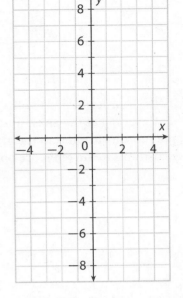

    a. State the function's domain and range.

    b. Identify the function's end behavior.

    c. Identify the graph's x- and y-intercepts.

    d. Identify the intervals where the function has positive values and where it has negative values.

    e. Identify the intervals where the function is increasing and where it is decreasing.

    f. Tell whether the function is even, odd, or neither. Explain.

    g. Describe the graph's symmetry.

Describe how the graph of $g(x)$ is related to the graph of $f(x) = x^3$.

2. $g(x) = (x - 4)^3$ **3.** $g(x) = -5x^3$

4. $g(x) = x^3 + 2$ **5.** $g(x) = (3x)^3$

6. $g(x) = (x + 1)^3$

7. $g(x) = \frac{1}{4}x^3$

8. $g(x) = x^3 - 3$

9. $g(x) = \left(-\frac{2}{3}x\right)^3$

Identify the transformations of the graph of $f(x) = x^3$ that produce the graph of the given function $g(x)$. Then graph $g(x)$ on the same coordinate plane as the graph of $f(x)$ by applying the transformations to the reference points $(-1, -1)$, $(0, 0)$, and $(1, 1)$.

10. $g(x) = \left(\frac{1}{3}x\right)^3$

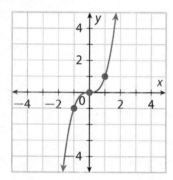

11. $g(x) = \frac{1}{3}x^3$

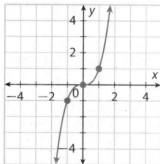

12. $g(x) = (x - 4)^3 - 3$

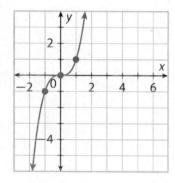

13. $g(x) = (x + 1)^3 + 2$

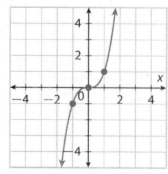

A general equation for a cubic function $g(x)$ is given along with the function's graph. Write a specific equation by identifying the values of the parameters from the reference points shown on the graph.

14. $g(x) = \left(\dfrac{1}{b}(x-h)\right)^3 + k$

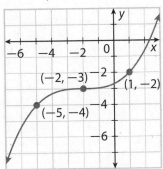

15. $g(x) = a(x-h)^3 + k$

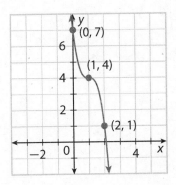

16. $g(x) = \left(\dfrac{1}{b}(x-h)\right)^3 + k$

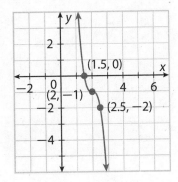

17. $g(x) = a(x-h)^3 + k$

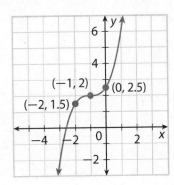

Use a cubic function to model the situation, and graph the function using calculated values of the function. Then use the graph to obtain the indicated estimate.

18. Estimate the edge length of a cube of gold with a mass of 1 kg. The density of gold is 0.019 kg/cm³.

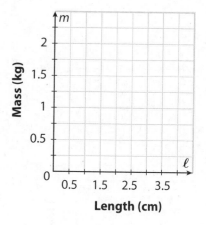

19. A proposed design for a habitable Mars colony is a hemispherical biodome used to maintain a breathable atmosphere for the colonists. Estimate the radius of the biodome if it is required to contain 5.5 billion cubic feet of air.

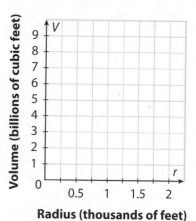

20. Multiple Response Select the transformations of the graph of the parent cubic function that result in the graph of $g(x) = \left(3(x-2)\right)^3 + 1$.

A. Horizontal stretch by a factor of 3

B. Horizontal compression by a factor of $\dfrac{1}{3}$

C. Vertical stretch by a factor of 3

D. Vertical compression by a factor of $\dfrac{1}{3}$

E. Translation 1 unit up

F. Translation 1 unit down

G. Translation 2 units left

H. Translation 2 units right

H.O.T. **Focus on Higher Order Thinking**

21. Justify Reasoning Explain how horizontally stretching (or compressing) the graph of $f(x) = x^3$ by a factor of b can be equivalent to vertically compressing (or stretching) the graph of $f(x) = x^3$ by a factor of a.

22. Critique Reasoning A student reasoned that $g(x) = (x-h)^3$ can be rewritten as $g(x) = x^3 - h^3$, so a horizontal translation of h units is equivalent to a vertical translation of $-h^3$ units. Is the student correct? Explain.

Lesson Performance Task

Julio wants to purchase a spherical aquarium and fill it with salt water, which has an average density of 1.027 g/cm^3. He has found a company that sells four sizes of spherical aquariums.

Aquarium Size	Diameter (cm)
Small	15
Medium	30
Large	45
Extra large	60

a. If the stand for Julio's aquarium will support a maximum of 50 kg, what is the largest size tank that he should buy? Explain your reasoning.

b. Julio's friend suggests that he could buy a larger tank if he uses fresh water, which has a density of 1.0 g/cm^3. Do you agree with the friend? Why or why not?

Name_____ Class_____ Date_____

5.2 Graphing Polynomial Functions

Essential Question: How do you sketch the graph of a polynomial function in intercept form?

Resource
Locker

⊘ Explore 1   Investigating the End Behavior of the Graphs of Simple Polynomial Functions

Linear, quadratic, and cubic functions belong to a more general class of functions called *polynomial functions*, which are categorized by their degree. Linear functions are polynomial functions of degree 1, quadratic functions are polynomial functions of degree 2, and cubic functions are polynomial functions of degree 3. In general, a **polynomial function of degree n** has the standard form $p(x) = a_n x^n + a_{n-1} x^{n-1} + ... + a_2 x^2 + a_1 x + a_0$, where $a_n, a_{n-1},..., a_2, a_1$, and a_0 are real numbers called the *coefficients* of the expressions $a_n x^n$, $a_{n-1} x^{n-1}$,..., $a_2 x^2$, $a_1 x$, and a_0, which are the *terms* of the polynomial function. (Note that the constant term, a_0, appears to have no power of x associated with it, but since $x^0 = 1$, you can write a_0 as $a_0 x^0$ and treat a_0 as the coefficient of the term.)

A polynomial function of degree 4 is called a *quartic* function, while a polynomial function of degree 5 is called a *quintic* function. After degree 5, polynomial functions are generally referred to by their degree, as in "a sixth-degree polynomial function."

Ⓐ Use a graphing calculator to graph the polynomial functions $f(x) = x$, $f(x) = x^2$, $f(x) = x^3$, $f(x) = x^4$, $f(x) = x^5$, and $f(x) = x^6$. Then use the graph of each function to determine the function's domain, range, and end behavior. (Use interval notation for the domain and range.)

Function	Domain	Range	End Behavior
$f(x) = x$			As $x \to +\infty$, $f(x) \to$ ▢ . As $x \to -\infty$, $f(x) \to$ ▢ .
$f(x) = x^2$			As $x \to +\infty$, $f(x) \to$ ▢ . As $x \to -\infty$, $f(x) \to$ ▢ .
$f(x) = x^3$			As $x \to +\infty$, $f(x) \to$ ▢ . As $x \to -\infty$, $f(x) \to$ ▢ .
$f(x) = x^4$			As $x \to +\infty$, $f(x) \to$ ▢ . As $x \to -\infty$, $f(x) \to$ ▢ .
$f(x) = x^5$			As $x \to +\infty$, $f(x) \to$ ▢ . As $x \to -\infty$, $f(x) \to$ ▢ .
$f(x) = x^6$			As $x \to +\infty$, $f(x) \to$ ▢ .

(B) Use a graphing calculator to graph the polynomial functions $f(x) = -x$, $f(x) = -x^2$, $f(x) = -x^3$, $f(x) = -x^4$, $f(x) = -x^5$, and $f(x) = -x^6$. Then use the graph of each function to determine the function's domain, range, and end behavior. (Use interval notation for the domain and range.)

Function	Domain	Range	End Behavior	
$f(x) = -x$			As $x \to +\infty$, $f(x) \to$ ☐ .	As $x \to -\infty$, $f(x) \to$ ☐ .
$f(x) = -x^2$			As $x \to +\infty$, $f(x) \to$ ☐ .	As $x \to -\infty$, $f(x) \to$ ☐ .
$f(x) = -x^3$			As $x \to +\infty$, $f(x) \to$ ☐ .	As $x \to -\infty$, $f(x) \to$ ☐ .
$f(x) = -x^4$			As $x \to +\infty$, $f(x) \to$ ☐ .	As $x \to -\infty$, $f(x) \to$ ☐ .
$f(x) = -x^5$			As $x \to +\infty$, $f(x) \to$ ☐ .	As $x \to -\infty$, $f(x) \to$ ☐ .
$f(x) = -x^6$			As $x \to +\infty$, $f(x) \to$ ☐ .	As $x \to -\infty$, $f(x) \to$ ☐ .

Reflect

1. How can you generalize the results of this Explore for $f(x) = x^n$ and $f(x) = -x^n$ where n is positive whole number?

_____

_____

_____

_____

_____

_____

The cubic function $f(x) = x^3$ has three factors, all of which happen to be x. One or more of the x's can be replaced with other linear factors in x, such as $x - 2$, without changing the fact that the function is cubic. In general, a polynomial function of the form $p(x) = a(x - x_1)(x - x_2)...(x - x_n)$ where a, x_1, x_2,..., and x_n are real numbers (that are not necessarily distinct) has degree n where n is the number of variable factors.

The graph of $p(x) = a(x - x_1)(x - x_2)...(x - x_n)$ has x_1, x_2,..., and x_n as its x-intercepts, which is why the polynomial is said to be in *intercept form*. Since the graph of $p(x)$ intersects the x-axis only at its x-intercepts, the graph must move away from and then move back toward the x-axis between each pair of successive x-intercepts, which means that the graph has a *turning point* between those x-intercepts. Also, instead of crossing the x-axis at an x-intercept, the graph can be *tangent* to the x-axis, and the point of tangency becomes a turning point because the graph must move toward the x-axis and then away from it near the point of tangency.

The y-coordinate of each turning point is a maximum or minimum value of the function at least near that turning point. A maximum or minimum value is called *global* or *absolute* if the function never takes on a value that is greater than the maximum or less than the minimum. A *local maximum* or *local minimum*, also called a *relative maximum* or *relative minimum*, is a maximum or minimum within some interval around the turning point that need not be (but may be) a global maximum or global minimum.

Ⓐ Use a graphing calculator to graph the cubic functions $f(x) = x^3$, $f(x) = x^2(x - 2)$, and $f(x) = x(x - 2)(x + 2)$. Then use the graph of each function to answer the questions in the table.

Function	$f(x) = x^3$	$f(x) = x^2(x - 2)$	$f(x) = x(x - 2)(x + 2)$
How many distinct factors does $f(x)$ have?			
What are the graph's x-intercepts?			
Is the graph tangent to the x-axis or does it cross the x-axis at each x-intercept?			
How many turning points does the graph have?			
How many global maximum values? How many local maximum values that are not global?			
How many global minimum values? How many local minimum values that are not global?			

Ⓑ Use a graphing calculator to graph the quartic functions $f(x) = x^4$, $f(x) = x^3(x - 2)$, $f(x) = x^2(x - 2)(x + 2)$, and $f(x) = x(x - 2)(x + 2)(x + 3)$. Then use the graph of each function to answer the questions in the table.

Function	$f(x) = x^4$	$f(x) = x^3(x - 2)$	$f(x) = x^2(x - 2)(x + 2)$	$f(x) = x(x - 2)(x + 2)(x + 3)$
How many distinct factors?				
What are the x-intercepts?				
Tangent to or cross the x-axis at x-intercepts?				
How many turning points?				
How many global maximum values? How many local maximum values that are not global?				
How many global minimum values? How many local minimum values that are not global?				

Reflect

2. What determines how many x-intercepts the graph of a polynomial function in intercept form has?

3. What determines whether the graph of a polynomial function in intercept form crosses the x-axis or is tangent to it at an x-intercept?

4. Suppose you introduced a factor of -1 into each of the quartic functions in Step B. (For instance, $f(x) = x^4$ becomes $f(x) = -x^4$.) How would your answers to the questions about the functions and their graphs change?

 **Sketching the Graph of Polynomial Functions in Intercept Form**

Given a polynomial function in intercept form, you can sketch the function's graph by using the end behavior, the x-intercepts, and the sign of the function values on intervals determined by the x-intercepts. The sign of the function values tells you whether the graph is above or below the x-axis on a particular interval. You can find the sign of the function values by determining the sign of each factor and recognizing what the sign of the product of those factors is.

Example 1 **Sketch the graph of the polynomial function.**

(A) $f(x) = x(x + 2)(x - 3)$

Identify the end behavior. For the function $p(x) = a(x - x_1)(x - x_2)\ldots(x - x_n)$, the end behavior is determined by whether the degree n is even or odd and whether the constant factor a is positive or negative. For the given function $f(x)$, the degree is 3 and the constant factor a, which is 1, is positive, so $f(x)$ has the following end behavior:

As $x \to +\infty$, $f(x) \to +\infty$.

As $x \to -\infty$, $f(x) \to -\infty$.

Identify the graph's x-intercepts, and then use the sign of $f(x)$ on intervals determined by the x-intercepts to find where the graph is above the x-axis and where it's below the x-axis.

The x-intercepts are $x = 0$, $x = -2$, and $x = 3$. These three x-intercepts divide the x-axis into four intervals: $x < -2$, $-2 < x < 0$, $0 < x < 3$, and $x > 3$.

Interval	Sign of the Constant Factor	Sign of x	Sign of x + 2	Sign of x − 3	Sign of $f(x) = x(x+2)(x-3)$
$x < -2$	+	−	−	−	−
$-2 < x < 0$	+	−	+	−	+
$0 < x < 3$	+	+	+	−	−
$x > 3$	+	+	+	+	+

So, the graph of $f(x)$ is above the x-axis on the intervals $-2 < x < 0$ and $x > 3$, and it's below the x-axis on the intervals $x < -2$ and $0 < x < 3$.

Sketch the graph.

While you should be precise about where the graph crosses the x-axis, you do not need to be precise about the y-coordinates of points on the graph that aren't on the x-axis. Your sketch should simply show where the graph lies above the x-axis and where it lies below the x-axis.

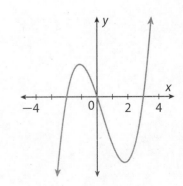

(B) $f(x) = -(x-4)(x-1)(x+1)(x+2)$

Identify the end behavior.

As $x \to +\infty$, $f(x) \to$ ☐ .

As $x \to -\infty$, $f(x) \to$ ☐ .

Identify the graph's x-intercepts, and then use the sign of $f(x)$ on intervals determined by the x-intercepts to find where the graph is above the x-axis and where it's below the x-axis.

The x-intercepts are $x =$ ☐ , $x =$ ☐ , $x =$ ☐ , $x =$ ☐ .

Interval	Sign of the Constant Factor	Sign of $x-4$	Sign of $x-1$	Sign of $x+1$	Sign of $x+2$	Sign of $f(x) = -(x-4)(x-1)(x+1)(x+2)$
$x <$ ☐	$-$		$-$		$-$	
☐ $< x <$ ☐	$-$		$-$		$+$	
☐ $< x <$ ☐	$-$		$+$		$+$	
☐ $< x <$ ☐	$-$		$+$		$+$	
$x >$ ☐	$-$		$+$		$+$	

So, the graph of $f(x)$ is above the x-axis on the intervals

☐ $< x <$ ☐ and ☐ $< x <$ ☐ , and

it's below the x-axis on the intervals $x <$ ☐ , ☐ $< x <$ ☐ ,

and $x >$ ☐ .

Sketch the graph.

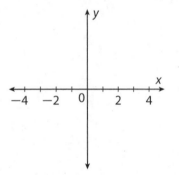

Sketch the graph of the polynomial function.

5. $f(x) = -x^2(x - 4)$

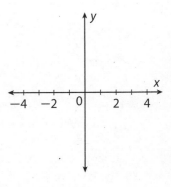

⚙ Explain 2   Modeling with a Polynomial Function

You can use cubic functions to model real-world situations. For example, you find the volume of a box (a rectangular prism) by multiplying the length, width, and height. If each dimension of the box is given in terms of x, then the volume is a cubic function of x.

Example 2

To create an open-top box out of a sheet of cardboard that is 9 inches long and 5 inches wide, you make a square flap of side length x inches in each corner by cutting along one of the flap's sides and folding along the other side. (In the first diagram, a solid line segment in the interior of the rectangle indicates a cut, while a dashed line segment indicates a fold.) After you fold up the four sides of the box (see the second diagram), you glue each flap to the side it overlaps. To the nearest tenth, find the value of x that maximizes the volume of the box.

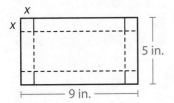

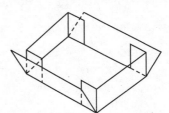

Analyze Information

Identify the important information.

A square flap of side length x inches is made in each corner of a rectangular sheet of cardboard.

The sheet of cardboard measures 9 inches by 5 inches.

 Formulate a Plan

Find the dimensions of the box once the flaps have been made and the sides have been folded up. Create a volume function for the box, graph the function on a graphing calculator, and use the graph to find the value of x that maximizes the volume.

Solve

1. Write expressions for the dimensions of the box.

   Length of box: $9 - \boxed{}$

   Width of box: $5 - \boxed{}$

   Height of box: $\boxed{}$

2. Write the volume function and determine its domain.

   $$V(x) = \left(9 - \boxed{}\right)\left(5 - \boxed{}\right)$$

   Because the length, width, and height of the box must all be positive, the volume function's domain is determined by the following three constraints:

   $9 - 2x > 0$, or $x < \boxed{}$

   $5 - 2x > 0$, or $x < \boxed{}$

   $x > 0$

   Taken together, these constraints give a domain of $0 < x < \boxed{}$.

3. Use a graphing calculator to graph the volume function on its domain.

   Adjust the viewing window so you can see the maximum. From the graphing calculator's **CALC** menu, select **4: maximum** to locate the point where the maximum value occurs.

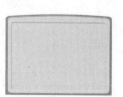

   So, $V(x) \approx 21.0$ when $x \approx \boxed{}$, which means that the box has a maximum volume of about 21 cubic inches when square flaps with a side length of 1 inch are made in the corners of the sheet of cardboard.

Making square flaps with a side length of 1 inch means that the box will be 7 inches long, 3 inches wide, and 1 inch high, so the volume is 21 cubic inches. As a check on this result, consider making square flaps with a side length of 0.9 inch and 1.1 inches:

$$V(0.9) = (9 - 1.8)(5 - 1.8)(0.9) = \boxed{}$$

$$V(1.1) = (9 - 2.2)(5 - 2.2)(1.1) = \boxed{}$$

Both volumes are slightly less than 21 cubic inches, which suggests that 21 cubic inches is the maximum volume.

Reflect

6. Discussion Although the volume function has three constraints on its domain, the domain involves only two of them. Why?

_____

_____

Your Turn

7. To create an open-top box out of a sheet of cardboard that is 25 inches long and 13 inches wide, you make a square flap of side length x inches in each corner by cutting along one of the flap's sides and folding along the other. (In the diagram, a solid line segment in the interior of the rectangle indicates a cut, while a dashed line segment indicates a fold.) Once you fold up the four sides of the box, you glue each flap to the side it overlaps. To the nearest tenth, find the value of x that maximizes the volume of the box.

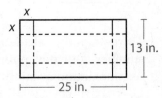

Elaborate

8. Compare and contrast the domain, range, and end behavior of $f(x) = x^n$ when n is even and when n is odd.

_____

_____

_____

_____

9. Essential Question Check-In For a polynomial function in intercept form, why is the constant factor important when graphing the function?

_____

_____

_____

Use a graphing calculator to graph the polynomial function. Then use the graph to determine the function's domain, range, and end behavior. (Use interval notation for the domain and range.)

1. $f(x) = x^7$

2. $f(x) = -x^9$

3. $f(x) = x^{10}$

4. $f(x) = -x^8$

Use a graphing calculator to graph the function. Then use the graph to determine the number of turning points and the number and type (global, or local but not global) of any maximum or minimum values.

5. $f(x) = x(x + 1)(x + 3)$

6. $f(x) = (x + 1)^2(x - 1)(x - 2)$

7. $f(x) = -x(x - 2)^2$

8. $f(x) = -(x - 1)(x + 2)^3$

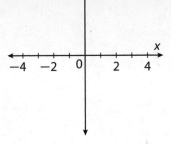

10. $f(x) = -(x+1)(x-2)(x-3)$

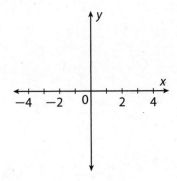

11. $f(x) = x(x+2)^2(x-1)$

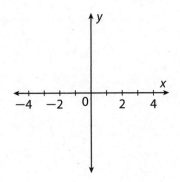

13. The template shows how to create a box from a square sheet of cardboard that has a side length of 36 inches. In the template, solid line segments indicate cuts, dashed line segments indicate folds, and grayed rectangles indicate pieces removed. The vertical strip that is 2 inches wide on the left side of the template is a flap that will be glued to the side of the box that it overlaps when the box is folded up. The horizontal strips that are $\frac{x}{2}$ inches wide at the top and bottom of the template are also flaps that will overlap to form the top and bottom of the box when the box is folded up. Write a volume function for the box in terms of x only. (You will need to determine a relationship between x and y first.) Then, to the nearest tenth, find the dimensions of the box with maximum volume.

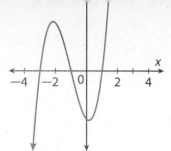
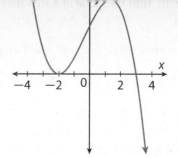

Write a quartic function in intercept form for the given graph, whose x-intercepts are integers. Assume that the constant factor a is either 1 or −1.

16.

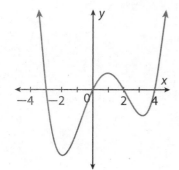

17.

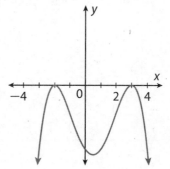

B. The x-intercepts are $x = -1$ and $x = 2$.

C. The graph crosses the x-axis at $x = 1$ and is tangent to the x-axis at $x = -2$.

D. The graph crosses the x-axis at $x = -1$ and is tangent to the x-axis at $x = 2$.

E. The graph is tangent to the x-axis at $x = 1$ and crosses the x-axis at $x = -2$.

F. The graph is tangent to the x-axis at $x = -1$ and crosses the x-axis at $x = 2$.

G. A local, but not global, minimum occurs on the interval $-2 < x < 1$, and a local, but not global, maximum occurs at $x = 1$.

H. A local, but not global, maximum occurs on the interval $-2 < x < 1$, and a local, but not global, minimum occurs at $x = 1$.

I. A local, but not global, minimum occurs on the interval $-1 < x < 2$, and a local, but not global, maximum occurs at $x = 2$.

J. A local, but not global, maximum occurs on the interval $-1 < x < 2$, and a local, but not global, minimum occurs at $x = 2$.

H.O.T. Focus on Higher Order Thinking

19. Explain the Error A student was asked to sketch the graph of the function $f(x) = x^2(x - 3)$. Describe what the student did wrong. Then sketch the correct graph.

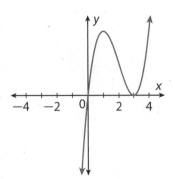 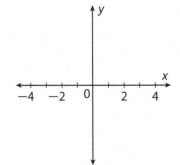

20. Make a Prediction Knowing the characteristics of the graphs of cubic and quartic functions in intercept form, sketch the graph of the quintic function $f(x) = x^2(x + 2)(x - 2)^2$.

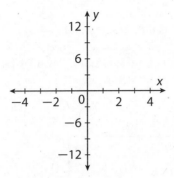

21. Represent Real-World Situations A rectangular piece of sheet metal is rolled and riveted to form a circular tube that is open at both ends, as shown. The sheet metal has a perimeter of 36 inches. Each of the two sides of the rectangle that form the two ends of the tube has a length of x inches, but the tube has a circumference of $x - 1$ inches because an overlap of 1 inch is needed for the rivets. Write a volume function for the tube in terms of x. Then, to the nearest tenth, find the value of x that maximizes the volume of the tube.

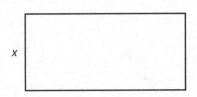

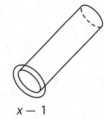

$x - 1$

Lesson Performance Task

The template shows how to create a box with a lid from a sheet of card stock that is 10 inches wide and 24 inches long. In the template, solid line segments indicate cuts, and dashed line segments indicate folds. The square flaps, each with a side length of x inches, are glued to the sides they overlap when the box is folded up. The box has a bottom and four upright sides. The lid, which is attached to one of the upright sides, has three upright sides of its own. Assume that the three sides of the lid can be tucked inside the box when the lid is closed.

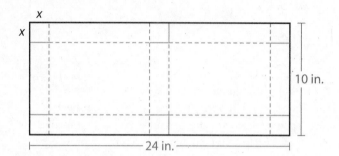

a. Write a polynomial function that represents the volume of the box, and state its domain.

b. Use a graphing calculator to find the value of x that will produce the box with maximum volume. What are the dimensions of that box?

Essential Question: How can polynomial functions help to solve real-world problems?

Key Vocabulary

cubic function *(función cúbica)*

polynomial function *(función polinomial)*

KEY EXAMPLE   (Lesson 5.1)

Identify the transformations of the graph $f(x) = x^3$ that produce the graph of the function $g(x) = \frac{1}{3}(x + 2)^3$. Then create a table with the corresponding input and output values.

- a vertical compression by a factor of $\frac{1}{3}$
- a translation of 2 units to the left

x	$f(x) = x^3$	$g(x) = \frac{1}{3}(x + 2)^3$
−2	−8	$\frac{1}{3}(-2 + 2)^3 = 0$
−1	−1	$\frac{1}{3}(-1 + 2)^3 = \frac{1}{3}$
0	0	$\frac{1}{3}(0 + 2)^3 = \frac{8}{3}$
1	1	$\frac{1}{3}(1 + 2)^3 = 9$
2	8	$\frac{1}{3}(2 + 2)^3 = \frac{64}{3}$

KEY EXAMPLE   (Lesson 5.2)

Use a graphing calculator to graph $g(x) = x(x - 2)^2 (x + 3)$. Then use the graph to determine the number of turning points, global maximums and minimums, and local maximums and minimums that are not global.

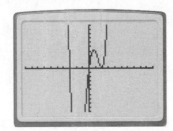

According to the graph, there are three turning points, one local maximum, one local minimum, and one global minimum.

EXERCISES

Identify the transformations of the graph $f(x) = x^3$ that produce the graph of the function. *(Lesson 5.1)*

1. $g(x) = \left(-\dfrac{1}{4}(x+2)\right)^3 + 3$

2. $h(x) = \dfrac{1}{3}(x-4)^3$

Use a graphing calculator to graph each function, then use the graph to determine the number of turning points, global maximums and minimums, and local maximums and minimums that are not global. *(Lesson 5.2)*

3. $s(x) = x(x+2)(x+1)^2$

4. $h(x) = x^2(x-3)(x+2)(x-2)$

5. Write a real world situation that could be modeled by the equation $V(w) = w(5w)(3w)$. *(Lesson 5.2)*

MODULE PERFORMANCE TASK

What's the Function of a Roller Coaster?

An engineer is designing part of a roller coaster track that can be modeled by the polynomial function

$$f(x) = 2.0 \times 10^{-6}x^4 - 0.0011x^3 + 0.195x^2 - 12.25x + 250$$

where $f(x)$ is the height in feet of a roller coaster car above ground level, and x is the horizontal distance in feet. For this section of track, the domain is $0 \le x \le 250$.

The factored form of this function is

$$f(x) = 2.0 \times 10^{-6}(x-200)(x-250)(x-50)^2.$$

Describe the experience of a rider who is riding a roller coaster on this track.

Use your own paper to complete the task. Be sure to write down all your data and assumptions. Then use graphs, numbers, words, or algebra to explain how you reached your conclusion.

Ready to Go On?

5.1–5.2 Polynomial Functions

• Online Homework
• Hints and Help
• Extra Practice

Identify the transformations of the graph of $f(x) = x^3$ that produce the graph of $g(x) = -\frac{1}{4}(x+4)^3$. Apply the transformations to the reference points $(-1, -1)$, $(0, 0)$, and $(1, 1)$ *(Lesson 5.1)*

1. Changes to x.

2. Changes to y.

3. Apply the transformations using the changes to x and y.

$f(x) = x^3$		$g(x) = -\frac{1}{4}(x+4)^3$	
x	y	x	y

Graph the given function on your graphing calculator. Use the graph to state the number of turning points in the graph and the x-intercepts. *(Lesson 5.2)*

4. $g(x) = x^2(x-3)$

5. $h(x) = (x-4)(x-3)(x+2)^2$

ESSENTIAL QUESTION

6. Give a real world example of a cubic function. *(Lesson 5.1)*

Assessment Readiness

1. Look at each equation. Is the vertex of the graph translated to the right and up when compared to $f(x) = x^3$?
   Select Yes or No for A–C.

   A. $y = (x + 6)^3 + 2$ ○ Yes   ○ No

   B. $y = 5x^3 + 7$ ○ Yes   ○ No

   C. $y = (x - 4)^3 + 2$ ○ Yes   ○ No

2. Consider the equation $h(x) = x(x - 1)(x + 3)^2$. Choose True or False for each statement.

   A. There are four turning points in the graph.   ○ True   ○ False

   B. The graph crosses the x-axis at $-3, -1, 0,$ and 1.   ○ True   ○ False

   C. The graph has a global maximum.   ○ True   ○ False

3. Write a quartic function in intercept form for the given graph. Assume that the constant factor a is either 1 or −1. Explain your answer.

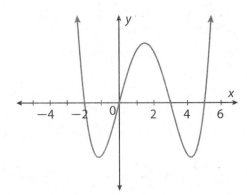

4. An ottoman shaped like a rectangular prism has a length of x, a width two inches shorter than the length, and a height two inches taller than the length. Write the function that represents the volume; then find the length, width, and height of the ottoman if the volume is 5760 in³.

Polynomials

Essential Question: How can you use polynomials to solve real-world problems?

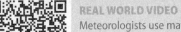

REAL WORLD VIDEO
Meteorologists use mathematics and computer models to analyze climate patterns and forecast weather. For example, polynomial functions can be used to model temperature patterns.

MODULE PERFORMANCE TASK PREVIEW
What's the Temperature?

The weather is always a topic for conversation. Is it hot or cold outside? Is it T-shirt and shorts weather, or should you bundle up? What were the high and low temperatures for a particular day? You might suspect that the outdoor temperature follows a pattern. How can you use a polynomial to model the temperature? Let's find out!

Complete these exercises to review skills you will need for this module.

• Online Homework
• Hints and Help
• Extra Practice

Adding and Subtracting Polynomials

Example 1   Subtract.

$$\left(7a^3 - 4a^2 + 11\right) - \left(3a^2 - 2a + 5\right)$$

$7a^3 - 4a^2 + 11 - 3a^2 + 2a - 5$ Multiply by -1.

$7a^3 - 7a^2 + 2a + 6$ Combine like terms.

Add or subtract the polynomials.

1. $\left(m^5 + 4m^2 + 6\right) - \left(3m^5 - 8m^2\right)$

2. $\left(k^2 + 3k + 1\right) + \left(k^2 - 8\right)$

Algebraic Expressions

Example 2   Simplify the expression $5x^3 - 10x^2 + x^3 + 10$.

$6x^3 - 10x^2 + 10$ Combine like terms.

Simplify each expression.

3. $6x - 2x^2 - 2x$

4. $(5x)(2x^2) - x^2$

5. $4(2x - 3y) + 2(x + y)$

6. $4(a + b) - 7(a + 2b)$

Multiplying Polynomials

Example 3   Multiply. $(2a - b)(a + ab + b)$

$(2a - b)(a + ab + b) = 2a(a + ab + b) - b(a + ab + b)$

$= 2a \cdot a + 2a \cdot ab + 2a \cdot b - b \cdot a - b \cdot ab - b \cdot b$

$= 2a^2 + 2a^2b + 2ab - ab - ab^2 - b^2$

$= 2a^2 + 2a^2b + ab - ab^2 - b^2$

Multiply the polynomials.

7. $\left(x^2 - 4\right)(x + y)$

8. $(3m + 2)\left(3m^2 - 2m + 1\right)$

6.1 Adding and Subtracting Polynomials

Essential Question: How do you add or subtract two polynomials, and what type of expression is the result?

Resource Locker

⊘ Explore   Identifying and Analyzing Monomials and Polynomials

A polynomial function of degree n has the *standard form* $p(x) = a_n x^n + a_{n-1} x^{n-1} + \ldots + a_2 x^2 + a_1 x + a_0$, where $a_n, a_{n-1}, \ldots, a_2, a_1$, and a_0 are real numbers and $a_n \neq 0$. The expression $a_n x^n + a_{n-1} x^{n-1} + \ldots a_2 x^2 + a_1 x + a_0$ is called a **polynomial**, and each term of a polynomial is called a **monomial**. A monomial is the product of a number and one or more variables with whole-number exponents. A polynomial is a monomial or a sum of monomials. The *degree of a monomial* is the sum of the exponents of the variables, and the *degree of a polynomial* is the degree of the monomial term with the greatest degree. The *leading coefficient* of a polynomial is the coefficient of the term with the greatest degree.

(A) Identify the monomials: x^3, $y + 3y^2 - 5y^3 + 10$, $a^2 bc^{12}$, 76

　　Monomials: _____

　　Not monomials: _____

(B) Identify the degree of each monomial.

Monomial	x^3	$a^2 bc^{12}$	76
Degree			

(C) Identify the terms of the polynomial $y + 3y^2 - 5y^3 + 10$. _____

(D) Identify the coefficient of each term.

Term	y	$3y^2$	$-5y^3$	10
Coefficient				

(E) Identify the degree of each term.

Term	y	$3y^2$	$-5y^3$	10
Degree				

(F) Write the polynomial in standard form. _____

(G) What is the leading coefficient of the polynomial? _____

1. **Discussion** How can you find the degree of a polynomial with multiple variables in each term?

_____

_____

⊘ Explain 1 Adding Polynomials

To add polynomials, combine like terms.

Example 1 Add the polynomials.

Ⓐ $\left(4x^2 - x^3 + 2 + 5x^4\right) + \left(-x + 6x^2 + 3x^4\right)$

$$
\begin{array}{cccccc}
5x^4 & -x^3 & +4x^2 & & +2 \\
+3x^4 & & +6x^2 & -x \\
\hline
8x^4 & -x^3 & +10x^2 & -x & +2
\end{array}
$$

Write in standard form.
Align like terms.
Add.

Ⓑ $\left(10x - 18x^3 + 6x^4 - 2\right) + \left(-7x^4 + 5 + x + 2x^3\right)$

$\left(6x^4 - 18x^3 + 10x - 2\right) + \left(-7x^4 + 2x^3 + x + 5\right)$ Write in standard form.

$= \left(6x^4 - \boxed{}\right) + \left(\boxed{} + 2x^3\right) + \left(\boxed{} + x\right) + \left(-2 + \boxed{}\right)$ Group like terms.

$= \boxed{} - 16x^3 + \boxed{} + 3$ Add.

Reflect

2. Is the sum of two polynomials always a polynomial? Explain.

_____

_____

Your Turn

Add the polynomials.

3. $\left(17x^4 + 8x^2 - 9x^7 + 4 - 2x^3\right) + \left(11x^3 - 8x^2 + 12\right)$

4. $\left(-8x + 3x^{11} + x^6\right) + \left(4x^4 - x + 17\right)$

Explain 2 Subtracting Polynomials

To subtract polynomials, combine like terms.

Example 2 Subtract the polynomials.

(A) $\left(12x^3 + 5x - 8x^2 + 19\right) - \left(6x^2 - 9x + 3 - 18x^3\right)$

Write in standard form.

Align like terms and add the opposite.

Add.

$$
\begin{array}{llll}
12x^3 & -8x^2 & +5x & +19 \\
+18x^3 & -6x^2 & +9x & -3 \\
\hline
30x^3 & -14x^2 & +14x & +16
\end{array}
$$

(B) $\left(-4x^2 + 8x^3 + 19 - 5x^5\right) - \left(9 + 2x^2 + 10x^5\right)$

Write in standard form and add the opposite.

$\left(-5x^5 + 8x^3 - 4x^2 + 19\right) + \left(-10x^5 - 2x^2 - 9\right)$

Group like terms

$= \left(-5x^5 - \boxed{}\right) + \left(\boxed{}\right) + \left(\boxed{} - 2x^2\right) + \left(\boxed{} - 9\right)$

Add

$= \boxed{} + 8x^3 - \boxed{} + 10$

Reflect

5. Is the difference of two polynomials always a polynomial? Explain.

_____

_____

_____

Your Turn

Subtract the polynomials.

6. $\left(23x^7 - 9x^4 + 1\right) - \left(-9x^4 + 6x^2 - 31\right)$

7. $\left(7x^3 + 13x - 8x^5 + 20x^2\right) - \left(-2x^5 + 9x^2\right)$

Modeling with Polynomial Addition and Subtraction

Polynomial functions can be used to model real-world quantities. If two polynomial functions model quantities that are two parts of a whole, the functions can be added to find a function that models the quantity as a whole. If the polynomial function for the whole and a polynomial function for a part are given, subtraction can be used to find the polynomial function that models the other part of the whole.

Example 3 **Find the polynomial that models the problem and use it to estimate the quantity.**

(A) The data from the U.S. Census Bureau for 2005–2009 shows that the number of male students enrolled in high school in the United States can be modeled by the function $M(x) = -10.4x^3 + 74.2x^2 - 3.4x + 8320.2$, where x is the number of years after 2005 and $M(x)$ is the number of male students in thousands. The number of female students enrolled in high school in the United States can be modeled by the function $F(x) = -13.8x^3 + 55.3x^2 + 141x + 7880$, where x is the number of years after 2005 and $F(x)$ is the number of female students in thousands. Estimate the total number of students enrolled in high school in the United States in 2009.

In the equation $T(x) = M(x) + F(x)$, $T(x)$ is the total number of students in thousands.

Add the polynomials.

$\left(-10.4x^3 + 74.2x^2 - 3.4x + 8320.2\right) + \left(-13.8x^3 + 55.3x^2 + 141x + 7880\right)$

$= \left(-10.4x^3 - 13.8x^3\right) + \left(74.2x^2 + 55.3x^2\right) + \left(-3.4x + 141x\right) + \left(8320.2 + 7880\right)$

$= -24.2x^3 + 129.5x^2 + 137.6x + 16{,}200.2$

The year 2009 is 4 years after 2005, so substitute 4 for x.

$-24.2(4)^3 + 129.5(4)^2 + 137.6(4) + 16{,}200.2 \approx 17{,}274$

About 17,274 thousand students were enrolled in high school in the United States in 2009.

(B) The data from the U.S. Census Bureau for 2000–2010 shows that the total number of overseas travelers visiting New York and Florida can be modeled by the function $T(x) = 41.5x^3 - 689.1x^2 + 4323.3x + 2796.6$, where x is the number of years after 2000 and $T(x)$ is the total number of travelers in thousands. The number of overseas travelers visiting New York can be modeled by the function $N(x) = -41.6x^3 + 560.9x^2 - 1632.7x + 6837.4$, where x is the number of years after 2000 and $N(x)$ is the number of travelers in thousands. Estimate the total number of overseas travelers to Florida in 2008.

In the equation $F(x) = T(x) \boxed{} N(x)$, $F(x)$ is the number of travelers to Florida in thousands.

Subtract the polynomials.

$\left(41.5x^3 - 689.1x^2 + 4323.3x + 2796.6\right) \boxed{} \left(-41.6x^3 + 560.9x^2 - 1632.7x + 6837.4\right)$

$= \left(41.5x^3 - 689.1x^2 + 4323.3x + 2796.6\right) + \left(41.6x^3 - 560.9x^2 + 1632.7x - 6837.4\right)$

$$= \left(41.5x^3 + \boxed{}\right) + \left(\boxed{} - 560.9x^2\right) + \left(\boxed{} + 1632.7x\right) + \left(2796.6 - \boxed{}\right)$$

$$= \boxed{}\, x^3 - \boxed{}\, x^2 + \boxed{}\, x - \boxed{}$$

The year 2008 is 8 years after 2000, so substitute $\boxed{}$ for x.

$$83.1(8)^3 - 1250(8)^2 + 5956(8) - 4040.8 \approx \boxed{}$$

About $\boxed{}$ thousand overseas travelers visited Florida in 2008.

Your Turn

8. According to the data from the U.S. Census Bureau for 1990–2009, the number of commercially owned automobiles in the United States can be modeled by the function $A(x) = 1.4x^3 - 130.6x^2 + 1831.3x + 128,141$, where x is the number of years after 1990 and $A(x)$ is the number of automobiles in thousands. The number of privately-owned automobiles in the United States can be modeled by the function $P(x) = -x^3 + 24.9x^2 - 177.9x + 1709.5$, where x is the number of years after 1990 and $P(x)$ is the number of automobiles in thousands. Estimate the total number of automobiles owned in 2005.

Elaborate

9. How is the degree of a polynomial related to the degrees of the monomials that comprise the polynomial?

10. How is polynomial subtraction based on polynomial addition?

11. How would you find the model for a whole if you have polynomial functions that are models for the two distinct parts that make up that whole?

12. **Essential Question Check-In** What is the result of adding or subtracting polynomials?

1. Write the polynomial $-23x^7 + x^9 - 6x^3 + 10 + 2x^2$ in standard form, and then identify the degree and leading coefficient.

Add the polynomials.

2. $\left(82x^8 + 21x^2 - 6\right) + \left(18x + 7x^8 - 42x^2 + 3\right)$

3. $\left(15x - 121x^{12} + x^9 - x^7 + 3x^2\right) + \left(x^7 - 68x^2 - x^9\right)$

4. $\left(16 - x^2\right) + \left(-18x^2 + 7x^5 - 10x^4 + 5\right)$

5. $\left(x + 1 - 3x^2\right) + \left(8x + 21x^2 - 1\right)$

6. $\left(64 + x^3 - 8x^2\right) + \left(7x + 3 - x^2\right) + \left(19x^2 - 7x - 2\right)$

7. $\left(x^4 - 7x^3 + 2 - x\right) + \left(2x^3 - 3\right) + \left(1 - 5x^3 - x^4 + x\right)$

Subtract the polynomials.

8. $\left(-2x + 23x^5 + 11\right) - \left(5 - 9x^3 + x\right)$

9. $\left(7x^3 + 68x^4 - 14x + 1\right) - \left(-10x^3 + 8x + 23\right)$

10. $\left(57x^{18} - x^2\right) - \left(6x - 71x^3 + 5x^2 + 2\right)$

11. $\left(9x - 12x^3\right) - \left(5x^3 + 7x - 2\right)$

12. $\left(3x^5 - 9\right) - \left(11 + 13x^2 - x^4\right) - \left(10x^2 + x^4\right)$

13. $\left(10x^2 - x + 4\right) - \left(5x + 7\right) + \left(6x - 11\right)$

Find the polynomial that models the problem and use it to estimate the quantity.

14. A rectangle has a length of x and a width of $5x^3 + 4 - x^2$. Find the perimeter of the rectangle when the length is 5 feet.

15. A rectangle has a perimeter of $6x^3 + 9x^2 - 10x + 5$ and a length of x. Find the width of the rectangle when the length is 21 inches.

16. Cho is making a rectangular garden, where the length is x feet and the width is $4x - 1$ feet. He wants to add garden stones around the perimeter of the garden once he is done. If the garden is 4 feet long, how many feet will Cho need to cover with garden stones?

17. Employment The data from the U.S. Census Bureau for 1980–2010 shows that the median weekly earnings of full-time male employees who have at least a bachelor's degree can be modeled by the function $M(x) = 0.009x^3 - 0.29x^2 + 30.7x + 439.6$, where x is the number of years after 1980 and $M(x)$ is the median weekly earnings in dollars. The median weekly earnings of all full-time employees who have at least a bachelor's degree can be modeled by the function $T(x) = 0.012x^3 - 0.46x^2 + 56.1x + 732.3$, where x is the number of years after 1980 and $T(x)$ is the median weekly earnings in dollars. Estimate the median weekly earnings of a full-time female employee with at least a bachelor's degree in 2010.

18. Business From data gathered in the period 2008–2012, the yearly value of U.S. exports can be modeled by the function $E(x) = -228x^3 + 2552.8x^2 - 6098.5x + 11,425.8$, where x is the number of years after 2008 and $E(x)$ is the value of exports in billions of dollars. The yearly value of U.S. imports can be modeled by the function $l(x) = -400.4x^3 + 3954.4x^2 - 11,128.8x + 17,749.6$, where x is the number of years after 2008 and $l(x)$ is the value of imports in billions of dollars. Estimate the total value the United States imported and exported in 2012.

19. Education From data gathered in the period 1970–2010, the number of full-time students enrolled in a degree-granting institution can be modeled by the function $F(x) = 8.7x^3 - 213.3x^2 + 2015.5x + 3874.9$, where x is the number of years after 1970 and $F(x)$ is the number of students in thousands. The number of part-time students enrolled in a degree-granting institution can be modeled by the function $P(x) = 12x^3 - 285.3x^2 + 2217x + 1230$, where x is the number of years after 1970 and $P(x)$ is the number of students in thousands. Estimate the total number of students enrolled in a degree-granting institution in 2000.

20. Geography The data from the U.S. Census Bureau for 1982–2003 shows that the surface area of the United States that is covered by rural land can be modeled by the function $R(x) = 0.003x^3 - 0.086x^2 - 1.2x + 1417.4$, where x is the number of years after 1982 and $R(x)$ is the surface area in millions of acres. The total surface area of the United States can be modeled by the function $T(x) = 0.0023x^3 + 0.034x^2 - 5.9x + 1839.4$, where x is the number of years after 1982 and $T(x)$ is the surface area in millions of acres. Estimate the surface area of the United States that is not covered by rural land in 2001.

21. Determine which polynomials are monomials. Choose all that apply.

a. $4x^3y$

b. $12 - x^2 + 5x$

c. $152 + x$

d. 783

e. x

f. $19x^{-2}$

g. $4x^4x^2$

H.O.T. Focus on Higher Order Thinking

22. Explain the Error Colin simplified $\left(16x + 8x^2y - 7xy^2 + 9y - 2xy\right) - \left(-9xy + 8xy^2 + 10x^2y + x - 7y\right)$. His work is shown below. Find and correct Colin's mistake.

$\left(16x + 8x^2y - 7xy^2 + 9y - 2xy\right) - \left(-9xy + 8xy^2 + 10x^2y + x - 7y\right)$
$= \left(16x + 8x^2y - 7xy^2 + 9y - 2xy\right) + \left(9xy - 8xy^2 - 10x^2y - x + 7y\right)$
$= \left(16x - x\right) + \left(8x^2y - 7xy^2 - 8xy^2 - 10x^2y\right) + \left(9y + 7y\right) + \left(-2xy + 9xy\right)$
$= 15x - 17x^2y^2 + 16y + 7xy$

23. Critical Reasoning Janice is building a fence around a portion of her rectangular yard. The length of yard she will enclose is x, and the width is $2x^2 - 98x + 5$, where the measurements are in feet. If the length of the enclosed yard is 50 feet and the cost of fencing is $13 per foot, how much will Janice need to spend on fencing?

24. Multi-Step Find a polynomial expression for the perimeter of a trapezoid with legs of length x and bases of lengths $0.1x^3 + 2x$ and $x^2 + 3x - 10$ where each is measured in inches.

   a. Find the perimeter of the trapezoid if the length of one leg is 6 inches.

   b. If the leg length is increased by 5 inches, will the perimeter also increase? By how much?

25. Communicate Mathematical Ideas Present a formal argument for why the set of polynomials is closed under addition and subtraction. Use the polynomials $ax^m + bx^m$ and $ax^m - bx^m$, for real numbers a and b and whole number m, to justify your reasoning.

Lesson Performance Task

The table shows the average monthly maximum and minimum temperatures for Death Valley throughout one year.

Month	Maximum Temperature	Minimum Temperature
January	67	40
February	73	46
March	82	55
April	91	62
May	101	73
June	110	81
July	116	88
August	115	86
September	107	76
October	93	62
November	77	48
December	65	38

Use a graphing calculator to find a good fourth-degree polynomial regression model for both the maximum and minimum temperatures. Then find a function that models the range in monthly temperatures and use the model to estimate the range during September. How does the range predicted by your model compare with the range shown in the table?

6.2 Multiplying Polynomials

Essential Question: How do you multiply polynomials, and what type of expression is the result?

⊘ Explore Analyzing a Visual Model for Polynomial Multiplication

The volume of a rectangular prism is the product of the length, width, and height of that prism. If the dimensions are all known, then the volume is a simple calculation. What if some of the dimensions are given as *binomials*? A **binomial** is a polynomial with two terms. How would you find the volume of a rectangular prism that is $x + 3$ units long, $x + 2$ units wide, and x units high? The images below show two methods for finding the solution.

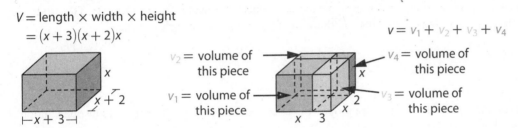

$V = $ length $\times$ width $\times$ height
$= (x + 3)(x + 2)x$

$v = v_1 + v_2 + v_3 + v_4$

$v_2 =$ volume of this piece

$v_4 =$ volume of this piece

$v_1 =$ volume of this piece

$v_3 =$ volume of this piece

(A) The first model shows the rectangular prism, and its volume is calculated directly as the product of two binomials and a monomial.

(B) The second image divides the rectangular prism into _____ smaller prisms, the dimensions of which are each _____.

(C) The volume of a cube (V_1) where all sides have a length of x, is _____.

(D) The volume of a rectangular prism (V_2) with dimensions x by x by 2 is _____.

(E) The volume of a rectangular prism (V_3) with dimensions x by x by 3 is _____.

(F) The volume of a rectangular prism (V_4) with dimensions x by 3 by 2 is _____.

(G) So the volume of the rectangular prism is the sum of the volumes of the four smaller regions.

$$V_1 + V_2 + V_3 + V_4 = \boxed{} + \boxed{} + \boxed{} + \boxed{}$$

$$= \boxed{}$$

1. If all three dimensions were binomials, how many regions would the rectangular prism be divided into?

_____

_____

_____

2. **Discussion** Can this method be applied to finding the volume of other simple solids? Are there solids that this process would be difficult to apply to? Are there any solids that this method cannot be applied to?

_____

_____

_____

🔑 Explain 1 Multiplying Polynomials

Multiplying polynomials involves using the product rule for exponents and the distributive property. The product of two monomials is the product of the coefficients and the sum of the exponents of each variable.

$$5x \cdot 6x^3 = 30x^{1+3} \qquad\qquad -2x^2y^4z \cdot 5y^2z = -10x^2y^{4+2}z^{1+1}$$

$$= 30x^4 \qquad\qquad\qquad\qquad = -10x^2y^6z^2$$

When multiplying two binomials, the distributive property is used. Each term of one polynomial must be multiplied by each term of the other.

$$(2 + 3x)(1 + x) = 2(1 + x) + 3x(x + 1)$$

$$= 2(1) + 2(x) + 3x(x) + 3x(1)$$

$$= 2 + 2x + 3x^{1+1} + 3x$$

$$= 2 + 5x + 3x^2$$

The polynomial $2 + 5x + 3x^2$ is called a **trinomial** because it has three terms.

Example 1 **Perform the following polynomial multiplications.**

Ⓐ $(x + 2)(1 - 4x + 2x^2)$

Find the product by multiplying horizontally.

$(x + 2)(2x^2 - 4x + 1)$	Write the polynomials in standard form.
$x(2x^2) + x(-4x) + x(1) + 2(2x^2) + 2(-4x) + 2(1)$	Distribute the x and the 2.
$2x^3 - 4x^2 + x + 4x^2 - 8x + 2$	Simplify.
$2x^3 - 7x + 2$	Combine like terms.

Therefore, $(x + 2)(2x^2 - 4x + 1) = 2x^3 - 7x + 2$.

Ⓑ $(3x - 4)(2 + x - 7x^2)$

Find the product by multiplying vertically.

$$-7x^2 + \boxed{} + 2$$
$$\underline{\qquad 3x - 4 \qquad}$$

Write each polynomial in standard form.

$$\boxed{} - 4x - 8$$

Multipy -4 and $(-7x^2 + x + 2)$.

$$\underline{\boxed{} + 3x^2 + 6x}$$

Multipy $\boxed{}$ and $(-7x^2 + x + 2)$.

$$-21x^3 + \boxed{} + 2x - 8$$

Combine like terms.

Therefore, $(3x - 4)(2 + x - 7x^2) = $ _____.

Your Turn

3. $(3 + 2x)(4 - 7x + 5x^2)$

4. $(x - 6)(3 - 8x - 4x^2)$

⊘ Explain 2   Modeling with Polynomial Multiplication

Many real-world situations can be modeled with polynomial functions. Sometimes, a situation will arise in which a model is needed that combines two quantities modeled by polynomial functions. In this case, the desired model would be the product of the two known models.

Example 2   Find the polynomial function modeling the desired relationship.

Ⓐ Mr. Silva manages a manufacturing plant. From 1990 through 2005, the number of units produced (in thousands) can be modeled by $N(x) = 0.02x^2 + 0.2x + 3$, where x is the number of years since 1990. The average cost per unit (in dollars) can be modeled by $C(x) = -0.002x^2 - 0.1x + 2$, where x is the number of years since 1990. Write a polynomial $T(x)$ that can be used to model Mr. Silva's total manufacturing cost for those years.

The total manufacturing cost is the product of the number of units made and the cost per unit.

$T(x) = N(x) \cdot C(x)$

Multiply the two polynomials.

$$
\begin{array}{r}
0.02x^2 + 0.2x + 3 \\
\times\ -0.002x^2 - 0.1x + 2 \\
\hline
0.04x^2 + 0.4x + 6 \\
-0.002x^3\ \ \ -0.02x^2 - 0.3x \\
-0.00004x^4 - 0.0004x^3\ \ \ -0.006x^2 \\
\hline
-0.00004x^4 - 0.0024x^3\ \ +0.014x^2 + 0.1x + 6
\end{array}
$$

Therefore, the total manufacturing cost can be modeled by the following polynomial, where x is the number of years since 1990.

$T(x) = -0.00004x^4 - 0.0024x^3 + 0.014x^2 + 0.1x + 6$

Ⓑ Ms. Liao runs a small dress company. From 1995 through 2005, the number of dresses she made can be modeled by $N(x) = 0.3x^2 - 1.6x + 14$, and the average cost to make each dress can be modeled by $C(x) = -0.001x^2 - 0.06x + 8.3$, where x is the number of years since 1995. Write a polynomial that can be used to model Ms. Liao's total dressmaking costs, $T(x)$, for those years.

The total dressmaking cost is the product of the number of dresses made and the cost per dress.

$T(x) = N(x) \cdot C(x)$

Multiply the two polynomials.

$$
\begin{array}{r}
0.3x^2 - 1.6x + 14 \\
\times\ -0.001x^2\ \boxed{} + 8.3 \\
\hline
2.49x^2 - 13.28x\ \boxed{} \\
-0.018x^3\ \boxed{} - 0.84x \\
-0.0003x^{\boxed{}} + 0.0016x^3 - 0.014x^2 \\
\hline
-0.0003x^{\boxed{}} - 0.0164x^3 + 2.572x^2\ \boxed{} + 116.2
\end{array}
$$

Therefore, the total dressmaking cost can be modeled by the following polynomial, where x is the number of years since 1995.

$T(x) = $ _____

5. Brent runs a small toy store specializing in wooden toys. From 2000 through 2012, the number of toys Brent made can be modeled by $N(x) = 0.7x^2 - 2x + 23$, and the average cost to make each toy can be modeled by $C(x) = -0.004x^2 - 0.08x + 25$, where x is the number of years since 2000. Write a polynomial that can be used to model Brent's total cost for making the toys, $T(x)$, for those years.

⚙ Explain 3 Verifying Polynomial Identities

You have already seen certain special polynomial relationships. For example, a difference of two squares can be easily factored: $x^2 - a^2 = (x + a)(x - a)$. This equation is an example of a **polynomial identity**, a mathematical relationship equating one polynomial quantity to another. Another example of a polynomial identity is

$$(x + a)^2 - (x - a)^2 = 4ax.$$

The identity can be verified by simplifying one side of the equation to match the other.

Example 3 Verify the given polynomial identity.

(A) $(x + a)^2 - (x - a)^2 = 4ax$

The right side of the identity is already fully simplified. Simplify the left-hand side.

$$(x + a)^2 - (x - a)^2 = 4ax$$

$x^2 + 2ax + a^2 - (x^2 - 2ax + a^2) = 4ax$ Square each binomial.

$x^2 + 2ax + a^2 - x^2 + 2ax - a^2 = 4ax$ Distribute the negative.

$\cancel{x^2} - \cancel{x^2} + 2ax + 2ax + \cancel{a^2} - \cancel{a^2} = 4ax$ Rearrange terms.

$$4ax = 4ax$$ Simplify.

Therefore, $(x + a)^2 - (x - a)^2 = 4ax$ is a true statement.

(B) $(a + b)(a^2 - ab + b^2) = a^3 + b^3$

The right side of the identity is already fully simplified. Simplify the left-hand side.

$$(a + b)(a^2 - ab + b^2) = a^3 + b^3$$

$a(a^2) + a\left(\boxed{}\right) + a(b^2) + b(a^2) + \boxed{}(-ab) + b(b^2) = a^3 + b^3$ Distribute a and b.

$a^3 - a^2b + ab^2 + \boxed{} - ab^2 + \boxed{} = a^3 + b^3$ _____

$a^3 - \boxed{} + a^2b + ab^2 - \boxed{} + b^3 = a^3 + b^3$ Rearrange terms.

$a^3 \boxed{} b^3 = a^3 + b^3$ Combine like terms.

Therefore, $(a + b)(a^2 - ab + b^2) = a^3 + b^3$ is a _____ statement.

Your Turn

6. Show that $a^5 - b^5 = (a - b)(a^4 + a^3b + a^2b^2 + ab^3 + b^4)$.

7. Show that $(a - b)(a^2 + ab + b^2) = a^3 - b^3$.

⊘ Explain 4 Using Polynomial Identities

The most obvious use for polynomial identities is simplifying algebraic expressions, but polynomial identities often turn out to have nonintuitive uses as well.

Example 4 For each situation, find the solution using the given polynomial identity.

(A) The polynomial identity $(x^2 + y^2)^2 = (x^2 - y^2)^2 + (2xy)^2$ can be used to identify Pythagorean triples. Generate a Pythagorean triple using $x = 4$ and $y = 3$.

Substitute the given values into the identity.

$$(4^2 + 3^2)^2 = (4^2 - 3^2)^2 + (2 \cdot 4 \cdot 3)^2$$
$$(16 + 9)^2 = (16 - 9)^2 + (24)^2$$
$$(25)^2 = (7)^2 + (24)^2$$
$$625 = 49 + 576$$
$$625 = 625$$

Therefore, 7, 24, 25 is a Pythagorean triple.

(B) The identity $(x + y)^2 = x^2 + 2xy + y^2$ can be used for mental-math calculations to quickly square numbers.

Find the square of 27.

Find two numbers whose sum is equal to 27.

Let $x = $ ☐ and $y = 7$

Evaluate

$$\left(20 + \boxed{}\right)^2 = 20^2 + \boxed{} + 7^2$$

$$27^2 = 400 + \boxed{} + 49$$

$$27^2 = \boxed{}$$

Verify by using a calculator to find 27^2.

$$27^2 = \boxed{}$$

Your Turn

8. The identity $(x + y)(x - y) = x^2 - y^2$ can be used for mental-math calculations to quickly multiply two numbers in specific situations.

   Find the product of 37 and 43. (Hint: What values should you choose for x and y so the equation calculates the product of 37 and 43?)

9. The identity $(x - y)^2 = x^2 - 2xy + y^2$ can also be used for mental-math calculations to quickly square numbers.

   Find the square of 18. (Hint: What values should you choose for x and y so the equation calculates the square of 18?)

10. What property is employed in the process of polynomial multiplication?

_____

_____

11. How can you use unit analysis to justify multiplying two polynomial models of real-world quantities?

_____

_____

12. Give an example of a polynomial identity and how it's useful.

_____

_____

13. **Essential Question Check-In** When multiplying polynomials, what type of expression is the product?

_____

_____

⭐ Evaluate: Homework and Practice

- Online Homework
- Hints and Help
- Extra Practice

1. The dimensions for a rectangular prism are $x + 5$ for the length, $x + 1$ for the width, and x for the height. What is the volume of the prism?

Perform the following polynomial multiplications.

2. $(3x - 2)(2x^2 + 3x - 1)$

3. $(x^3 + 3x^2 + 1)(3x^2 + 6x - 2)$

4. $(x^2 + 9x + 7)(3x^2 + 9x + 5)$

5. $(2x + 5y)(3x^2 - 4xy + 2y^2)$

6. $(x^3 + x^2 + 1)(x^2 - x - 5)$

7. $(4x^2 + 3x + 2)(3x^2 + 2x - 1)$

Write a polynomial function to represent the new value.

8. The volume of a stock, or number of shares traded, is modeled over time during a given day by $S(x) = x^5 - 3x^4 + 10x^2 - 6x + 30$. The cost per share of that stock during that day is modeled by $C(x) = 0.004x^4 - 0.02x^2 + 0.3x + 4$. Write a polynomial function $V(x)$ to model the changing value during that day of the trades made of shares of that stock.

9. A businessman models the number of items (in thousands) that his company sold from 1998 through 2004 as $N(x) = -0.1x^3 + x^2 - 3x + 4$ and the average price per item (in dollars) as $P(x) = 0.2x + 5$, where x represents the number of years since 1998. Write a polynomial $R(x)$ that can be used to model the total revenue for this company.

10. Biology A biologist has found that the number of branches on a certain rare tree can be modeled by the polynomial $b(y) = 4y^2 + y$ where y is the number of years after the tree reaches a height of 6 feet. The number of leaves on each branch can be modeled by the polynomial $l(y) = 2y^3 + 3y^2 + y$. Write a polynomial describing the total number of leaves on the tree.

11. Physics An object thrown in the air has a velocity after t seconds that can be described by $v(t) = -9.8t + 24$ (in meters/second) and a height $h(t) = -4.9t^2 + 24t + 60$ (in meters). The object has mass $m = 2$ kilograms. The kinetic energy of the object is given by $K = \frac{1}{2}mv^2$, and the potential energy is given by $U = 9.8mh$. Find an expression for the total kinetic and potential energy $K + U$ as a function of time. What does this expression tell you about the energy of the falling object?

Verify the given polynomial identity.

12. $(x + y + z)^2 = x^2 + y^2 + z^2 + 2xy + 2xz + 2yz$

13. $a^5 + b^5 = (a + b)(a^4 - a^3b + a^2b^2 - ab^3 + b^4)$

14. $x^4 - y^4 = (x - y)(x + y)(x^2 + y^2)$

15. $\left(a^2 + b^2\right)\left(x^2 + y^2\right) = \left(ax - by\right)^2 + \left(bx + ay\right)^2$

Find the square of the number or the product of the numbers using one or more of these identities.

$\left(x + y\right)^2 = x^2 + 2xy + y^2$, $\left(x + y\right)\left(x - y\right) = x^2 - y^2$, or $\left(x - y\right)^2 = x^2 - 2xy + y^2$.

16. 43^2

17. 32^2

18. 89^2

19. 47^2

20. $54 \cdot 38$

21. $58 \cdot 68$

22. Explain the Error A polynomial identity for the difference of two cubes is $a^3 - b^3 = (a - b)(a^2 + ab + b^2)$. A student uses the identity to factor $64 - 27x^6$. Identify the error the student made, and then correct it.

Each term of $64 - 27x^6$ is a perfect cube. Let $a = 4$ and $b = 3x^2$. Then:

$64 - 27x^6 = 4^3 - (3x^2)^3$

$\qquad\qquad = (4 - 3x^2)(4^2 + 4(-3x^2) + (-3x^2)^2)$

$\qquad\qquad = (4 - 3x^2)(16 - 12x^2 + 9x^4)$

23. Determine how many terms there will be after performing the polynomial multiplication.

a. $(5x)(3x)$ ☐ 1   ☐ 2   ☐ 3   ☐ 4

b. $(3x)(2x + 1)$ ☐ 1   ☐ 2   ☐ 3   ☐ 4

c. $(x + 1)(x - 1)$ ☐ 1   ☐ 2   ☐ 3   ☐ 4

d. $(x + 2)(3x^2 - 2x + 1)$ ☐ 1   ☐ 2   ☐ 3   ☐ 4

24. Multi-Step Given the polynomial identity: $x^6 + y^6 = (x^2 + y^2)(x^4 - x^2y^2 + y^4)$

a. Verify directly by expanding the right hand side.

b. Use another polynomial identity to verify this identity. $\left(\text{Note that } a^6 = (a^2)^3 = (a^3)^2\right)$

25. Communicate Mathematical Ideas Explain why the set of polynomials is closed under multiplication.

26. Critical Thinking Explain why every other term of the polynomial product $(x - y)^5$ written in standard form is subtracted when $(x - y)$ is raised to the fifth power.

Lesson Performance Task

The table presents data about oil wells in the state of Oklahoma from 1992 through 2008.

Year	Number of Wells	Average Daily Oil Production per Well (Barrels)
2008	83,443	2.178
2007	82,832	2.053
2006	82,284	2.108
2005	82,551	2.006
2004	83,222	2.10
2003	83,415	2.12
2002	83,730	2.16
2001	84,160	2.24
2000	84,432	2.24
1999	85,043	2.29
1998	85,691	2.49
1997	86,765	2.62
1996	88,144	2.66
1995	90,557	2.65
1994	91,289	2.73
1993	92,377	2.87
1992	93,192	2.99

a. Given the data in this table, use regression to find models for the number of producing wells (cubic regression) and average daily well output (quadratic regression) in terms of t years since 1992.

b. Find a function modeling the total daily oil output for the state of Oklahoma.

6.3 The Binomial Theorem

Essential Question: How is the Binomial Theorem useful?

Resource
Locker

⊘ Explore 1   Generating Pascal's Triangle

Pascal's Triangle is a famous number pattern named after the French mathematician Blaise Pascal (1623–1662). You can use Pascal's Triangle to help you expand a power of a binomial of the form $(a + b)^n$.

Use the tree diagram shown to generate Pascal's Triangle. Notice that from each node in the diagram to the nodes immediately below it there are two paths, a left path (L) and a right path (R). You can describe a path from the single node in row 0 to any other node in the diagram using a string of Ls and Rs.

First, notice that there is only one possible path to each node in row 1, which is why a 1 appears in those nodes. In row 2, there is only one possible path, LL, to the first node and only one possible path, RR, to the last node, but there are two possible paths, LR and RL, to the center node.

Ⓐ Complete only rows 3 and 4 of Pascal's Triangle. (You will complete rows 5 and 6 in Step C.) In each node, write the number of possible paths from the top down to that node.

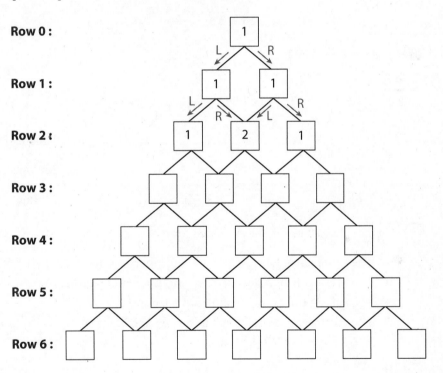

Ⓑ Look for patterns in the tree diagram.

What is the value in the first and last node in each row? _____

For every other node, the value in the node is the _____ of the two values above it.

Ⓒ Using the patterns in Step B, go back to Pascal's Triangle in Step A and complete rows 5 and 6.

---

1. Using strings of Ls and Rs, write the paths that lead to the second node in row 3 of Pascal's Triangle. How are the paths alike, and how are they different?

2. The path LLRLR leads to which node in which row of Pascal's Triangle? What is the value of that node?

Explore 2 Relating Pascal's Triangle to Powers of Binomials

As shown, the value in position r of row n of Pascal's Triangle is written as $_nC_r$, where the position numbers in each row start with 0. In this Explore, you will see how the values in Pascal's Triangle are related to powers of a binomial.

Row 0 : $\longrightarrow$ $_0C_0$

Row 1 : $\longrightarrow$ $_1C_0$ $\quad$ $_1C_1$

Row 2 : $\longrightarrow$ $_2C_0$ $\quad$ $_2C_1$ $\quad$ $_2C_2$

Row 3 : $\longrightarrow$ $_3C_0$ $\quad$ $_3C_1$ $\quad$ $_3C_2$ $\quad$ $_3C_3$

(A) Expand each power.

$(a+b)^0 = \boxed{}$

$(a+b)^1 = \boxed{}$

$(a+b)^2 = \boxed{}$ $\qquad$ Square of a binomial

$(a+b)^3 = \boxed{}$ $\qquad$ Multiply $(a+b)^2$ by $(a+b)$.

$(a+b)^4 = \boxed{}$ $\qquad$ Multiply $(a+b)^3$ by $(a+b)$.

(B) Identify the patterns in the expanded form of $(a+b)^n$.

- The exponents of a start at _____ and [increase/decrease] by _____ each term.
- The exponents of b start at _____ and [increase/decrease] by _____ each term.
- The sum of the exponents in each term is _____ .
- The coefficients of the terms in the expanded form of $(a+b)^n$ are the values in row _____ of Pascal's Triangle.

Reflect

3. How many terms are in the expanded form of $(a+b)^n$?

4. Without expanding the power, determine the middle term of $(a+b)^6$. Explain how you found your answer.

5. Without expanding the power, determine the first term of $(a+b)^{15}$. Explain how you found your answer.

⚙ Explain 1 Expanding Powers of Binomials Using the Binomial Theorem

The **Binomial Theorem** states the connection between the terms of the expanded form of $(a + b)^n$ and Pascal's Triangle.

> ### Binomial Theorem
> For any whole number n, the binomial expansion of $(a + b)^n$ is given by
> $$(a + b)^n = {}_nC_0 a^n b^0 + {}_nC_1 a^{n-1} b^1 + {}_nC_2 a^{n-2} b^2 + \ldots + {}_nC_{n-1} a^1 b^{n-1} + {}_nC_n a^0 b^n$$
> where ${}_nC_r$ is the value in position r (where r starts at 0) of the nth row of Pascal's Triangle.

Since it can be cumbersome to look up numbers from Pascal's Triangle each time you want to expand a power of a binomial, you can use a calculator instead. To do so, enter the value of n, press MATH, go to the **PRB** menu, select **3:nCr**, and then enter the value of r. The calculator screen shows the values for ${}_6C_1$, ${}_6C_2$, and ${}_6C_3$.

Example 1 Use the Binomial Theorem to expand each power of a binomial.

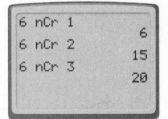

(A) $(x - 2)^3$

    Step 1 Identify the values in row 3 of Pascal's Triangle.

        1, 3, 3, and 1

    Step 2 Expand the power as described by the Binomial Theorem, using the values from Pascal's Triangle as coefficients.

$$(x - 2)^3 = 1x^3(-2)^0 + 3x^2(-2)^1 + 3x^1(-2)^2 + 1x^0(-2)^3$$

    Step 3 Simplify.

$$(x - 2)^3 = x^3 - 6x^2 + 12x - 8$$

(B) $(x + y)^7$

    Step 1 Use a calculator to determine the values of ${}_7C_0$, ${}_7C_1$, ${}_7C_2$, ${}_7C_3$, ${}_7C_4$, ${}_7C_5$, ${}_7C_6$, and ${}_7C_7$.

    Step 2 Expand the power as described by the Binomial Theorem, using the values of ${}_7C_0$, ${}_7C_1$, ${}_7C_2$, ${}_7C_3$, ${}_7C_4$, ${}_7C_5$, ${}_7C_6$, and ${}_7C_7$ as coefficients.

$$(x + y)^7 = \boxed{}\, x^{\square} y^{\square} + \boxed{}\, x^{\square} y^{\square} + \boxed{}\, x^{\square} y^{\square} + \boxed{}\, x^{\square} y^{\square}$$
$$+ \boxed{}\, x^{\square} y^{\square} + \boxed{}\, x^{\square} y^{\square} + \boxed{}\, x^{\square} y^{\square} + \boxed{}\, x^{\square} y^{\square}$$

    Step 3 Simplify.

$$(x + y)^7 = x^{\square} + \boxed{}\, x^{\square} y + \boxed{}\, x^{\square} y^{\square} + \boxed{}\, x^{\square} y^{\square} + \boxed{}\, x^{\square} y^{\square}$$
$$+ \boxed{}\, x^{\square} y^{\square} + \boxed{}\, xy^{\square} + y^{\square}$$

6. What happens to the signs of the terms in the expanded form of $(x - 2)^3$? Why does this happen?

_____

_____

7. If the number 11 is written as the binomial $(10 + 1)$, how can you use the Binomial Theorem to find 11^2, 11^3, and 11^4? What is the pattern in the digits?

_____

_____

_____

Your Turn

8. Use the Binomial Theorem to expand $(x - y)^4$.

⚙ Explain 2   Solving a Real-World Problem Using Binomial Probabilities

Recall that the probability of an event A is written as $P(A)$ and is expressed as a number between 0 and 1, where 0 represents impossibility and 1 represents certainty.

When dealing with probabilities, you will find these two rules helpful.

1. Addition Rule for Mutually Exclusive Events: If events A and B are *mutually exclusive* (that is, they cannot occur together), then $P(A \text{ or } B) = P(A) + P(B)$. For example, when rolling a die, getting a 1 and getting a 2 are mutually exclusive events, so $P(1 \text{ or } 2) = P(1) + P(2) = \frac{1}{6} + \frac{1}{6} = \frac{1}{3}$.

2. Complement Rule: The *complement* of event A consists of all of the possible outcomes that are not part of A, and the probability that A does not occur is $P(\text{not } A) = 1 - P(A)$. For example, when rolling a die, the probability of not getting a 2 is $P(\text{not } 2) = 1 - P(2) = 1 - \frac{1}{6} = \frac{5}{6}$.

A **binomial experiment** involves many trials where each trial has only two possible outcomes: success or failure. If the probability of success in each trial is p and the probability of failure in each trial is $q = 1 - p$, the **binomial probability** of exactly r successes in n trials is given by $P(r) = {}_nC_r p^r q^{n-r}$. Since ${}_nC_r = {}_nC_{n-r}$, you can rewrite $P(r)$ as $P(r) = {}_nC_{n-r} p^r q^{n-r}$, which represents the $(n - r)$th term in the expanded form of $(p + q)^n$.

Example 2   One in 5 boats traveling down a river bypass a harbor at the mouth of the
river and head out to sea. Currently, 4 boats are traveling down the river
and approaching the mouth of the river.

(A) What is the probability that exactly 2 of the 4 boats head
out to sea?

The probability that a boat will head out to sea is $\frac{1}{5}$,
or 0.2.

Substitute 4 for n, 2 for r, 0.2 for p, and 0.8 for q.

$$P(2) = {}_4C_2(0.2)^2(0.8)^{4-2}$$

$$= 6(0.2)^2(0.8)^2$$

$$= 6(0.04)(0.64)$$

$$= 0.1536$$

So, the probability that exactly 2 of the 4 boats will head out to sea is 0.1536, or 15.36%.

(B) What is the probability that at least 2 of the 4 boats will head out to sea?

To find the probability that at least 2 of the 4 boats will head out to sea, find the probability that 2,

_____, or _____ boats will head out to sea and add the probabilities.

From Part A, you know that $P(2) = 0.1536$.

$$P(3) = {}_4C_{\boxed{}}(0.2)^{\boxed{}}(0.8)^{\boxed{}}$$

$$= 4\left(\boxed{}\right)\left(\boxed{}\right)$$

$$= \boxed{}$$

$$P(4) = {}_4C_{\boxed{}}(0.2)^{\boxed{}}(0.8)^{\boxed{}}$$

$$= 1\left(\boxed{}\right)\left(\boxed{}\right)$$

$$= \boxed{}$$

$$P(\text{at least } 2) = P(2 \text{ or } 3 \text{ or } 4)$$

$$= P(2) + P(3) + P(4)$$

$$= 0.1536 + \boxed{} + \boxed{}$$

$$= \boxed{}$$

So, the probability that at least 2 of the 4 boats will head out to sea is 0.1808, or 18.08%.

9. In words, state the complement of the event that at least 2 of the 4 boats will head out to sea. Then find the probability of the complement.

_____

_____

_____

_____

Your Turn

10. Students are assigned randomly to 1 of 3 guidance counselors at a school. What is the probability that Ms. Banks, one of the school's guidance counselors, will get exactly 2 of the next 3 students assigned?

💬 **Elaborate**

11. How do the numbers in one row of Pascal's Triangle relate to the numbers in the previous row?

_____

_____

12. How does Pascal's Triangle relate to the power of a binomial?

_____

_____

13. The expanded form of $(p + q)^3$ is $p^3 + 3p^2q + 3pq^2 + q^3$. In terms of a binomial experiment with a probability p of success and a probability q of failure on each trial, what do each of the terms p^3, $3p^2q$, $3pq^2$, and q^3 represent?

_____

_____

14. **Essential Question Check-In** The Binomial Theorem says that the expanded form of $(a + b)^n$ is a sum of terms of the form $_nC_r a^{n-r}b^r$ for what values of r?

_____

_____

1. The path LLRRLLR leads to which node in which row of Pascal's Triangle? What is the value of that node?

2. Without expanding the power, determine the middle term of $(a + b)^8$. Explain how you found your answer.

Use the Binomial Theorem to expand each power of a binomial.

3. $(x + 6)^3$

4. $(x - 5)^4$

5. $(x + 3)^6$

6. $(2x - 1)^3$

7. $(3x + 4)^5$

8. $(2x - 3)^7$

9. $\left(x + 2y\right)^5$

10. $\left(3x - y\right)^4$

11. $\left(5x + y\right)^4$

12. $\left(x - 6y\right)^5$

13. $\left(5x - 4y\right)^3$

14. $\left(4x + 3y\right)^6$

Use the Binomial Theorem to find the specified term of the given power of a binomial. (Remember that r starts at 0 in the Binomial Theorem, so finding, say, the second term means that $r = 1$.)

15. Find the fourth term in the expanded form of $(x - 1)^6$.

16. Find the second term in the expanded form of $\left(2x + 1\right)^4$.

17. Find the third term in the expanded form of $\left(3x - 2y\right)^5$.

18. Find the fifth term in the expanded form of $\left(6x + 8y\right)^7$.

**Ellen takes a multiple-choice quiz that has 5 questions, with
4 answer choices for each question.**

19. What is the probability that she will get exactly 2 answers correct by guessing?

20. What is the probability that Ellen will get at least 3 answers correct by guessing?

Manufacturing A machine that makes a part used
in cars has a 98% probability of producing the part
within acceptable tolerance levels. The machine makes
25 parts per hour.

21. What is the probability that the machine will make
exactly 20 acceptable parts in an hour?

22. What is the probability that the machine makes 23 or fewer acceptable parts?

23. Match each term of an expanded power of a binomial on the right with the corresponding description of the term on the left. (Remember that r starts at 0 in the Binomial Theorem, so finding, say, the second term means that $r = 1$.)

A. Fifth term in the expanded form of $(x + 2)^6$ _____ $640x^2$

B. Fourth term in the expanded form of $(x + 4)^5$ _____ $48x^2$

C. Third term in the expanded form of $(x + 8)^4$ _____ $240x^2$

D. Second term in the expanded form of $(x + 16)^3$ _____ $384x^2$

H.O.T. Focus on Higher Order Thinking

24. Construct Arguments Identify the symmetry in the rows of Pascal's Triangle and give an argument based on strings of Ls and Rs to explain why the symmetry exists.

25. Communicate Mathematical Ideas Explain why the numbers from Pascal's Triangle show up in the Binomial Theorem.

26. Represent Real-World Situations A small airline overbooks flights on the assumption that some passengers will not show up. The probability that a passenger shows up is 0.8. What number of tickets can the airline sell for a 20-seat flight and still have a probability of seating everyone that is at least 90%? Explain your reasoning.

Lesson Performance Task

Suppose that a basketball player has just been fouled while attempting a 3-point shot and is awarded three free throws. Given that the player is 85% successful at making free throws, calculate the probability that the player successfully makes zero, one, two, or all three of the free throws. Which situation is most likely to occur?

6.4 Factoring Polynomials

Resource
Locker

Essential Question: What are some ways to factor a polynomial, and how is factoring useful?

⊘ Explore   Analyzing a Visual Model for Polynomial Factorization

Factoring a polynomial of degree n involves finding factors of a lesser degree that can be multiplied together to produce the polynomial. When a polynomial has degree 3, for example, you can think of it as the volume of a rectangular prism whose dimensions you need to determine.

(A) The volumes of the parts of the rectangular prism are as follows:

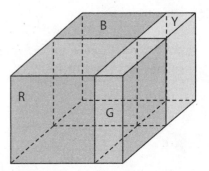

Red(R): $V = x^3$

Green(G): $V = 2x^2$

Yellow(Y): $V = 8x$

Blue(B): $V = 4x^2$

Total volume: $V = x^3 + 6x^2 + 8x$

(B) The volume of the red piece is found by cubing the length of one edge. What is the height of this piece?

_____

(C) The volume of a rectangular prism is $V = lwh$, where l is the length, w is the width, and h is the height of the prism. Notice that the green prism shares two dimensions with the cube. What are these dimensions?

_____

(D) What is the length of the third edge of the green prism?

_____

_____

(E) You showed that the width of the cube is _____ and the width of the green prism

is _____. What is the width of the entire prism?

_____

_____

You determined that the length of the green piece is x. Use the volume of the yellow piece and the information you have derived to find the length of the prism.

_____

_____

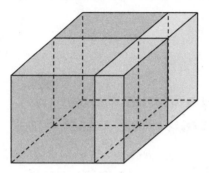

Ⓖ Since the dimensions of the overall prism are x, $x + 2$, and $x + 4$, the volume of the overall prism can be rewritten in factored form as $V = (x)(x + 2)(x + 4)$. Multiply these polynomials together to verify that this is equal to the original given expression for the volume of the overall figure.

_____

_____

Reflect

1. **Discussion** What is one way to double the volume of the prism?

_____

_____

⌾ Explain 1 Factoring Out the Greatest Common Monomial First

Most polynomials cannot be *factored over the integers*, which means to find factors that use only integer coefficients. But when a polynomial can be factored, each factor has a degree less than the polynomial's degree. While the goal is to write the polynomial as a product of linear factors, this is not always possible. When a factor of degree 2 or greater cannot be factored further, it is called an **irreducible factor**.

Example 1 Factor each polynomial over the integers.

Ⓐ $6x^3 + 15x^2 + 6x$

$6x^3 + 15x^2 + 6x$	Write out the polynomial.
$x(6x^2 + 15x + 6)$	Factor out a common monomial, an x.
$3x(2x^2 + 5x + 2)$	Factor out a common monomial, a 3.
$3x(2x + 1)(x + 2)$	Factor into simplest terms.

Note: The second and third steps can be combined into one step by factoring out the greatest common monomial.

Ⓑ $2x^3 - 20x$

$$\underline{\quad}^3 - \underline{\quad}x \qquad\qquad \text{Write out the polynomial.}$$

$$\underline{\quad}(x^2 - 10) \qquad\qquad \text{Factor out the greatest common monomial.}$$

Reflect

2. Why wasn't the factor $x^2 - 10$ further factored?

_____

_____

3. Consider what happens when you factor $x^2 - 10$ over the real numbers and not merely the integers. Find a such that $x^2 - 10 = (x - a)(x + a)$.

_____

Your Turn

4. $3x^3 + 7x^2 + 4x$

⚡ Explain 2 Recognizing Special Factoring Patterns

Remember the factoring patterns you already know:

Difference of two squares: $a^2 - b^2 = (a + b)(a - b)$

Perfect square trinomials: $a^2 + 2ab + b^2 = (a + b)^2$ and $a^2 - 2ab + b^2 = (a - b)^2$

There are two other factoring patterns that will prove useful:

Sum of two cubes: $a^3 + b^3 = (a + b)(a^2 - ab + b^2)$

Difference of two cubes: $a^3 - b^3 = (a - b)(a^2 + ab + b^2)$

Notice that in each of the new factoring patterns, the quadratic factor is irreducible over the integers.

Example 2 Factor the polynomial using a factoring pattern.

Ⓐ $27x^3 + 64$

$27x^3 + 64$ Write out the polynomial.

$27x^3 = (3x)^3$ Check if $27x^3$ is a perfect cube.

$64 = (4)^3$ Check if 64 is a perfect cube.

$a^3 + b^3 = (a + b)(a^2 - ab + b^2)$ Use the sum of two cubes formula to factor.

$(3x)^3 + 4^3 = (3x + 4)\big((3x)^2 - (3x)(4) + 4^2\big)$

$27x^3 + 64 = (3x + 4)(9x^2 - 12x + 16)$

Ⓑ $8x^3 - 27$

$$8\underline{}^3 - 27$$ Write out the polynomial.

$$8x^3 = (\underline{}x)^3$$ Check if $8x^3$ is a perfect cube.

$$27 = (\underline{})^3$$ Check if 27 is a perfect cube.

$$a^3 - b^3 = (a - b)(a^2 + ab + b^2)$$ Use the difference of two cubes formula to factor.

$$8x^3 - 27 = (\underline{}x - \underline{})(\underline{}x^2 + \underline{}x + \underline{})$$

Reflect

5. The equation $8x^3 - 27 = 0$ has three roots. How many of them are real, what are they, and how many are nonreal?

Your Turn

6. $40x^4 + 5x$

🛠 Explain 3   Factoring by Grouping

Another technique for factoring a polynomial is grouping. If the polynomial has pairs of terms with common factors, factor by grouping terms with common factors and then factoring out the common factor from each group. Then look for a common factor of the groups in order to complete the factorization of the polynomial.

Example 3   Factor the polynomial by grouping.

(A) $x^3 - x^2 + x - 1$

Write out the polynomial.	$x^3 - x^2 + x - 1$
Group by common factor.	$(x^3 - x^2) + (x - 1)$
Factor.	$x^2(x - 1) + 1(x - 1)$
Regroup.	$(x^2 + 1)(x - 1)$

(B) $x^4 + x^3 + x + 1$

Write out the polynomial.	$x^4 + x^3 + x + 1$
Group by common factor.	$(\underline{\quad} + \underline{\quad}) + (x + 1)$
Factor.	$\underline{\quad}(x + 1) + \underline{\quad}(x + 1)$
Regroup.	$(\underline{\quad} + \underline{\quad})(x + 1)$
Apply sum of two cubes to the first term.	$(\underline{\quad} - \underline{\quad} + 1)(x + 1)(x + 1)$
Substitute this into the expression and simplify.	$(\underline{\quad})^2(\underline{\quad}^2 - \underline{\quad} + 1)$

Your Turn

7. $x^3 + 3x^2 + 3x + 2$

🛠 Explain 4   Solving a Real-World Problem by Factoring a Polynomial

Remember that the zero-product property is used in solving factorable quadratic equations. It can also be used in solving factorable polynomial equations.

A water park is designing a new pool in the shape of a rectangular prism. The sides and bottom of the pool are made of material 5 feet thick. The interior length must be twice the interior height (depth), and the interior width must be three times the interior height. The volume of water that the pool holds must be 6000 cubic feet. What are the exterior dimensions of the pool?

Let x represent the exterior height of the pool, that is, including its bottom. Let h, l, and w represent the interior dimensions. Then the dimensions of the interior of the pool are the following:

$h = x - 5$

$l = 2x - 10$

$w = 3x - 15$

The formula for the volume of a rectangular prism is $V = lwh$. Plug the values into the volume equation.

$V = (2x - 10)(3x - 15)(x - 5)$

$V = (6x^2 - 60x + 150)(x - 5)$

$V = 6x^3 - 90x^2 + 450x - 750$

Now solve for $V = 6000$.

$6000 = 6x^3 - 90x^2 + 450x - 750$

$0 = 6x^3 - 90x^2 + 450x - 6750$

Factor the resulting new polynomial.

$6x^3 - 90x^2 + 450x - 6750$

$= 6x^2(x - 15) + 450(x - 15)$

$= (6x^2 + 450)(x - 15)$

The only real root is $x = 15$. This is the exterior height of the pool.

The interior height of the pool will be 10 feet, the interior length 20 feet, and the interior width 30 feet. Because each side wall of the pool is 5 feet thick, the exterior length is 30 feet and the exterior width is 40 feet.

 Engineering To build a hefty wooden feeding trough for a zoo, its sides and bottom should be 2 feet thick, and its outer length should be twice its outer width and height.

What should the outer dimensions of the trough be if it is to hold 288 cubic feet of water?

Volume = Interior Length(feet) · Interior Width(feet) · Interior Height(feet)

$288 = (\underline{\quad} - 4)(\underline{\quad} - 4)(\underline{\quad} - 2)$

$288 = \underline{\quad} x^3 - \underline{\quad} x^2 + \underline{\quad} x - \underline{\quad}$

$0 = \underline{\quad} x^3 - \underline{\quad} x^2 + \underline{\quad} x - \underline{\quad}$

$0 = \underline{\quad}(x - \underline{\quad}) + \underline{\quad}(x - \underline{\quad})$

$0 = \underline{\quad}(x^2 + \underline{\quad})(x - \underline{\quad})$

The only real solution is $x = \underline{\quad}$. The trough is $\underline{\quad}$ feet long, $\underline{\quad}$ feet wide, and $\underline{\quad}$ feet high.

8. **Engineering** A small bank vault is being designed in the shape of a rectangular prism. The vault's sides and top should all be 3 feet thick. The outer length of the vault should be twice the outer width. The outer height should be the same as the outer width.

   What should the outer dimensions of the vault be if it is to have 972 cubic feet of space?

Elaborate

9. Describe how the method of grouping incorporates the method of factoring out the greatest common monomial.

   _____

   _____

   _____

10. How do you decide if an equation fits in the sum of two cubes pattern?

    _____

    _____

11. How can factoring be used to solve a polynomial equation of the form $p(x) = a$, where a is a nonzero constant?

    _____

    _____

12. **Essential Question Check-In** What are two ways to factor a polynomial?

    _____

    _____

Factor the polynomial, or identify it as irreducible.

1. $x^3 + x^2 - 12x$

2. $x^3 + 5$

3. $x^3 - 125$

4. $x^3 + 5x^2 + 6x$

5. $8x^3 + 125$

6. $2x^3 + 6x$

7. $216x^3 + 64$

8. $8x^3 - 64$

9. $10x^3 - 80$

10. $2x^4 + 7x^3 + 5x^2$

11. $x^3 + 10x^2 + 16x$

12. $x^3 + 9769$

Factor the polynomial by grouping.

13. $x^3 + 8x^2 + 6x + 48$

14. $x^3 + 4x^2 - x - 4$

15. $8x^4 + 8x^3 + 27x + 27$

16. $27x^4 + 54x^3 - 64x - 128$

17. $x^3 + 2x^2 + 3x + 6$

18. $4x^4 - 4x^3 - x + 1$

Write and solve a polynomial equation for the situation described.

19. Engineering A rectangular two-story horse barn is being designed for a farm. The upper floor will be used for storing hay, and the lower floor will have horse stalls that extend 5 feet from both of the longer walls. The barn's length is twice the barn's width, and the lower floor's ceiling height is 6 feet less than the barn's width. What should the dimensions of the lower floor be if the space not used for stalls is to have a volume of 1920 cubic feet?

20. Arts A piece of rectangular crafting supply is being cut for a new sculpture. You want its length to be 4 times its height and its width to be 2 times its height. If you want the wood to have a volume of 64 cubic centimeters, what will its length, width, and height be?

21. Engineering A new rectangular holding tank is being built. The tank's sides and bottom should be 1 foot thick. Its outer length should be twice its outer width and height.

What should the outer dimensions of the tank be if it is to have a volume of 36 cubic feet?

22. Construction A piece of granite is being cut for a building foundation. You want its length to be 8 times its height and its width to be 3 times its height. If you want the granite to have a volume of 648 cubic yards, what will its length, width, and height be?

23. State which, if any, special factoring pattern each of the following polynomial expressions follows:

a. $x^2 - 4$

b. $3x^3 + 5$

c. $4x^2 + 25$

d. $27x^3 + 1000$

e. $64x^3 - x^2 + 1$

H.O.T. Focus on Higher Order Thinking

24. Communicate Mathematical Ideas What is the relationship between the degree of a polynomial and the degree of its factors?

25. Critical Thinking Why is there no sum-of-two-squares factoring pattern?

26. Explain the Error Jim was trying to factor a polynomial and produced the following result:

$3x^3 + x^2 + 3x + 1$ Write out the polynomial.

$3x^2(x + 1) + 3(x + 1)$ Group by common factor.

$3(x^2 + 1)(x + 1)$ Regroup.

Explain Jim's error.

27. Factoring can also be done over the complex numbers. This allows you to find all the roots of an equation, not just the real ones.

Complete the steps showing how to use a special factor identity to factor $x^2 + 4$ over the complex numbers.

$x^2 + 4$ Write out the polynomial.

$x^2 - (-4)$ _____

$(x + \underline{\hspace{1cm}})(x - \underline{\hspace{1cm}})$ Factor.

$(x + 2i)(\underline{\hspace{1cm}})$ Simplify.

28. Find all the imaginary roots of the equation $x^4 - 16 = 0$.

29. Factor $x^3 + x^2 + x + 1$ over the complex numbers.

Lesson Performance Task

Sabrina is building a rectangular raised flower bed. The boards on the two shorter sides are 6 inches thick, and the boards on the two longer sides are 4 inches thick. Sabrina wants the outer length of her bed to be 4 times its height and the outer width to be 2 times its height. She also wants the boards to rise 4 inches above the level of the soil in the bed. What should the outer dimensions of the bed be if she wants it to hold 3136 cubic inches of soil?

Name_____ Class_____ Date_____

6.5 Dividing Polynomials

Essential Question: What are some ways to divide polynomials, and how do you know when the divisor is a factor of the dividend?

Resource
Locker

⊘ Explore Evaluating a Polynomial Function Using Synthetic Substitution

Polynomials can be written in something called nested form. A polynomial in nested form is written in such a way that evaluating it involves an alternating sequence of additions and multiplications. For instance, the nested form of $p(x) = 4x^3 + 3x^2 + 2x + 1$ is $p(x) = x\left(x(4x + 3) + 2\right) + 1$, which you evaluate by starting with 4, multiplying by the value of x, adding 3, multiplying by x, adding 2, multiplying by x, and adding 1.

(A) Given $p(x) = 4x^3 + 3x^2 + 2x + 1$, find $p(-2)$.

_____

_____

_____

_____

_____

_____

You can set up an array of numbers that captures the sequence of multiplications and additions needed to find $p(a)$. Using this array to find $p(a)$ is called **synthetic substitution**.

Given $p(x) = 4x^3 + 3x^2 + 2x + 1$, find $p(-2)$ by using synthetic substitution. The dashed arrow indicates bringing down, the diagonal arrows represent multiplication by -2, and the solid down arrows indicate adding.

The first two steps are to bring down the leading number, 4, then multiply by the value you are evaluating at, -2.

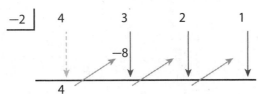

(B) Add 3 and -8.

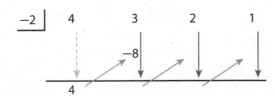

Module 6

321

Lesson 5

(C) Multiply the previous answer by –2.

(D) Continue this sequence of steps until you reach the last addition.

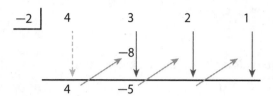

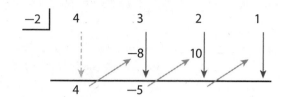

(E) $p(-2) = \boxed{}$

Reflect

1. **Discussion** After the final addition, what does this sum correspond to?

_____

_____

⚙ Explain 1 Dividing Polynomials Using Long Division

Recall that arithmetic long division proceeds as follows.

$$
\begin{array}{r}
\text{Divisor} \quad \quad 23 \leftarrow \text{Quotient} \\
12\overline{)\,277\,} \leftarrow \text{Dividend} \\
\underline{24} \\
37 \\
\underline{36} \\
1 \leftarrow \text{Remainder}
\end{array}
$$

Notice that the long division leads to the result $\frac{dividend}{divisor} = quotient + \frac{remainder}{divisor}$. Using the numbers from above, the arithmetic long division leads to $\frac{277}{12} = 23 + \frac{1}{12}$. Multiplying through by the divisor yields the result $dividend = (divisor)(quotient) + remainder$. (This can be used as a means of checking your work.)

Example 1 Given a polynomial divisor and dividend, use long division to find the quotient and remainder. Write the result in the form $dividend = (divisor)(quotient) + remainder$ and then carry out the multiplication and addition as a check.

(A) $\left(4x^3 + 2x^2 + 3x + 5\right) \div \left(x^2 + 3x + 1\right)$

Begin by writing the dividend in standard form, including terms with a coefficient of 0 (if any).

$4x^3 + 2x^2 + 3x + 5$

Write division in the same way as you would when dividing numbers.

$$x^2 + 3x + 1 \overline{)\,4x^3 + 2x^2 + 3x + 5\,}$$

Find the value you need to multiply the divisor by so that the first term matches with the first term of the dividend. In this case, in order to get $4x^2$, we must multiply x^2 by $4x$. This will be the first term of the quotient.

$$\begin{array}{r} 4x \phantom{{}+ 2x^2 + 3x + 5} \\ x^2 + 3x + 1 \overline{)\, 4x^3 + 2x^2 + 3x + 5} \end{array}$$

Next, multiply the divisor through by the term of the quotient you just found and subtract that value from the dividend. $(x^2 + 3x + 1)(4x) = 4x^3 + 12x^2 + 4x$, so subtract $4x^3 + 12x^2 + 4x$ from $4x^3 + 2x^2 + 3x + 5$.

$$\begin{array}{r} 4x \phantom{{}+ 2x^2 + 3x + 5} \\ x^2 + 3x + 1 \overline{)\, 4x^3 + 2x^2 + 3x + 5} \\ \underline{-\left(4x^3 + 12x^2 + 4x\right)} \\ -10x^2 - x + 5 \end{array}$$

Taking this difference as the new dividend, continue in this fashion until the largest term of the remaining dividend is of lower degree than the divisor.

$$\begin{array}{r} 4x - 10 \\ x^2 + 3x + 1 \overline{)\, 4x^3 + 2x^2 + 3x + 5} \\ \underline{-\left(4x^3 + 12x^2 + 4x\right)} \\ -10x^2 - x + 5 \\ \underline{-\left(-10x^2 - 30x - 10\right)} \\ 29x + 15 \end{array}$$

Since $29x + 5$ is of lower degree than $x^2 + 3x + 1$, stop. $29x + 15$ is the remainder.

Write the final answer.

$$4x^3 + 2x^2 + 3x + 5 = \left(x^2 + 3x + 1\right)(4x - 10) + 29x + 15$$

Check.

$$4x^3 + 2x^2 + 3x + 5 = \left(x^2 + 3x + 1\right)(4x - 10) + 29x + 15$$
$$= 4x^3 + 12x^2 + 4x - 10x^2 - 30x - 10 + 29x + 15$$
$$= 4x^3 + 2x^2 + 3x + 5$$

Ⓑ $\left(6x^4 + 5x^3 + 2x + 8\right) \div \left(x^2 + 2x - 5\right)$

Write the dividend in standard form, including terms with a coefficient of 0.

$$\boxed{}$$

Write the division in the same way as you would when dividing numbers.

$$x^2 + 2x - 5 \overline{)\, 6x^4 + 5x^3 + 0x^2 + 2x + 8}$$

Divide.

$$
\begin{array}{r}
6x^2 - \boxed{} + \boxed{} \\[4pt]
x^2 + 2x - 5 \overline{)\, 6x^4 + 5x^3 + 0x^2 + 2x + 8}
\end{array}
$$

$$-\left(6x^4 + 12x^3 - 30x^2\right)$$

$$-7x^3 + 30x^2 + 2x$$

$$-\left(-7x^3 \ \boxed{}\,\right)$$

$$\boxed{} + 8$$

$$-\left(\boxed{}\right)$$

$$\boxed{}$$

Write the final answer.

$$6x^4 + 5x^3 + 2x + 8 = \boxed{}$$

Check.

Reflect

2. How do you include the terms with coefficients of 0?

_____

_____

Your Turn

Use long division to find the quotient and remainder. Write the result in the form *dividend* $=$ (*divisor*)(*quotient*) $+$ *remainder* and then carry out a check.

3. $\left(15x^3 + 8x - 12\right) \div \left(3x^2 + 6x + 1\right)$

4. $\left(9x^4 + x^3 + 11x^2 - 4\right) \div \left(x^2 + 16\right)$

Explain 2 **Dividing $p(x)$ by $x - a$ Using Synthetic Division**

Compare long division with synthetic substitution. There are two important things to notice. The first is that $p(a)$ is equal to the remainder when $p(x)$ is divided by $x - a$. The second is that the numbers to the left of $p(a)$ in the bottom row of the synthetic substitution array give the coefficients of the quotient. For this reason, synthetic substitution is also called **synthetic division**.

Long Division	Synthetic Substitution
$\begin{array}{r} 3x^2 + 10x + 20 \\ x - 2 \overline{)\, 3x^3 + 4x^2 + 0x + 10} \\ \underline{-\left(3x^3 - 6x^2\right)} \\ 10x^2 + 0x \\ \underline{-\left(10x^2 - 20x\right)} \\ 20x + 10 \\ \underline{-20x - 40} \\ 50 \end{array}$	$\begin{array}{r} \underline{2\,|}\;\; 3\quad 4\quad 0\quad 10 \\ 6\quad 20\quad 40 \\ \hline 3\;\; 10\;\; 20\;\underline{|\;50} \end{array}$

Example 2 Given a polynomial $p(x)$, use synthetic division to divide by $x - a$ and obtain the quotient and the (nonzero) remainder. Write the result in the form $p(x) = (x - a)(quotient) + p(a)$, then carry out the multiplication and addition as a check.

(A) $\left(7x^3 - 6x + 9\right) \div (x + 5)$

By inspection, $a = -5$. Write the coefficients and a in the synthetic division format.

$$\underline{-5\,|}\qquad 7\quad 0\quad -6\quad 9$$

Bring down the first coefficient. Then multiply and add for each column.

$$\begin{array}{r} \underline{-5\,|}\qquad 7\qquad 0\qquad -6\qquad 9 \\ -35\quad 175\quad -845 \\ \hline 7\quad -35\quad 169\;\underline{|-836} \end{array}$$

Write the result, using the non-remainder entries of the bottom row as the coefficients.

$$\left(7x^3 - 6x + 9\right) = (x + 5)\left(7x^2 - 35x + 169\right) - 836$$

Check.

$$\left(7x^3 - 6x + 9\right) = (x + 5)\left(7x^2 - 35x + 169\right) - 836$$

$$= 7x^3 - 35x^2 - 35x^2 - 175x + 169x + 845 - 836$$

$$= 7x^3 - 6x + 9$$

(B) $\left(4x^4 - 3x^2 + 7x + 2\right) \div \left(x - \dfrac{1}{2}\right)$

Find a. Then write the coefficients and a in the synthetic division format.

Find $a =$ ☐

$$\underline{} \rfloor \quad 4 \quad 0 \quad -3 \quad 7 \quad 2$$

Bring down the first coefficient. Then multiply and add for each column.

$$\underline{} \rfloor 4 \quad 0 \quad -3 \quad 7 \quad 2$$

$$4 \qquad\qquad \llcorner$$

Write the result.

$\left(4x^4 - 3x^2 + 7x + 2\right) =$ ☐

Check.

Reflect

5. Can you use synthetic division to divide a polynomial by $x^2 + 3$? Explain.

_____

Your Turn

Given a polynomial $p(x)$, use synthetic division to divide by $x - a$ and obtain the quotient and the (nonzero) remainder. Write the result in the form $p(x) = (x - a)(quotient) + p(a)$. You may wish to perform a check.

6. $\left(2x^3 + 5x^2 - x + 7\right) \div (x - 2)$

7. $\left(6x^4 - 25x^3 - 3x + 5\right) \div \left(x + \dfrac{1}{3}\right)$

Using the Remainder Theorem and Factor Theorem

When $p(x)$ is divided by $x - a$, the result can be written in the form $p(x) = (x - a)q(x) + r$ where $q(x)$ is the quotient and r is a number. Substituting a for x in this equation gives $p(a) = (a - a)q(a) + r$. Since $a - a = 0$, this simplifies to $p(a) = r$. This is known as the **Remainder Theorem**.

If the remainder $p(a)$ in $p(x) = (x - a)q(x) + p(a)$ is 0, then $p(x) = (x - a)q(x)$, which tells you that $x - a$ is a factor of $p(x)$. Conversely, if $x - a$ is a factor of $p(x)$, then you can write $p(x)$ as $p(x) = (x - a)q(x)$, and when you divide $p(x)$ by $x - a$, you get the quotient $q(x)$ with a remainder of 0. These facts are known as the Factor Theorem .

Example 3 Determine whether the given binomial is a factor of the polynomial $p(x)$. If so, find the remaining factors of $p(x)$.

Ⓐ $p(x) = x^3 + 3x^2 - 4x - 12; (x + 3)$

Use synthetic division.

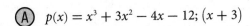

$$\begin{array}{r|rrrr} -3 & 1 & 3 & -4 & -12 \\ & & -3 & 0 & 12 \\ \hline & 1 & 0 & -4 & \enclose{box}{0} \end{array}$$

Since the remainder is 0, $x + 3$ is a factor.

Write $q(x)$ and then factor it.

$q(x) = x^2 - 4 = (x + 2)(x - 2)$

So, $p(x) = x^3 + 3x^2 - 4x - 12 = (x + 2)(x - 2)(x + 3)$.

Ⓑ $p(x) = x^4 - 4x^3 - 6x^2 + 4x + 5; (x + 1)$

Use synthetic division.

$$\begin{array}{r|rrrrr} -1 & 1 & -4 & -6 & 4 & 5 \\ & & & & & \\ \hline & 1 & & & \enclose{box}{} \end{array}$$

Since the remainder is _____, $(x + 1)$ _____ a factor. Write $q(x)$.

$q(x) = $ [ ]

Now factor $q(x)$ by grouping.

$q(x) = $ [ ]

$= $ [ ]

$= $ [ ]

$= $ [ ]

So, $p(x) = x^4 - 4x^3 - 6x^2 + 4x + 5 = $ [ ].

Determine whether the given binomial is a factor of the polynomial $p(x)$. If it is, find the remaining factors of $p(x)$.

8. $p(x) = 2x^4 + 8x^3 + 2x + 8; (x + 4)$

9. $p(x) = 3x^3 - 2x + 5; (x - 1)$

Elaborate

10. Compare long division and synthetic division of polynomials.

11. How does knowing one linear factor of a polynomial help find the other factors?

12. What conditions must be met in order to use synthetic division?

13. **Essential Question Check-In** How do you know when the divisor is a factor of the dividend?

Given $p(x)$, find $p(-3)$ by using synthetic substitution.

1. $p(x) = 8x^3 + 7x^2 + 2x + 4$

2. $p(x) = x^3 + 6x^2 + 7x - 25$

3. $p(x) = 2x^3 + 5x^2 - 3x$

4. $p(x) = -x^4 + 5x^3 - 8x + 45$

Given a polynomial divisor and dividend, use long division to find the quotient and remainder. Write the result in the form $dividend = (divisor)(quotient) + remainder$. You may wish to carry out a check.

5. $(18x^3 - 3x^2 + x - 1) \div (x^2 - 4)$

6. $(6x^4 + x^3 - 9x + 13) \div (x^2 + 8)$

7. $\left(x^4 + 6x - 2.5\right) \div \left(x^2 + 3x + 0.5\right)$

8. $\left(x^3 + 250x^2 + 100x\right) \div \left(\frac{1}{2}x^2 + 25x + 9\right)$

Given a polynomial $p(x)$, use synthetic division to divide by $x - a$ and obtain the quotient and the (nonzero) remainder. Write the result in the form $p(x) = (x - a)(\text{quotient}) + p(a)$. You may wish to carry out a check.

9. $\left(7x^3 - 4x^2 - 400x - 100\right) \div (x - 8)$

10. $\left(8x^4 - 28.5x^2 - 9x + 10\right) \div (x + 0.25)$

11. $\left(2.5x^3 + 6x^2 - 5.5x - 10\right) \div (x + 1)$

Determine whether the given binomial is a factor of the polynomial $p(x)$.
If so, find the remaining factors of $p(x)$.

12. $p(x) = x^3 + 2x^2 - x - 2; (x + 2)$

13. $p(x) = 2x^4 + 6x^3 - 5x - 10; (x + 2)$

14. $p(x) = x^3 - 22x^2 + 157x - 360; (x - 8)$

15. $p(x) = 4x^3 - 12x^2 + 2x - 5; (x - 3)$

16. The volume of a rectangular prism whose dimensions are binomials with integer coefficients is modeled by the function $V(x) = x^3 - 8x^2 + 19x - 12$.
Given that $x - 1$ and $x - 3$ are two of the dimensions, find the missing dimension of the prism.

17. Given that the height of a rectangular prism is $x + 2$ and the volume is $x^3 - x^2 - 6x$, write an expression that represents the area of the base of the prism.

18. Physics A Van de Graaff generator is a machine that produces very high voltages by using small, safe levels of electric current. One machine has a current that can be modeled by $I(t) = t + 2$, where $t > 0$ represents time in seconds. The power of the system can be modeled by $P(t) = 0.5t^3 + 6t^2 + 10t$. Write an expression that represents the voltage of the system. Recall that $V = \frac{P}{I}$.

19. Geometry The volume of a hexagonal pyramid is modeled by the function $V(x) = \frac{1}{3}x^3 + \frac{4}{3}x^2 + \frac{2}{3}x - \frac{1}{3}$. Given the height $x + 1$, use polynomial division to find an expression for the area of the base.

(Hint: For a pyramid, $V = \frac{1}{3}Bh$.)

20. Explain the Error Two students used synthetic division to divide $3x^3 - 2x - 8$ by $x - 2$. Determine which solution is correct. Find the error in the other solution.

A.			
2⌋	3 0 −2 −8		
	6 12 20		
	3 6 10 12		

B.			
−2⌋	3 0 −2 −8		
	−6 12 −20		
	3 −6 10 −28		

21. Multi-Step Use synthetic division to divide $p(x) = 3x^3 - 11x^2 - 56x - 50$ by $(3x + 4)$. Then check the solution.

22. Critical Thinking The polynomial $ax^3 + bx^2 + cx + d$ is factored as $3(x - 2)(x + 3)(x - 4)$. What are the values of a and d? Explain.

23. Analyze Relationships Investigate whether the set of whole numbers, the set of integers, and the set of rational numbers are closed under each of the four basic operations. Then consider whether the set of polynomials in one variable is closed under the four basic operations, and determine whether polynomials are like whole numbers, integers, or rational numbers with respect to closure. Use the table to organize.

	Whole Numbers	Integers	Rational Numbers	Polynomials
Addition				
Subtraction				
Multiplication				
Division (by nonzero)				

Lesson Performance Task

The table gives the attendance data for all divisions of NCAA Women's Basketball.

NCAA Women's Basketball Attendance			
Season	Years since 2006–2007	Number of teams in all 3 divisions	Attendance (in thousands) for all 3 divisions
2006–2007	0	1003	10,878.3
2007–2008	1	1013	11,120.8
2008–2009	2	1032	11,160.3
2009–2010	3	1037	11,134.7
2010–2011	4	1048	11,160.0
2011–2012	5	1055	11,201.8

Enter the data from the second, third, and fourth columns of the table and perform linear regression on the data pairs (t, T) and cubic regression on the data pairs (t, A) where $t =$ years since the 2006–2007 season, $T =$ number of teams, and $A =$ attendance (in thousands).

Then create a model for the average attendance per team: $A_{avg}(t) = \frac{A(t)}{T(t)}$. Carry out the division to write $A_{avg}(t)$ in the form $quadratic\ quotient + \frac{remainder}{T(t)}$.

Use an online computer algebra system to carry out the division of $A(t)$ by $T(t)$.

Polynomials

Essential Question: How can you use polynomials to solve real-world problems?

Key Vocabulary

binomial *(binomio)*

monomial *(monomio)*

polynomial *(polinomio)*

synthetic division *(división sintética)*

trinomial *(trinomio)*

KEY EXAMPLE *(Lesson 6.1)*

Subtract: $(5x^4 - x^3 + 2x + 1) - (2x^3 + 3x^2 - 4x - 7)$

$$
\begin{array}{l}
5x^4 - x^3 + 0x^2 + 2x + 1 \\
\underline{+ -2x^3 - 3x^2 + 4x + 7} \\
5x^4 - 3x^3 - 3x^2 + 6x + 8
\end{array}
$$

Write in standard form.

Align like terms and add the opposite.

Add.

Therefore, $(5x^4 - x^3 + 2x + 1) - (2x^3 + 3x^2 - 4x - 7) = 5x^4 - 3x^3 - 3x^2 + 6x + 8$.

KEY EXAMPLE *(Lesson 6.2)*

Multiply: $(3x - 2)(2x^2 - 5x + 1)$

$(3x - 2)(2x^2 - 5x + 1)$

$3x(2x^2) + 3x(-5x) + 3x(1) + (-2)(2x^2) + (-2)(-5x) + (-2)(1)$

$6x^3 - 15x^2 + 3x - 4x^2 + 10x - 2$

$6x^3 - 19x^2 + 13x - 2$

Write in standard form.

Distribute the 3x and the −2.

Simplify.

Combine like terms.

Therefore, $(3x - 2)(2x^2 - 5x + 1) = 6x^3 - 19x^2 + 13x - 2$.

KEY EXAMPLE *(Lesson 6.5)*

Divide: $(x^3 + 10x^2 + 13x + 36) \div (x + 9)$

$$
\begin{array}{r}
x^2 + x + 4 \\
x + 9 \overline{\smash{)}\, x^3 + 10x^2 + 13x + 36} \\
\underline{-(x^3 + 9x^2)} \\
x^2 + 13x \\
\underline{-(x^2 + 9x)} \\
4x + 36 \\
\underline{-(4x + 36)} \\
0
\end{array}
$$

In order to get x^3, multiply by x^2.

Multiply the divisor through by x^2, then subtract.

In order to get x^2, multiply by x.

Multiply the divisor through by x, then subtract.

In order to get $4x$, multiply by 4.

Multiply the divisor through by 4, then subtract.

Therefore, $(x^3 + 10x^2 + 13x + 36) \div (x + 9) = x^2 + x + 4$.

EXERCISES

Simplify. *(Lessons 6.1, 6.2, 6.5)*

1. $(9x^2 + 2x + 12) + (7x^2 + 10x - 13)$

2. $(6x^6 - 4x^5) - (10x^5 - 15x^4 + 8)$

3. $(x - 3)(4x^2 - 2x + 3)$

4. $(9x^4 + 27x^3 + 23x^2 + 10x) \div (x^2 + 2x)$

5. Mr. Alonzo runs a car repair garage. The average income from repairing a car can be modeled by $C(x) = 45x + 150$. If, for one year, the number of cars repaired can be modeled by $N(x) = 9x^2 + 7x + 6$, write a polynomial that can be used to model Mr. Alonzo's business income for that year. Explain. *(Lesson 6.2)*

MODULE PERFORMANCE TASK

What's the Temperature?

A meteorologist studying the temperature patterns for Redding, California, found the average of the daily minimum and maximum temperatures for each month, but the August temperatures are missing.

Month	Jan	Feb	Mar	Apr	May	June	July	Aug	Sep	Oct	Nov	Dec
Average Max Temperature (°F)	55.3	61.3	62.5	69.6	80.5	90.4	98.3	?	89.3	77.6	62.1	54.7
Average Min Temperature (°F)	35.7	40	41.7	46	52.3	61.8	64.7	?	58.8	49.2	41.4	35.2

How can she find the averages for August? She began by fitting the polynomial function shown below to the data for the average maximum temperature, where x is the month, with $x = 1$ corresponding to January, and the temperature is in degrees Fahrenheit.

$$T_{max}(x) = 0.0095x^5 - 0.2719x^4 + 2.5477x^3 - 9.1882x^2 + 17.272x + 45.468$$

She also thinks that a vertical compression of this function will create a function that fits the average minimum temperature data for Redding.

Use this information to find the average high and low temperature for August. Use graphs, numbers, words, or algebra to explain how you reached your conclusion.

(Ready) to Go On?

6.1–6.5 Polynomials

Factor the polynomial. *(Lesson 6.4)*

1. $3x^2 + 4x - 4$

2. $2x^3 + 4x^2 - 30x$

3. $9x^2 - 25$

4. $4x^2 - 16x + 16$

Complete the polynomial operation. *(Lesson 6.1, 6.2, 6.3, 6.5)*

5. $(8x^3 - 2x^2 - 4x + 8) + (5x^2 + 6x - 4)$

6. $(-4x^2 - 2x + 8) - (x^2 + 8x - 5)$

7. $5x(x + 2)(3x - 7)$

8. $(3x^3 + 12x^2 + 11x - 2) \div (x + 2)$

9. $(x + y)^6$

ESSENTIAL QUESTION

10. Write a real-world situation that would require adding polynomials. *(Lesson 6.1)*

Assessment Readiness

1. Look at each polynomial division problem. Can the polynomials be divided without a remainder?
   Select Yes or No for A–C.

   A. $(3x^3 - 5x^2 + 10x + 4) \div (3x + 1)$ ◯ Yes ◯ No

   B. $(2x^2 - 5x - 1) \div (x - 3)$ ◯ Yes ◯ No

   C. $(x^3 - 4x^2 + 2x - 3) \div (x + 2)$ ◯ Yes ◯ No

2. Consider the polynomial $x^3 - x^2 - 6x$.
   Select True or False for each statement.

   A. $6x$ can be factored out of every term. ◯ True ◯ False

   B. The completely factored polynomial is
   $x(x + 2)(x - 3)$. ◯ True ◯ False

   C. $f(x) = x^3 - x^2 - 6x$
   has a global minimum. ◯ True ◯ False

3. Alana completed a problem where she had to find the sum of the polynomials $(3x^2 + 8x - 4)$ and $(-8x^3 - 3x + 4)$. Her answer is 0. Describe and correct her mistake. When graphed, how many times does the sum change directions?

4. A rectangular plot of land has a length of $(2x^2 + 5x - 20)$ and a width of $(3x + 4)$. What polynomial represents the area of the plot of land? Explain how you got your answer.

Polynomial Equations

Essential Question: How can you use polynomial equations to solve real-world problems?

REAL WORLD VIDEO
The population of the Texas horned lizard has decreased rapidly, and the species is now considered threatened. Biologists use polynomials and other mathematical models to study threatened and endangered species.

MODULE PERFORMANCE TASK PREVIEW
What Do Polynomials Have to Do with Endangered Species?

A species is considered to be endangered when the population is so low that the species is at risk of becoming extinct. Biologists use mathematics to model the population of species, and they use their models to help them predict the future population and to determine whether or not a species is at risk of extinction. How can a polynomial be used to model a species population? Let's find out!

JeppsonShutterstock

Are YOU Ready?

Complete these exercises to review skills you will need for this module.

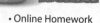

Real Numbers

Example 1

Compare $2\sqrt{64}$ and $\sqrt{225}$.

$2\sqrt{64} = 2 \cdot 8$ and $\sqrt{225} = 15$ Evaluate the radicals.

$16 > 15$ Multiply and compare.

Since $16 > 15$, $2\sqrt{64} > \sqrt{225}$.

Compare. Use $>$ or $<$.

1. $4\sqrt{25}$ _____ $25\sqrt{4}$

2. $0.75\sqrt{144}$ _____ $8\sqrt{16}$

3. $2.2\sqrt{100}$ _____ $3\sqrt{36}$

Add and Subtract Rational Numbers

Example 2

Add $\dfrac{3}{4} + \dfrac{5}{6}$.

$\left(\dfrac{3}{3}\right) \cdot \dfrac{3}{4} + \left(\dfrac{2}{2}\right) \cdot \dfrac{5}{6}$ The LCM is 12. Multiply by 1.

$\dfrac{9}{12} + \dfrac{10}{12}$ Add.

$\dfrac{19}{12}$

Add or subtract.

4. $\dfrac{1}{3} + \dfrac{5}{8}$

5. $\dfrac{7}{12} - \dfrac{4}{9}$

6. $\dfrac{9}{8} - \dfrac{5}{6}$

_____

_____

_____

Solving Quadratic Equations by Factoring

Example 3

Solve $x^2 + 3x - 10 = 0$ for x.

$(x - 2)(x + 5) = 0$ Factor.

Either $(x - 2) = 0$ or $(x + 5) = 0$

$x = 2$ or $x = -5$ Solve.

The solutions for x are 2 and −5.

Solve for x.

7. $x^2 - 5x + 4 = 0$

8. $x^2 + 11x + 30 = 0$

9. $x^2 + 6x = 16$

_____

_____

_____

7.1 Finding Rational Solutions of Polynomial Equations

Resource Locker

Essential Question: How do you find the rational roots of a polynomial equation?

Explore   Relating Zeros and Coefficients of Polynomial Functions

The zeros of a polynomial function and the coefficients of the function are related. Consider the polynomial function $f(x) = (x + 2)(x - 1)(x + 3)$.

(A) Identify the zeros of the polynomial function. _____

(B) Multiply the factors to write the function in standard form.

(C) How are the zeros of $f(x)$ related to the standard form of the function? _____

_____

(D) Now consider the polynomial function $g(x) = (2x + 3)(4x - 5)(6x - 1)$. Identify the zeros of this function.

_____

(E) Multiply the factors to write the function in standard form.

(F) How are the zeros of $g(x)$ related to the standard form of the function?

_____

_____

Reflect

1. In general, how are the zeros of a polynomial function related to the function written in standard form?

_____

_____

2. Discussion Does the relationship from the first Reflect question hold if the zeros are all integers? Explain.

_____

_____

3. If you use the zeros, you can write the factored form of $g(x)$ as $g(x) = \left(x + \frac{3}{2}\right)\left(x - \frac{5}{4}\right)\left(x - \frac{1}{6}\right)$, rather than as $g(x) = (2x + 3)(4x - 5)(6x - 1)$. What is the relationship of the factors between the two forms? Give this relationship in a general form.

_____

_____

⊘ Explain 1   Finding Zeros Using the Rational Zero Theorem

If a polynomial function $p(x)$ is equal to $(a_1x + b_1)(a_2x + b_2)(a_3x + b_3)$, where $a_1, a_2, a_3, b_1, b_2,$ and b_3 are integers, the leading coefficient of $p(x)$ will be the product $a_1a_2a_3$ and the constant term will be the product $b_1b_2b_3$. The zeros of $p(x)$ will be the rational numbers $-\frac{b_1}{a_1}, -\frac{b_2}{a_2}, -\frac{b_3}{a_3}$.

Comparing the zeros of $p(x)$ to its coefficient and constant term shows that the numerators of the polynomial's zeros are factors of the constant term and the denominators of the zeros are factors of the leading coefficient. This result can be generalized as the Rational Zero Theorem.

Rational Zero Theorem

If $p(x)$ is a polynomial function with integer coefficients, and if $\frac{m}{n}$ is a zero of $p(x)$ $\left(p\left(\frac{m}{n}\right) = 0\right)$, then m is a factor of the constant term of $p(x)$ and n is a factor of the leading coefficient of $p(x)$.

Example 1 Find the rational zeros of the polynomial function; then write the function as a product of factors. Make sure to test the possible zeros to find the actual zeros of the function.

(A) $f(x) = x^3 + 2x^2 - 19x - 20$

    a. Use the Rational Zero Theorem to find all possible rational zeros.
    Factors of -20: $\pm 1, \pm 2, \pm 4, \pm 5, \pm 10, \pm 20$

    b. Test the possible zeros. Use a synthetic division table to organize the work. In this table, the first row (shaded) represents the coefficients of the polynomial, the first column represents the divisors, and the last column represents the remainders.

$\dfrac{m}{n}$	1	2	-19	-20
1	1	3	-16	-36
2	1	4	-11	-42
4	1	6	5	0
5	1	7	16	60

c. Factor the polynomial. The synthetic division by 4 results in a remainder of 0, so 4 is a zero and the polynomial in factored form is given as follows:

$$(x - 4)(x^2 + 6x + 5) = 0$$

$$(x - 4)(x + 5)(x + 1) = 0$$

$$x = 4, x = -5, \text{ or } x = -1$$

The zeros are $x = 4$, $x = -5$, and $x = -1$.

B $f(x) = x^4 - 4x^3 - 7x^2 + 22x + 24$

a. Use the Rational Zero Theorem to find all possible rational zeros.

Factors of 24: $\pm$_____, $\pm$_____, $\pm$_____, $\pm$_____, $\pm$_____, $\pm$_____, $\pm$_____, $\pm$_____

b. Test the possible zeros. Use a synthetic division table.

$\dfrac{m}{n}$	1	−4	−7	22	24
1					
2					
3					

c. Factor the polynomial. The synthetic division by _____ results in a remainder of 0, so _____ is a zero and the polynomial in factored form is given as follows:

$$(x - \text{_____})(x^3 - x^2 - \text{_____}x - \text{_____}) = 0$$

d. Use the Rational Zero Theorem again to find all possible rational zeros of

$$g(x) = x^3 - x^2 - \text{_____}x - \text{_____}.$$

Factors of −8: $\pm$_____, $\pm$_____, $\pm$_____, $\pm$_____

e. Test the possible zeros. Use a synthetic division table.

$\dfrac{m}{n}$	1	−1	−10	−8
1				
2				
4				

f. Factor the polynomial. The synthetic division by _____ results in a remainder of 0, so _____ is a zero and the polynomial in factored form is:

$$(x - \text{_____})(x - \text{_____})(\text{_____}x^2 + \text{_____}x + \text{_____}) = 0$$

$$(x - \text{_____})(x - \text{_____})(x + \text{_____})(x + \text{_____}) = 0$$

$$x = \text{_____}, x = \text{_____}, x = \text{_____}, \text{ or } x = \text{_____}$$

The zeros are _____.

4. How is using synthetic division on a 4th degree polynomial to find its zeros different than using synthetic division on a 3rd degree polynomial to find its zeros?

_____

_____

_____

5. Suppose you are trying to find the zeros the function $f(x) = x^2 + 1$. Would it be possible to use synthetic division on this polynomial? Why or why not?

_____

_____

6. Using synthetic division, you find that $\frac{1}{2}$ is a zero of $f(x) = 2x^3 + x^2 - 13x + 6$. The quotient from the synthetic division array for $f\left(\frac{1}{2}\right)$ is $2x^2 + 2x - 12$. Show how to write the factored form of $f(x) = 2x^3 + x^2 - 13x + 6$ using integer coefficients.

7. Find the zeros of $f(x) = x^3 + 3x^2 - 13x - 15$.

Explain 2 · Solving a Real-World Problem Using the Rational Root Theorem

Since a zero of a function $f(x)$ is a value of x for which $f(x) = 0$, finding the zeros of a polynomial function $p(x)$ is the same thing as find the solutions of the polynomial equation $p(x) = 0$. Because a solution of a polynomial equation is known as a **root**, the Rational Zero Theorem can be also expressed as the Rational Root Theorem.

Rational Root Theorem

If the polynomial $p(x)$ has integer coefficients, then every rational root of the polynomial equation $p(x) = 0$ can be written in the form $\frac{m}{n}$, where m is a factor of the constant term of $p(x)$ and n is a factor of the leading coefficient of $p(x)$.

Engineering A pen company is designing a gift container for their new premium pen. The marketing department has designed a pyramidal box with a rectangular base. The base width is 1 inch shorter than its base length and the height is 3 inches taller than 3 times the base length. The volume of the box must be 6 cubic inches. What are the dimensions of the box? Graph the volume function and the line $y = 6$ on a graphing calculator to check your solution.

A. Analyze Information

The important information is that the base width must be _____ inch shorter than

the base length, the height must be _____ inches taller than 3 times the base length,

and the box must have a volume of _____ cubic inches.

B. Formulate a Plan

Write an equation to model the volume of the box.

Let x represent the base length in inches. The base width is _____ and the

height is _____, or _____.

$$\frac{1}{3}\, \ell w\, h = V$$

$$\frac{1}{3}\,(\underline{\quad})(x - \underline{\quad})(3)(x + \underline{\quad}) = \underline{\quad}$$

$$\underline{\quad}x^3 - \underline{\quad}x - \underline{\quad} = 0$$

C. Solve

Use the Rational Root Theorem to find all possible rational roots.

Factors of −6: ±_____ , ±_____ , ±_____ , ±_____

Test the possible roots. Use a synthetic division table.

$\frac{m}{n}$	1	0	−1	−6
1				
2				
3				

Factor the polynomial. The synthetic division by _____ results in a remainder of 0,

so _____ is a root and the polynomial in factored form is as follows:

$(\underline{\quad}x - \underline{\quad})(\underline{\quad}x^2 + \underline{\quad}x + \underline{\quad}) = 0$

The quadratic polynomial produces only _____ roots, so the only possible

answer for the base length is _____ inches. The base width is _____ inch and the

height is _____ inches.

D. Justify and Evaluate

The x-coordinates of the points where the graphs of two functions, f and g, intersect
is the solution of the equation $f(x) = g(x)$. Using a graphing calculator to graph the
volume function and $y = 6$ results in the graphs intersecting at the point _____.
Since the x-coordinate is _____, the answer is correct.

Your Turn

8. **Engineering** A box company is designing a new rectangular gift container. The marketing department
has designed a box with a width 2 inches shorter than its length and a height 3 inches taller than its length.
The volume of the box must be 56 cubic inches. What are the dimensions of the box?

Elaborate

9. For a polynomial function with integer coefficients, how are the function's coefficients and rational zeros related?

10. Describe the process for finding the rational zeros of a polynomial function with integer coefficients.

11. How is the Rational Root Theorem useful when solving a real-world problem about the volume of an object when the volume function is a polynomial and a specific value of the function is given?

12. **Essential Question Check-In** What does the Rational Root Theorem find?

Find the rational zeros of each polynomial function. Then write each function in factored form.

1. $f(x) = x^3 - x^2 - 10x - 8$

2. $f(x) = x^3 + 2x^2 - 23x - 60$

3. $j(x) = 2x^3 - x^2 - 13x - 6$

4. $g(x) = x^3 - 9x^2 + 23x - 15$

5. $h(x) = x^3 - 5x^2 + 2x + 8$

6. $h(x) = 6x^3 - 7x^2 - 9x - 2$

7. $s(x) = x^3 - x^2 - x + 1$

8. $t(x) = x^3 + x^2 - 8x - 12$

9. $k(x) = x^4 + 5x^3 - x^2 - 17x + 12$

10. $g(x) = x^4 - 6x^3 + 11x^2 - 6x$

11. $h(x) = x^4 - 2x^3 - 3x^2 + 4x + 4$

12. $f(x) = x^4 - 5x^2 + 4$

13. Manufacturing A laboratory supply company is designing a new rectangular box in which to ship glass pipes. The company has created a box with a width 2 inches shorter than its length and a height 9 inches taller than twice its length. The volume of each box must be 45 cubic inches. What are the dimensions?

14. Engineering A natural history museum is building a pyramidal glass structure for its tree snake exhibit. Its research team has designed a pyramid with a square base and with a height that is 2 yards more than a side of its base. The volume of the pyramid must be 147 cubic yards. What are the dimensions?

15. Engineering A paper company is designing a new, pyramid-shaped paperweight. Its development team has decided that to make the length of the paperweight 4 inches less than the height and the width of the paperweight 3 inches less than the height. The paperweight must have a volume of 12 cubic inches. What are the dimensions of the paperweight?

16. Match each set of roots with its polynomial function.

A. $x = 2, x = 3, x = 4$ _____ $f(x) = (x + 2)(x + 4)\left(x - \dfrac{3}{2}\right)$

B. $x = -2, x = -4, x = \dfrac{3}{2}$ _____ $f(x) = \left(x - \dfrac{1}{2}\right)\left(x - \dfrac{5}{4}\right)\left(x + \dfrac{7}{3}\right)$

C. $x = \dfrac{1}{2}, x = \dfrac{5}{4}, x = -\dfrac{7}{3}$ _____ $f(x) = (x - 2)(x - 3)(x - 4)$

D. $x = -\dfrac{4}{5}, x = \dfrac{6}{7}, x = 4$ _____ $f(x) = \left(x + \dfrac{4}{5}\right)\left(x - \dfrac{6}{7}\right)(x - 4)$

17. Identify the zeros of $f(x) = (x + 3)(x - 4)(x - 3)$, write the function in standard form, and state how the zeros are related to the standard form.

18. Critical Thinking Consider the polynomial function $g(x) = 2x^3 - 6x^2 + \pi x + 5$. Is it possible to use the Rational Zero Theorem and synthetic division to factor this polynomial? Explain.

19. Explain the Error Sabrina was told to find the zeros of the polynomial function $h(x) = x(x - 4)(x + 2)$. She stated that the zeros of this polynomial are $x = 0$, $x = -4$, and $x = 2$. Explain her error.

20. Justify Reasoning If $\dfrac{c}{b}$ is a rational zero of a polynomial function $p(x)$, explain why $bx - c$ must be a factor of the polynomial.

21. Justify Reasoning A polynomial function $p(x)$ has degree 3, and its zeros are -3, 4, and 6. What do you think is the equation of $p(x)$? Do you think there could be more than one possibility? Explain.

Lesson Performance Task

For the years from 2001–2010, the number of Americans traveling to other countries by plane can be represented by the polynomial function $A(t) = 20t^4 - 428t^3 + 2760t^2 - 4320t + 33,600$, where A is the number of thousands of Americans traveling abroad by airplane and t is the number of years since 2001. In which year were there 40,000,000 Americans traveling abroad? Use the Rational Root Theorem to find your answer.
[Hint: consider the function's domain and range before finding all possible rational roots.]

7.2 Finding Complex Solutions of Polynomial Equations

Resource Locker

Essential Question: What do the Fundamental Theorem of Algebra and its corollary tell you about the roots of the polynomial equation p(x) = 0 where p(x) has degree n?

⊘ Explore   Investigating the Number of Complex Zeros of a Polynomial Function

You have used various algebraic and graphical methods to find the roots of a polynomial equation $p(x) = 0$ or the zeros of a polynomial function $p(x)$. Because a polynomial can have a factor that repeats, a zero or a root can occur multiple times.

The polynomial $p(x) = x^3 + 8x^2 + 21x + 18 = (x + 2)(x + 3)^2$ has -2 as a zero once and -3 as a zero twice, or *with multiplicity 2*. The **multiplicity** of a zero of $p(x)$ or a root of $p(x) = 0$ is the number of times that the related factor occurs in the factorization.

In this Explore, you will use algebraic methods to investigate the relationship between the degree of a polynomial function and the number of zeros that it has.

(A) Find all zeros of $p(x) = x^3 + 7x^2$. Include any multiplicities greater than 1.

$$p(x) = x^3 + 7x^2$$

Factor out the GCF. $p(x) = \boxed{}(x + 7)$

What are all the zeros of $p(x)$? _____

(B) Find all zeros of $p(x) = x^3 - 64$. Include any multiplicities greater than 1.

$$p(x) = x^3 - 64$$

Factor the difference of two cubes. $p(x) = \left(x \boxed{} 4\right)\left(x^2 + \boxed{} + \boxed{}\right)$

What are the real zeros of $p(x)$? _____

Solve $x^2 + 4x + 16 = 0$ using the quadratic formula.

$$x = \frac{-b \pm \sqrt{b^2 - 4ac}}{2a}$$

$$x = \frac{\boxed{} \pm \sqrt{4^2 - 4 \cdot 1 \cdot \boxed{}}}{2 \cdot \boxed{}} \quad x = \frac{-4 \pm \sqrt{\boxed{}}}{2} \quad x = \frac{-4 \pm \boxed{}\sqrt{3}}{2}$$

$$x = -2 \pm 2i\sqrt{3}$$

What are the non-real zeros of $p(x)$? _____

(C) Find all zeros of $p(x) = x^4 + 3x^3 - 4x^2 - 12x$. Include any multiplicities greater than 1.

$$p(x) = x^4 + 3x^3 - 4x^2 - 12x$$

Factor out the GCF. $p(x) = x\left(\boxed{}\right)$

Group terms to begin $p(x) = x\left((x^3 + 3x^2) - \left(\boxed{}\right)\right)$
factoring by grouping.

Factor out common monomials. $p(x) = x\left(\boxed{}(x+3) - \boxed{}(x+3)\right)$

Factor out the common binomial. $p(x) = x(x+3)(x^2 - 4)$

Factor the difference of squares. $p(x) = x(x+3)\left(\boxed{}\right)\left(\boxed{}\right)$

What are all the zeros of $p(x)$? _____

(D) Find all zeros of $p(x) = x^4 - 16$. Include any multiplicities greater than 1.

$$p(x) = x^4 - 16$$

Factor the difference of squares. $p(x) = \left(\boxed{}\right)(x^2 + 4)$

Factor the difference of squares. $p(x) = \left(\boxed{}\right)\left(\boxed{}\right)(x^2 + 4)$

What are the real zeros of $p(x)$? _____

Solve $x^2 + 4 = 0$ by taking square roots.

$x^2 + 4 = 0$
$x^2 = -4$
$x = \pm\sqrt{-4}$
$x = \pm\boxed{}$

What are the non-real zeros of $p(x)$? _____

Find all zeros of $p(x) = x^4 + 5x^3 + 6x^2 - 4x - 8$. Include multiplicities greater than 1.

By the Rational Zero Theorem, possible rational zeros are $\pm 1, \pm 2, \pm 4,$ and ± 8.
Use a synthetic division table to test possible zeros.

$\frac{m}{n}$	1	5	6	−4	−8
1	1	6	12	8	0

The remainder is 0, so 1 is/is not a zero.

$p(x)$ factors as $(x - 1)\left(\right)$.

Test for zeros in the cubic polynomial.

$\frac{m}{n}$	1	6	12	8
1	1	7	19	27
−1	1	5	7	1
2	1	8	28	64
−2	1	4	4	0

_____ a zero.

$p(x)$ factors as $(x - 1)(x + 2)\left(\right)$. The quadratic is a perfect square trinomial.

So, $p(x)$ factors completely as $p(x) = (x - 1)\,\boxed{}$.

What are all the zeros of $p(x)$? _____

Complete the table to summarize your results from Steps A–E.

Polynomial Function in Standard Form	Polynomial Function Factored over the Integers	Real Zeros and Their Multiplicities	Non-real Zeros and Their Multiplicities
$p(x) = x^3 + 7x^2$			
$p(x) = x^3 - 64$			
$p(x) = x^4 + 3x^3 - 4x^2 - 12x$			
$p(x) = x^4 - 16$			
$p(x) = x^4 + 5x^3 + 6x^2 - 4x - 8$			

1. Examine the table. For each function, count the number of unique zeros, both real and non-real. How does the number of unique zeros compare with the degree?

2. Examine the table again. This time, count the total number of zeros for each function, where a zero of multiplicity m is counted as m zeros. How does the total number of zeros compare with the degree?

3. **Discussion** Describe the apparent relationship between the degree of a polynomial function and the number of zeros it has.

⚙ Explain 1   Applying the Fundamental Theorem of Algebra to Solving Polynomial Equations

The Fundamental Theorem of Algebra and its corollary summarize what you have observed earlier while finding rational zeros of polynomial functions and in completing the Explore.

> ### The Fundamental Theorem of Algebra
>
> Every polynomial function of degree $n \geq 1$ has at least one zero, where a zero may be a complex number.
>
> **Corollary:** Every polynomial function of degree $n \geq 1$ has exactly n zeros, including multiplicities.

Because the zeros of a polynomial function $p(x)$ give the roots of the equation $p(x) = 0$, the theorem and its corollary also extend to finding all roots of a polynomial equation.

Example 1   Solve the polynomial equation by finding all roots.

(A) $2x^3 - 12x^2 - 34x + 204 = 0$

The polynomial has degree 3, so the equation has exactly 3 roots.

$$2x^3 - 12x^2 - 34x + 204 = 0$$

Divide both sides by 2.	$x^3 - 6x^2 - 17x + 102 = 0$
Group terms.	$\left(x^3 - 6x^2\right) - (17x - 102) = 0$
Factor out common monomials.	$x^2(x - 6) - 17(x - 6) = 0$
Factor out the common binomial.	$\left(x^2 - 17\right)(x - 6) = 0$

One root is $x = 6$. Solving $x^2 - 17 = 0$ gives $x^2 = 17$, or $x = \pm\sqrt{17}$.

The roots are $-\sqrt{17}$, $\sqrt{17}$, and 6.

(B) $x^4 - 6x^2 - 27 = 0$

The polynomial has degree _____, so the equation has exactly _____ roots.

Notice that $x^4 - 6x^2 - 27$ has the form $u^2 - 6u - 27$, where $u = x^2$. So, you can factor it like a quadratic trinomial.

$$x^4 - 6x^2 - 27 = 0$$

Factor the trinomial.
$$\left(x^2 - \boxed{}\right)\left(x^2 + \boxed{}\right) = 0$$

Factor the difference of squares.
$$\left(x + \boxed{}\right)\left(x - \boxed{}\right)(x^2 + 3) = 0$$

The real roots are _____ and _____. Solving $x^2 + 3 = 0$ gives $x^2 = -3$, or

$$x = \pm\sqrt{-3} = \pm \boxed{} \sqrt{\boxed{}}.$$

The roots are _____.

Reflect

4. Restate the Fundamental Theorem of Algebra and its corollary in terms of the roots of equations.

   _____

   _____

   _____

   _____

Your Turn

Solve the polynomial equation by finding all roots.

5. $8x^3 - 27 = 0$

6. $p(x) = x^4 - 13x^3 + 55x^2 - 91x$

Writing a Polynomial Function From Its Zeros

You may have noticed in finding roots of quadratic and polynomial equations that any irrational or complex roots come in pairs. These pairs reflect the "±" in the quadratic formula. For example, for any of the following number pairs, you will never have a polynomial equation for which only one number in the pair is a root.

$$\sqrt{5} \text{ and } -\sqrt{5};\ 1 + \sqrt{7} \text{ and } 1 - \sqrt{7};\ i \text{ and } -i;\ 2 + 14i \text{ and } 2 - 14i;\ \frac{11}{6} + \frac{1}{6}i\sqrt{3} \text{ and } \frac{11}{6} - \frac{1}{6}i\sqrt{3}$$

The irrational root pairs $a + b\sqrt{c}$ and $a - b\sqrt{c}$ are called *irrational conjugates*. The complex root pairs $a + bi$ and $a - bi$ are called *complex conjugates*.

Irrational Root Theorem

If a polynomial $p(x)$ has rational coefficients and $a + b\sqrt{c}$ is a root of the equation $p(x) = 0$, where a and b are rational and $\sqrt{c}$ is irrational, then $a - b\sqrt{c}$ is also a root of $p(x) = 0$.

Complex Conjugate Root Theorem

If $a + bi$ is an imaginary root of a polynomial equation with real-number coefficients, then $a - bi$ is also a root.

Because the roots of the equation $p(x) = 0$ give the zeros of a polynomial function, corresponding theorems apply to the zeros of a polynomial function. You can use this fact to write a polynomial function from its zeros. Because irrational and complex conjugate pairs are a sum and difference of terms, the product of irrational conjugates is always a rational number and the product of complex conjugates is always a real number.

$$\left(2 - \sqrt{10}\right)\left(2 + \sqrt{10}\right) = 2^2 - \left(\sqrt{10}\right)^2 = 4 - 10 = -6$$
$$\left(1 - i\sqrt{2}\right)\left(1 + i\sqrt{2}\right) = 1^2 - \left(i\sqrt{2}\right)^2 = 1 - (-1)(2) = 3$$

Example 2 Write the polynomial function with least degree and a leading coefficient of 1 that has the given zeros.

Ⓐ   5 and $3 + 2\sqrt{7}$

Because irrational zeros come in conjugate pairs, $3 - 2\sqrt{7}$ must also be a zero of the function. Use the 3 zeros to write a function in factored form, then multiply to write it in standard form.

$$p(x) = \left[x - \left(3 + 2\sqrt{7}\right)\right]\left[x - \left(3 - 2\sqrt{7}\right)\right](x - 5)$$

Multiply the first two factors using FOIL.
$$= \left[x^2 - \left(3 - 2\sqrt{7}\right)x - \left(3 + 2\sqrt{7}\right)x + \left(3 + 2\sqrt{7}\right)\left(3 - 2\sqrt{7}\right)\right](x - 5)$$

Multipy the conjugates.
$$= \left[x^2 - \left(3 - 2\sqrt{7}\right)x - \left(3 + 2\sqrt{7}\right)x + (9 - 4 \cdot 7)\right](x - 5)$$

Combine like terms.
$$= \left[x^2 + \left(-3 + 2\sqrt{7} - 3 - 2\sqrt{7}\right)x + (-19)\right](x - 5)$$

Simplify.
$$= \left[x^2 - 6x - 19\right](x - 5)$$

Distributive property
$$= x\left(x^2 - 6x - 19\right) - 5\left(x^2 - 6x - 19\right)$$

Multiply.
$$= x^3 - 6x^2 - 19x - 5x^2 + 30x + 95$$

Combine like terms.
$$= x^3 - 11x^2 + 11x + 95$$

The polynomial function is $p(x) = x^3 - 11x^2 + 11x + 95$.

(B) 2, 3 and $1 - i$

Because complex zeros come in conjugate pairs, _____ must also be a zero of the function.

Use the 4 zeros to write a function in factored form, then multiply to write it in standard form.

$$p(x) = \Big[x - (1 + i)\Big]\Big[x - \Big(\boxed{}\Big)\Big](x - 2)(x - 3)$$

Multiply the first two factors using FOIL.
$$= \Big[x^2 - (1 - i)x - \boxed{}x + (1 + i)(1 - i)\Big](x - 2)(x - 3)$$

Multipy the conjugates.
$$= \Big[x^2 - (1 - i)x - (1 + i)x + \Big(1 - \boxed{}\Big)\Big](x - 2)(x - 3)$$

Combine like terms.
$$= \Big[x^2 + (-1 + i - 1 - i)x + 2\Big](x - 2)(x - 3)$$

Simplify.
$$= \Big(\boxed{}\Big)(x - 2)(x - 3)$$

Multipy the binomials.
$$= (x^2 - 2x + 2)\boxed{}$$

Distributive property
$$= x^2(x^2 - 5x + 6)\boxed{}(x^2 - 5x + 6) + 2(x^2 - 5x + 6)$$

Multipy.
$$= (x^4 - 5x^3 + 6x^2) + (-2x^3 + 10x^2 - 12x) + (2x^2 - 10x + 12)$$

Combine like terms.
$$= \boxed{}$$

The polynomial function is $p(x) = $ _____.

Reflect

7. Restate the Irrational Root Theorem in terms of the zeros of polynomial functions.

_____

_____

_____

8. Restate the Complex Conjugates Zero Theorem in terms of the roots of equations.

_____

_____

Write the polynomial function with the least degree and a leading coefficient of 1 that has the given zeros.

9. $2 + 3i$ and $4 - 7\sqrt{2}$

⚙ Explain 3 Solving a Real-World Problem by Graphing Polynomial Functions

You can use graphing to help you locate or approximate any real zeros of a polynomial function. Though a graph will not help you find non-real zeros, it can indicate that the function has non-real zeros. For example, look at the graph of $p(x) = x^4 - 2x^2 - 3$.

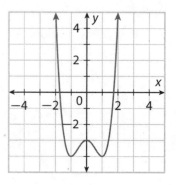

The graph intersects the x-axis twice, which shows that the function has two real zeros. By the corollary to the Fundamental Theorem of Algebra, however, a fourth degree polynomial has four zeros. So, the other two zeros of $p(x)$ must be non-real. The zeros are $-\sqrt{3}$, $\sqrt{3}$, i, and $-i$. (A polynomial whose graph has a turning point on the x-axis has a real zero of even multiplicity at that point. If the graph "bends" at the x-axis, there is a real zero of odd multiplicity greater than 1 at that point.)

Ⓐ The following polynomial models approximate the total oil consumption C (in millions of barrels per day) for North America (NA) and the Asia Pacific region (AP) over the period from 2001 to 2011, where t is in years and $t = 0$ represents 2001.

$$C_{NA}(t) = 0.00494t^4 - 0.0915t^3 + 0.442t^2 - 0.239t + 23.6$$

$$C_{AP}(t) = 0.00877t^3 - 0.139t^2 + 1.23t + 21.1$$

Use a graphing calculator to plot the functions and approximate the x-coordinate of the intersection in the region of interest. What does this represent in the context of this situation? Determine when oil consumption in the Asia Pacific region overtook oil consumption in North America using the requested method.

Graph $Y1 = 0.00494x^4 - 0.0915x^3 + 0.442x^2 - 0.239x + 23.6$ and $Y2 = 0.00877x^3 - 0.139x^2 + 1.23x + 21.1$. Use the "Calc" menu to find the point of intersection. Here are the results for Xmin = 0, Xmax = 10, Ymin = 20, Ymax = 30. (The graph for the Asia Pacific is the one that rises upward on all segments.)

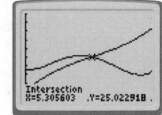

The functions intersect at about $x = 5$, which represents the year 2006. This means that the models show oil consumption in the Asia Pacific equaling and then overtaking oil consumption in North America about 2006.

Ⓑ Find a single polynomial model for the situation in Example 3A whose zero represents the time that oil consumption for the Asia Pacific region overtakes consumption for North America. Plot the function on a graphing calculator and use it to find the x-intercept.

Let the function $C_D(t)$ represent the difference in oil consumption in the Asia Pacific and North America.

A difference of 0 indicates _____.

$$\boxed{} = \boxed{} - C_{NA}(t)$$

$$= 0.00877t^3 - 0.139t^2 + 1.23t + 21.1 - \left(0.00494t^4 - 0.0915t^3 + 0.442t^2 - 0.239t + 23.6\right)$$

Remove parentheses and rearrange terms.

$$= -0.00494t^4 + 0.00877t^3 + 0.0915t^3 - 0.139t^2 - 0.442t^2 + 1.23t + 0.239t + 21.1 - 23.6$$

Combine like terms. Round to three significant digits.

$$= \boxed{}$$

Graph $C_D(t)$ and find the x-intercept. (The graph with Ymin $= -4$, Ymax $= 6$ is shown.)

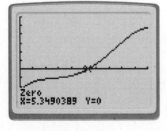

Within the rounding error, the results for the x-coordinate of the intersection of $C_{NA}(t)$ and $C_{AP}(t)$ and the x-intercept of $C_D(t)$ are the same.

10. An engineering class is designing model rockets for a competition. The body of the rocket must be cylindrical with a cone-shaped top. The cylinder part must be 60 cm tall, and the height of the cone must be twice the radius. The volume of the payload region must be 558π cm^3 in order to hold the cargo. Use a graphing calculator to graph the rocket's payload volume as a function of the radius x. On the same screen, graph the constant function for the desired payload. Find the intersection to find x.

Elaborate

11. What does the degree of a polynomial function $p(x)$ tell you about the zeros of the function or the roots of the equation $p(x) = 0$?

_____

_____

12. A polynomial equation of degree 5 has the roots 0.3, 2, 8, and 10.6 (each of multiplicity 1). What can you conclude about the remaining root? Explain your reasoning.

_____

_____

_____

13. **Discussion** Describe two ways you can use graphing to determine when two polynomial functions that model a real-world situation have the same value.

_____

_____

_____

_____

14. **Essential Question Check-In** What are possible ways to find all the roots of a polynomial equation?

_____

_____

_____

_____

Find all zeros of $p(x)$. Include any multiplicities greater than 1.

1. $p(x) = 3x^3 - 10x^2 + 10x - 4$

2. $p(x) = x^3 - 3x^2 + 4x - 12$

Solve the polynomial equation by finding all roots.

3. $2x^3 - 3x^2 + 8x - 12 = 0$

4. $x^4 - 5x^3 + 3x^2 + x = 0$

Write the polynomial function with least degree and a leading coefficient of 1 that has the given zeros.

5. $0, \sqrt{5}$, and 2

6. $4i$, 2, and -2

7. $1, -1$ (multiplicity 3), and $3i$

8. 3(multiplicity of 2) and $3i$

9. Forestry Height and trunk volume measurements from 10 giant sequoias between the heights of 220 and 275 feet in California give the following model, where h is the height in feet and V is the volume in cubic feet.

$$V(h) = 0.131h^3 - 90.9h^2 + 21{,}200h - 1{,}627{,}400$$

The "President" tree in the Giant Forest Grove in Sequoia National Park has a volume of about 45,100 cubic feet. Use a graphing calculator to plot the function $V(h)$ and the constant function representing the volume of the President tree together. (Use a window of 220 to 275 for X and 30,000 to 55,000 for Y.) Find the x-coordinate of the intersection of the graphs. What does this represent in the context of this situation?

10. Business Two competing stores, store A and store B, opened the same year in the same neighborhood. The annual revenue R (in millions of dollars) for each store t years after opening can be approximated by the polynomial models shown.

$$R_A(t) = 0.0001\left(-t^4 + 12t^3 - 77t^2 + 600t + 13{,}650\right)$$

$$R_B(t) = 0.0001\left(-t^4 + 36t^3 - 509t^2 + 3684t + 3390\right)$$

Using a graphing calculator, graph the models from $t = 0$ to $t = 10$, with a range of 0 to 2 for R. Find the x-coordinate of the intersection of the graphs, and interpret the graphs.

11. Personal Finance A retirement account contains cash and stock in a company. The cash amount is added to each week by the same amount until week 32, then that same amount is withdrawn each week. The functions shown model the balance B (in thousands of dollars) over the course of the past year, with the time t in weeks.

$$B_C(t) = -0.12|t - 32| + 13$$

$$B_S(t) = 0.00005t^4 - 0.00485t^3 + 0.1395t^2 - 1.135t + 15.75$$

Use a graphing calculator to graph both models (Use 0 to 50 for the domain and 0 to 20 for the range.). Find the x-coordinate of any points of intersection. Then interpret your results in the context of this situation.

12. Match the roots with their equation.

A. 1   _____ $x^4 + x^3 + 2x^2 + 4x - 8 = 0$

B. -2 _____ $x^4 - 5x^2 + 4 = 0$

C. 2

D. -1

E. $2i$

F. $-2i$

13. Draw Conclusions Find all of the roots of $x^6 - 5x^4 - 125x^2 + 15{,}625 = 0$. (Hint: Rearrange the terms with a sum of cubes followed by the two other terms.)

14. Explain the Error A student is asked to write the polynomial function with least degree and a leading coefficient of 1 that has the zeros $1 + i$, $1 - i$, $\sqrt{2}$, and -3. The student uses these zeros to find the corresponding factors, and multiplies them together to obtain $p(x) = x^4 + \left(1 - \sqrt{2}\right)x^3 - \left(4 + \sqrt{2}\right)x^2 + \left(6 + 4\sqrt{2}\right)x - 6\sqrt{2}$. What error did the student make? What is the correct function?

15. Critical Thinking What is the least degree of a polynomial equation that has $3i$ as a root with a multiplicity of 3, and $2 - \sqrt{3}$ as a root with multiplicity 2? Explain.

Lesson Performance Task

In 1984 the MPAA introduced the PG-13 rating to their movie rating system. Recently, scientists measured the incidences of a specific type of violence depicted in movies. The researchers used specially trained coders to identify the specific type of violence in one half of the top grossing movies for each year since 1985. The trend in the average rate per hour of 5-minute segments of this type of violence in movies rated G/PG, PG-13, and R can be modeled as a function of time by the following equations:

$$V_{G/PG}(t) = -0.015t + 1.45$$

$$V_{PG-13}(t) = 0.000577t^3 - 0.0225t^2 + 0.26t + 0.8$$

$$V_R(t) = 2.15$$

V is the average rate per hour of 5-minute segments containing the specific type of violence in movies, and t is the number of years since 1985.

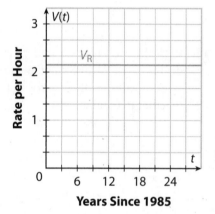

a. Interestingly, in 1985 or $t = 0$, $V_{G/PG}(0) > V_{PG-13}(0)$. Can you think of any reasons why this would be true?

b. What do the equations indicate about the relationship between $V_{G/PG}(t)$ and $V_{PG-13}(t)$ as t increases?

c. Graph the models for $V_{G/PG}(t)$ and $V_{PG-13}(t)$ and find the year in which $V_{PG-13}(t)$ will be greater than $V_{G/PG}(t)$.

Essential Question: How can you use polynomial equations to solve real-world problems?

KEY EXAMPLE   *(Lesson 7.1)*

Find the rational zeros of $f(x) = x^3 + 6x^2 + 11x + 6$; then write the function as a product of factors.

Factors of 6: $\pm 1, \pm 2, \pm 3, \pm 6$

$\dfrac{m}{n}$	1	6	11	6
1	1	7	18	24
2	1	8	27	60
3	1	9	38	120
6	1	12	83	504
−1	1	5	6	0

Use the Rational Zero Theorem.

Test the roots in a synthetic division table.

$(x + 1)(x^2 + 5x + 6)$

$(x + 1)(x + 2)(x + 3)$

$x = -1, x = -2, x = -3$

Factor the trinomial.

KEY EXAMPLE   *(Lesson 7.2)*

Find all the zeros of $m(x) = 2x^4 - 4x^3 + 8x^2 - 16x$.

$2x^4 - 4x^3 - 8x^2 - 16x$

$2x(x^3 - 2x^2 - 4x + 8)$ Factor out the GCF.

$2x((x^3 - 2x^2) - (4x - 8))$ Group the terms.

$2x(x^2(x - 2) - 4(x - 2))$ Factor out common monomials.

$2x(x^2 - 4)(x - 2)$ Factor out the common binomial.

$2x(x + 2)(x - 2)(x - 2)$ Difference of two squares

So, the zeros of $m(x)$ are $0, -2, 2$ (mult. 2).

Rewrite the function as a product of factors, and state all of the zeros. *(Lessons 7.1, 7.2)*

1. $r(x) = x^3 + 13x^2 + 48x + 36$

2. $m(x) = 3x^4 - 3x^2$

3. $n(x) = x^3 + 5x^2 - 8x - 12$

4. $p(x) = x^3 - 8$

5. $b(x) = x^4 - 81$

6. $t(x) = 15x^3 + 27x^2 - 6x$

7. Give an example of a fourth-degree polynomial function with all real zeros. Explain how you got your function. *(Lesson 7.1)*

MODULE PERFORMANCE TASK

What Do Polynomials Have to Do With Endangered Species?

A biologist has been studying a particular species of frog in an area for many years and has compiled population data. She used the data to create a model of the population, given here, where x is the years since 2000.

$$P(x) = -x^4 + 27x^3 - 198x^2 + 372x + 1768$$

Describe the trends for the population, and explain what the model predicts for the future population of this species of frog.

Use your own paper to complete the task. Be sure to write down all your data and assumptions. Then use graphs, numbers, words, or algebra to explain how you reached your conclusions.

(Ready) to Go On?

7.1–7.2 Polynomial Functions

- Online Homework
- Hints and Help
- Extra Practice

Write the function as a product of factors. *(Lesson 7.1)*

1. $f(x) = 7x^3 - 14x^2 - x + 2$

2. $g(x) = 3x^2 + 2x - 8$

3. $h(x) = 4x^2 - 25$

4. $t(x) = 8x^3 - 512$

List the zeros. *(Lessons 7.1, 7.2)*

5. $m(x) = x^4 + 3x^2 - 18$

6. $r(x) = x^3 + 3x^2 - x - 3$

7. $q(x) = x^3 - 1$

8. $p(x) = 9x^2 - 100$

ESSENTIAL QUESTION

9. Give an example of how factoring polynomials might be used in geometry. *(Lesson 7.1)*

Assessment Readiness

1. Look at each equation. Does the polynomial function have all real zeros? Select Yes or No for A–C?

   A. $f(x) = x^4 - 2x^2 - 5$ ○ Yes   ○ No

   B. $g(x) = x^2 - 9$ ○ Yes   ○ No

   C. $h(x) = x^4 - 256$ ○ Yes   ○ No

2. Consider the polynomial function $m(x) = x^4 - 16x^2$. Choose True or False for each statement.

   A. There will be both real and imaginary zeros of this function.   ○ True   ○ False

   B. Factoring the polynomial involves the difference of two squares.   ○ True   ○ False

   C. The zeros of the function are 0 (mult. 2), 4, −4.   ○ True   ○ False

3. Explain why some polynomial functions with real coefficients have non-real zeros.

4. By analyzing a quickly growing oil town, an analyst states that the predicted population P of the town t years from now can be modeled by the function $P(t) = 5t^3 - 2t^2 + 15{,}000$. If we assume the function is accurate, in approximately how many years will the town have a population of 225,000? How did you get your answer?

1. Identify the transformations of the graph of $f(x) = x^3$ that produce the graph of the function $g(x) = -2(x - 5)^3$. Select True or False for each statement.

   A. When compared with $f(x)$, the graph of $g(x)$ is vertically compressed by a factor of $\frac{1}{2}$. ○ True ○ False

   B. When compared with $f(x)$, the graph of $g(x)$ is translated 5 units to the right. ○ True ○ False

   C. When compared with $f(x)$, the graph of $g(x)$ is reflected across the x-axis. ○ True ○ False

2. Consider the polynomial $3x^3 + 9x^2 - 12x$. Select True or False for each statement.

   A. $3x$ can be factored out of every term. ○ True ○ False

   B. The polynomial cannot be factored as it is written. ○ True ○ False

   C. The completely factored polynomial is $3x(x - 1)(x + 4)$. ○ True ○ False

3. Consider the factored polynomial $3x(x - 2)(5x + 2)$. Is the expression equivalent? Select Yes or No for A–D

   A. $(3x^2 - 6x)(5x + 2)$ ○ Yes ○ No

   B. $3x(5x^2 - 8x - 4)$ ○ Yes ○ No

   C. $15x^3 - 24x^2 - 12x$ ○ Yes ○ No

   D. $3x(5x^2 - 5x - 2)$ ○ Yes ○ No

4. Consider the polynomial function $g(x) = 3x^3 + 6x^2 - 9x$. Select True or False for each statement.

   A. The polynomial has only real zeros. ○ True ○ False

   B. Factoring the polynomial involves a common monomial. ○ True ○ False

   C. The zeros of the polynomial are 0, –3, 1, 3. ○ True ○ False

5. Consider the function $m(x) = x^4 - 16$. Are these zeros of the function? Select Yes or No for A–C.

   A. $-2i, 2i$ ○ Yes ○ No

   B. $2 \pm 2i$ ○ Yes ○ No

   C. $-2, 2$ ○ Yes ○ No

6. Use a graphing calculator to graph the function $f(x) = -x(x + 1)(x - 4)^2$, and then use the graph to determine the number of turning points and global maximums and minimums, and local maximums and minimums that are not global.

7. Ms. Flores grows tomatoes on her farm. The price per pound of tomatoes can be modeled by $P(x) = 20x + 4$. If the total income that she wants to earn from tomatoes for one year can be modeled by $I(x) = 60x^3 - 8x^2 + 136x + 28$, write a polynomial that can be used to model the number of pounds of tomatoes Ms. Flores needs to grow in one year. Explain your answer.

8. During a discussion in class, Hannah stated that she liked the quadratic formula more than completing the square and factoring, because it works on every quadratic equation. The teacher then proposed the equation $-3x(x + 7) = 14$. Explain how Hannah can adjust this equation so she can use the quadratic formula to solve it.

Performance Tasks

★ **9.** A bottom for a box can be made by cutting congruent squares from each of the four corners of a piece of cardboard. The volume of a box made from an 8.5-by-11-inch piece of cardboard would be represented by $V(x) = x(11 - 2x)(8.5 - 2x)$, where x is the side length of one square.

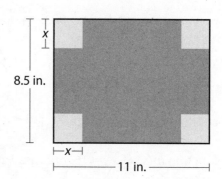

8.5 in.

x

11 in.

 A. Express the volume as a sum of monomials.

 B. Find the volume when $x = 1$ inch.

★★**10.** The volume of several planets in cubic kilometers can be modeled by $v(d) = \frac{1}{6}\pi d^3$, where d is the diameter of the planet in kilometers. The mass of each planet in kilograms in terms of diameter d can be modeled by $M(d) = (3.96 \times 10^{12})d^3 - (6.50 \times 10^{17})d^2 + (2.56 \times 10^{22})d - 5.56 \times 10^{25}$.

    A. The density of a planet in kilograms per cubic kilometer can be found by dividing the planet's mass by its volume. Use polynomial division to find a model for the density of a planet in terms of its diameter.

    B. Use the model to estimate the density of Jupiter, with diameter $d = 142{,}984$ km.

★★★**11.** The profit of a small business (in thousands of dollars) since it was founded can be modeled by the polynomial $f(t) = -t^4 + 44t^3 - 612t^2 + 2592t$, where t represents the number of years since 1980.

    A. Factor $f(t)$ completely.

    B. What was the company's profit in 1985?

    C. Find and interpret $f(15)$.

    D. What can you say about the company's long-term prospects?

Statistician According to data from the U.S. Census Bureau, the total number of people in the United States labor force can be approximated by the function $T(x) = -0.011x^2 + 2x + 107$, where x is the number of years since 1980 and $T(x)$ is the number of workers in millions. The number of women in the United States labor force can be approximated by the function $W(x) = -0.012x^2 + 1.26x + 45.5$.

a. Use the function $T(x)$ to estimate the number of workers in millions in 2010.

b. Write a polynomial function $M(x)$ that models the number of men in the labor force, and explain how you found your function.

c. Use the function found in part b to estimate the number of male workers in millions in 2010.

d. Explain how you could have found the answer to part c without using the function $M(x)$.

UNIT 4

Rational Functions, Expressions, and Equations

MATH IN CAREERS

Chemist Chemists study the properties and composition of substances. They use the mathematics of ratios and proportions to determine the atomic composition of materials and the quantities of atoms needed to synthesize materials. They use geometry to understand the physical structures of chemical compounds. Chemists also use mathematical models to understand and predict behavior of chemical interactions, including reaction rates and activation energies.

If you are interested in a career as a chemist, you should study these mathematical subjects:

- Geometry
- Algebra
- Calculus
- Differential Equations
- Statistics

Research other careers that require using mathematical models to predict behavior. Check out the career activity at the end of the unit to find out how **Chemists** use math.

isakson/Blend Images/Corbis

Reading Start-Up

Visualize Vocabulary

Use the ✓ words to complete the chart.

	the set of output values of a function or relation
	a linear relationship between two variables, x and y, that can be written in the form $y = kx$, where k is a nonzero constant
	the multiplicative inverse of a number
	the simplest function with the defining characteristics of the function family
	the set of all possible input values of a relation or function
	an algebraic expression whose numerator and denominator are polynomials

Understand Vocabulary

To become familiar with some of the vocabulary terms in the module, consider the following. You may refer to the module, the glossary, or a dictionary.

1. _____ is a relationship between two variables, x and y, that can be written in the form $y = \frac{k}{x}$, where k is a nonzero constant and $x \neq 0$.

2. A line that a graph approaches as the value of the variable becomes extremely large or small is a/an _____.

3. A function whose rule can be written as a rational expression is a/an _____.

Active Reading

Double-Door Fold Before beginning each lesson, create a double-door fold to compare the characteristics of two expressions, functions, or variations. This can help you identify the similarities and differences between the topics.

Rational Functions

Essential Question: How can you use rational functions to solve real-world problems?

REAL WORLD VIDEO
As a consumer, you may shop around for the best deal on a new bike helmet. Check out the video to see how sporting goods manufacturers can use rational functions to help set pricing and sales goals.

MODULE PERFORMANCE TASK PREVIEW

What Is the Profit?

Like any business, a manufacturer of bike helmets must pay attention to ways to minimize costs and maximize profit. Businesses use mathematical functions to calculate and predict various quantities, including profits, costs, and revenue. What are some of the ways a business can use a profit function? Let's find out!

Zero Creatives/Getty Images

Are (YOU) Ready?

Complete these exercises to review skills you will need for this module.

Graphing Linear Nonproportional Relationships

Personal Math Trainer
• Online Homework
• Hints and Help
• Extra Practice

Example 1

Graph $y = -\frac{1}{2}x - 3$

Plot the y-intercept $(0, -3)$

The slope is $-\frac{1}{2}$, so from $(0, -3)$, plot the next point up 1 and left 2.

Draw a line through the two points.

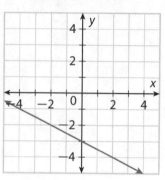

Graph each relationship.

1. $y = 3x - 4$

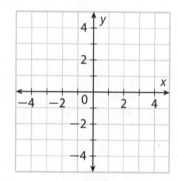

2. $y = -\frac{3}{4}x + 1$

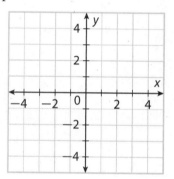

Direct and Inverse Variation

Example 2

The graph of a direct variation function passes through $(1, 10)$. Write the equation for the function.

$k = \frac{y}{x} = \frac{10}{1} = 10$,

so the equation is $y = 10x$.

Example 3

The graph of an inverse variation function passes through $(4, 3)$. Write the equation for the function.

$k = xy = 4 \cdot 3 = 12$,

so the equation is $y = \frac{12}{x}$.

Write a direct variation equation for the graph that passes through the point.

3. $(2, 5)$ _____

4. $(3, 6)$ _____

5. $(4, 1)$ _____

Write an inverse variation equation for the graph that passes through the point.

6. $(8, 1)$ _____

7. $(5, 10)$ _____

8. $(2, 6)$ _____

8.1 Graphing Simple Rational Functions

Resource
Locker

Essential Question: How are the graphs of $f(x) = a\left(\frac{1}{x-h}\right) + k$ and $f(x) = \frac{1}{\frac{1}{b}(x-h)} + k$ related to the graph of $f(x) = \frac{1}{x}$?

⊘ Explore 1 Graphing and Analyzing $f(x) = \frac{1}{x}$

A **rational function** is a function of the form $f(x) = \frac{p(x)}{q(x)}$ where $p(x)$ and $q(x)$ are polynomials, where $q(x) \neq 0$. The most basic rational function with a variable expression in the denominator is $f(x) = \frac{1}{x}$.

(A) State the domain of $f(x) = \frac{1}{x}$.

The function accepts all real numbers except ____, because division by ____ is undefined. So, the function's domain is as follows:

• As an inequality: $x < \boxed{}$ or $x > \boxed{}$

• In set notation: $\left\{ x \mid x \neq \boxed{} \right\}$

• In interval notation (where the symbol $\cup$ means *union*):

$$\left(-\infty, \boxed{} \right) \cup \left(\boxed{}, +\infty \right)$$

(B) Determine the end behavior of $f(x) = \frac{1}{x}$.

First, complete the tables.

x Increases without Bound			x Decreases without Bound	
x	$f(x) = \frac{1}{x}$		x	$f(x) = \frac{1}{x}$
100			-100	
1000			-1000	
10,000			$-10,000$	

Next, summarize the results.

• As $x \to +\infty$, $f(x) \to \boxed{}$.

• As $x \to -\infty$, $f(x) \to \boxed{}$.

(C) Be more precise about the end behavior of $f(x) = \frac{1}{x}$, and determine what this means for the graph of the function.

You can be more precise about the end behavior by using the notation $f(x) \rightarrow 0^+$, which means that the value of $f(x)$ approaches 0 from the positive direction (that is, the value of $f(x)$ is positive as it approaches 0), and the notation $f(x) \rightarrow 0^-$, which means that the value of $f(x)$ approaches 0 from the negative direction. So, the end behavior of the function is more precisely summarized as follows:

- As $x \rightarrow +\infty$, $f(x) \rightarrow \boxed{}$.
- As $x \rightarrow -\infty$, $f(x) \rightarrow \boxed{}$.

The end behavior indicates that the graph of $f(x)$ approaches, but does not cross, the [x-axis/y-axis], so that axis is an asymptote for the graph.

(D) Examine the behavior of $f(x) = \frac{1}{x}$ near $x = 0$, and determine what this means for the graph of the function.

First, complete the tables.

x Approaches 0 from the Positive Direction	
x	$f(x) = \frac{1}{x}$
0.01	
0.001	
0.0001	

x Approaches 0 from the Negative Direction	
x	$f(x) = \frac{1}{x}$
−0.01	
−0.001	
−0.0001	

Next, summarize the results.

- As $x \rightarrow 0^+$, $f(x) \rightarrow \boxed{}$.
- As $x \rightarrow 0^-$, $f(x) \rightarrow \boxed{}$.

The behavior of $f(x) = \frac{1}{x}$ near $x = 0$ indicates that the graph of $f(x)$ approaches, but does not cross, the [x-axis/y-axis], so that axis is also an asymptote for the graph.

(E) Graph $f(x) = \frac{1}{x}$.

First, determine the sign of $f(x)$ on the two parts of its domain.

- When x is a negative number, $f(x)$ is a [positive/negative] number.
- When x is a positive number, $f(x)$ is a [positive/negative] number.

Next, complete the tables.

Negative Values of x	
x	$f(x) = \frac{1}{x}$
−2	
−1	
−0.5	

Positive Values of x	
x	$f(x) = \frac{1}{x}$
0.5	
1	
2	

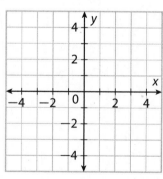

Finally, use the information from this step and all previous steps to draw the graph. Draw asymptotes as dashed lines.

(F) State the range of $f(x) = \frac{1}{x}$.

The function takes on all real numbers except _____, so the function's range is as follows:

- As an inequality: $y < \boxed{}$ or $y > \boxed{}$

- In set notation: $\left\{ y \mid y \neq \boxed{} \right\}$

- In interval notation (where the symbol $\cup$ means *union*): $\left(-\infty, \boxed{} \right) \cup \left(\boxed{}, +\infty \right)$

(G) Identify the intervals where the function is increasing and where it is decreasing.

_____

_____

(H) Determine whether $f(x) = \frac{1}{x}$ is an even function, an odd function, or neither.

_____

Reflect

1. How does the graph of $f(x) = \frac{1}{x}$ show that the function has no zeros?

_____

_____

_____

2. **Discussion** A graph is said to be *symmetric about the origin* (and the origin is called the graph's *point of symmetry*) if for every point (x, y) on the graph, the point $(-x, -y)$ is also on the graph. Is the graph of $f(x) = \frac{1}{x}$ symmetric about the origin? Explain.

_____

_____

_____

3. Give any line(s) of symmetry for the graph of $f(x) = \frac{1}{x}$.

_____

_____

_____

⚙ Explain 1 Graphing Simple Rational Functions

When graphing transformations of $f(x) = \frac{1}{x}$, it helps to consider the effect of the transformations on the following features of the graph of $f(x)$: the vertical asymptote, $x = 0$; the horizontal asymptote, $y = 0$; and two reference points, $(-1, -1)$ and $(1, 1)$. The table lists these features of the graph of $f(x)$ and the corresponding features of the graph of $g(x) = a\left(\dfrac{1}{\frac{1}{b}(x - h)}\right) + k$. Note that the asymptotes are affected only by the parameters h and k, while the reference points are affected by all four parameters.

Feature	$f(x) = \frac{1}{x}$	$g(x) = a\left(\dfrac{1}{\frac{1}{b}(x-h)}\right) + k$
Vertical asymptote	$x = 0$	$x = h$
Horizontal asymptote	$y = 0$	$y = k$
Reference point	$(-1, -1)$	$(-b + h, -a + k)$
Reference point	$(1, 1)$	$(b + h, a + k)$

Example 1 Identify the transformations of the graph of $f(x) = \frac{1}{x}$ that produce the graph of the given function $g(x)$. Then graph $g(x)$ on the same coordinate plane as the graph of $f(x)$ by applying the transformations to the asymptotes $x = 0$ and $y = 0$ to the reference points $(-1, -1)$ and $(1, 1)$. Also state the domain and range of $g(x)$ using inequalities, set notation, and interval notation.

Ⓐ $g(x) = 3\left(\dfrac{1}{x - 1}\right) + 2$

The transformations of the graph of $f(x)$ that produce the graph of $g(x)$ are:

- a vertical stretch by a factor of 3
- a translation of 1 unit to the right and 2 units up

Note that the translation of 1 unit to the right affects only the x-coordinates, while the vertical stretch by a factor of 3 and the translation of 2 units up affect only the y-coordinates.

Feature	$f(x) = \frac{1}{x}$	$g(x) = 3\left(\dfrac{1}{x-1}\right) + 2$
Vertical asymptote	$x = 0$	$x = 1$
Horizontal asymptote	$y = 0$	$y = 2$
Reference point	$(-1, -1)$	$\left(-1 + 1, 3(-1) + 2\right) = (0, -1)$
Reference point	$(1, 1)$	$\left(1 + 1, 3(1) + 2\right) = (2, 5)$

Domain of $g(x)$:

    Inequality: $x < 1$ or $x > 1$

    Set notation: $\{x | x \neq 1\}$

    Interval notation: $(-\infty, 1) \cup (1, +\infty)$

Range of $g(x)$:

    Inequality: $y < 2$ or $y > 2$

    Set notation: $\{y | y \neq 2\}$

    Interval notation: $(-\infty, 2) \cup (2, +\infty)$

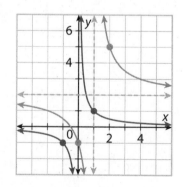

(B) $g(x) = \dfrac{1}{2(x+3)} - 1$

The transformations of the graph of $f(x)$ that produce the graph of $g(x)$ are:

- a horizontal compression by a factor of $\frac{1}{2}$
- a translation of 3 units to the left and 1 unit down

Note that the horizontal compression by a factor of $\frac{1}{2}$ and the translation of 3 units to the left affect only the x-coordinates of points on the graph of $f(x)$, while the translation of 1 unit down affects only the y-coordinates.

Feature	$f(x) = \dfrac{1}{x}$	$g(x) = \dfrac{1}{2(x+3)} - 1$
Vertical asymptote	$x = 0$	$x = \boxed{}$
Horizontal asymptote	$y = 0$	$y = \boxed{}$
Reference point	$(-1, -1)$	$\left(\frac{1}{2}\left(\boxed{}\right) - 3,\ \boxed{} - 1 \right) = \left(\boxed{}, \boxed{} \right)$
Reference point	$(1, 1)$	$\left(\frac{1}{2}\left(\boxed{}\right) - 3,\ \boxed{} - 1 \right) = \left(\boxed{}, \boxed{} \right)$

Domain of $g(x)$:

Inequality: $x < \boxed{}$ or $x > \boxed{}$

Set notation: $\left\{ x \mid x \neq \boxed{} \right\}$

Interval notation: $\left(-\infty, \boxed{} \right) \cup \left(\boxed{}, +\infty \right)$

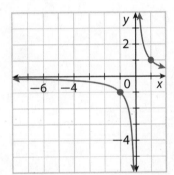

Range of $g(x)$:

Inequality: $y < \boxed{}$ or $y > \boxed{}$

Set notation: $\left\{ y \mid y \neq \boxed{} \right\}$

Interval notation: $\left(-\infty, \boxed{} \right) \cup \left(\boxed{}, +\infty \right)$

Identify the transformations of the graph of $f(x) = \frac{1}{x}$ that produce the graph of the given function $g(x)$. Then graph $g(x)$ on the same coordinate plane as the graph of $f(x)$ by applying the transformations to the asymptotes $x = 0$ and $y = 0$ to the reference points $(-1, -1)$ and $(1, 1)$. Also state the domain and range of $g(x)$ using inequalities, set notation, and interval notation.

4. $g(x) = -0.5\left(\dfrac{1}{x+1}\right) - 3$

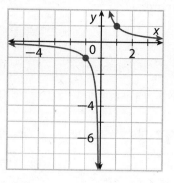

5. $g(x) = \dfrac{1}{-0.5(x-2)} + 1$

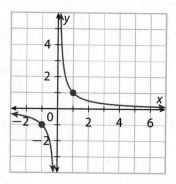

⚙ Explain 2 Rewriting Simple Rational Functions in Order to Graph Them

When given a rational function of the form $g(x) = \frac{mx + n}{px + q}$, where $m \neq 0$ and $p \neq 0$, you can carry out the division of the numerator by the denominator to write the function in the form $g(x) = a\left(\frac{1}{x-h}\right) + k$ or $g(x) = \frac{1}{\frac{1}{b}(x-h)} + k$ in order to graph it.

Example 2 Rewrite the function in the form $g(x) = a\left(\frac{1}{x-h}\right) + k$ or $g(x) = \frac{1}{\frac{1}{b}(x-h)} + k$ and graph it. Also state the domain and range using inequalities, set notation, and interval notation.

Ⓐ $g(x) = \dfrac{3x - 4}{x - 1}$

Use long division.

$$
\begin{array}{r}
3 \\
x - 1 \overline{)\, 3x - 4} \\
\underline{3x - 3} \\
-1
\end{array}
$$

So, the quotient is 3, and the remainder is -1. Using the fact that $dividend = quotient + \frac{remainder}{divisor}$, you have $g(x) = 3 + \frac{-1}{x-1}$, or $g(x) = -\frac{1}{x-1} + 3$.

The graph of $g(x)$ has vertical asymptote $x = 1$, horizontal asymptote $y = 3$, and reference points $\left(-1 + 1, -(-1) + 3\right) = (0, 4)$ and $(1 + 1, -(1) + 3) = (2, 2)$.

Domain of $g(x)$:

Inequality: $x < 1$ or $x > 1$

Set notation: $\left\{x \mid x \neq 1\right\}$

Interval notation: $(-\infty, 1) \cup (1, +\infty)$

Range of $g(x)$:

Inequality: $y < 3$ or $y > 3$

Set notation: $\left\{y \mid y \neq 3\right\}$

Interval notation: $(-\infty, 3) \cup (3, +\infty)$

Ⓑ $g(x) = \dfrac{4x - 7}{-2x + 4}$

Use long division.

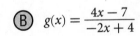

$$
\begin{array}{r}
-2 \\
-2x + 4 \overline{)\, 4x - 7} \\
\underline{4x - 8} \\
\boxed{}
\end{array}
$$

So, the quotient is -2, and the remainder is ____. Using the fact that $dividend = quotient + \frac{remainder}{divisor}$, you have

$$g(x) = -2 + \frac{\boxed{}}{-2x + 4}, \text{ or } g(x) = \frac{\boxed{}}{-2\left(x - \boxed{}\right)} - 2.$$

The graph of $g(x)$ has vertical asymptote $x = \boxed{}$, horizontal asymptote $y = -2$, and reference points

$\left(-\dfrac{1}{2}(-1) + \boxed{}, -1 - 2\right) = \left(\boxed{}, -3\right)$ and $\left(-\dfrac{1}{2}(1) + \boxed{}, 1 - 2\right) = \left(\boxed{}, -1\right)$.

Domain of $g(x)$:

  Inequality: $x < \boxed{}$ or $x > \boxed{}$

  Set notation: $\left\{ x \mid x \neq \boxed{} \right\}$

  Interval notation: $\left(-\infty, \boxed{}\right) \cup \left(\boxed{}, +\infty\right)$

Range of $g(x)$:

  Inequality: $y < \boxed{}$ or $y > \boxed{}$

  Set notation: $\left\{ y \mid y \neq \boxed{} \right\}$

  Interval notation: $\left(-\infty, \boxed{}\right) \cup \left(\boxed{}, +\infty\right)$

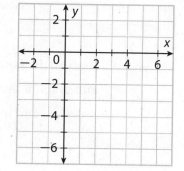

Reflect

6. In Part A, the graph of $g(x)$ is the result of what transformations of the graph of $f(x) = \dfrac{1}{x}$?

_____

_____

_____

_____

7. In Part B, the graph of $g(x)$ is the result of what transformations of the graph of $f(x) = \dfrac{1}{x}$?

_____

_____

_____

_____

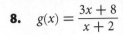

Rewrite the function in the form $g(x) = a\left(\dfrac{1}{x-h}\right) + k$ or $g(x) = \dfrac{1}{\frac{1}{b}(x-h)} + k$ and

graph it. Also state the domain and range using inequalities, set notation, and interval notation.

8. $g(x) = \dfrac{3x+8}{x+2}$

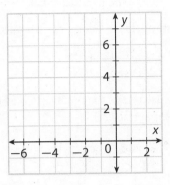

🔑 Explain 3 Writing Simple Rational Functions

When given the graph of a simple rational function, you can write its equation using one of the general forms $g(x) = a\left(\dfrac{1}{x-h}\right) + k$ and $g(x) = \dfrac{1}{\frac{1}{b}(x-h)} + k$ after identifying the values of the parameters using information obtained from the graph.

Example 3

(A) **Write the function whose graph is shown. Use the form $g(x) = a\left(\dfrac{1}{x-h}\right) + k$.**

Since the graph's vertical asymptote is $x = 3$, the value of the parameter h is 3. Since the graph's horizontal asymptote is $y = 4$, the value of the parameter k is 4.

Substitute these values into the general form of the function.

$g(x) = a\left(\dfrac{1}{x-3}\right) + 4$

Now use one of the points, such as $(4, 6)$, to find the value of the parameter a.

$g(x) = a\left(\dfrac{1}{x-3}\right) + 4$

$6 = a\left(\dfrac{1}{4-3}\right) + 4$

$6 = a + 4$

$2 = a$

So, $g(x) = 2\left(\dfrac{1}{x-3}\right) + 4.$

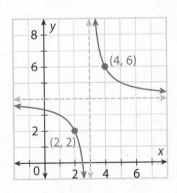

B Write the function whose graph is shown. Use the form $g(x) = \dfrac{1}{\frac{1}{b}(x-h)} + k$.

Since the graph's vertical asymptote is $x = -3$, the value of the

parameter h is -3. Since the graph's horizontal asymptote is $y = \boxed{}$,

the value of the parameter k is _____.

Substitute these values into the general form of the function.

$$g(x) = \dfrac{1}{\frac{1}{b}(x+3)} + \boxed{}$$

Now use one of the points, such as $(-5, 0)$, to find the value of the parameter a.

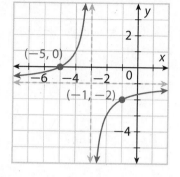
$(-5, 0)$
$(-1, -2)$

$$g(x) = \dfrac{1}{\frac{1}{b}(x+3)} + \boxed{}$$

$$0 = \dfrac{1}{\frac{1}{b}(-5+3)} + \boxed{}$$

$$\boxed{} = \dfrac{1}{\frac{1}{b}(-2)}$$

$$\frac{1}{b}(-2) \cdot \boxed{} = 1$$

$$\frac{1}{b} = \boxed{}$$

$$b = \boxed{}$$

So, $g(x) = \dfrac{1}{\frac{1}{\boxed{}}(x+3)} + \boxed{}$, or $g(x) = \dfrac{1}{-0.5(x+3)} - 1$.

Reflect

9. **Discussion** In Parts A and B, the coordinates of a second point on the graph of $g(x)$ are given. In what way can those coordinates be useful?

_____

_____

Your Turn

10. Write the function whose graph is shown.
Use the form $g(x) = a\left(\dfrac{1}{x-h}\right) + k$.

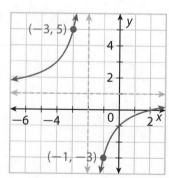
$(-3, 5)$
$(-1, -3)$

11. Write the function whose graph is shown. Use the form $g(x) = \dfrac{1}{\frac{1}{b}(x-h)} + k$.

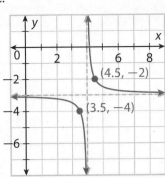
(4.5, −2)
(3.5, −4)

🔑 Explain 4 Modeling with Simple Rational Functions

In a real-world situation where there is a shared cost and a per-person or per-item cost, you can model the situation using a rational function that has the general form $f(x) = \dfrac{a}{x-h} + k$ where $f(x)$ is the total cost for each person or item.

Example 4

Ⓐ Mary and some of her friends are thinking about renting a car while staying at a beach resort for a vacation. The cost per person for staying at the beach resort is $300, and the cost of the car rental is $220. If the friends agree to share the cost of the car rental, what is the minimum number of people who must go on the trip so that the total cost for each person is no more than $350?

🧩 Analyze Information

Identify the important information.

- The cost per person for the resort is _____.

- The cost of the car rental is _____.

- The most that each person will spend is _____.

🧩 Formulate a Plan

Create a rational function that gives the total cost for each person. Graph the function, and use the graph to answer the question.

Let p be the number of people who agree to go on the trip. Let $C(p)$ be the cost (in dollars) for each person.

$$C(p) = \dfrac{\boxed{}}{p} + \boxed{}$$

Graph the function, recognizing that the graph involves two transformations of the graph of the parent rational function:

- a vertical stretch by a factor of _____

- a vertical translation of _____ units up

Also draw the line $C(p) = 350$.

The graphs intersect between $p = \boxed{}$ and $p = \boxed{}$, so the minimum number of people who must go on the trip in order for the total cost for each person to be no more than $350

is _____.

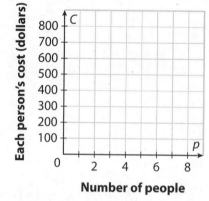

Justify and Evaluate

Check the solution by evaluating the function $C(p)$. Since $C(4) = \boxed{} > 350$ and $C(5) = \boxed{} < 350$, the minimum number of people who must go on the trip is _____.

Your Turn

12. Justin has purchased a basic silk screening kit for applying designs to fabric. The kit costs $200. He plans to buy T-shirts for $10 each, apply a design that he creates to them, and then sell them. Model this situation with a rational function that gives the average cost of a silk-screened T-shirt when the cost of the kit is included in the calculation. Use the graph of the function to determine the minimum number of T-shirts that brings the average cost below $17.50.

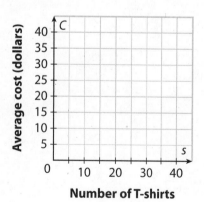

13. Compare and contrast the attributes of $f(x) = \frac{1}{x}$ and the attributes of $g(x) = -\frac{1}{x}$.

_____

_____

_____

_____

_____

_____

14. State the domain and range of $f(x) = a\left(\frac{1}{x-h}\right) + k$ using inequalities, set notation, and interval notation.

15. Given that the model $C(p) = \frac{100}{p} + 50$ represents the total cost C (in dollars) for each person in a group of p people when there is a shared expense and an individual expense, describe what the expressions $\frac{100}{p}$ and 50 represent.

_____

_____

_____

16. **Essential Question Check-In** Describe the transformations you must perform on the graph of $f(x) = \frac{1}{x}$ to obtain the graph of $f(x) = a\left(\frac{1}{x-h}\right) + k$.

_____

_____

_____

_____

Describe how the graph of $g(x)$ is related to the graph of $f(x) = \frac{1}{x}$.

1. $g(x) = \frac{1}{x} + 4$

2. $g(x) = 5\left(\frac{1}{x}\right)$

3. $g(x) = \frac{1}{x + 3}$

4. $g(x) = \frac{1}{0.1x}$

5. $g(x) = \frac{1}{x} - 7$

6. $g(x) = \frac{1}{x - 8}$

7. $g(x) = -0.1\left(\frac{1}{x}\right)$

8. $g(x) = \frac{1}{-3x}$

Identify the transformations of the graph of $f(x)$ that produce the graph of the given function $g(x)$. Then graph $g(x)$ on the same coordinate plane as the graph of $f(x)$ by applying the transformations to the asymptotes $x = 0$ and $y = 0$ and to the reference points $(-1, -1)$ and $(1, 1)$. Also state the domain and range of $g(x)$ using inequalities, set notation, and interval notation.

9. $g(x) = 3\left(\frac{1}{x + 1}\right) - 2$

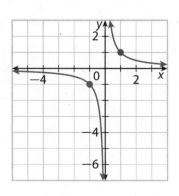

10. $g(x) = \dfrac{1}{-0.5(x - 3)} + 1$

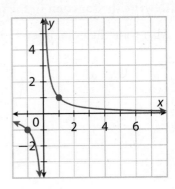

11. $g(x) = -0.5\left(\dfrac{1}{x - 1}\right) - 2$

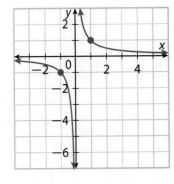

12. $g(x) = \dfrac{1}{2(x + 2)} + 3$

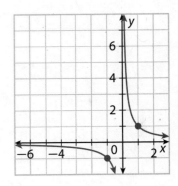

Rewrite the function in the form $g(x) = a\dfrac{1}{(x-h)} + k$ or $g(x) = \dfrac{1}{\frac{1}{b}(x-h)} + k$ and graph it.

Also state the domain and range using inequalities, set notation, and interval notation.

13. $g(x) = \dfrac{3x-5}{x-1}$

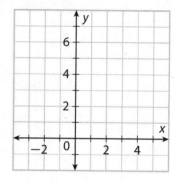

14. $g(x) = \dfrac{x+5}{0.5x+2}$

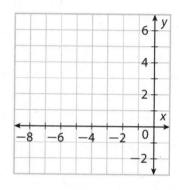

15. $g(x) = \dfrac{-4x+11}{x-2}$

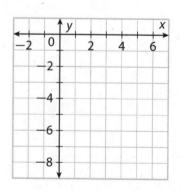

16. $g(x) = \dfrac{4x + 13}{-2x - 6}$

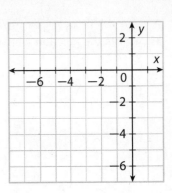

17. Write the function whose graph is shown. Use the form $g(x) = a\left(\dfrac{1}{x - h}\right) + k$.

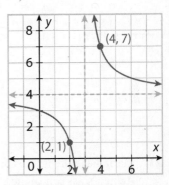

18. Write the function whose graph is shown. Use the form $g(x) = \dfrac{1}{\frac{1}{b}(x - h)} + k$

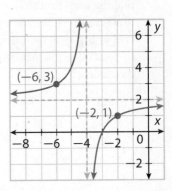

19. Write the function whose graph is shown. Use the form $g(x) = \dfrac{1}{\frac{1}{b}(x-h)} + k$.

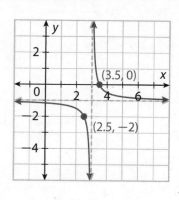

20. Write the function whose graph is shown. Use the form $g(x) = a\left(\dfrac{1}{x-h}\right) + k$

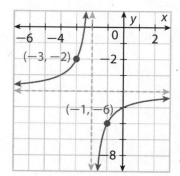

21. Maria has purchased a basic stained glass kit for $100. She plans to make stained glass suncatchers and sell them. She estimates that the materials for making each suncatcher will cost $15. Model this situation with a rational function that gives the average cost of a stained glass suncatcher when the cost of the kit is included in the calculation. Use the graph of the function to determine the minimum number of suncatchers that brings the average cost below $22.50.

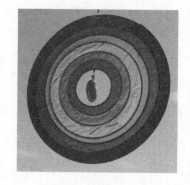

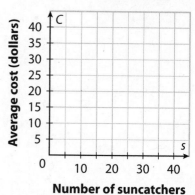

22. Amy has purchased a basic letterpress kit for $140. She plans to make wedding invitations. She estimates that the cost of the paper and envelope for each invitation is $2. Model this situation with a rational function that gives the average cost of a wedding invitation when the cost of the kit is included in the calculation. Use the graph of the function to determine the minimum number of invitations that brings the average cost below $5.

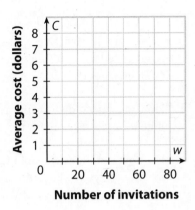

23. Multiple Response Select the transformations of the graph of the parent rational function that result in the graph of $g(x) = \dfrac{1}{2(x-3)} + 1$

A. Horizontal stretch by a factor of 2

B. Horizontal compression by a factor of $\frac{1}{2}$

C. Vertical stretch by a factor of 2

D. Vertical compression by a factor of $\frac{1}{2}$

E. Translation 1 unit up

F. Translation 1 unit down

G. Translation 3 units right

H. Translation 3 units left

> **H.O.T. Focus on Higher Order Thinking**

24. Justify Reasoning Explain why, for positive numbers a and b, a vertical stretch or compression of the graph of $f(x) = \frac{1}{x}$ by a factor of a and, separately, a horizontal stretch or compression of the graph of $f(x)$ by a factor of b result in the same graph when a and b are equal.

25. Communicate Mathematical Ideas Determine the domain and range of the rational function $g(x) = \dfrac{mx + n}{px + q}$ where $p \neq 0$. Give your answer in set notation, and explain your reasoning. Assume that there is a remainder when dividing $mx + n$ by $px + q$.

Lesson Performance Task

Graham wants to take snowboarding lessons at a nearby ski resort that charges $40 per week. The resort also charges a one-time equipment-rental fee of $99 for uninterrupted enrollment in classes. The resort requires that learners pay for three weeks of classes at a time.

a. Write a model that gives Graham's average weekly enrollment cost (in dollars) as a function of the time (in weeks) that Graham takes classes.

b. How much would Graham's average weekly enrollment cost be if he took classes only for the minimum of three weeks?

c. For how many weeks would Graham need to take classes for his average weekly enrollment cost to be at most $60? Describe how you can use a graphing calculator to graph the function from part a in order to answer this question, and then state the answer.

8.2 Graphing More Complicated Rational Functions

Essential Question: What features of the graph of a rational function should you identify in order to sketch the graph? How do you identify those features?

Resource
Locker

Explore 1 Investigating Domains and Vertical Asympotes of More Complicated Rational Functions

You know that the rational function $f(x) = \frac{1}{x-2} + 3$ has the domain $\{x|x \neq 2\}$ because the function is undefined at $x = 2$. Its graph has the vertical asymptote $x = 2$ because as $x \rightarrow 2^+$ (x approaches 2 from the right), $f(x) \rightarrow +\infty$, and as $x \rightarrow 2^-$ (x approaches 2 from the left), $f(x) \rightarrow -\infty$. In this Explore, you will investigate the domains and vertical asymptotes of other rational functions.

(A) Complete the table by identifying each function's domain based on the x-values for which the function is undefined. Write the domain using an inequality, set notation, and interval notation. Then state the equations of what you think the vertical asymptotes of the function's graph are.

Function	Domain	Possible Vertical Asymptotes
$f(x) = \dfrac{x+3}{x-1}$		
$f(x) = \dfrac{(x+5)(x-1)}{x+1}$		
$f(x) = \dfrac{x-4}{(x+1)(x-1)}$		
$f(x) = \dfrac{2x^2 - 3x + 9}{x^2 - x - 6}$		

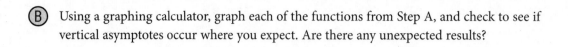

(B) Using a graphing calculator, graph each of the functions from Step A, and check to see if vertical asymptotes occur where you expect. Are there any unexpected results?

_____

_____

(C) Examine the behavior of $f(x) = \dfrac{x+3}{x-1}$ near $x = 1$.

First, complete the tables.

x approaches 1 from the right	
x	$f(x) = \dfrac{x+3}{x-1}$
1.1	
1.01	
1.001	

x approaches 1 from the left	
x	$f(x) = \dfrac{x+3}{x-1}$
0.9	
0.99	
0.999	

Next, summarize the results.

- As $x \to 1^+$, $f(x) \to$ ⬚ .
- As $x \to 1^-$, $f(x) \to$ ⬚ .

The behaviour of $f(x) = \dfrac{x+3}{x-1}$ near $x = 1$ shows that the graph of $f(x)$ [has/does not] have a vertical asymptote at $x = 1$.

(D) Examine the behavior of $f(x) = \dfrac{(x+5)(x-1)}{(x+1)}$ near $x = -1$.

First, complete the tables.

x approaches −1 from the right	
x	$f(x) = \dfrac{(x+5)(x-1)}{x+1}$
−0.9	
−0.99	
−0.999	

x approaches −1 from the left	
x	$f(x) = \dfrac{(x+5)(x-1)}{x+1}$
−1.1	
−1.01	
−1.001	

Next, summarize the results.

- As $x \to -1^+$, $f(x) \to$ ⬚ .
- As $x \to -1^-$, $f(x) \to$ ⬚ .

The behavior of $f(x) = \dfrac{(x+5)(x-1)}{(x+1)}$ near $x = -1$ shows that the graph of $f(x)$ [has/does not have] a vertical asymptote at $x = -1$.

(E) Examine the behavior of $f(x) = \dfrac{x - 4}{(x + 1)(x - 1)}$ near $x = -1$ and $x = 1$.

First, complete the tables. Round results to the nearest tenth.

x approaches −1 from the right	
x	$f(x) = \dfrac{x - 4}{(x + 1)(x - 1)}$
−0.9	
−0.99	
−0.999	

x approaches −1 from the left	
x	$f(x) = \dfrac{x - 4}{(x + 1)(x - 1)}$
−1.1	
−1.01	
−1.001	

x approaches 1 from the right	
x	$f(x) = \dfrac{x - 4}{(x + 1)(x - 1)}$
1.1	
1.01	
1.001	

x approaches 1 from the left	
x	$f(x) = \dfrac{x - 4}{(x + 1)(x - 1)}$
0.9	
0.99	
0.999	

Next, summarize the results.

- As $x \to -1^+$, $f(x) \to$ _____ .
- As $x \to -1^-$, $f(x) \to$ _____ .

- As $x \to 1^+$, $f(x) \to$ _____ .
- As $x \to 1^-$, $f(x) \to$ _____ .

The behavior of $f(x) = \dfrac{x-4}{(x+1)(x-1)}$ near $x = -1$ shows that the graph of $f(x)$ has/does not have a vertical asymptote at $x = -1$. The behavior of $f(x) = \dfrac{x-4}{(x+1)(x-1)}$ near $x = 1$ shows that the graph of $f(x)$ has/does not have a vertical asymptote at $x = 1$.

(F) Examine the behavior of $f(x) = \dfrac{2x^2 - 3x - 9}{x^2 - x - 6}$ near $x = -2$ and $x = 3$.

First, complete the tables. Round results to the nearest ten thousandth if necessary.

x approaches −2 from the right	
x	$f(x) = \dfrac{2x^2 - 3x - 9}{x^2 - x - 6}$
−1.9	
−1.99	
−1.999	

x approaches −2 from the left	
x	$f(x) = \dfrac{2x^2 - 3x - 9}{x^2 - x - 6}$
−2.1	
−2.01	
−2.001	

x approaches 3 from the right			x approaches 3 from the left	
x	$f(x) = \dfrac{2x^2 - 3x - 9}{x^2 - x - 6}$		x	$f(x) = \dfrac{2x^2 - 3x - 9}{x^2 - x - 6}$
3.1			2.9	
3.01			2.99	
3.001			2.999	

Next, summarize the results.

- As $x \to -2^+$, $f(x) \to$ ☐.
- As $x \to -2^-$, $f(x) \to$ ☐.

- As $x \to 3^+$, $f(x) \to$ ☐.
- As $x \to 3^-$, $f(x) \to$ ☐.

The behavior of $f(x) = \dfrac{2x^2 - 3x - 9}{x^2 - x - 6}$ near $x = -2$ shows that the graph of $f(x)$ has/does not have a vertical asymptote at $x = -2$. The behavior of $f(x) = \dfrac{2x^2 - 3x - 9}{x^2 - x - 6}$ near $x = 3$ shows that the graph of $f(x)$ has/does not have a vertical asymptote at $x = 3$.

Reflect

1. Rewrite $f(x) = \dfrac{2x^2 - 3x - 9}{x^2 - x - 6}$ so that its numerator and denominator are factored. How does this form of the function explain the behavior of the function near $x = 3$?

_____

_____

_____

_____

2. **Discussion** When you graph $f(x) = \dfrac{2x^2 - 3x - 9}{x^2 - x - 6}$ on a graphing calculator, you can't tell that the function is undefined for $x = 3$. How does using the calculator's table feature help? What do you think the graph should look like to make it clear that the function is undefined at $x = 3$?

_____

_____

Sketching the Graphs of More Complicated Rational Functions

As you have seen, there can be breaks in the graph of a rational function. These breaks are called *discontinuities*, and there are two kinds:

1. When a rational function has a factor in the denominator that is not also in the numerator, an *infinite discontinuity* occurs at the value of x for which the factor equals 0. On the graph of the function, an infinite discontinuity appears as a vertical asymptote.

2. When a rational function has a factor in the denominator that is also in the numerator, a *point discontinuity* occurs at the value of x for which the factor equals 0. On the graph of the function, a point discontinuity appears as a "hole."

The graph of a rational function can also have a horizontal asymptote, or even an asymptote that is a line that is neither horizontal nor vertical. This is determined by the degrees and leading coefficients of the function's numerator and denominator. Examine the following rational expressions, which include polynomial quotients rewritten using long division as a quotient plus a remainder that approaches 0 as x increases or decreases without bound.

$$\frac{1}{x-1} \to 0 \text{ as } x \to \pm\infty$$

$$\frac{x+1}{x^2-1} = \frac{x+1}{(x+1)(x-1)} = \frac{1}{x-1}\ (x \neq -1), \text{ so } \frac{x+1}{x^2-1} \to 0 \text{ as } x \to \pm\infty$$

$$\frac{x+3}{x-1} = 1 + \frac{4}{x-1} \to 1 \text{ as } x \to \pm\infty$$

$$\frac{4x+3}{x-1} = 4 + \frac{7}{x-1} \to 4 \text{ as } x \to \pm\infty$$

$$\frac{3x^2+x-1}{x-1} = 3x+4 + \frac{3}{x-1} \to 3x+4 \text{ as } x \to \pm\infty$$

In general, if the numerator is a polynomial $p(x)$ in standard form with leading coefficient a and the denominator is a polynomial $q(x)$ in standard form with leading coefficient b, then an examination of the function's end behavior gives the following results.

Relationship between Degree of $p(x)$ and Degree of $q(x)$	Equation of Horizontal Asymptote (if one exists)
Degree of $p(x)$ < degree of $q(x)$	$y = 0$
Degree of $p(x)$ = degree of $q(x)$	$y = \dfrac{a}{b}$
Degree of $p(x)$ > degree of $q(x)$	There is no horizontal asymptote. The function instead increases or decreases without bound as x increases or decreases without bound. In particular, when the degree of the numerator is 1 more than the degree of the denominator, the function's graph approaches a slanted line, called a *slant asymptote*, as x increases or decreases without bound.

You can sketch the graph of a rational function by identifying where vertical asymptotes, "holes," horizontal asymptotes, and slant asymptotes occur. Using the factors of the numerator and denominator, you can also establish intervals on the x-axis where either an x-intercept or a discontinuity occurs and then check the signs of the factors on those intervals to determine whether the graph lies above or below the x-axis.

Example 1 Sketch the graph of the given rational function. (If the degree of the numerator is 1 more than the degree of the denominator, find the graph's slant asymptote by dividing the numerator by the denominator.) Also state the function's domain and range using inequalities, set notation, and interval notation. (If your sketch indicates that the function has maximum or minimum values, use a graphing calculator to find those values to the nearest hundredth when determining the range.)

(A) $f(x) = \dfrac{x+1}{x-2}$

Identify vertical asymptotes and "holes."

The function is undefined when $x - 2 = 0$, or $x = 2$. Since $x - 2$ is not a factor of the numerator, there is a vertical asymptote rather than a "hole" at $x = 2$.

Identify horizontal asymptotes and slant asymptotes.

The numerator and denominator have the same degree and the leading coefficient of each is 1, so there is a horizontal asymptote at $y = \frac{1}{1} = 1$.

Identify x-intercepts.

An x-intercept occurs when $x + 1 = 0$, or $x = -1$.

Check the sign of the function on the intervals $x < -1$, $-1 < x < 2$, and $x > 2$.

Interval	Sign of $x+1$	Sign of $x-2$	Sign of $f(x) = \dfrac{x+1}{x-2}$
$x < -1$	$-$	$-$	$+$
$-1 < x < 2$	$+$	$-$	$-$
$x > 2$	$+$	$+$	$+$

Sketch the graph using all this information. Then state the domain and range.

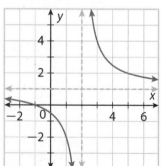

Domain:

Inequality: $x < 2$ or $x > 2$

Set notation: $\{x | x \neq 2\}$

Interval notation: $(-\infty, 2) \cup (2, +\infty)$

Range:

Inequality: $y < 1$ or $y > 1$

Set notation: $\{y | y \neq 1\}$

Interval notation: $(-\infty, 1) \cup (1, +\infty)$

Ⓑ $f(x) = \dfrac{x^2 + x - 2}{x + 3}$

Factor the function's numerator.

$f(x) = \dfrac{x^2 + x - 2}{x + 3} = \dfrac{(x - 1)(x + 2)}{x + 3}$

Identify vertical asymptotes and "holes."

The function is undefined when $x + 3 = 0$, or $x = \boxed{}$. Since $x + 3$ is not a factor of the numerator, there is a vertical asymptote rather than a "hole" at $x = \boxed{}$.

Identify horizontal asymptotes and slant asymptotes.

Because the degree of the numerator is 1 more than the degree of the denominator, there is no horizontal asymptote, but there is a slant asymptote. Divide the numerator by the denominator to identify the slant asymptote.

$$
\begin{array}{r}
x - \boxed{} \\
x + 3 \overline{)\, x^2 + x - 2} \\
\underline{x^2 + 3x} \\
-2x - 2 \\
\underline{-2x - 6} \\
4
\end{array}
$$

So, the line $y = x - \boxed{}$ is the slant asymptote.

Identify x-intercepts.

There are two x-intercepts: when $x - 1 = 0$, or $x = \boxed{}$, and when $x + 2 = 0$, or $x = \boxed{}$.

Check the sign of the function on the intervals $x < -3$, $-3 < x < -2$, $-2 < x < 1$, and $x > 1$.

Interval	Sign of $x+3$	Sign of $x+2$	Sign of $x-1$	Sign of $f(x) = \dfrac{(x-1)(x+2)}{x+3}$
$x < -3$	$-$	$-$	$-$	$-$
$-3 < x < -2$				
$-2 < x < 1$				
$x > 1$				

Sketch the graph using all this information. Then state the domain and range.

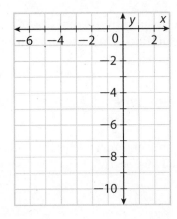

Domain:

Inequality: $x < \boxed{}$ or $x > \boxed{}$

Set notation: $\left\{ x \mid x \neq \boxed{} \right\}$

Interval notation: $\left(-\infty, \boxed{} \right) \cup \left(\boxed{}, +\infty \right)$

The sketch indicates that the function has a maximum value and a minimum value. Using **3:minimum** from the **CALC** menu on a graphing calculator gives -1 as the minimum value. Using **4:maximum** from the **CALC** menu on a graphing calculator gives -5 as the maximum value.

Range: Inequality: $y < \boxed{}$ or $y > \boxed{}$

Set notation: $\left\{ y \mid y < \boxed{} \text{ or } y > \boxed{} \right\}$ Interval notation: $\left(-\infty, \boxed{} \right) \cup \left(\boxed{}, +\infty \right)$

Your Turn

Sketch the graph of the given rational function. (If the degree of the numerator is 1 more than the degree of the denominator, find the graph's slant asymptote by dividing the numerator by the denominator.) Also state the function's domain and range using inequalities, set notation, and interval notation. (If your sketch indicates that the function has maximum or minimum values, use a graphing calculator to find those values to the nearest hundredth when determining the range.)

3. $f(x) = \dfrac{x+1}{x^2 + 3x - 4}$

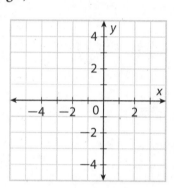

⚙ Explain 2   Modeling with More Complicated Rational Functions

When two real-world variable quantities are compared using a ratio or rate, the comparison is a rational function. You can solve problems about the ratio or rate by graphing the rational function.

Example 2   Write a rational function to model the situation, or use the given rational function. State a reasonable domain and range for the function using set notation. Then use a graphing calculator to graph the function and answer the question.

(A) A baseball team has won 32 games out of 56 games played, for a winning percentage of $\frac{32}{56} \approx 0.571$. How many consecutive games must the team win to raise its winning percentage to 0.600?

Let w be the number of consecutive games to be won. Then the total number of games won is the function $T_{\text{won}}(w) = 32 + w$, and the total number of games played is the function $T_{\text{played}}(w) = 56 + w$.

The rational function that gives the team's winning percentage p (as a decimal) is

$$p(w) = \frac{T_{\text{won}}(w)}{T_{\text{played}}(w)} = \frac{32 + w}{56 + w}.$$

The domain of the rational function is $\left\{w \mid w \geq 0 \text{ and } w \text{ is a whole number}\right\}$. Note that you do not need to exclude -56 from the domain, because only nonnegative whole-number values of w make sense in this situation.

Since the function models what happens to the team's winning percentage from consecutive wins (no losses), the values of $p(w)$ start at 0.571 and approach 1 as w increases without bound. So, the range is

$$\left\{p \mid 0.571 \leq p < 1\right\}.$$

Graph $y = \frac{32 + x}{56 + x}$ on a graphing calculator using a viewing window that shows 0 to 10 on the x-axis and 0.5 to 0.7 on the y-axis. Also graph the line $y = 0.6$. To find where the graphs intersect, select **5: intersect** from the **CALC** menu.

So, the team's winning percentage (as a decimal) will be 0.600 if the team wins 4 consecutive games.

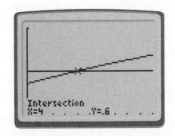

Intersection
X=4 · · · · .Y=.6 . · · · ·

(B) Two friends decide spend an afternoon canoeing on a river. They travel 4 miles upstream and 6 miles downstream. In still water, they know that their average paddling speed is 5 miles per hour. If their canoe trip takes 4 hours, what is the average speed of the river's current? To answer the question, use the rational function $t(c) = \frac{4}{5 - c} + \frac{6}{5 + c} = \frac{50 - 2c}{(5 - c)(5 + c)}$ where c is the average speed of the current (in miles per hour) and t is the time (in hours) spent canoeing 4 miles against the current at a rate of $5 - c$ miles per hour and 6 miles with the current at a rate of $5 + c$ miles per hour.

In order for the friends to travel upstream, the speed of the current must be less than their average paddling speed, so the domain of the function is $\left\{c \mid 0 \leq c < \boxed{}\right\}$. If the friends canoed in still water $(c = 0)$, the trip would take a total of $\frac{4}{5} + \frac{6}{5} = \boxed{}$ hours.

As c approaches 5 from the left, the value of $\frac{6}{5 + c}$ approaches $\frac{6}{10} = 0.6$ hour, but the value of $\frac{4}{5 - c}$ $\text{........................}$. So, the range of the function is $\left\{t \mid t \geq \boxed{}\right\}$.

Graph $y = \frac{50 - 2x}{(5 - x)(5 + x)}$ on a graphing calculator using a viewing window that shows 0 to 5 on the x-axis and 2 to 5 on the y-axis. Also graph the line $y = \boxed{}$. To find where the graphs intersect, select **5:intersect** from the **CALC** menu. The calculator shows that the

average speed of the current is about _____ miles per hour.

Write a rational function to model the situation, or use the given rational function.
State a reasonable domain and range for the function using set notation. Then use a
graphing calculator to graph the function and answer the question.

4. A saline solution is a mixture of salt and water. A $p\%$ saline solution contains $p\%$ salt
and $(100 - p)\%$ water by mass. A chemist has 300 grams of a 4% saline solution that needs
to be strengthened to a 6% solution by adding salt. How much salt should the chemist add?

Elaborate

5. How can you show that the vertical line $x = c$, where c is a constant, is an asymptote
for the graph of a rational function?

_____

_____

6. How can you determine the end behavior of a rational function?

_____

_____

_____

_____

7. **Essential Question Check-In** How do you identify any vertical asymptotes
and "holes" that the graph of a rational function has?

_____

_____

_____

_____

☆ Evaluate: Homework and Practice

• Online Homework
• Hints and Help
• Extra Practice

State the domain using an inequality, set notation, and interval notation. For any
x-value excluded from the domain, state whether the graph has a vertical asymptote
or a "hole" at that x-value. Use a graphing calculator to check your answer.

1. $f(x) = \dfrac{x + 5}{x + 1}$

2. $f(x) = \dfrac{x^2 + 2x - 3}{x^2 - 4x + 3}$

Divide the numerator by the denominator to write the function in the form $f(x) = \text{quotient} + \dfrac{\text{remainder}}{\text{divisor}}$
and determine the function's end behavior. Then, using a graphing calculator to examine the function's
graph, state the range using an inequality, set notation, and interval notation.

3. $f(x) = \dfrac{3x + 1}{x - 2}$

4. $f(x) = \dfrac{x}{(x - 2)(x + 3)}$

5. $f(x) = \dfrac{x^2 - 5x + 6}{x - 1}$

6. $f(x) = \dfrac{4x^2 - 1}{x^2 + x - 2}$

Sketch the graph of the given rational function. (If the degree of the numerator is 1 more than the degree of the denominator, find the graph's slant asymptote by dividing the numerator by the denominator.) Also state the function's domain and range using inequalities, set notation, and interval notation. (If your sketch indicates that the function has maximum or minimum values, use a graphing calculator to find those values to the nearest hundredth when determining the range.)

7. $f(x) = \dfrac{x-1}{x+1}$

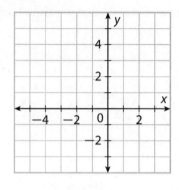

8. $f(x) = \dfrac{x-1}{(x-2)(x+3)}$

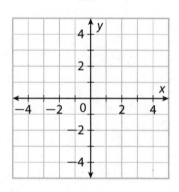

9. $f(x) = \dfrac{(x+1)(x-1)}{x+2}$

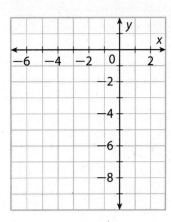

10. $f(x) = \dfrac{-3x(x-2)}{(x-2)(x+2)}$

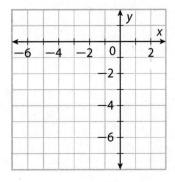

413

11. $f(x) = \dfrac{x^2 + 2x - 8}{x - 1}$

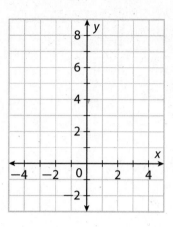

12. $f(x) = \dfrac{2x^2 - 4x}{x^2 + 4x + 4}$

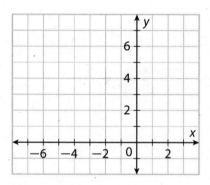

Write a rational function to model the situation, or use the given rational function. State a reasonable domain and range for the function using set notation. Then use a graphing calculator to graph the function and answer the question.

13. A basketball team has won 16 games out of 23 games played, for a winning percentage (expressed as a decimal) of $\frac{16}{23} \approx 0.696$. How many consecutive games must the team win to raise its winning percentage to 0.750?

14. So far this season, a baseball player has had 84 hits in 294 times at bat, for a batting average of $\frac{84}{294} \approx 0.286$. How many consecutive hits must the player get to raise his batting average to 0.300?

15. A kayaker traveled 5 miles upstream and then 8 miles downstream on a river. The average speed of the current was 3 miles per hour. If the kayaker was paddling for 5 hours, what was the kayaker's average paddling speed? To answer the question, use the rational function

$t(s) = \dfrac{5}{s-3} + \dfrac{8}{s+3} = \dfrac{13s-9}{(s-3)(s+3)}$ where s is the kayaker's

average paddling speed (in miles per hour) and t is the time (in hours) spent kayaking 5 miles against the current at a rate of $s - 3$ miles per hour and 8 miles with the current at a rate of $s + 3$ miles per hour.

16. In aviation, *air speed* refers to a plane's speed in still air. A small plane maintains a certain air speed when flying to and from a city that is 400 miles away. On the trip out, the plane flies against a wind, which has an average speed of 40 miles per hour. On the return trip, the plane flies with the wind. If the total flight time for the round trip is 3.5 hours, what is the plane's average air speed? To answer this question, use

the rational function $t(s) = \dfrac{400}{s-40} + \dfrac{400}{s+40} = \dfrac{800s}{(s-40)(s+40)}$, where s is the air speed

(in miles per hour) and t is the total flight time (in hours) for the round trip.

17. Multiple Response Select the statements that apply to the rational function

$f(x) = \dfrac{x - 2}{x^2 - x - 6}$.

A. The function's domain is $\left\{x | x \neq -2 \text{ and } x \neq 3\right\}$.

B. The function's domain is $\left\{x | x \neq -2 \text{ and } x \neq -3\right\}$.

C. The function's range is $\left\{y | y \neq 0\right\}$.

D. The function's range is $\left\{y | -\infty < y < +\infty\right\}$.

E. The function's graph has vertical asymptotes at $x = -2$ and $x = 3$.

F. The function's graph has a vertical asymptote at $x = -3$ and a "hole" at $x = 2$.

G. The function's graph has a horizontal asymptote at $y = 0$.

H. The function's graph has a horizontal asymptote at $y = 1$.

H.O.T. Focus on Higher Order Thinking

18. Draw Conclusions For what value(s) of a does the graph of $f(x) = \dfrac{x + a}{x^2 + 4x + 3}$ have a "hole"? Explain. Then, for each value of a, state the domain and the range of $f(x)$ using interval notation.

19. Critique Reasoning A student claims that the functions $f(x) = \dfrac{4x^2 - 1}{4x + 2}$ and $g(x) = \dfrac{4x + 2}{4x^2 - 1}$ have different domains but identical ranges. Which part of the student's claim is correct, and which is false? Explain.

Lesson Performance Task

In professional baseball, the smallest allowable volume of a baseball is 92.06% of the largest allowable volume, and the range of allowable radii is 0.04 inch.

a. Let r be the largest allowable radius (in inches) of a baseball. Write expressions, both in terms of r, for the largest allowable volume of the baseball and the smallest allowable volume of the baseball. (Use the formula for the volume of a sphere, $V = \frac{4}{3}\pi r^3$.)

b. Write and simplify a function that gives the ratio R of the smallest allowable volume of a baseball to the largest allowable volume.

c. Use a graphing calculator to graph the function from part b, and use the graph to find the smallest allowable radius and the largest allowable radius of a baseball. Round your answers to the nearest hundredth.

Rational Functions

Essential Question: How can you use rational functions to solve real-world problems?

KEY EXAMPLE *(Lesson 8.1)*

Graph $y = -\dfrac{1}{x-2}$. State the domain, range, y-intercept, and identify any asymptotes.

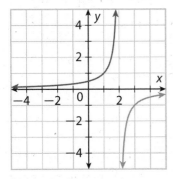

Domain: $x < 2$ or $x > 2$

Range: $y < 0$ or $y > 0$

y-intercept: $\left(0, \frac{1}{2}\right)$

The graph has a vertical asymptote at $x = 2$ and a horizontal asymptote at $y = 0$.

KEY EXAMPLE *(Lesson 8.2)*

Graph $y = \dfrac{2x^2}{x+2}$. State the domain, range, x-intercept, and identify any asymptotes.

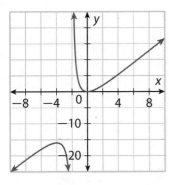

Domain: $x < -2$ or $x > -2$

Range: $y \le -16$ or $y \ge 0$

The numerator has 0 as its only zero, so the x-intercept is $(0, 0)$.

The denominator has -2 as its only zero, so the graph has a vertical asymptote at $x = -2$.

EXERCISES

Describe how the graph of $g(x)$ is related to the graph of $f(x) = \frac{1}{x}$. *(Lesson 8.1)*

1. $g(x) = \dfrac{1}{x + 4}$

2. $g(x) = \dfrac{1}{x - 2} + 3$

3. $g(x) = \dfrac{-1}{x + 3}$

Graph the function using a graphing calculator. State the domain, x-intercept(s), and identify asymptotes. *(Lesson 8.2)*

4. $f(x) = \dfrac{x^2 - 3x}{x + 4}$

5. $f(x) = \dfrac{x - 3}{x^2 + 6x + 5}$

6. $f(x) = -\dfrac{(x^2 - 4)}{(x + 1)}$

MODULE PERFORMANCE TASK

What Is the Profit?

A sporting goods store sells two styles of bike helmets: Style A for $30 each and Style B for $40 each. The store is trying to calculate its average profit on each style of helmet, using the rational function $A(x) = \frac{P(x)}{x}$, where $P(x)$ is the profit on the sale of x helmets. The helmet supplier offers a volume discount for orders up to 500 helmets, using the cost formulas shown in the table. For each style, how does per-helmet profit change as the number of helmets increases? What is the maximum per-helmet profit?

Number of Helmets (x)	100	200	300	400	500
Style A					
Revenue					
Cost: $100 + (20 - 0.01x)x$					
Profit					
Style B					
Revenue					
Cost: $250 + (30 - 0.03x)x$					
Profit					

Start by organizing your data in the table. Then use your own paper to complete the task. Use graphs, numbers, words, or algebra to explain how you reached your conclusion.

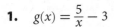

8.1–8.2 Rational Functions

Describe how the graph of $g(x)$ is related to the graph

of $f(x) = \frac{1}{x}$. *(Lesson 8.2)*

• Online Homework
• Hints and Help
• Extra Practice

1. $g(x) = \frac{5}{x} - 3$

2. $g(x) = \dfrac{1}{-0.5(x-2)} + 4$

3. $g(x) = \frac{-1}{x} + 5$

Graph the function using a graphing calculator. State the domain, x-intercept(s), and identify asymptotes. *(Lessons 8.2, 8.3)*

4. $f(x) = \dfrac{2x-4}{x+3}$

5. $f(x) = \dfrac{x^2-9}{x-2}$

6. $f(x) = -\dfrac{(x+2)}{(x^2+3x)}$

ESSENTIAL QUESTION

7. How do you identify any linear asymptotes of a rational function?

Assessment Readiness

1. Consider the inequality $x^2 - 64 < 0$. Tell whether each of the following is a solution set of the inequality.
   Select Yes or No for A–C.

   A. $x < -8$ or $x > -8$ ⬤ Yes   No

   B. $-8 < x < -8$ Yes ⬤ No

   C. $-64 < x < -64$ ⬤ Yes   No

2. Consider the equation $y = \frac{2x + 5}{x - 1}$. Select True or False for each statement.

   A. The line $x = 1$ is an asymptote.   True ⬤ False

   B. The point $(0, -5)$ lies on the graph.   True ⬤ False

   C. The function is undefined for $x = -1$. ⬤ True   False

3. Consider the function $y = \frac{x^2 + 5x + 4}{x^2 - 9}$. State the domain, range, and x- and y-intercepts, and identify any asymptotes.

4. You have subscribed to a cable television service. The cable company charges a one-time installation fee of $30 and a monthly fee of $50. Write a model that gives the average cost per month as a function of months subscribed to the service. After how many months will the average cost be $56? Explain your thinking and identify any asymptotes on the graph of the function.

Rational Expressions and Equations

Essential Question: How can you use rational expressions and equations to solve real-world problems?

REAL WORLD VIDEO
Robotic arms and other prosthetic devices are among the wonders of robotics. Check out some of the other cutting-edge applications of modern robotics.

MODULE PERFORMANCE TASK PREVIEW

Robots and Resistors

Robotics engineers design robots and develop applications for them, such as executing high-precision tasks in factories, cleaning toxic waste, and locating and defusing bombs. People who work in robotics are skilled in areas such as electronics and computer programming. How can a rational expression be used to help design the circuitry for a robot? Let's find out!

Benoist/BSIP/Corbis

Are YOU Ready?

Complete these exercises to review skills you will need for this module.

Graphing Linear Proportional Relationships

Example 1   Graph $y = \frac{1}{2}x$.

When $x = 0$, $y = 0$, so plot $(0, 0)$ on the graph.

The slope is $\frac{1}{2}$, so from $(0, 0)$, plot the next point up 1 and over 2.

Draw a line through the two points.

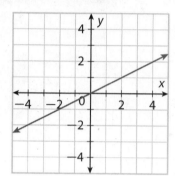

- Online Homework
- Hints and Help
- Extra Practice

Graph each proportional relationship.

1. $y = 2x$

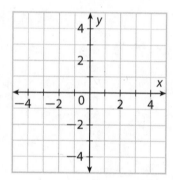

2. $y = \frac{2}{3}x$

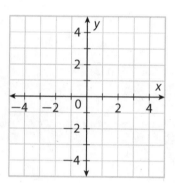

Direct and Inverse Variation

Example 2   In a direct variation the constant is 4 and its graph passes through $(x, 10)$. Find x.

$y = kx \rightarrow 10 = 4x \rightarrow x = 2.5$

Example 3   In an inverse variation the constant is 2.4 and its graph passes through $(6, y)$. Find y.

$k = xy \rightarrow 2.4 = 6y \rightarrow y = 0.4$

Find the missing variable for each direct variation.

3. $k = -1; (x, -5)$ _____   **4.** $k = 3; (9, y)$ _____   **5.** $k = \frac{1}{3}; (x, -2)$ _____

Find the missing variable for each inverse variation.

6. $k = 8; (x, -10)$ _____   **7.** $k = -2; (5, y)$ _____   **8.** $k = 6; (x, 1.5)$ _____

Module 9   **424**

9.1 Adding and Subtracting Rational Expressions

Essential Question: How can you add and subtract rational expressions?

Resource Locker

⊘ Explore   Identifying Excluded Values

Given a rational expression, identify the excluded values by finding the zeroes of the denominator. If possible, simplify the expression.

(A) $\dfrac{(1 - x^2)}{x - 1}$

The denominator of the expression is _____.

(B) Since division by 0 is not defined, the excluded values for this expression are all the values that would make the denominator equal to 0.

$x - 1 = 0$

$x = \boxed{}$

(C) Begin simplifying the expression by factoring the numerator.

$\dfrac{(1 - x^2)}{x - 1} = \dfrac{\left(\boxed{}\right)\left(\boxed{}\right)}{x - 1}$

(D) Divide out terms common to both the numerator and the denominator.

$\dfrac{(1 - x^2)}{x - 1} = \dfrac{\left(\boxed{}\right)\left(\boxed{}\right)}{-(1 - x)} = \boxed{} = \boxed{}$

(E) The simplified expression is

$\dfrac{(1 - x^2)}{x - 1} = \boxed{}$, whenever $x \neq \boxed{}$

(F) What is the domain for this function? What is its range?

_____

Reflect

1. What factors can be divided out of the numerator and denominator?

_____

⚙ Explain 1 Writing Equivalent Rational Expressions

Given a rational expression, there are different ways to write an equivalent rational expression. When common terms are divided out, the result is an equivalent but simplified expression.

Example 1 Rewrite the expression as indicated.

(A) Write $\dfrac{3x}{(x+3)}$ as an equivalent rational expression that has a denominator of $(x+3)(x+5)$.

The expression $\dfrac{3x}{(x+3)}$ has a denominator of $(x+3)$.

The factor missing from the denominator is $(x+5)$.

Introduce a common factor, $(x+5)$.

$$\frac{3x}{(x+3)} = \frac{3x(x+5)}{(x+3)(x+5)}$$

$\dfrac{3x}{(x+3)}$ is equivalent to $\dfrac{3x(x+5)}{(x+3)(x+5)}$.

(B) Simplify the expression $\dfrac{(x^2+5x+6)}{(x^2+3x+2)(x+3)}$.

Write the expression. $\qquad\qquad\qquad\qquad \dfrac{(x^2+5x+6)}{(x^2+3x+2)(x+3)}$

Factor the numerator and denominator. _____

Divide out like terms. _____

Your Turn

2. Write $\dfrac{5}{5x-25}$ as an equivalent expression with a denominator of $(x-5)(x+1)$.

3. Simplify the expression $\dfrac{(x+x^3)(1-x^2)}{(x^2-x^6)}$.

⚙ Explain 2 Identifying the LCD of Two Rational Expressions

Given two or more rational expressions, the least common denominator (LCD) is found by factoring each denominator and finding the least common multiple (LCM) of the factors. This technique is useful for the addition and subtraction of expressions with unlike denominators.

Least Common Denominator (LCD) of Rational Expressions
To find the LCD of rational expressions: **1.** Factor each denominator completely. Write any repeated factors as powers.   **2.** List the different factors. If the denominators have common factors, use the highest power of each common factor.

Example 2 Find the LCD for each set of rational expressions.

 $\dfrac{-2}{3x-15}$ and $\dfrac{6x}{4x+28}$

Factor each denominator completely.

$3x - 15 = 3(x - 5)$

$4x + 28 = 4(x + 7)$

List the different factors.

$3, 4, x - 5, x + 7$

The LCD is $3 \cdot 4(x - 5)(x + 7)$,

or $12(x - 5)(x + 7)$.

 $\dfrac{-14}{x^2-11x+24}$ and $\dfrac{9}{x^2-6x+9}$

Factor each denominator completely.

$x^2 - 11x + 24 = $ ☐

$x^2 - 6x + 9 = $ ☐

List the different factors.

_____ and _____

Taking the highest power of $(x - 3)$,

the LCD is _____.

Reflect

4. Discussion When is the LCD of two rational expressions not equal to the product of their denominators?

_____

Your Turn

Find the LCD for each set of rational expressions.

5. $\dfrac{x+6}{8x-24}$ and $\dfrac{14x}{10x-30}$

6. $\dfrac{12x}{15x+60} = \dfrac{5}{x^2+9x+20}$

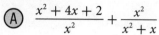

Adding and subtracting rational expressions is similar to adding and subtracting fractions.

Example 3 **Add or subtract. Identify any excluded values and simplify your answer.**

(A) $\dfrac{x^2 + 4x + 2}{x^2} + \dfrac{x^2}{x^2 + x}$

Factor the denominators. $\dfrac{x^2 + 4x + 2}{x^2} + \dfrac{x^2}{x(x + 1)}$

Identify where the expression is not defined. The first expression is undefined when $x = 0$. The second expression is undefined when $x = 0$ and when $x = -1$.

Find a common denominator. The LCM for x^2 and $x(x + 1)$ is $x^2(x + 1)$.

Write the expressions with a common denominator by multiplying both by the appropriate form of 1.

$$\dfrac{(x + 1)}{(x + 1)} \cdot \dfrac{x^2 + 4x + 2}{x^2} + \dfrac{x^2}{x(x + 1)} \cdot \dfrac{x}{x}$$

Simplify each numerator.

$$= \dfrac{x^3 + 5x^2 + 6x + 2}{x^2(x + 1)} + \dfrac{x^3}{x^2(x + 1)}$$

Add.

$$= \dfrac{2x^3 + 5x^2 + 6x + 2}{x^2(x + 1)}$$

Since none of the factors of the denominator are factors of the numerator, the expression cannot be further simplified.

(B) $\dfrac{2x^2}{x^2 - 5x} - \dfrac{x^2 + 3x - 4}{x^2}$

Factor the denominators.

$$\dfrac{2x^2}{\boxed{}} - \dfrac{x^2 + 3x - 4}{x^2}$$

Identify where the expression is not defined. The first expression is undefined when $x = 0$ and when $x = 5$. The second expression is undefined when $x = 0$.

Find a common denominator. The LCM for $x(x - 5)$ and x^2 is _____.

Write the expressions with a common denominator by multiplying both by the appropriate form of 1.

$$\boxed{} \cdot \dfrac{2x^2}{x(x - 5)} - \dfrac{x^2 + 3x - 4}{x^2} \cdot \dfrac{x - 5}{x - 5}$$

Simplify each numerator.

$$= \dfrac{2x^3}{x^2(x - 5)} - \dfrac{x^3 - 2x^2 - 19x + 20}{x^2(x - 5)}$$

Subtract.

$$= \dfrac{\boxed{} + 2x^2 + 19x - 20}{x^2(x - 5)}$$

Since none of the factors of the denominator are factors of the numerator, the expression cannot be further simplified.

Add each pair of expressions, simplifying the result and noting the combined excluded values. Then subtract the second expression from the first, again simplifying the result and noting the combined excluded values.

7. $-x^2$ and $\dfrac{1}{(1 - x^2)}$

8. $\dfrac{x^2}{(4 - x^2)}$ and $\dfrac{1}{(2 - x)}$

🎸 Explain 4 Adding and Subtracting with Rational Models

Rational expressions can model real-world phenomena, and can be used to calculate measurements of those phenomena.

Example 4   Find the sum or difference of the models to solve the problem.

(A) Two groups have agreed that each will contribute $2000 for an upcoming trip. Group A has 6 more people than group B. Let x represent the number of people in group A. Write and simplify an expression in terms of x that represents the difference between the number of dollars each person in group A must contribute and the number each person in group B must contribute.

$$\frac{2000}{x} - \frac{2000}{x-6} = \frac{2000(x-6)}{x(x-6)} - \frac{2000x}{(x-6)x}$$

$$= \frac{2000x - 12,000 - 2000x}{x(x-6)}$$

$$= -\frac{12,000}{x(x-6)}$$

(B) A freight train averages 30 miles per hour traveling to its destination with full cars and 40 miles per hour on the return trip with empty cars. Find the total time in terms of d. Use the formula $t = \frac{d}{r}$.

Let d represent the one-way distance.

Total time: $\dfrac{d}{30} + \dfrac{d}{40}$ $= \dfrac{d \cdot \Box}{30 \cdot \Box} + \dfrac{d \cdot \Box}{40 \cdot \Box}$

$$= \frac{d \cdot \Box + d \cdot \Box}{\Box}$$

$$= \frac{\Box}{\Box} d$$

Your Turn

9. A hiker averages 1.4 miles per hour when walking downhill on a mountain trail and 0.8 miles per hour on the return trip when walking uphill. Find the total time in terms of d. Use the formula $t = \frac{d}{r}$.

10. Yvette ran at an average speed of 6.20 feet per second during the first two laps of a race and an average speed of 7.75 feet per second during the second two laps of a race. Find her total time in terms of d, the distance around the racecourse.

💬 Elaborate

11. Why do rational expressions have excluded values?

_____

_____

_____

12. How can you tell if your answer is written in simplest form?

_____

_____

_____

13. Essential Question Check-In Why must the excluded values of each expression in a sum or difference of rational expressions also be excluded values for the simplified expression?

_____

_____

_____

_____

_____

☆ Evaluate: Homework and Practice

• Online Homework
• Hints and Help
• Extra Practice

Given a rational expression, identify the excluded values by finding the zeroes of the denominator.

1. $\dfrac{x-1}{x^2+3x-4}$

2. $\dfrac{4}{x(x+17)}$

Write the given expression as an equivalent rational expression that has the given denominator.

3. Expression: $\dfrac{x-7}{x+8}$

Denominator: x^3+8x^2

4. Expression: $\dfrac{3x^3}{3x-6}$

Denominator: $(2-x)(x^2+9)$

Simplify the given expression.

5. $\dfrac{(-4-4x)}{(x^2-x-2)}$

6. $\dfrac{-x-8}{x^2+9x+8}$

7. $\dfrac{6x^2+5x+1}{3x^2+4x+1}$

8. $\dfrac{x^4-1}{x^2+1}$

Find the LCD for each set of rational expressions.

9. $\dfrac{x}{2x+16}$ and $\dfrac{-4x}{3x-27}$

10. $\dfrac{x^2-4}{5x-30}$ and $\dfrac{5x+13}{7x-42}$

11. $\dfrac{4x + 12}{x^2 + 5x + 6}$ and $\dfrac{5x + 15}{10x + 20}$

12. $\dfrac{-11}{x^2 - 3x - 28}$ and $\dfrac{2}{x^2 - 2x - 24}$

13. $\dfrac{12}{3x^2 - 21x - 54}$ and $\dfrac{-1}{21x^2 - 84}$

14. $\dfrac{3x}{5x^2 - 40x + 60}$ and $\dfrac{17}{-7x^2 + 56x + 84}$

Add or subtract the given expressions, simplifying each result and noting the combined excluded values.

15. $\dfrac{1}{1 + x} + \dfrac{1 - x}{x}$

16. $\dfrac{x + 4}{x^2 - 4} + \dfrac{-2x - 2}{x^2 - 4}$

17. $\dfrac{1}{2+x} - \dfrac{2-x}{x}$

18. $\dfrac{4x^4 + 4}{x^2 + 1} - \dfrac{8}{x^2 + 1}$

19. $\dfrac{x^4 - 2}{x^2 - 2} + \dfrac{2}{-x^2 + 2}$

20. $\dfrac{1}{x^2 + 3x - 4} - \dfrac{1}{x^2 - 3x + 2}$

21. $\dfrac{3}{x^2 - 4} - \dfrac{x + 5}{x + 2}$

22. $\dfrac{-3}{9x^2 - 4} + \dfrac{1}{3x^2 + 2x}$

23. $\dfrac{x-2}{x+2} + \dfrac{1}{x^2-4} - \dfrac{x+2}{2-x}$

24. $\dfrac{x-3}{x+3} - \dfrac{1}{x-3} + \dfrac{x+2}{3-x}$

25. A company has two factories, factory A and factory B. The cost per item to produce q items in factory A is $\dfrac{200 + 13q}{q}$. The cost per item to produce q items in factory B is $\dfrac{300 + 25q}{2q}$. Find an expression for the sum of these costs per item. Then divide this expression by 2 to find an expression for the average cost per item to produce q items in each factory.

26. An auto race consists of 8 laps. A driver completes the first 3 laps at an average speed of 185 miles per hour and the remaining laps at an average speed of 200 miles per hour. Let d represent the length of one lap. Find the time in terms of d that it takes the driver to complete the race.

Crisman/Corbis

27. The junior and senior classes of a high school are cleaning up a beach. Each class has pledged to clean 1600 meters of shoreline. The junior class has 12 more students than the senior class. Let s represent the number of students in the senior class. Write and simplify an expression in terms of s that represents the difference between the number of meters of shoreline each senior must clean and the number of meters each junior must clean.

28. Architecture The Renaissance architect Andrea Palladio believed that the height of a room with vaulted ceilings should be the harmonic mean of the length and width. The harmonic mean of two positive numbers a and b is equal to $\dfrac{2}{\frac{1}{a} + \frac{1}{b}}$. Simplify this expression. What are the excluded values? What do they mean in this problem?

29. Match each expression with the correct excluded value(s).

a. $\dfrac{3x + 5}{x + 2}$ _____ no excluded values

b. $\dfrac{1 + x}{x^2 - 1}$ _____ $x \neq 0, -2$

c. $\dfrac{3x^4 - 12}{x^2 + 4}$ _____ $x \neq 1, -1$

d. $\dfrac{3x + 6}{x^2(x + 2)}$ _____ $x \neq -2$

30. **Explain the Error** George was asked to write the expression $2x - 3$ three times, once each with excluded values at $x = 1$, $x = 2$, and $x = -3$. He wrote the following expressions:

  a. $\dfrac{2x - 3}{x - 1}$

  b. $\dfrac{2x - 3}{x - 2}$

  c. $\dfrac{2x - 3}{x + 3}$

  What error did George make? Write the correct expressions, then write an expression that has all three excluded values.

31. **Communicate Mathematical Ideas** Write a rational expression with excluded values at $x = 0$ and $x = 17$.

32. **Critical Thinking** Sketch the graph of the rational equation $y = \dfrac{x^2 + 3x + 2}{x + 1}$. Think about how to show graphically that a graph exists over a domain except at one point.

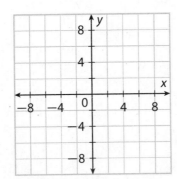

Lesson Performance Task

A kayaker spends an afternoon paddling on a river. She travels 3 miles upstream and 3 miles downstream in a total of 4 hours. In still water, the kayaker can travel at an average speed of 2 miles per hour. Based on this information, can you estimate the average speed of the river's current? Is your answer reasonable?

Next, assume the average speed of the kayaker is an unknown, k, and not necessarily 2 miles per hour. What is the range of possible average kayaker speeds under the rest of the constraints?

9.2 Multiplying and Dividing Rational Expressions

Resource Locker

Essential Question: How can you multiply and divide rational expressions?

⊘ Explore **Relating Multiplication Concepts**

Use the facts you know about multiplying rational numbers to determine how to multiply rational expressions.

Ⓐ How do you multiply $\frac{4}{5} \cdot \frac{5}{6}$?

Multiply 4 by ___ to find the _____ of the product, and multiply 5 by ___ to find

the _____.

Ⓑ $\frac{4}{5} \cdot \frac{5}{6} = \dfrac{\boxed{}}{\boxed{}}$

Ⓒ To simplify, factor the numerator and denominator.

$20 = \boxed{}$

$30 = \boxed{}$

Ⓓ Cancel common factors in the numerator and denominator to simplify the product.

$\frac{4}{5} \cdot \frac{5}{6} = \frac{20}{30} = \frac{2 \cdot 2 \cdot 5}{2 \cdot 3 \cdot 5} = \dfrac{\boxed{}}{\boxed{}}$

Ⓔ Based on the steps used for multiplying rational numbers, how can you multiply the rational

expression $\frac{x+1}{x-1} \cdot \frac{3}{2(x+1)}$?

_____

_____

Reflect

1. **Discussion** Multiplying rational expressions is similar to multiplying rational numbers. Likewise, dividing rational expressions is similar to dividing rational numbers. How could you use the steps for dividing rational numbers to divide rational expressions?

_____

_____

_____

⊘ Explain 1 Multiplying Rational Expressions

To multiply rational expressions, multiply the numerators to find the numerator of the product, and multiply the denominators to find the denominator. Then, simplify the product by cancelling common factors.

Note the excluded values of the product, which are any values of the variable for which the expression is undefined.

Example 1 Find the products and any excluded values.

(A) $\dfrac{3x^2}{x^2-2x-8} \cdot \dfrac{2x^2-6x-20}{x^2-3x-10}$

$\dfrac{3x^2}{x^2-2x-8} \cdot \dfrac{2x^2-6x-20}{x^2-3x-10} = \dfrac{3x^2}{(x+2)(x-4)} \cdot \dfrac{2(x+2)(x-5)}{(x+2)(x-5)}$ Factor the numerators and denominators.

$= \dfrac{6x^2(x+2)(x-5)}{(x+2)(x-4)(x+2)(x-5)}$ Multiply the numerators and multiply the denominators.

$= \dfrac{6x^2\cancel{(x+2)}\cancel{(x-5)}}{\cancel{(x+2)}(x-4)(x+2)\cancel{(x-5)}}$ Cancel the common factors in the numerator and denominator.

$= \dfrac{6x^2}{(x+2)(x-4)}$

Determine what values of x make each expression undefined.

$\dfrac{3x^2}{x^2-2x-8}$:   The denominator is 0 when $x=-2$ and $x=4$.

$\dfrac{2x^2-6x-20}{x^2-3x-10}$:   The denominator is 0 when $x=-2$ and $x=5$.

Excluded values: $x=-2$, $x=4$, and $x=5$

(B) $\dfrac{x^2-8x}{14(x^2+8x+15)} \cdot \dfrac{7x+35}{x+8}$

$\dfrac{x^2-8x}{14(x^2+8x+15)} \cdot \dfrac{7x+35}{x+8} = \dfrac{\boxed{}(x-8)}{14\boxed{}(x+5)} \cdot \dfrac{7\left(\boxed{}\right)}{x+8}$ Factor the numerators and denominators.

$= \dfrac{7x(x-8)\left(\boxed{}\right)}{14\left(\boxed{}\right)(x+5)(x+8)}$ Multiply the numerators and multiply the denominators.

$= \dfrac{\boxed{}}{\boxed{}}$ Cancel the common factors in the numerator and denominator.

Determine what values of x make each expression undefined.

$\dfrac{x^2-8x}{14(x^2+8x+15)}$:   The denominator is 0 when $\boxed{}$.

$\dfrac{7x+35}{x+8}$:   The denominator is 0 when $\boxed{}$.

Excluded values: $\boxed{}$

Find the products and any excluded values.

2. $\dfrac{x^2 - 9}{x^2 - 5x - 24} \cdot \dfrac{x - 8}{2x^2 - 18x}$

3. $\dfrac{x}{x - 9} \cdot \dfrac{3x - 27}{x + 1}$

🎻 Explain 2 Dividing Rational Expressions

To divide rational expressions, change the division problem to a multiplication problem by multiplying by the reciprocal. Then, follow the steps for multiplying rational expressions.

Example 2 Find the quotients and any excluded values.

Ⓐ $\dfrac{(x + 7)^2}{x^2} \div \dfrac{x^2 + 9x + 14}{x^2 + x - 2}$

$\dfrac{(x + 7)^2}{x^2} \div \dfrac{x^2 + 9x + 14}{x^2 + x - 2} = \dfrac{(x + 7)^2}{x^2} \cdot \dfrac{x^2 + x - 2}{x^2 + 9x + 14}$ Multiply by the reciprocal.

$= \dfrac{(x + 7)(x + 7)}{x^2} \cdot \dfrac{(x + 2)(x - 1)}{(x + 7)(x + 2)}$ Factor the numerators and denominators.

$= \dfrac{(x + 7)(x + 7)(x + 2)(x - 1)}{x^2(x + 7)(x + 2)}$ Multiply the numerators and multiply the denominators.

$= \dfrac{(x\!\!\not\!+\!7)(x + 7)(x\!\!\not\!+\!2)(x - 1)}{x^2(x\!\!\not\!+\!7)(x\!\!\not\!+\!2)}$ Cancel the common factors in the numerator and denominator.

$= \dfrac{(x + 7)(x - 1)}{x^2}$

Determine what values of x make each expression undefined.

$\dfrac{(x + 7)^2}{x}:$ The denominator is 0 when $x = 0$.

$\dfrac{x^2 + 9x + 14}{x^2 + x - 2}:$ The denominator is 0 when $x = -2$ and $x = 1$.

$\dfrac{x^2 + x - 2}{x^2 + 9x + 14}:$ The denominator is 0 when $x = -7$ and $x = -2$.

Excluded values: $x = 0$, $x = -7$, $x = 1$, and $x = -2$

B $\dfrac{6x}{3x - 30} \div \dfrac{9x^2 - 27x - 36}{x^2 - 10x}$

$\dfrac{6x}{3x - 30} \div \dfrac{9x^2 - 27x - 36}{x^2 - 10x} = \dfrac{6x}{3x - 30} \cdot \dfrac{\boxed{}}{\boxed{}}$ Multiply by the reciprocal.

$= \dfrac{6x}{3\left(\boxed{}\right)} \cdot \dfrac{x\left(\boxed{}\right)}{9(x + 1)\left(\boxed{}\right)}$ Factor the numerators and denominators.

$= \dfrac{6x^2\left(\boxed{}\right)}{27\left(\boxed{}\right)(x + 1)\left(\boxed{}\right)}$ Multiply the numerators and multiply the denominators.

$= \dfrac{\boxed{}}{\boxed{}}.$ Cancel the common factors in the numerator and denominator.

Determine what values of x make each expression undefined.

$\dfrac{6x}{3x - 30}$:   The denominator is 0 when $\boxed{}$.

$\dfrac{9x^2 - 27x - 36}{x^2 - 10x}$:   The denominator is 0 when $\boxed{}$.

$\dfrac{x^2 - 10x}{9x^2 - 27x - 36}$:   The denominator is 0 when $\boxed{}$.

Excluded values: $\boxed{}$

Your Turn

Find the quotients and any excluded values.

4. $\dfrac{x + 11}{4x} \div \dfrac{2x + 6}{x^2 + 2x - 3}$

5. $\dfrac{20}{x^2 - 7x} \div \dfrac{5x^2 - 40x}{x^2 - 15x + 56}$

Activity: Investigating Closure

A set of numbers is said to be closed, or to have **closure**, under a given operation if the result of the operation on any two numbers in the set is also in the set.

(A) Recall whether the set of whole numbers, the set of integers, and the set of rational numbers are closed under each of the four basic operations.

	Addition	Subtraction	Multiplication	Division
Whole Numbers				
Integers				
Rational Numbers				

(B) Look at the set of rational expressions. Use the rational expressions $\frac{p(x)}{q(x)}$ and $\frac{r(x)}{s(x)}$ where $p(x)$, $q(x)$, $r(x)$ and $s(x)$ are nonzero. Add the rational expressions.

$$\frac{p(x)}{q(x)} + \frac{r(x)}{s(x)} = \boxed{}$$

(C) Is the set of rational expressions closed under addition? Explain.

_____

_____

(D) Subtract the rational expressions.

$$\frac{p(x)}{q(x)} - \frac{r(x)}{s(x)} = \boxed{}$$

(E) Is the set of rational expressions closed under subtraction? Explain.

_____

_____

(F) Multiply the rational expressions.

$$\frac{p(x)}{q(x)} \cdot \frac{r(x)}{s(x)} = \boxed{}$$

(G) Is the set of rational expressions closed under multiplication? Explain.

_____

_____

(H) Divide the rational expressions.

$$\frac{p(x)}{q(x)} \div \frac{r(x)}{s(x)} = \boxed{}$$

(I) Is the set of rational expressions closed under division? Explain.

_____

_____

6. Are rational expressions most like whole numbers, integers, or rational numbers? Explain.

🔧 Explain 4 Multiplying and Dividing with Rational Models

Models involving rational expressions can be solved using the same steps to multiply or divide rational expressions.

Example 3 **Solve the problems using rational expressions.**

(A) Leonard drives 40 miles to work every day. One-fifth of his drive is on city roads, where he averages 30 miles per hour. The other part of his drive is on a highway, where he averages 55 miles per hour. The expression $\frac{d_c r_h + d_h r_c}{r_c r_h}$ represents the total time spent driving, in hours. In the expression, d_c represents the distance traveled on city roads, d_h represents the distance traveled on the highway, r_c is the average speed on city roads, and r_h is the average speed on the highway. Use the expression to find the average speed of Leonard's drive.

The total distance traveled is 40 miles. Find an expression for the average speed, r, of Leonard's drive.

$r =$ Total distance traveled $\div$ Total time

$$= 40 \div \frac{d_c r_h + d_h r_c}{r_c r_h}$$

$$= 40 \cdot \frac{r_c r_h}{d_c r_h + d_h r_c}$$

$$= \frac{40 r_c r_h}{d_c r_h + d_h r_c}$$

Find the values of d_c and d_h.

$d_c = \frac{1}{5}(40) = 8$ miles

$d_h = 40 - 8 = 32$ miles

Solve for r by substituting in the given values from the problem.

$$r = \frac{d r_c r_h}{d_c r_h + d_h r_c}$$

$$= \frac{40 \cdot 55 \cdot 30}{8 \cdot 55 + 32 \cdot 30}$$

$$\approx 47 \text{ miles per hour}$$

The average speed of Leonard's drive is about 47 miles per hour.

(B) The fuel efficiency of Tanika's car at highway speeds is 35 miles per gallon. The expression $\frac{48E - 216}{E(E - 6)}$ represents the total gas consumed, in gallons, when Tanika drives 36 miles on a highway and 12 miles in a town to get to her relative's house. In the expression, E represents the fuel efficiency, in miles per gallon, of Tanika's car at highway speeds. Use the expression to find the average rate of gas consumed on her trip.

The total distance traveled is ☐ miles. Find an expression for the average rate of gas consumed, g, on Tanika's trip.

g = Total gas consumed ÷ Total distance traveled

$$= \frac{48E - 216}{E(E - 6)} \div \boxed{}$$

$$= \frac{48E - 216}{\boxed{}\, E(E - 6)}$$

The value of E is ☐.

Solve for g by substituting in the value of E.

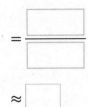

$$g = \frac{48\left(\boxed{}\right) - 216}{48\left(\boxed{}\right)\left(\boxed{} - 6\right)}$$

$$= \frac{\boxed{}}{\boxed{}}$$

$$\approx \boxed{}$$

The average rate of gas consumed on Tanika's trip is about ☐ gallon per mile.

Your Turn

7. The distance traveled by a car undergoing constant acceleration, a, for a time, t, is given by $d = v_0 t + \frac{1}{2}at^2$, where v_0 is the initial velocity of the car. Two cars are side by side with the same initial velocity. One car accelerates and the other car does not. Write an expression for the ratio of the distance traveled by the accelerating car to the distance traveled by the nonaccelerating car as a function of time.

🗨 Elaborate

8. Explain how finding excluded values when dividing one rational expression by another is different from multiplying two rational expressions.

_____

_____

_____

_____

9. **Essential Question Check-In** How is dividing rational expressions related to multiplying rational expressions?

_____

_____

_____

• Online Homework
• Hints and Help
• Extra Practice

1. Explain how to multiply the rational expressions.

$$\frac{x-3}{2} \cdot \frac{x^2-3x+4}{x^2-2x}$$

Find the products and any excluded values.

2. $\dfrac{x}{3x-6} \cdot \dfrac{x-2}{x+9}$

3. $\dfrac{5x^2+25x}{2} \cdot \dfrac{4x}{x+5}$

4. $\dfrac{x^2-2x-15}{10x+30} \cdot \dfrac{3}{x^2-3x-10}$

5. $\dfrac{x^2-1}{x^2+5x+4} \cdot \dfrac{x^2}{x^2-x}$

6. $\dfrac{x^2 + 14x + 33}{4x} \cdot \dfrac{x^2 - 3x}{x + 3} \cdot \dfrac{8x - 56}{x^2 + 4x - 77}$

7. $\dfrac{9x^2}{x - 6} \cdot \dfrac{x^2 - 36}{3x - 6} \cdot \dfrac{3}{4x^2 + 24x}$

Find the quotients and any excluded values.

8. $\dfrac{5x^2 + 10x}{x^2 + 2x + 1} \div \dfrac{20x + 40}{x^2 - 1}$

9. $\dfrac{x^2 - 9x + 18}{x^2 + 9x + 18} \div \dfrac{x^2 - 36}{x^2 - 9}$

10. $\dfrac{-x^2 + x + 20}{5x^2 - 25x} \div \dfrac{x + 4}{2x - 14}$

11. $\dfrac{x + 3}{x^2 + 8x + 15} \div \dfrac{x^2 - 25}{x - 5}$

12. $\dfrac{x^2 - 10x + 9}{3x} \div \dfrac{x^2 - 7x - 18}{x^2 + 2x}$

13. $\dfrac{8x + 32}{x^2 + 8x + 16} \div \dfrac{x^2 - 6x}{x^2 - 2x - 24}$

Let $p(x) = \dfrac{1}{x+1}$ and $q(x) = \dfrac{1}{x-1}$. **Perform the operation, and show that it results in another rational expression.**

14. $p(x) + q(x)$

15. $p(x) - q(x)$

16. $p(x) \cdot q(x)$

17. $p(x) \div q(x)$

18. The distance a race car travels is given by the equation $d = v_0 t + \frac{1}{2}at^2$, where v_0 is the initial speed of the race car, a is the acceleration, and t is the time travelled. Near the beginning of a race, the driver accelerates for 9 seconds at a rate of 4 m/s². The driver's initial speed was 75 m/s. Find the driver's average speed during the acceleration.

19. Julianna is designing a circular track that will consist of three concentric rings. The radius of the middle ring is 6 meters greater than that of the inner ring and 6 meters less than that of the outer ring. Find an expression for the ratio of the length of the outer ring to the length of the middle ring and another for the ratio of the length of the outer ring to length of the inner ring. If the radius of the inner ring is set at 90 meters, how many times longer is the outer ring than the middle ring and the inner ring?

20. Geometry Find a rational expression for the ratio of the surface area of a cylinder to the volume of a cylinder. Then find the ratio when the radius is 3 inches and the height is 10 inches.

21. Explain the Error Maria finds an expression equivalent to
$\dfrac{x^2 - 4x - 45}{3x - 15} \div \dfrac{6x^2 - 150}{x^2 - 5x}$.
Her work is shown. Find and correct Maria's mistake.

$$\frac{x^2 - 4x - 45}{3x - 15} \div \frac{6x^2 - 150}{x^2 - 5x} = \frac{(x - 9)(x + 5)}{3(x - 5)} \div \frac{6(x + 5)(x - 5)}{x(x - 5)}$$

$$= \frac{6(x - 9)(x + 5)(x + 5)(x - 5)}{3x(x - 5)(x - 5)}$$

$$= \frac{2(x - 9)(x + 5)^2}{x(x - 5)}$$

22. Critical Thinking Multiply the expressions. What do you notice about the resulting expression?

$$\left(\frac{3}{x - 4} + \frac{x^3 - 4x}{8x^2 - 32} \right)\left(\frac{3x + 18}{x^2 + 2x - 24} - \frac{x}{8} \right)$$

23. Multi-Step Jordan is making a garden with an area of $x^2 + 13x + 30$ square feet and a length of $x + 3$ feet.

a. Find an expression for the width of Jordan's garden.

b. If Karl makes a garden with an area of $3x^2 + 48x + 180$ square feet and a length of $x + 6$, how many times larger is the width of Jon's garden than Jordan's?

c. If x is equal to 4, what are the dimensions of both Jordan's and Karl's gardens?

Lesson Performance Task

Who has the advantage, taller or shorter runners? Almost all of the energy generated by a long-distance runner is released in the form of heat. For a runner with height H and speed V, the rate h_g of heat generated and the rate h_r of heat released can be modeled by $h_g = k_1 H^3 V^2$ and $h_r = k_2 H^2$, k_1 and k_2 being constants. So, how does a runner's height affect the amount of heat she releases as she increases her speed?

9.3 Solving Rational Equations

Essential Question: What methods are there for solving rational equations?

Explore   Solving Rational Equations Graphically

A rational equation is an equation that contains one or more rational expressions. The time t in hours it takes to travel d miles can be determined by using the equation $t = \frac{d}{r}$, where r is the average rate of speed. This equation is an example of a rational equation. One method to solving rational equations is by graphing.

Solve the rational equation $\frac{x}{x-3} = 2$ by graphing.

(A) First, identify any excluded values. A number is an excluded value of a rational expression if substituting the number into the expression results in a division by 0, which is undefined. Solve $x - 3 = 0$ for x.

$x - 3 = 0$

$x = \boxed{}$

(B) So, 3 is an excluded value of the rational equation. Rewrite the equation with 0 on one side.

$\frac{x}{x-3} = 2$

$\boxed{} = 0$

(C) Graph the left side of the equation as a function. Substitute y for 0 and complete the table below.

x	y	(x, y)
0		
1		
2		
4		
5		
9		

(D) Use the table to graph the function.

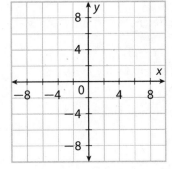

(E) Identify any x-intercepts of the graph.

There is an x-intercept at $\boxed{}$.

(F) Is the value of x an excluded value? What is the solution of $\frac{x}{x-3} = 2$?

_____

_____

1. **Discussion** Why does rewriting a rational equation with 0 on one side help with solving the equation?

_____

_____

_____

_____

⊘ Explain 1   Solving Rational Equations Algebraically

Rational equations can be solved algebraically by multiplying through by the LCD and solving the resulting polynomial equation. However, this eliminates the information about the excluded values of the original equation. Sometimes an excluded value of the original equation is a solution of the polynomial equation, and in this case the excluded value will be an **extraneous solution** of the polynomial equation. Extraneous solutions are not solutions of an equation.

Example 1   Solve each rational equation algebraically.

 $\dfrac{3x + 7}{x - 5} = \dfrac{5x + 17}{2x - 10}$

Identify any excluded values.

$$x - 5 = 0 \qquad\qquad 2x - 10 = 0$$
$$x = 5 \qquad\qquad\qquad x = 5$$

The excluded value is 5.
Identify the LCD by finding all factors of the denominators.

$$2x - 10 = 2(x - 5)$$

The different factors are 2 and $x - 5$.

The LCD is $2(x - 5)$.
Multiply each term by the LCD.

$$\dfrac{3x + 7}{x - 5} \cdot 2(x - 5) = \dfrac{5x + 17}{2(x - 5)} \cdot 2(x - 5)$$

Divide out common factors.

$$\dfrac{3x + 7}{\cancel{x - 5}} \cdot 2\,\cancel{(x - 5)} = \dfrac{5x + 17}{\cancel{2}\,\cancel{(x - 5)}} \cdot \cancel{2}\,\cancel{(x - 5)}$$

Simplify.

$$(3x + 7)2 = 5x + 17$$

Use the Distributive Property.

$$6x + 14 = 5x + 17$$

Solve for x.

$$x + 14 = 17$$

$$x = 3$$

The solution $x = 3$ is not an excluded value. So, $x = 3$ is the solution of the equation.

Ⓑ $\dfrac{2x-9}{x-7}+\dfrac{x}{2}=\dfrac{5}{x-7}$

Identify any excluded values.

$x-7=0$

$x=\boxed{}$

The excluded value is _____.

Identify the LCD.

The different factors are _____.

The LCD is _____.

Multiply each term by the LCD. $\quad\dfrac{2x-9}{x-7}\cdot\boxed{}+\dfrac{x}{2}\cdot\boxed{}=\dfrac{5}{x-7}\cdot\boxed{}$

Divide out common factors. $\quad\dfrac{2x-9}{\cancel{x-7}}\cdot\boxed{}+\dfrac{x}{\cancel{2}}\cdot\boxed{}=\dfrac{5}{\cancel{x-7}}\cdot\boxed{}$

Simplify. $\quad\boxed{}(2x-9)+x\left(\boxed{}\right)=5\left(\boxed{}\right)$

Use the Distributive Property. $\quad\boxed{}+x^2-7x=\boxed{}$

Write in standard form. $\quad\boxed{}=0$

Factor. $\quad\left(\boxed{}\right)\left(\boxed{}\right)=0$

Use the Zero Product Property. $\quad x-7=0 \text{ or } \boxed{}=0$

Solve for x. $\quad x=7 \text{ or } x=\boxed{}$

The solution $x=\boxed{}$ is extraneous because it is an excluded value. The only solution is $x=\boxed{}$.

Your Turn

Solve each rational equation algebraically.

2. $\dfrac{8}{x+3}=\dfrac{x+1}{x+6}$

Explain 2 Solving a Real-world Problem with a Rational Equation

Rational equations are used to model real-world situations. These equations can be solved algebraically.

Example 2 Use a rational equation to solve the problem.

(A) Kelsey is kayaking on a river. She travels 5 miles upstream and 5 miles downstream in a total of 6 hours. In still water, Kelsey can travel at an average speed of 3 miles per hour. What is the average speed of the river's current?

Analyze Information

Identify the important information:
- The answer will be the average speed

  of _____.

- Kelsey spends _____ kayaking.

- She travels _____ upstream and _____ downstream.

- Her average speed in still water is _____.

Formulate a Plan

Let c represent the speed of the current in miles per hour. When Kelsey is going

upstream, her speed is equal to her speed in still water _____ c. When Kelsey is

going downstream, her speed is equal to her speed in still water _____ c.

The variable c is restricted to _____.

Complete the table.

	Distance (mi)	Average speed (mi/h)	Time (h)
Upstream	5		
Downstream	5		

Use the results from the table to write an equation.
total time = time upstream + time downstream

$$6 = \boxed{} + \boxed{}$$

Solve

$3 - c = 0$ $3 + c = 0$

$\boxed{} = c$ $c = \boxed{}$

Excluded values: _____

LCD: _____

Multiply by the LCD.	$6 \cdot \boxed{} = \dfrac{5}{3 - c} \cdot \boxed{} + \dfrac{5}{3 + c} \cdot \boxed{}$
Divide out common factors.	$6 \cdot \boxed{} = \dfrac{5}{3\!\!\!\!\diagdown\, c} \cdot \boxed{} + \dfrac{5}{3\!\!\!\!\diagup\! c} \cdot \boxed{}$
Simplify.	$6 \cdot \boxed{} = 5 \cdot \boxed{} + 5 \cdot \boxed{}$
Use the Distributive Property.	$\boxed{} = 15 + 5c + \boxed{}$
Write in standard form.	$0 = \boxed{}$
Factor.	$0 = 6\,(c + 2)\left(\boxed{}\right)$
Use the Zero Product Property.	$c + 2 = 0$ or $\boxed{} = 0$
Solve for c.	$c = \boxed{}$ or $c = \boxed{}$

There _____ extraneous solutions. The solutions are _____ .

Justify and Evaluate

The solution $c = \boxed{}$ is unreasonable because the speed of the current cannot

be _____ but the solution $c = \boxed{}$ is reasonable because the speed of the

current can be _____ . If the speed of the current is _____ , it

would take Kelsey _____ hour(s) to go upstream and _____ hour(s) to go

downstream, which is a total of _____ hours.

Reflect

3. Why does the domain of the variable have to be restricted in real-world problems that can be modeled with a rational equation?

_____

_____

4. Kevin can clean a large aquarium tank in about 7 hours. When Kevin and Lara work together, they can clean the tank in 4 hours. Write and solve a rational equation to determine how long, to the nearest tenth of an hour, it would take Lara to clean the tank if she works by herself. Explain whether the answer is reasonable.

💬 Elaborate

5. Why is it important to check solutions to rational equations?

_____

_____

6. Why can extraneous solutions to rational equations exist?

_____

_____

_____

7. **Essential Question Check In** How can you solve a rational equation without graphing?

_____

_____

_____

Solve each rational equation by graphing using a table of values.

1. $\dfrac{x}{x+4} = -3$

x	y	(x, y)
−8		
−6		
−5		
−3.5		
−2		
0		

2. $\dfrac{x}{2x - 10} = 3$

x	y	(x, y)
0		
3		
4		
5.5		
7		
10		

Solve each rational equation algebraically.

3. $\dfrac{9}{4x} - \dfrac{5}{6} = -\dfrac{13}{12x}$

4. $\dfrac{3}{x+1} + \dfrac{2}{7} = 2$

5. $\dfrac{56}{x^2 - 2x - 15} - \dfrac{6}{x + 3} = \dfrac{7}{x - 5}$

6. $\dfrac{x^2 - 29}{x^2 - 10x + 21} = \dfrac{6}{x - 7} + \dfrac{5}{x - 3}$

7. $\dfrac{5}{2x+6} - \dfrac{1}{6} = \dfrac{2}{x+4}$

8. $\dfrac{5}{x^2-3x+2} - \dfrac{1}{x-2} = \dfrac{x+6}{3x-3}$

For 9 and 10, write a rational equation for each real-world application. Do not solve.

9. A save percentage in lacrosse is found by dividing the number of saves by the number of shots faced. A lacrosse goalie saved 9 of 12 shots. How many additional consecutive saves s must the goalie make to raise his save percentage to 0.850?

10. Jake can mulch a garden in 30 minutes. Together, Jake and Ross can mulch the same garden in 16 minutes. How much time t, in minutes, will it take Ross to mulch the garden when working alone?

11. **Geometry** A new ice skating rink will be approximately rectangular in shape and will have an area of 18,000 square feet. Using an equation for the perimeter P, of the skating rink in terms of its width W, what are the dimensions of the skating rink if the perimeter is 580 feet?

12. Water flowing through both a small pipe and a large pipe can fill a water tank in 9 hours. Water flowing through the large pipe alone can fill the tank in 17 hours. Write an equation that can be used to find the amount of time t, in hours, it would take to fill the tank using only the small pipe.

13. A riverboat travels at an average of 14 km per hour in still water. The riverboat travels 110 km east up the Ohio River and 110 km west down the same river in a total of 17.5 hours. To the nearest tenth of a kilometer per hour, what was the speed of the current of the river?

14. A baseball player's batting average is equal to the number of hits divided by the number of at bats. A professional player had 139 hits in 515 at bats in 2012 and 167 hits in 584 at bats in 2013. Write and solve an equation to find how many additional consecutive hits h the batter would have needed to raise his batting average in 2012 to be at least equal to his average in 2013.

15. The time required to deliver and install a computer network at a customer's location is $t = 5 + \frac{2d}{r}$, where t is time in hours, d is the distance (in miles) from the warehouse to the customer's location, and r is the average speed of the delivery truck. If it takes 8.2 hours for an employee to deliver and install a network for a customer located 80 miles from the warehouse, what is the average speed of the delivery truck?

16. **Art** A glassblower can produce several sets of simple glasses in about 3 hours. When the glassblower works with an apprentice, the job takes about 2 hours. How long would it take the apprentice to make the same number of sets of glasses when working alone?

17. Which of the following equations have at least two excluded values? Select all that apply.

A. $\dfrac{3}{x} + \dfrac{1}{5x} = 1$

B. $\dfrac{x-4}{x-2} + \dfrac{3}{x} = \dfrac{5}{6}$

C. $\dfrac{x}{x-6} + 1 = \dfrac{5}{2x-12}$

D. $\dfrac{2x-3}{x^2-10x+25} + \dfrac{3}{7} = \dfrac{1}{x-5}$

E. $\dfrac{7}{x+2} + \dfrac{3x-4}{x^2+5x+6} = 9$

18. **Critical Thinking** An equation has the form $\frac{a}{x} + \frac{x}{b} = c$, where a, b, and c are constants and $b \neq 0$. How many solutions could this equation have? Explain.

19. **Multiple Representations** Write an equation whose graph is a straight line, but with an open circle at $x = 4$.

20. **Justify Reasoning** Explain why the excluded values do not change when multiplying by the LCD to add or subtract rational expressions.

21. **Critical Thinking** Describe how you would find the inverse of the rational function $f(x) = \frac{x - 1}{x - 2}$, $x \neq 2$. Then find the inverse.

Lesson Performance Task

Kasey creates comedy sketch videos and posts them on a popular video website and is selling an exclusive series of sketches on DVD. The total cost to make the series of sketches is $989. The materials cost $1.40 per DVD and the shipping costs $2.00 per DVD. Kasey plans to sell the DVDs for $12 each.

a. Let d be the number of DVDs Kasey sells. Create a profit-per-item model from the given information by writing a rule for $C(d)$, the total costs in dollars, $S(d)$, the total sales income in dollars, $P(d)$, the profit in dollars, and $P_{PI}(d)$, the profit per item sold in dollars.

b. What is the profit per DVD if Kasey sells 80 DVDs? Does this value make sense in the context of the problem?

c. Then use the function $P_{PI}(d)$ from part a to find how many DVDs Kasey would have to sell to break even. Identify all excluded values.

Rational Expressions and Equations

Essential Question: How can you use rational expressions and equations to solve real-world problems?

KEY EXAMPLE   *(Lesson 9.1)*

Add $\dfrac{1}{3+x}$ and $\dfrac{3-x}{x}$, simplify the result, and note the excluded values.

$$\dfrac{1}{3+x} + \dfrac{3-x}{x} = \dfrac{1x}{(3+x)x} + \dfrac{(3-x)(3+x)}{x(3+x)}$$ Write with like denominators.

$$= \dfrac{x+(9-x^2)}{x(x+3)}$$ Add.

$$= \dfrac{-x^2+x+9}{x(x+3)}, x \neq -3, 0$$ Simplify.

KEY EXAMPLE   *(Lesson 9.2)*

Find the quotient $\dfrac{x+3}{x+2} \div \dfrac{x^2-9}{2x-4}$ and note any excluded values.

$$\dfrac{x+3}{x+2} \div \dfrac{x^2-9}{2x-4} = \dfrac{x+3}{x+2} \cdot \dfrac{2x-4}{x^2-9}$$ Multiply by the reciprocal.

$$= \dfrac{x+3}{x+2} \cdot \dfrac{2(x-2)}{(x+3)(x-3)}$$ Factor the numerators and denominators.

$$= \dfrac{2(x+3)(x-2)}{(x+2)(x+3)(x-3)}$$ Multiply and cancel the common factors.

$$= \dfrac{2(x-2)}{(x+2)(x-3)}; x \neq \pm 2, \pm 3$$ Simplify.

KEY EXAMPLE   *(Lesson 9.3)*

Solve the rational equation algebraically.

$$\dfrac{x}{x-3} + \dfrac{x}{2} = \dfrac{6x}{2x-6}$$

$$2(x-3)\dfrac{x}{x-3} + 2(x-3)\dfrac{x}{2} = 2(x-3)\dfrac{6x}{2x-6}$$ Multiply each term by the LCD and divide out common factors.

$$2x + x(x-3) = 6x$$ Simplify.

$$x^2 - 7x = 0$$ Write in standard form.

$$x(x-7) = 0$$ Factor.

$$x = 0 \text{ or } x = 7$$ Solve for x.

EXERCISES

Add or subtract the given expressions, simplify the result, and note the excluded values. *(Lesson 9.1)*

1. $\dfrac{6x + 6}{x^2 - 9} + \dfrac{-3x + 3}{x^2 - 9}$

2. $\dfrac{4}{x^2 - 1} - \dfrac{x + 2}{x - 1}$

Multiply or divide the given expressions, simplify the result, and note the excluded values. *(Lesson 9.2)*

3. $\dfrac{x^2 - 4x - 5}{3x - 15} \cdot \dfrac{4}{x^2 - 2x - 3}$

4. $\dfrac{x + 2}{x - 4} \div \dfrac{x}{3x - 12}$

Solve each rational equation algebraically. *(Lesson 9.3)*

5. $x - \dfrac{10}{x} = 3$

6. $\dfrac{5}{x + 1} = \dfrac{2}{x + 4}$

MODULE PERFORMANCE TASK

Robots and Resistors

An engineer is designing part of a circuit that will control a robot. The circuit must have a certain total resistance to function properly. The engineer plans to use several resistors in *parallel*, which means each resistor is on its own branch of the circuit. The resistors available for this project are 20, 50, 80, and 200-ohm.

How can the engineer design a parallel circuit with a total resistance of 10 ohms using a maximum of 5 resistors, at least two of which must be different values? Find at least two possible circuit configurations that meet these criteria.

For another part of the circuit, the engineer wants to use resistors in parallel to create a total resistance of 6 ohms. Can she do it using the available resistor values? If so, how? If not, explain why not.

Begin by listing in the space below all of the information you will need to solve the problem. Then use your own paper to complete the task. Be sure to write down all your data and assumptions. Then use graphs, numbers, words, or algebra to explain how you reached your conclusion.

9.1–9.3 Rational Expressions and Equations

Personal Math Trainer

• Online Homework
• Hints and Help
• Extra Practice

Perform the indicated operations, simplify the result, and note any excluded values.
(Lessons 9.1, 9.2)

1. $\dfrac{4}{x+5} + \dfrac{2x}{x^2-25}$

2. $\dfrac{3x+2}{x-2} - \dfrac{x+5}{x-2}$

3. $\dfrac{x+3}{x+2} \cdot \dfrac{2x-4}{x^2-9}$

4. $\dfrac{x-3}{x-4} \div \dfrac{x-2}{x^2-16}$

Solve each rational equation. *(Lesson 9.3)*

5. $\dfrac{3}{x+2} + \dfrac{3}{2x+4} = \dfrac{x}{2x+4}$

6. $\dfrac{x}{x-8} = \dfrac{24-2x}{x-8}$

7. $\dfrac{8x}{x^2-4} - \dfrac{4}{x+2} = \dfrac{8}{x^2-4}$

8. $\dfrac{3x}{x+1} + \dfrac{6}{2x} = \dfrac{7}{x}$

ESSENTIAL QUESTION

9. How do you add or subtract rational expressions and identify any excluded values?

Assessment Readiness

1. Look at each expression. Is it equivalent to $x - 3$? Select Yes or No for A–C.

   A. $\dfrac{(x-3)(x+5)}{x+3} + \dfrac{x+3}{x+5}$ ⚪ Yes   ⚪ No

   B. $\dfrac{x+3}{x+5} + \dfrac{x-3}{x+5}$ ⚪ Yes   ⚪ No

   C. $\dfrac{(x+3)(x+5)}{x-5} \div \dfrac{x+5}{x-5}$ ⚪ Yes   ⚪ No

2. Consider finding how many roots a quadratic equation has. Choose True or False for each statement.

   A. The quadratic equation $x^2 - 12 = 0$ has real roots.   ⚪ True   ⚪ False

   B. The quadratic equation $x^2 + 25 = 0$ has imaginary roots.   ⚪ True   ⚪ False

   C. The quadratic equation $-8x^2 + 20 = 0$ has one real root, and one imaginary root.   ⚪ True   ⚪ False

3. A hiker averages 0.6 mile per hour walking up a mountain trail and 1.3 miles per hour walking down the trail. Find the total time in terms of d. Explain your answer.

4. A restaurant has two pastry ovens. When both ovens are used, it takes about 3 hours to bake the bread needed for one day. When only the large oven is used, it takes about 4 hours to bake the bread for one day. About how long would it take to bake the bread for one day if only the small oven were used? Explain how you got your answer.

1. Consider the equations. Does the graph of the equation have an asymptote at $x = 5$? Choose Yes or No for A–C.

   A. $y = \dfrac{3x^3}{x - 5}$ ◯ Yes   ◯ No

   B. $y = \dfrac{x^2(x - 4)}{x - 4}$ ◯ Yes   ◯ No

   C. $y = \dfrac{3x^2 - 6}{(x - 2)(x - 5)}$ ◯ Yes   ◯ No

2. Consider the equations $f(x) = \dfrac{1}{x}$ and $g(x) = 1 + \dfrac{1}{x + 5}$. Select True or False for each statement.

   A. $g(x)$ is translated 1 unit up and 5 units left from $f(x)$.   ◯ True   ◯ False

   B. $g(x)$ is translated 1 unit up and 5 units right from $f(x)$.   ◯ True   ◯ False

   C. $g(x)$ is reflected over the x-axis in comparison to $f(x)$.   ◯ True   ◯ False

3. Consider each equation. Does the equation have the solutions $x = -6, 4$? Choose Yes or No for A–C.

   A. $x + 2 = \dfrac{24}{x + 6}$ ◯ Yes   ◯ No

   B. $\dfrac{x + 2}{x} = 24$ ◯ Yes   ◯ No

   C. $x + 2 = \dfrac{24}{x}$ ◯ Yes   ◯ No

4. Consider each expression. Are the values $x = 0$ and $x = 2$ excluded? Choose Yes or No for A–C.

   A. $\dfrac{1}{x + 2} + \dfrac{4 + x}{x}$ ◯ Yes   ◯ No

   B. $\dfrac{1}{x - 2} + \dfrac{4 + x}{x}$ ◯ Yes   ◯ No

   C. $\dfrac{1}{x^2 - 2} + \dfrac{4 + x}{x^2 + 2}$ ◯ Yes   ◯ No

5. The time t it takes Sam to drive to his grandmother's house is inversely proportional to the speed v at which he drives. Write an equation for the one-way travel time. If it takes Sam 5 hours driving 50 miles per hour, how long would it take him if he drove at 65 miles per hour? Explain your answer.

6. A town has two trucks to collect garbage. When both trucks are in use, they take 6 hours to collect all the garbage. When only the small truck is in use, it takes 24 hours to collect the garbage. How long would it take to collect the garbage if only the large truck is in service? Explain your answer.

7. A farmer needs $3x^2 - 4x + 10$ seeds for each of $x^3 + 5x - 20$ fields. What expression would represent the seeds the farmer needs to plant all of the fields? Is $x = 1$ a reasonable value for this representation? Explain your answers.

Performance Tasks

★ **8.** For a car moving with initial speed v_0 and acceleration a, the distance d that the car travels in time t is given by $d = v_0 t + \frac{1}{2}at^2$.

    A. Write a rational expression in terms of t for the average speed of the car during a period of acceleration. Simplify the expression.

    B. During a race, a driver accelerates for 3 s at a rate of 10 ft/s^2 in order to pass another car. The driver's initial speed was 264 ft/s. What was the driver's average speed during the acceleration?

9. The average speed for the winner of the 2002 Indy 500 was 25 mi/h greater than the average speed for the 2001 winner. In addition, the 2002 winner completed the 500 mi race 32 min faster than the 2001 winner.

   A. Let s represent the average speed of the 2001 winner in miles per hour. Write expressions in terms of s for the time in hours that it took the 2001 and 2002 winners to complete the race.

   B. Write a rational equation that can be used to determine s. Solve your equation to find the average speed of the 2001 winner to the nearest mile per hour.

10. The Renaissance architect Andrea Palladio preferred that the length and width of rectangular rooms be limited to certain ratios. These ratios are listed in the table. Palladio also believed that the height of a room with vaulted ceilings should be the harmonic mean of the length and width.

Rooms with a Width of 30 ft		
Length-to-Width Ratio	**Length (ft)**	**Height (ft)**
2:1		
3:2		
4:3		
5:3		
$\sqrt{2}$:1		

   A. The harmonic mean of two positive numbers a and b is equal to $\dfrac{2}{\frac{1}{a}+\frac{1}{b}}$. Simplify this expression.

   B. Complete the table for a rectangular room with a width of 30 feet that meets Palladio's requirements for its length and height. If necessary, round to the nearest tenth.

   C. A Palladian room has a length-to-width ratio of 4:3. If the length of this room is doubled, what effect should this change have on the room's width and height, according to Palladio's principles?

Chemist A chemist mixes 5 mL of an acid with 15 mL of water. The concentration of acid in the acid-and-water mix is $\frac{5}{5+15} = \frac{5}{20} = 25\%$. If the chemist adds more acid to the mix, then the concentration C becomes a function of the additional amount a of acid added to the mix.

a. Write a rule for the function $C(a)$.

b. What is a reasonable domain for this function? Explain.

c. What concentration of acid does pure water have? What concentration of acid does pure acid have? So, what are the possible values of $C(a)$?

d. Graph the function. Be sure to label the axes with the quantities they represent and indicate the axis scales by showing numbers for some grid lines.

e. Analyze the function's rule to determine the vertical asymptote of the function's graph. Why is the asymptote irrelevant in this situation?

f. Analyze the function's rule to determine the horizontal asymptote of the function's graph. What is the relevance of the asymptote in this situation?

Radical Functions, Expressions, and Equations

MATH IN CAREERS

Nutritionist Nutritionists provide services to individuals and institutions, such as schools and hospitals. Nutritionists must be able to calculate the amounts of different substances in a person's diet, including calories, fat, vitamins, and minerals. They must also calculate measures of fitness, such as body mass index. Nutritionists must use statistics when reviewing nutritional studies in scientific journals.

If you are interested in a career as a nutritionist, you should study these mathematical subjects:

- Algebra
- Statistics
- Business Math

Research other careers that require proficiency in understanding statistics in scientific articles. Check out the career activity at the end of the unit to find out how **Nutritionists** use math.

Reading Start-Up

Vocabulary

Review Words

✔ composition of functions
(*composición de funciones*)
extraneous solution
(*solución extraña*)

✔ inverse function
(*función inversa*)

✔ many-to-one function
(*función muchos a uno*)

✔ one-to-one function
(*función uno a uno*)
radical expression
(*expresión radical*)

Preview Words

cube root function
(*función de raíz cúbica*)
index (*índice*)
square root function
(*función de raíz cuadrada*)

Visualize Vocabulary

Use the ✓ words to complete the graphic. Put just one word in each section of the square.

The function that results from exchanging the input and output values of a function.	A function where each element of the range may correspond to more than one element of the domain.
A function where each element of the range corresponds to only one element of the domain.	A situation with two functions in which the output of one function is used as the input for the other.

Function Types

Understand Vocabulary

To become familiar with some of the vocabulary terms in the module, consider the following. You may refer to the module, the glossary, or a dictionary.

1. A function whose rule contains a variable under a square-root sign

   is a _____.

2. A function whose rule contains a variable under a cube-root sign

   is a _____.

3. In the radical expression $\sqrt[n]{x}$, n is the _____.

Active Reading

Pyramid Fold Before beginning a module, create a pyramid fold to help you take notes from each lesson in the module. The three sides of the pyramid can summarize information about function families, their graphs, and their characteristics.

Radical Functions

Essential Question: How can you use radical functions to solve real-world problems?

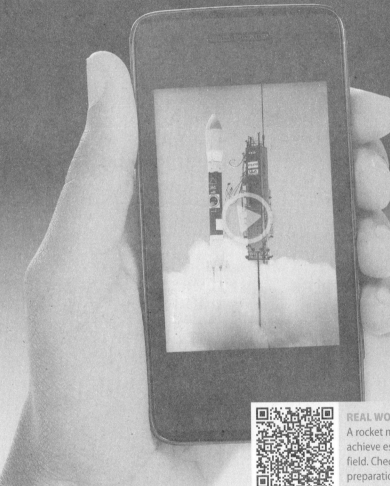

REAL WORLD VIDEO
A rocket must generate enough thrust to achieve escape velocity from Earth's gravitational field. Check out some of the calculations and preparations that go into a successful launch.

MODULE PERFORMANCE TASK PREVIEW
We Have Liftoff!

If you throw a ball straight up, it will eventually come back down. But if you could throw it with enough initial velocity, it would escape Earth's surface and go into orbit. If you could throw it even faster, it might even escape the solar system. What is the escape velocity for Earth, the minimum velocity for an object to leave Earth's surface and not return? What about the velocity necessary to escape other planets? Let's take off and find out!

Are(YOU)Ready?

Complete these exercises to review skills you will need for this module.

Exponents

Example 1   Simplify .

$$x^2 \cdot x^3 - 2x^4 \cdot x = x^{2+3} - 2x^{4+1}$$
$$= x^5 - 2x^5$$
$$= -x^5$$

• Online Homework
• Hints and Help
• Extra Practice

Simplify each expression.

1. $5x^3 \cdot 2x$

2. $-x^4 \cdot x^3$

3. $4x^2 \left(2xy - x^2 \right)$

Inverse Linear Functions

Example 2   Write the inverse function of $y = x + 9$.

$$y - 9 = x + 9 - 9 \qquad\qquad \text{Subtract.}$$
$$y - 9 = x \qquad\qquad\qquad \text{Simplify.}$$
$$x - 9 = y \qquad\qquad\qquad \text{Switch } x \text{ and } y.$$

The inverse function of $y = x + 9$ is $y = x - 9$.

Example 3   Write the inverse function of $y = \frac{x}{-22}$.

$$(-22)y = -\frac{x}{22}(-22) \qquad \text{Multiply.}$$
$$-22y = x \qquad\qquad\qquad \text{Simplify.}$$
$$-22x = y \qquad\qquad\qquad \text{Switch } x \text{ and } y.$$

The inverse function of $y = \frac{x}{-22}$ is $y = -22x$.

Write the inverse of each function.

4. $y = x - 6$

5. $y = 7x$

6. $y = \frac{1}{2}x$

7. $y = x + 11$

8. $y = -18x$

9. $y = 21 + x$

10.1 Inverses of Simple Quadratic and Cubic Functions

Essential Question: What functions are the inverses of quadratic functions and cubic functions, and how can you find them?

⊘ Explore   Finding the Inverse of a Many-to-One Function

The function $f(x)$ is defined by the following ordered pairs: $(-2, 4)$, $(-1, 2)$, $(0, 0)$, $(1, 2)$, and $(2, 4)$.

(A) Find the inverse function of $f(x)$, $f^{-1}(x)$, by reversing the coordinates in the ordered pairs.

_____

(B) Is the inverse also a function? Explain.

_____

(C) If necessary, restrict the domain of $f(x)$ such that the inverse, $f^{-1}(x)$, is a function.

To restrict the domain of $f(x)$ so that its inverse is a function, you can restrict it

to $\left\{ x \mid x \geq \boxed{} \right\}$

(D) With the restricted domain of $f(x)$, what ordered pairs define the inverse function $f^{-1}(x)$?

_____

Reflect

1. **Discussion** Look again at the ordered pairs that define $f(x)$. Without reversing the order of the coordinates, how could you have known that the inverse of $f(x)$ would not be a function?

_____

_____

_____

2. How will restricting the domain of $f(x)$ affect the range of its inverse?

_____

_____

_____

_____

Finding and Graphing the Inverse of a Simple Quadratic Function

The function $f(x) = x^2$ is a many-to-one function, so its domain must be restricted in order to find its inverse function. If the domain is restricted to $x \geq 0$, then the inverse function is $f^{-1}(x) = \sqrt{x}$; if the domain is restricted to $x \leq 0$, then the inverse function is $f^{-1}(x) = -\sqrt{x}$.

The inverse of a quadratic function is a **square root function**, which is a function whose rule involves $\sqrt{x}$. **The parent square root function** is $g(x) = \sqrt{x}$. A square root function is defined only for values of x that make the expression under the radical sign nonnegative.

Example 1   Restrict the domain of each quadratic function and find its inverse. Confirm the inverse relationship using composition. Graph the function and its inverse.

(A) $f(x) = 0.5x^2$

Restrict the domain. $\left\{ x \mid x \geq 0 \right\}$

Find the inverse.

Replace $f(x)$ with y.	$y = 0.5x^2$
Multiply both sides by 2.	$2y = x^2$
Use the definition of positive square root.	$\sqrt{2y} = x$
Switch x and y to write the inverse.	$\sqrt{2x} = y$
Replace y with $f^{-1}(x)$.	$f^{-1}(x) = \sqrt{2x}$

Confirm the inverse relationship using composition.

$$f^{-1}(f(x)) = f^{-1}(0.5x^2) \qquad\qquad f(f^{-1}(x)) = 0.5(\sqrt{2x})^2$$
$$= \sqrt{2(0.5x^2)} \qquad\qquad\qquad = 0.5(2x)$$
$$= \sqrt{x^2} \qquad\qquad\qquad\qquad = x \text{ for } x \geq 0$$
$$= x \text{ for } x \geq 0$$

Since $f^{-1}(f(x)) = x$ for $x \geq 0$ and $f(f^{-1}(x)) = x$ for $x \geq 0$, it has been confirmed that $f^{-1}(x) = \sqrt{2x}$ for $x \geq 0$ is the inverse function of $f(x) = 0.5x^2$ for $x \geq 0$.

Graph $f^{-1}(x)$ by graphing $f(x)$ over the restricted domain and reflecting the graph over the line $y = x$.

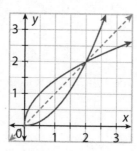

Ⓑ $f(x) = x^2 - 7$

Find the inverse.

Restrict the domain. _____

Replace $f(x)$ with y.   ☐ $= x^2 - 7$

Add 7 to both sides.   ☐ $= x^2$

Use the definition of positive square root.   ☐ $= x$

Switch x and y to write the inverse.   _____

Replace y with $f^{-1}(x)$.   _____

Confirm the inverse relationship using composition.

$f^{-1}(f(x)) = f^{-1}\left(\boxed{} \right)$ $f(f^{-1}(x)) = f\left(\boxed{} \right)$

$= \boxed{}$ $= \left(\boxed{} \right)^2 - 7$

$= \boxed{}$ $= \boxed{} - 7$

$= \boxed{}$ $= \boxed{}$

Since $f^{-1}(f(x)) = \boxed{}$ for _____ and $f\left(\boxed{} \right) = x$ for $x \geq \boxed{}$, it has been confirmed that

$f^{-1}(x) = \boxed{}$ for $\boxed{}$ is the inverse function of $f(x) = x^2 - 7$ for _____.

Graph $f^{-1}(x)$ by graphing $f(x)$ over the restricted domain and reflecting the graph over the line $y = x$.

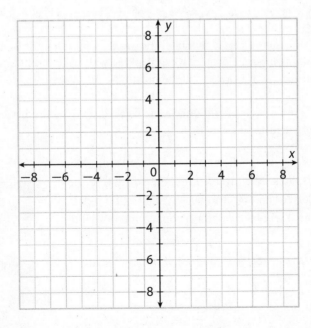

Restrict the domain of each quadratic function and find its inverse. Confirm the inverse relationship using composition. Graph the function and its inverse.

3. $f(x) = 3x^2$

⚙ Explain 2 Finding the Inverse of a Quadratic Model

In many instances, quadratic functions are used to model real-world applications. It is often useful to find and interpret the inverse of a quadratic model. Note that when working with real-world applications, it is more useful to use the notation $x(y)$ for the inverse of $y(x)$ instead of the notation $y^{-1}(x)$.

Example 2 Find the inverse of each of the quadratic functions. Use the inverse to solve the application.

(A) The function $d(t) = 16t^2$ gives the distance d in feet that a dropped object falls in t seconds. Write the inverse function $t(d)$ to find the time t in seconds it takes for an object to fall a distance of d feet. Then estimate how long it will take a penny dropped into a well to fall 48 feet.

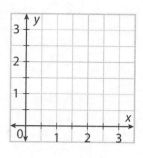
©CreativeNature.nl/Shutterstock

The original function $d(t) = 16t^2$ is a quadratic function with a domain restricted to $t \geq 0$.

Find the inverse function.

Write $d(t)$ as d. $\qquad\qquad\qquad d = 16t^2$

Divide both sides by 16. $\qquad\qquad \dfrac{d}{16} = t^2$

Use the definition of positive square root. $\qquad \sqrt{\dfrac{d}{16}} = t$

Write t as $t(d)$.

$$\sqrt{\dfrac{d}{16}} = t(d)$$

The inverse function is $t(d) = \sqrt{\dfrac{d}{16}}$ for $d \geq 0$.

Use the inverse function to estimate how long it will take a penny dropped into a well to fall 48 feet. Substitute $d = 48$ into the inverse function.

Write the function.

$$t(d) = \sqrt{\dfrac{d}{16}}$$

Substitute 48 for d.

$$t(48) = \sqrt{\dfrac{48}{16}}$$

Simplify.

$$t(48) = \sqrt{3}$$

Use a calculator to estimate.

$$t(48) \approx 1.7$$

So, it will take about 1.7 seconds for a penny to fall 48 feet into the well.

(B) The function $E(v) = 4v^2$ gives the kinetic energy E in Joules of an 8-kg object that is traveling at a velocity of v meters per second. Write and graph the inverse function $v(E)$ to find the velocity v in meters per second required for an 8-kg object to have a kinetic energy of E Joules. Then estimate the velocity required for an 8-kg object to have a kinetic energy of 60 Joules.

The original function $E(v) = 4v^2$ is a _____ function with a domain restricted

to v _____.

Find the inverse function.

Write $E(v)$ as E.

$\boxed{} = 4v^2$

Divide both sides by 4.

$\boxed{} = v^2$

Use the definition of positive square root.

$\boxed{} = v$

Write v as $v(E)$.

_____

The inverse function is $v(E) =$ _____ for E _____.

Use the inverse function to estimate the velocity required for an 8-kg object to have a kinetic energy of 60 Joules.

Substitute $E = 60$ into the inverse function.

Write the function.

$v(E) = \boxed{}$

Substitute 60 for E.

$v\left(\boxed{}\right) = \boxed{}$

Simplify.

_____

Use a calculator to estimate.

_____

So, an 8-kg object with kinetic energy of 60 Joules is traveling at a velocity of _____ meters per second.

Find the inverse of the quadratic function. Use the inverse to solve the application.

4.   The function $A(r) = \pi r^2$ gives the area of a circular object with respect to its radius r. Write the inverse function $r(A)$ to find the radius r required for area of A. Then estimate the radius of a circular object that has an area of 40 cm².

⚙ Explain 3 Finding and Graphing the Inverse of a Simple Cubic Function

Note that the function $f(x) = x^3$ is a one-to-one function, so its domain does not need to be restricted in order to find its inverse function. The inverse of $f(x) = x^3$ is $f^{-1}(x) = \sqrt[3]{x}$.

The inverse of a cubic function is a **cube root function**, which is a function whose rule involves $\sqrt[3]{x}$. The **parent cube root function** is $g(x) = \sqrt[3]{x}$.

Example 3   **Find the inverse of each cubic function. Confirm the inverse relationship using composition. Graph the function and its inverse.**

Ⓐ $f(x) = 0.5x^3$

Find each inverse. Graph the function and its inverse.

Replace $f(x)$ with y.	$y = 0.5x^3$
Multiply both sides by 2.	$2y = x^3$
Use the definition of cube root.	$\sqrt[3]{2y} = x$
Switch x and y to write the inverse.	$\sqrt[3]{2x} = y$
Replace y with $f^{-1}(x)$.	$\sqrt[3]{2x} = f^{-1}(x)$

Confirm the inverse relationship using composition.

$$f^{-1}(f(x)) = f^{-1}(0.5x^3)$$
$$= \sqrt[3]{2(0.5x^3)}$$
$$= \sqrt[3]{x^3}$$
$$= x$$

$$f(f^{-1}(x)) = f(\sqrt[3]{2x})$$
$$= 0.5(\sqrt[3]{2x})^3$$
$$= 0.5(2x)$$
$$= x$$

Since $f^{-1}\!\left(f(x)\right) = x$ and $f\!\left(f^{-1}(x)\right) = x$, it has been confirmed that $f^{-1}(x) = \sqrt[3]{2x}$ is the inverse function of $f(x) = 0.5x^3$.

Graph $f^{-1}(x)$ by graphing $f(x)$ and reflecting $f(x)$ over the line $y = x$.

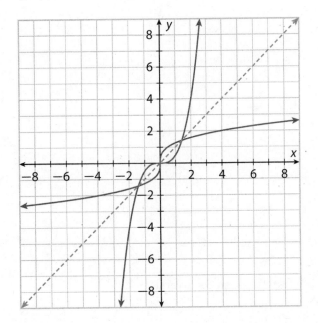

B $f(x) = x^3 - 9$

Find the inverse.

Replace $f(x)$ with y. $\boxed{} = x^3 - 9$

Add 9 to both sides. $\boxed{} = x^3$

Use the definition of cube root. $\boxed{} = x$

Switch x and y to write the inverse. _____

Replace y with $f^{-1}(x)$. _____

Confirm the inverse relationship using composition.

$f^{-1}\!\left(f(x)\right) = f^{-1}\!\left(\boxed{}\right)$ $f\!\left(f^{-1}(x)\right) = f\left(\boxed{}\right)$

$= \boxed{}$ $= \boxed{}$

$= \boxed{}$ $= \boxed{}$

$= \boxed{}$ $= \boxed{}$

Since $f^{-1}\!\left(f(x)\right) = \boxed{}$ and $f\!\left(f^{-1}(x)\right) = \boxed{}$, it has been confirmed that $f^{-1}(x) = \boxed{}$ is the inverse function of $f(x) = x^3 - 9$.

Graph $f^{-1}(x)$ by graphing $f(x)$ and reflecting $f(x)$ over the line $y = x$.

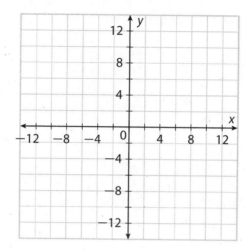

Your Turn

Find each inverse. Graph the function and its inverse.

5. $f(x) = 2x^3$

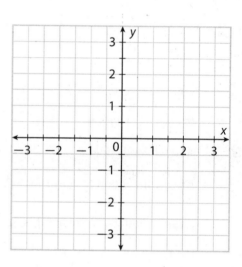

⭐ Explain 4 Finding the Inverse of a Cubic Model

In many instances, cubic functions are used to model real-world applications.
It is often useful to find and interpret the inverse of cubic models. As with
quadratic real-world applications, it is more useful to use the notation $x(y)$
for the inverse of $y(x)$ instead of the notation $y^{-1}(x)$.

Example 4 Find the inverse of each of the following cubic functions.

(A) The function $m(L) = 0.00001L^3$ gives the mass m in kilograms of a red snapper of length L centimeters. Find the inverse function $L(m)$ to find the length L in centimeters of a red snapper that has a mass of m kilograms.

The original function $m(L) = 0.00001L^3$ is a cubic function.

Find the inverse function.

Write $m(L)$ as m. $\qquad\qquad\qquad\qquad$ $m = 0.00001L^3$

Multiply both sides by 100,000. $\qquad$ $100{,}000m = L^3$

Use the definition of cube root. $\sqrt[3]{100{,}000m} = L$

Write L as $L(m)$. $\qquad\qquad\qquad$ $\sqrt[3]{100{,}000m} = L(m)$

The inverse function is $L(m) = \sqrt[3]{100{,}000m}$.

(B) The function $V(r) = \frac{4}{3}\pi r^3$ gives the volume V of a sphere with radius r. Find the inverse function $r(V)$ to find the radius r of a sphere with volume V.

The original function $V(r) = \frac{4}{3}\pi r^3$ is a _____ function.

Find the inverse function.

Write $V(r)$ as V. $\qquad\qquad\qquad$ $\boxed{} = \frac{4}{3}\pi r^3$

Divide both sides by $\frac{4}{3}\pi$. $\qquad\qquad$ $\boxed{} = r^3$

Use the definition of cube root. $\qquad$ $\boxed{} = r$

Write r as $r(V)$. $\qquad\qquad\qquad\qquad$ _____

The inverse function is $r(V) =$ _____.

6. The function $m(r) = \frac{44}{3}\pi r^3$ gives the mass in grams of a spherical lead ball with a radius of r centimeters. Find the inverse function $r(m)$ to find the radius r of a lead sphere with mass m.

7. What is the general form of the inverse function for the function $f(x) = ax^2$? State any restrictions on the domains.

_____

_____

_____

8. What is the general form of the inverse function for the function $f(x) = ax^3$? State any restrictions on the domains.

_____

_____

_____

9. Essential Question Check-In Why must the domain be restricted when finding the inverse of a quadratic function, but not when finding the inverse of a cubic function?

_____

_____

_____

 Evaluate: Homework and Practice

- Online Homework
- Hints and Help
- Extra Practice

Restrict the domain of the quadratic function and find its inverse. Confirm the inverse relationship using composition. Graph the function and its inverse.

1. $f(x) = 0.2x^2$

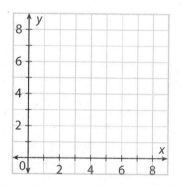

2. $f(x) = 8x^2$

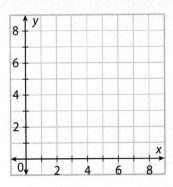

3. $f(x) = x^2 + 10$

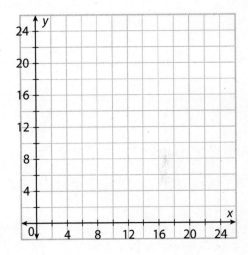

Restrict the domain of the quadratic function and find its inverse. Confirm the inverse relationship using composition.

4. $f(x) = 15x^2$

5. $f(x) = x^2 - \dfrac{3}{4}$

6. $f(x) = 0.7x^2$

7. The function $d(s) = \dfrac{1}{14.9}s^2$ models the average depth d in feet of the water over which a tsunami travels, where s is the speed in miles per hour. Write the inverse function $s(d)$ to find the speed required for a depth of d feet. Then estimate the speed of a tsunami over water with an average depth of 1500 feet.

8. The function $x(T) = 9.8\left(\frac{T}{2\pi}\right)^2$ gives the length x in meters for a

pendulum to swing for a period of T seconds. Write the inverse function to find the period of a pendulum in seconds. The period of a pendulum is the time it takes the pendulum to complete one back-and-forth swing. Find the period of a pendulum with length of 5 meters.

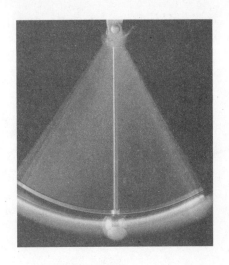

Find the inverse of each cubic function. Confirm the inverse relationship using composition. Graph the function and its inverse.

9. $f(x) = 0.25x^3$

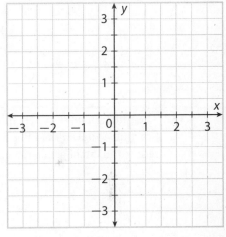

10. $f(x) = -12x^3$

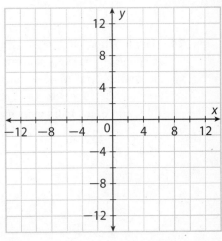

Find the inverse of the cubic function. Confirm the inverse relationship using composition.

11. $f(x) = x^3 - \dfrac{5}{6}$

12. $f(x) = x^3 + 9$

13. The function $m(r) = 31r^3$ models the mass in grams of a spherical zinc ball as a function of the ball's radius in centimeters. Write the inverse model to represent the radius r in cm of a spherical zinc ball as a function of the ball's mass m in g.

14. The function $m(r) = 21r^3$ models the mass in grams of a spherical titanium ball as a function of the ball's radius in centimeters. Write the inverse model to represent the radius r in centimeters of a spherical titanium ball as a function of the ball's mass m in grams.

15. After an initial deposit of $2000, a bank account pays interest at an annual rate $r\%$ compounded annually. The value V of the account after 3 years can be represented by the model $V(r) = 2000(1 + r)^3$. Write the inverse function $r(V)$ to find the interest rate needed for the account to have value V after the 3 years.

16. Explain the Error A student was asked to find the inverse of the function $f(x) = \left(\frac{x}{2}\right)^3 + 9$. What did the student do wrong? Find the correct inverse.

$$f(x) = \left(\frac{x}{2}\right)^3 + 9$$

$$y = \left(\frac{x}{2}\right)^3 + 9$$

$$y - 9 = \left(\frac{x}{2}\right)^3$$

$$2y - 18 = x^3$$

$$\sqrt[3]{2y - 18} = x$$

$$y = \sqrt[3]{2x - 18}$$

$$f^{-1}(x) = \sqrt[3]{2x - 18}$$

17. Multi-Step A framing store uses the function $\left(\frac{c - 0.2}{0.5}\right)^2 = a$ to determine the total area of a piece of glass with respect to the cost before installation of the glass. Write the inverse function for the cost c in dollars of glass for a picture with an area of a in square centimeters. Then write a new function to represent the total cost C the store charges if it costs $6.00 for installation. Use the total cost function to estimate the cost if the area of the glass is 192 cm^2.

18. Make a Conjecture The function $f(x) = x^2$ must have its domain restricted to have its inverse be a function. The function $f(x) = x^3$ does not need to have its domain restricted to have its inverse be a function. Make a conjecture about which power functions need to have their domains restricted to have their inverses be functions and which do not.

Lesson Performance Task

One method used to irrigate crops is the center-pivot irrigation system. In this method, sprinklers rotate in a circle to water crops. The challenge for the farmer is to determine where to place the pivot in order to water the desired number of acres. The farmer knows the area but needs to find the radius of the circle necessary to define that area. How can the farmer determine this from the formula for the area of a circle $A = \pi r^2$? Find the formula the farmer could use to determine the radius necessary to irrigate a given number of acres, A. (Hint: One acre is 43,560 square feet.) What would be the radius necessary for the sprinklers to irrigate an area of 133 acres?

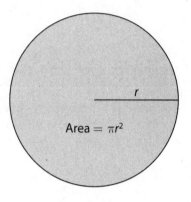

$$\text{Area} = \pi r^2$$

10.2 Graphing Square Root Functions

Essential Question: How can you use transformations of a parent square root function to graph functions of the form $g(x) = a\sqrt{(x-h)} + k$ or $g(x) = \sqrt{\frac{1}{b}(x-h)} + k$?

Resource Locker

⊘ Explore   Graphing and Analyzing the Parent Square Root Function

Although you have seen how to use imaginary numbers to evaluate square roots of negative numbers, graphing complex numbers and complex valued functions is beyond the scope of this course. For purposes of graphing functions based on the square roots (and in most cases where a square root function is used in a real-world example), the domain and range should both be limited to real numbers.

The square root function is the inverse of a quadratic function with a domain limited to positive real numbers. The quadratic function must be a one-to-one function in order to have an inverse, so the domain is limited to one side of the vertex. The square root function is also a one-to-one function as all inverse functions are.

Ⓐ The domain of the square root function (limited to real numbers) is given by $\left\{ x \mid x \geq \boxed{} \right\}$

Ⓑ Fill in the table.

x	$f(x) = \sqrt{x}$
0	
1	
4	
9	

Ⓒ Plot the points on the graph, and connect them with a smooth curve.

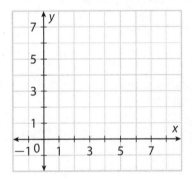

Ⓓ Recall that this function is the inverse of the parent quadratic $\left(f(x) = x^2 \right)$ with a domain limited to the nonnegative real numbers. Write the range of this square root function:

$\left\{ y \mid y \geq \boxed{} \right\}$.

Ⓔ The graph appears to be getting flatter as x increases, indicating that the rate of change _____ as x increases.

Ⓕ Describe the end behavior of the square root function, $f(x) = \sqrt{x}$. $f(x) \to \boxed{}$ as $x \to \boxed{}$

1. **Discussion** Why does the end behavior of the square root function only need to be described at one end?

_____

_____

_____

_____

2. The solution to the equation $x^2 = 4$ is sometimes written as $x = \pm 2$. Explain why the inverse of $f(x) = x^2$ cannot similarly be written as $g(x) = \pm\sqrt{x}$ in order to use all reals as the domain of $f(x)$.

_____

_____

_____

_____

_____

⊘ Explore 2 Predicting the Effects of Parameters on the Graphs of Square Root Functions

You have learned how to transform the graph of a function using reflections across the x- and y-axes, vertical and horizontal stretches and compressions, and translations. Here, you will apply those transformations to the graph of the square root function $f(x) = \sqrt{x}$.

When transforming the parent function $f(x) = \sqrt{x}$, you can get functions of the form

$g(x) = a\sqrt{(x - h)} + k$ or $g(x) = \sqrt{\frac{1}{b}(x - h)} + k$.

For each parameter, predict the effect on the graph of the parent function, and then confirm your prediction with a graphing calculator.

Ⓐ Predict the effect of the parameter, h, on the graph of $g(x) = \sqrt{x - h}$ for each function.

   a. $g(x) = \sqrt{x - 2}$: The graph is a _____ of the graph of $f(x)$ [right/left/up/down] 2 units.

   b. $g(x) = \sqrt{x + 2}$: The graph is a _____ of the graph of $f(x)$ [right/left/up/down] 2 units.

   Check your answers using a graphing calculator.

Ⓑ Predict the effect of the parameter k on the graph of $g(x) = \sqrt{x} + k$ for each function.

   a. $g(x) = \sqrt{x} + 2$: The graph is a _____ of the graph of $f(x)$ [right/up/left/down] 2 units.

   b. $g(x) = \sqrt{x} - 2$: The graph is a _____ of the graph of $f(x)$ [right/up/left/down] 2 units.

   Check your answers using a graphing calculator.

(C) Predict the effect of the parameter a on the graph of $g(x) = a\sqrt{x}$ for each function.

a. $g(x) = 2\sqrt{x}$: The graph is a _____ stretch of the graph of $f(x)$ by a factor of ____.

b. $g(x) = \frac{1}{2}\sqrt{x}$: The graph is a _____ compression of the graph of $f(x)$ by a factor of ____.

c. $g(x) = -\frac{1}{2}\sqrt{x}$: The graph is a _____ compression of the graph of $f(x)$ by a factor of ____ as well as a _____ across the _____.

d. $g(x) = -2\sqrt{x}$: The graph is a _____ stretch of the graph of $f(x)$ by a factor of ____ as well as a _____ across the _____.

Check your answers using a graphing calculator.

(D) Predict the effect of the parameter, b, on the graph of $g(x) = \sqrt{\frac{1}{b}x}$ for each function.

a. $g(x) = \sqrt{\frac{1}{2}x}$: The graph is a _____ stretch of the graph of $f(x)$ by a factor of ____.

b. $g(x) = \sqrt{2x}$: The graph is a _____ compression of the graph of $f(x)$ by a factor of ____.

c. $g(x) = \sqrt{-\frac{1}{2}x}$: The graph is a _____ stretch of the graph of $f(x)$ by a factor of ____ as well as a _____ across the _____.

d. $g(x) = \sqrt{-2x}$: The graph is a _____ compression of the graph of $f(x)$ by a factor of ____ as well as a _____ across the _____.

Check your answers using a graphing calculator.

Reflect

3. **Discussion** Describe what the effect of each of the transformation parameters is on the domain and range of the transformed function.

_____

_____

_____

_____

_____

⊘ Explain 1   Graphing Square Root Functions

When graphing transformations of the square root function, it is useful to consider the effect of the transformation on two reference points, $(0, 0)$ and $(1, 1)$, that lie on the parent function, and where they map to on the transformed function, $g(x)$.

$f(x) = \sqrt{x}$		$g(x) = a\sqrt{x - h} + k$		$g(x) = \sqrt{\frac{1}{b}(x - h)} + k$	
x	y	x	y	x	y
0	0	h	k	h	k
1	1	$h + 1$	$k + a$	$h + b$	$k + 1$

The transformed reference points can be found by recognizing that the initial point of the graph is translated from $(0, 0)$ to (h, k). When $g(x)$ involves the parameters a, h, and k, the second transformed reference point is 1 unit to the right of (h, k) and $|a|$ units up or down from (h, k), depending on the sign of a. When $g(x)$ involves the parameters b, h, and k, the second transformed reference point is $|b|$ units left or right from (h, k), depending on the sign of b, and 1 unit above (h, k).

Transformations of the square root function also affect the domain and range. In order to work with real valued inputs and outputs, the domain of the square root function cannot include values of x that result in a negative-valued expression. Negative values of x can be in the domain, as long as they result in nonnegative values of the expression that is inside the square root. Similarly, the value of the square root function is positive by definition, but multiplying the square root function by a negative number, or adding a constant to it changes the range and can result in negative values of the transformed function.

Example 1   For each of the transformed square root functions, find the transformed reference points and use them to plot the transformed function on the same graph with the parent function. Describe the domain and range using set notation.

Ⓐ $g(x) = 2\sqrt{x - 3} - 2$

To find the domain:

Square root input must be nonnegative. $x - 3 \geq 0$

Solve the inequality for x. $x \geq 3$

The domain is $\left\{ x \mid x \geq 3 \right\}$.

To find the range:

The square root function is nonnegative. $\sqrt{x - 3} \geq 0$

Multiply by 2 $2\sqrt{x - 3} \geq 0$

Subtract 2. $2\sqrt{x - 3} - 2 \geq -2$

The expression on the left is $g(x)$. $g(x) \geq -2$

Since $g(x)$ is greater than or equal to -2 for all x in the domain, the range is $\left\{ y \mid y \geq -2 \right\}$.

$(0, 0) \rightarrow (3, -2)$

$(1, 1) \rightarrow (4, 0)$

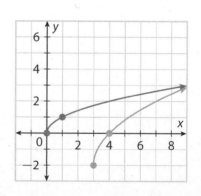

ⓑ $g(x) = \sqrt{-\frac{1}{2}(x - 2)} + 1$

To find the domain:

Square root input must be nonnegative. $\qquad -\frac{1}{2}(x - 2) \geq \boxed{}$

Multiply both sides by −2. $\qquad\qquad x - 2 \boxed{} \;\; 0$

Add 2 to both sides. $\qquad\qquad\qquad \boxed{} \leq 2$

Expressed in set notation, the domain is $\left\{ x \mid \boxed{} \right\}$.

To find the range:

The square root function is nonnegative. $\qquad \sqrt{-\frac{1}{2}(x - 2)} \;\boxed{}\; 0$

Add 1 both sides $\qquad\qquad\qquad\qquad \sqrt{-\frac{1}{2}(x - 2)} + 1 \geq \boxed{}$

Substistute in $\boxed{}$. $\qquad\qquad g(x) \geq 1$

Since $g(x)$ is greater than 1 for all x in the domain,

the range (in set notation) is $\left\{ y \mid \boxed{} \right\}$.

$(0, 0) \rightarrow \boxed{}$

$(1, 1) \rightarrow \boxed{}$

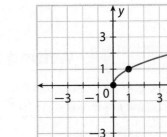

Your Turn

For each of the transformed square root functions, find the transformed reference points and use them to plot the transformed function on the same graph with the parent function. Describe the domain and range using set notation.

4. $g(x) = -3\sqrt{x - 2} + 3$

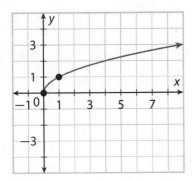

5. $g(x) = \sqrt{\frac{1}{3}(x+2)} + 1$

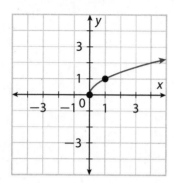

⚙ Explain 2 Writing Square Root Functions

Given the graph of a square root function and the form of the transformed function, either
$g(x) = a\sqrt{x-h} + k$ or $g(x) = \sqrt{\frac{1}{b}(x-h)} = k$, the transformation parameters can be determined from the transformed reference points. In either case, the initial point will be at (h, k) and readily apparent. The parameter a can be determined by how far up or down the second point (found at $x = h + 1$) is from the initial point, or the parameter b can be determined by how far to the left or right the second point (found at $y = k + 1$) is from the initial point.

Example 2 **Write the function that matches the graph using the indicated transformation format.**

Ⓐ $g(x) = \sqrt{\frac{1}{b}(x-h)} + k$

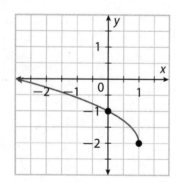

Initial point: $(h, k) = (1, -2)$

Second point:

$$(h + b, k + 1) = (0, -1)$$

$$1 + b = 0$$

$$b = -1$$

The function is $g(x) = \sqrt{-1(x-1)} - 2$.

Ⓑ $g(x) = a\sqrt{x - h} + k$

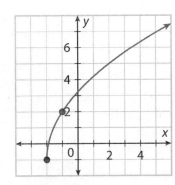

Initial point: $(h, k) = \left(\boxed{}, \boxed{} \right)$

Second point:

$\left(h + 1, k + \boxed{} \right) = \left(-1, \boxed{} \right)$

$\boxed{} + a = 2$

$a = \boxed{}$

The function is $g(x) = \boxed{} \sqrt{x \boxed{} 2} - \boxed{}$.

Your Turn

Write the function that matches the graph using the indicated transformation format.

6. $g(x) = \sqrt{\dfrac{1}{b}(x - h)} + k$

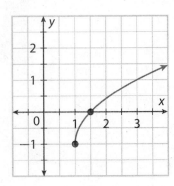

7. $g(x) = a\sqrt{(x - h)} + k$

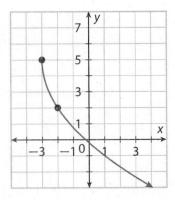

⏱ Explain 3 Modeling with Square Root Functions

Square root functions that model real-world situations can be used to investigate average rates of change.

Recall that the average rate of change of the function $f(x)$ over an interval from x_1 to x_2 is given by

$$\frac{f(x_2) - f(x_1)}{x_2 - x_1.}$$

Example 3 **Use a calculator to evaluate the model at the indicated points, and connect the points with a curve to complete the graph of the model. Calculate the average rates of change over the first and last intervals and explain what the rate of change represents.**

Ⓐ The approximate period T of a pendulum (the time it takes a pendulum to complete one swing) is given in seconds by the formula $T = 0.32\sqrt{\ell}$, where ℓ is the length of the pendulum in inches. Use lengths of 2, 4, 6, 8, and 10 inches.

First find the points for the given x-values.

Length (inches)	Period (seconds)
2	0.45
4	0.64
6	0.78
8	0.91
10	1.01

Plot the points and draw a smooth curve through them.

Find the average increase in period per inch increase in the pendulum length for the first interval and the last interval.

First interval:

$$\text{rate of change} = \frac{0.64 - 0.45}{4 - 2}$$

$$= 0.095$$

Last Interval:

$$\text{rate of change} = \frac{1.01 - 0.91}{10 - 8}$$

$$= 0.05$$

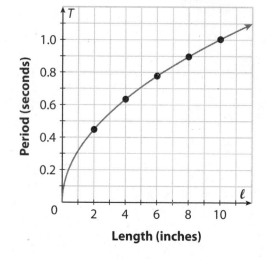

The average rate of change is less for the last interval. The average rate of change represents the increase in pendulum period with each additional inch of length. As the length of the pendulum increases, the increase in period time per inch of length becomes less.

Ⓑ A car with good tires is on a dry road. The speed, in miles per hour, from which the car can stop in a given distance d, in feet, is given by $s(d) = \sqrt{96d}$. Use distances of 20, 40, 60, 80, and 100 feet. •

First, find the points for the given x-values.

Distance	20	40	60	80	100
Speed					

Plot the points and draw a smooth curve through them.

First interval:

rate of change $= \dfrac{\boxed{} - \boxed{}}{40 - 20}$

$= \boxed{}$

Last Interval:

rate of change $= \dfrac{\boxed{} - \boxed{}}{100 - 80}$

$= \boxed{}$

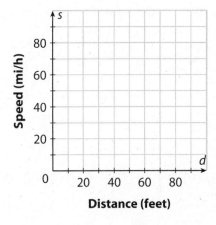

The average rate of change is _____ for the last interval. The average rate of change represents the increase in _____ with each additional _____. As the available stopping distance increases, the additional increase in speed per foot of stopping distance _____.

Your Turn

Use a calculator to evaluate the model at the indicated points, and connect the points with a curve to complete the graph of the model. Calculate the average rates of change over the first and last intervals and explain what the rate of change represents.

8. The speed in miles per hour of a tsunami can be modeled by the function $s(d) = 3.86\sqrt{d}$, where d is the average depth in feet of the water over which the tsunami travels. Graph this function from depths of 1000 feet to 5000 feet and compare the change in speed with depth from the shallowest interval to the deepest. Use depths of 1000, 2000, 3000, 4000, and 5000 feet for the x-values.

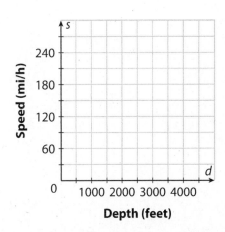

9. What is the difference between the parameters inside the radical (b and h) and the parameters outside the radical (a and k)?

_____

_____

_____

10. Which transformations change the square root function's end behavior?

_____

_____

11. Which transformations change the square root function's initial point location?

_____

_____

12. Which transformations change the square root function's domain?

_____

_____

13. Which transformations change the square root function's range?

_____

_____

14. **Essential Question Check-In** Describe in your own words the steps you would take to graph a function of the form $g(x) = a\sqrt{x - h} + k$ or $g(x) = \sqrt{\frac{1}{b}(x - h)} + k$ if you were given the values of h and k and using either a or b.

_____

_____

_____

_____

_____

1. Graph the functions $f(x) = \sqrt{x}$ and $g(x) = -\sqrt{x}$ on the same grid. Describe the domain, range and end behavior of each function. How are the functions related?

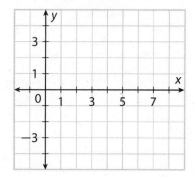

Describe the transformations of $g(x)$ from the parent function $f(x) = \sqrt{x}$.

2. $g(x) = \sqrt{\dfrac{1}{2}x} + 1$

3. $g(x) = -5\sqrt{x+1} - 3$

4. $g(x) = \dfrac{1}{4}\sqrt{x-5} - 2$

5. $g(x) = \sqrt{-7(x-7)}$

Describe the domain and range of each function using set notation.

6. $g(x) = \sqrt{\dfrac{1}{3}(x-1)}$

7. $g(x) = 3\sqrt{x+4} + 3$

8. $g(x) = \sqrt{-5(x+1)} + 2$

9. $g(x) = -7\sqrt{x-3} - 5$

Plot the transformed function $g(x)$ on the grid with the parent function, $f(x) = \sqrt{x}$.
Describe the domain and range of each function using set notation.

10. $g(x) = -\sqrt{x} + 3$

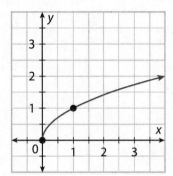

11. $g(x) = \sqrt{\frac{1}{3}(x + 4)} - 1$

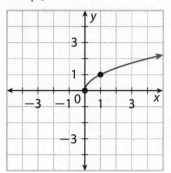

12. $g(x) = \sqrt{-\frac{2}{3}\left(x - \frac{1}{2}\right)} - 2$

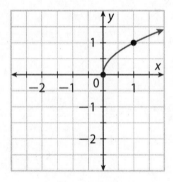

13. $g(x) = 4\sqrt{x + 3} - 4$

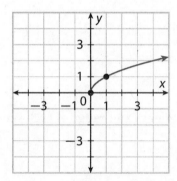

Write the function that matches the graph using the indicated transformation format.

14. $g(x) = \sqrt{\frac{1}{b}(x-h)} + k$

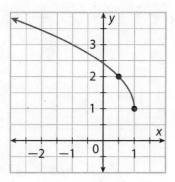

15. $g(x) = \sqrt{\frac{1}{b}(x-h)} + k$

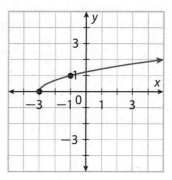

16. $g(x) = a\sqrt{x-h} + k$

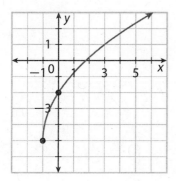

17. $g(x) = a\sqrt{x-h} + k$

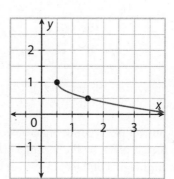

Use a calculator to evaluate the model at the indicated points, and connect the points with a curve to complete the graph of the model. Calculate the average rates of change over the first and last intervals and explain what the rate of change represents.

18. A farmer is trying to determine how much fencing to buy to make a square holding pen with a 6-foot gap for a gate. The length of fencing, f, in feet, required as a function of area, A, in square feet, is given by $f(A) = 4\sqrt{A} - 6$. Evaluate the function from 20 ft^2 to 100 ft^2 by calculating points every 20 ft^2.

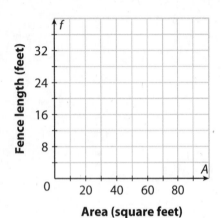

19. The speed, s, in feet per second, of an object dropped from a height, h, in feet, is given by the formula $s(h) = \sqrt{64h}$. Evaluate the function for heights of 0 feet to 25 feet by calculating points every 5 feet.

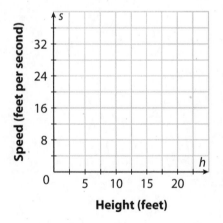

20. Water is draining from a tank at an average speed, s, in feet per second, characterized by the function $s(d) = 8\sqrt{d-2}$, where d is the depth of the water in the tank in feet. Evaluate the function for depths of 2, 3, 4, and 5 feet.

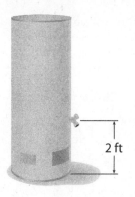

2 ft

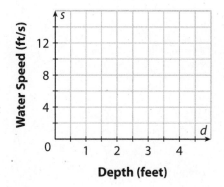

21. A research team studies the effects from an oil spill to develop new methods in oil clean-up. In the spill they are studying, the damaged oil tanker spilled oil into the ocean, forming a roughly circular spill pattern. The spill expanded out from the tanker, increasing the area at a rate of 100 square meters per hour. The radius of the circle is given by the function $r = \sqrt{\frac{100}{\pi}t}$, where t is the time (in hours) after the spill begins. Evaluate the function at hours 0, 1, 2, 3, and 4.

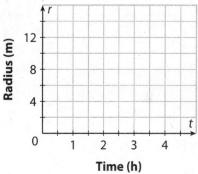

22. Give all of the transformations of the parent function $f(x) = \sqrt{x}$ that result in the function $g(x) = \sqrt{-2(x-3)} + 2$.

A. Horizontal stretch   **E.** Vertical stretch

B. Horizontal compression   **F.** Vertical compression

C. Horizontal reflection   **G.** Vertical reflection

D. Horizontal translation   **H.** Vertical translation

H.O.T. Focus on Higher Order Thinking

23. Draw Conclusions Describe the transformations to $f(x) = \sqrt{x}$ that result in the function $g(x) = \sqrt{-8x + 16} + 3$.

24. Analyze Relationships Show how a horizontally stretched square root function can sometimes be replaced by a vertical compression by equating the two forms of the transformed square root function.

$$g(x) = a\sqrt{x} = \sqrt{\frac{1}{b}x}$$

What must you assume about a and b for this replacement to result in the same function?

25. Multi-Step On a clear day, the view across the ocean is limited by the curvature of Earth. Objects appear to disappear below the horizon as they get farther from an observer. For an observer at height h above the water looking at an object with a height of H (both in feet), the approximate distance (d) in miles at which the object drops below the horizon is given by $d(h) = 1.21\sqrt{h + H}$.

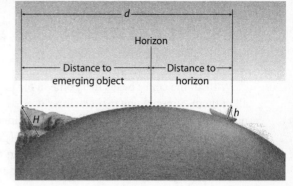

a. What is the effect of the object height, H, on the graph of $d(h)$?

b. What is the domain of the function $d(h)$? Explain your answer.

c. Plot two functions of distance required to see an object over the horizon versus observer height: one for seeing a 2-foot-tall buoy and one for seeing a 20-foot-tall sailboat. Calculate points every 10 feet from 0 to 40 feet.

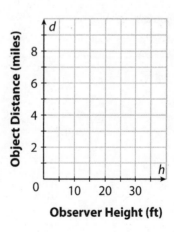

d. Where is the greatest increase in viewing distance with observer height?

Lesson Performance Task

With all the coffee beans that come in for processing, a coffee manufacturer cannot sample all of them. Suppose one manufacturer uses the function $s(x) = \sqrt{x} + 1$ to determine how many samples that it must take from x containers in order to obtain a good representative sampling of beans. How does this function relate to the function $f(x) = \sqrt{x}$? Graph both functions. How many samples should be taken from a shipment of 45 containers of beans? Explain why this can only be a whole number answer.

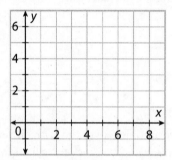

10.3 Graphing Cube Root Functions

Resource Locker

Essential Question: How can you use transformations of the parent cube root function to graph functions of the form $f(x) = a\sqrt[3]{(x-h)} + k$ or $g(x) = \sqrt[3]{\frac{1}{b}(x-h)} + k$?

⊕ Explore   Graphing and Analyzing the Parent Cube Root Function

The cube root parent function is $f(x) = \sqrt[3]{x}$. To graph $f(x)$, choose values of x and find corresponding values of y. Choose both negative and positive values of x.

Graph the function $f(x) = \sqrt[3]{x}$. Identify the domain and range of the function.

Ⓐ Make the table of values.

x	y	x, y
−8		
−1		
0		
1		
8		

Ⓑ Use the table to graph the function.

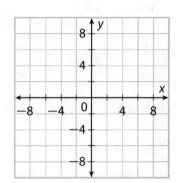

Ⓒ Identify the domain and range of the function.

The domain is the _____.

The range is _____.

Ⓓ Does the graph of $f(x) = \sqrt[3]{x}$ have any symmetry?

The graph has _____.

Reflect

1. Can the radicand in a cube root function be negative?

_____

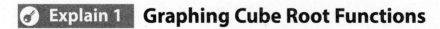

Explain 1 **Graphing Cube Root Functions**

Transformations of the Cube Root Parent Function $f(x) = \sqrt[3]{x}$		
Transformation	**$f(x)$ Notation**	**Examples**
Vertical translation	$f(x) + k$	$y = \sqrt[3]{x} + 3$ 3 units up $y = \sqrt[3]{x} - 4$ 4 units down
Horizontal translation	$f(x - h)$	$y = \sqrt[3]{x - 2}$ 2 units right $y = \sqrt[3]{x + 1}$ 1 units left
Vertical stretch/compression	$af(x)$	$y = 6\sqrt[3]{x}$ vertical stretch by a factor of 6 $y = \frac{1}{2}\sqrt[3]{x}$ vertical compression by a factor of $\frac{1}{2}$
Horizontal stretch/ compression	$f\left(\frac{1}{b}x\right)$	$y = \sqrt[3]{\frac{1}{5}x}$ horizontal stretch by a factor of 5 $y = \sqrt[3]{3x}$ horizontal compression by a factor of $\frac{1}{3}$
Reflection	$-f(x)$ $f(-x)$	$y = -\sqrt[3]{x}$ across x-axis $y = \sqrt[3]{-x}$ across y-axis

For the function $f(x) = a\sqrt[3]{x - h} + k$, (h, k) is the graph's point of symmetry. Use the values of a, h, and k to draw each graph. Note that the point $(1, 1)$ on the graph of the parent function becomes the point $(1 + h, a + k)$ on the graph of the given function.

For the function $f(x) = \sqrt[3]{\frac{1}{b}(x - h)} + k$, (h, k) remains the graph's point of symmetry. Note that the point $(1, 1)$ on the graph of the parent function becomes the point $(b + h, 1 + k)$ on the graph of the given function.

Example 1 **Graph the cube root functions.**

(A) Graph $g(x) = 2\sqrt[3]{x - 3} + 5$.

The transformations of the graph of $f(x) = \sqrt[3]{x}$ that produce the graph of $g(x)$ are:

- a vertical stretch by a factor of 2

- a translation of 3 units to the right and 5 units up

Choose points on $f(x) = \sqrt[3]{x}$ and find the transformed corresponding points on $g(x) = 2\sqrt[3]{x - 3} + 5$.

Graph $g(x) = 2\sqrt[3]{x - 3} + 5$ using the transformed points.

(See the table and graph on the next page.)

$f(x) = \sqrt[3]{x}$	$g(x) = 2\sqrt[3]{x-3}+5$
$(-8, -2)$	$(-5, 1)$
$(-1, -1)$	$(2, 3)$
$(0, 0)$	$(3, 5)$
$(1, 1)$	$(4, 7)$
$(8, 2)$	$(11, 9)$

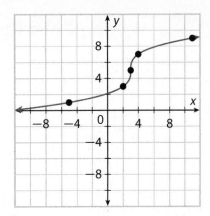

B Graph $g(x) = \sqrt[3]{\frac{1}{2}(x-10)} + 4$.

The transformations of the graph of $f(x) = \sqrt[3]{x}$ that produce the graph of $g(x)$ are:

- a horizontal stretch by a factor of 2
- a translation of 10 units to the right and 4 units up

Choose points on $f(x) = \sqrt[3]{x}$ and find the transformed corresponding points on $g(x) = \sqrt[3]{\frac{1}{2}(x-10)} + 4$.

Graph $g(x) = \sqrt[3]{\frac{1}{2}(x-10)} + 4$ using the transformed points.

$f(x) = \sqrt[3]{x}$	$g(x) = \sqrt[3]{\frac{1}{2}(x-10)}+4$
$(-8, -2)$	
$(-1, -1)$	
$(0, 0)$	
$(1, 1)$	
$(8, 2)$	

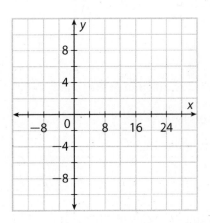

Your Turn

Graph the cube root function.

2. Graph $g(x) = \sqrt[3]{x-3} + 6$.

$f(x) = \sqrt[3]{x}$	$g(x) = \sqrt[3]{x-3}+6$
$(-8, -2)$	
$(-1, -1)$	
$(0, 0)$	
$(1, 1)$	
$(8, 2)$	

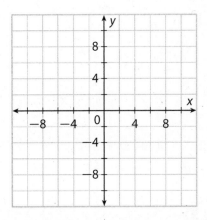

Explain 2 **Writing Cube Root Functions**

Given the graph of the transformed function $g(x) = a\sqrt[3]{\frac{1}{b}(x-h)} + k$, you can determine the values of the parameters by using the reference points $(-1, 1)$, $(0, 0)$, and $(1, 1)$ that you used to graph $g(x)$ in the previous example.

Example 2 For the given graphs, write a cube root function.

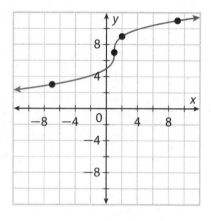

(A) Write the function in the form $g(x) = a\sqrt[3]{x-h} + k$.

Identify the values of a, h, and k.

Identify the values of h and k from the point of symmetry.

$(h, k) = (1, 7)$, so $h = 1$ and $k = 7$.

Identify the value of a from either of the other two reference points $(-1, 1)$ or $(1, 1)$.

The reference point $(1, 1)$ has general coordinates $(h + 1, a + k)$. Substituting 1 for h and 7 for k and setting the general coordinates equal to the actual coordinates gives this result:

$(h + 1, a + k) = (2, a + 7) = (2, 9)$, so $a = 2$.

$a = 2$ $h = 1$ $k = 7$

The function is $g(x) = 2\sqrt[3]{x-1} + 7$.

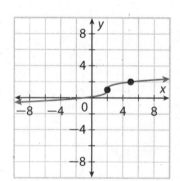

(B) Write the function in the form $g(x) = \sqrt[3]{\frac{1}{b}(x-h)} + k$.

Identify the values of b, h, and k.

Identify the values of h and k from the point of symmetry.

$(h, k) = \left(2, \boxed{}\right)$ so $h = 2$ and $k = \boxed{}$.

Identify the value of b from either of the other two reference points.

The rightmost reference point has general coordinates $(b + h, 1 + k)$. Substituting 2 for h and _____ for k and setting the general coordinates equal to the actual coordinates gives this result:

$\left(b + h, 1 + \boxed{}\right) = \left(b + 2, \boxed{}\right) = (5, 2)$, so $b = \boxed{}$.

$b = \boxed{}$ $h = \boxed{}$ $k = \boxed{}$

The function is $g(x) = $ _____ .

For the given graphs, write a cube root function.

3. Write the function in the form $g(x) = a\sqrt[3]{x-h} + k$.

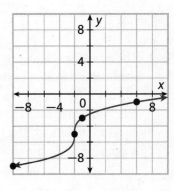

4. Write the function in the form $g(x) = \sqrt[3]{\frac{1}{b}(x-h)} + k$.

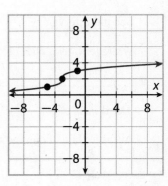

You can use cube root functions to model real-world situations.

Example 3

(A) The shoulder height h (in centimeters) of a particular elephant is modeled by the function $h(t) = 62.1\sqrt[3]{t} + 76$, where t is the age (in years) of the elephant. Graph the function and examine its average rate of change over the equal t-intervals $(0, 20)$, $(20, 40)$, and $(40, 60)$. What is happening to the average rate of change as the t-values of the intervals increase? Use the graph to find the height when $t = 35$.

Graph $h(t) = 62.1\sqrt[3]{t} + 76$.

The graph is the graph of $f(x) = \sqrt[3]{x}$ translated up 76 and stretched vertically by a factor of 62.1. Graph the transformed points $(0, 76)$, $(8, 200.2)$, $(27, 262.3)$, and $(64, 324.4)$. Connect the points with a smooth curve.

First interval:

$$\text{Average Rate of change} \approx \frac{244.6 - 76}{20 - 0}$$

$$= 8.43$$

Second interval:

$$\text{Average Rate of change} \approx \frac{288.4 - 244.6}{40 - 20}$$

$$= 2.19$$

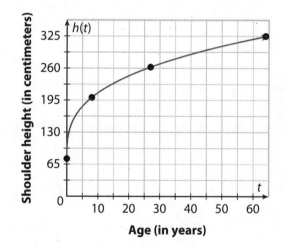

Third interval:

$$\text{Average Rate of change} \approx \frac{319.1 - 288.4}{60 - 40}$$

$$= 1.54$$

The average rate of change is becoming less.

Drawing a vertical line up from 35 gives a value of about 280 cm.

(B) The velocity of a 1400-kilogram car at the end of a 400-meter run is modeled by the function $v = 15.2\sqrt[3]{p}$, where v is the velocity in kilometers per hour and p is the power of its engine in horsepower. Graph the function and examine its average rate of change over the equal p-intervals $(0, 60)$, $(60, 120)$, and $(120, 180)$. What is happening to the average rate of change as the p-values of the intervals increase? Use the function to find the velocity when p is 100 horsepower.

Graph $v = 15.2\sqrt[3]{p}$.

The graph is the graph of $f(x) = \sqrt[3]{x}$ stretched _____ by a factor of 15.2. Graph the transformed points $(0, 0)$, $(8, \underline{\quad})$, $(27, \underline{\quad})$, $(64, \underline{\quad})$, $(125, \underline{\quad})$, and $(216, \underline{\quad})$.

Connect the points with a smooth curve.

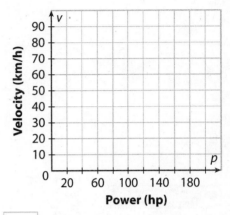

The average rate of change over the interval $(0, 60)$ is

$$\frac{\boxed{} - \boxed{}}{60 - 0}$$ which is about _____.

The average rate of change over the interval $(60, 120)$ is $\dfrac{\boxed{} - \boxed{}}{120 - 60}$ which is about _____.

The average rate of change over the interval $(120, 180)$ is $\dfrac{\boxed{} - \boxed{}}{180 - 120}$ which is about _____.

The average rate of change is becoming _____.

Substitute $p = 100$ in the function.

$v = 15.2\sqrt[3]{p}$

$v = 15.2\sqrt[3]{\boxed{}}$

$v \approx 15.2\left(\boxed{}\right)$

$v \approx \boxed{}$

The velocity is about _____ km/h.

5. The fetch is the length of water over which the wind is blowing in a certain direction. The function $s(f) = 7.1\sqrt[3]{f}$, relates the speed of the wind s in kilometers per hour to the fetch f in kilometers. Graph the function and examine its average rate of change over the intervals $(20, 80)$, $(80, 140)$, and $(140, 200)$. What is happening to the average rate of change as the f-values of the intervals increase? Use the function to find the speed of the wind when $f = 64$.

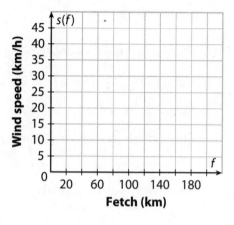

Elaborate

6. **Discussion** Why is the domain of $f(x) = \sqrt[3]{x}$ all real numbers?

_____

_____

_____

7. Identify which transformations (stretches or compressions, reflections, and translations) of $f(x) = \sqrt[3]{x}$ change the following attributes of the function.

a. Location of the point of symmetry

b. Symmetry about a point

_____

_____

_____

8. **Essential Question Check-In** How do parameters a, b, h, and k effect the graphs of $f(x) = a\sqrt[3]{(x-h)} + k$ and $g(x) = \sqrt[3]{\frac{1}{b}(x-h)} + k$?

_____

_____

_____

_____

_____

_____

_____

_____

1. Graph the function $g(x) = \sqrt[3]{x} + 3$. Identify the domain and range of the function.

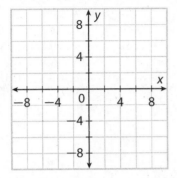

2. Graph the function $g(x) = \sqrt[3]{x} - 5$. Identify the domain and range of the function.

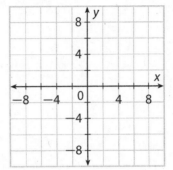

Describe how the graph of the function compares to the graph of $f(x) = \sqrt[3]{x}$.

3. $g(x) = \sqrt[3]{x} + 6$

4. $g(x) = \sqrt[3]{x} - 5$

5. $g(x) = \frac{1}{3}\sqrt[3]{-x}$

6. $g(x) = \sqrt[3]{5x}$

7. $g(x) = -2\sqrt[3]{x} + 3$

8. $g(x) = \sqrt[3]{x + 4} - 3$

Graph the cube root functions.

9. $g(x) = 3\sqrt[3]{x} + 4$

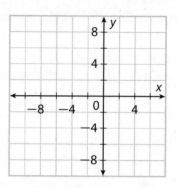

10. $g(x) = 2\sqrt[3]{x} + 3$

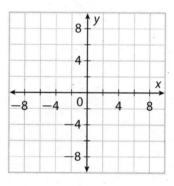

11. $g(x) = \sqrt[3]{x - 3} + 2$

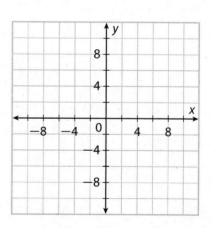

For the given graphs, write a cube root function.

12. Write the function in the form $g(x) = a\sqrt[3]{x - h} + k$.

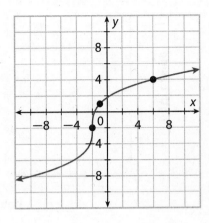

13. Write the function in the form $g(x) = a\sqrt[3]{x - h} + k$.

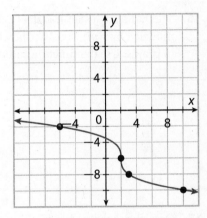

14. Write the function in the form $g(x) = \sqrt[3]{\dfrac{1}{b}(x - h)} + k$.

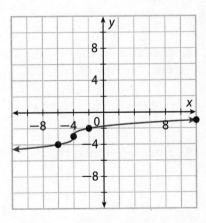

15. The length of the side of a cube is modeled by $s = \sqrt[3]{V}$. Graph the function. Use the graph to find s when $V = 48$.

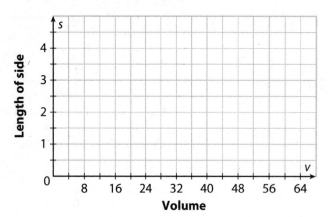

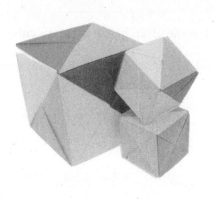

16. The radius of a stainless steel ball, in centimeters, can be modeled by $r(m) = 0.31\sqrt[3]{m}$, where m is the mass of the ball in grams. Use the function to find r when $m = 125$.

17. Describe the steps for graphing $g(x) = \sqrt[3]{x + 8} - 11$.

18. **Modeling** Write a situation that can be modeled by a cube root function. Give the function.

19. Find the y-intercept for the function $y = a\sqrt[3]{x - h} + k$.

20. Find the x-intercept for the function $y = a\sqrt[3]{x - h} + k$.

21. Describe the translation(s) used to get $g(x) = \sqrt[3]{x - 9} + 12$ from $f(x) = \sqrt[3]{x}$. Select all that apply.

    A. translated 9 units right   **E.** translated 12 units right

    B. translated 9 units left   **F.** translated 12 units left

    C. translated 9 units up   **G.** translated 12 units up

    D. translated 9 units down   **H.** translated 12 units down

H.O.T. Focus on Higher Order Thinking

22. Explain the Error Tim says that to graph $g(x) = \sqrt[3]{x - 6} + 3$, you need to translate the graph of $f(x) = \sqrt[3]{x}$ 6 units to the left and then 3 units up. What mistake did he make?

23. Communicate Mathematical Ideas Why does the square root function have a restricted domain but the cube root function does not?

24. Justify Reasoning Does a horizontal translation and a vertical translation of the function $f(x) = \sqrt[3]{x}$ affect the function's domain or range? Explain.

Lesson Performance Task

The side length of a 243-gram copper cube is 3 centimeters. Use this information to write a model for the radius of a copper sphere as a function of its mass. Then, find the radius of a copper sphere with a mass of 50 grams. How would changing the material affect the function?

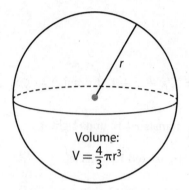

Volume:
$$V = \frac{4}{3}\pi r^3$$

Radical Functions

Essential Question: How can you use radical functions to solve real-world problems?

KEY EXAMPLE   *(Lesson 10.1)*

Find the inverse function $f^{-1}(x)$ for $f(x) = 2x^3 + 10$.

Replace $f(x)$ with y. $y = 2x^3 + 10$

Solve for x^3. $\frac{y - 10}{2} = x^3$

Take the cube root. $\sqrt[3]{\frac{y - 10}{2}} = x$

Switch x and y. $y = \sqrt[3]{\frac{x - 10}{2}}$

Replace y with $f^{-1}(x)$. $f^{-1}(x) = \sqrt[3]{\frac{x - 10}{2}}$

KEY EXAMPLE   *(Lesson 10.2)*

Graph $y = -\sqrt{x - 3} + 2$. Describe the domain and range.

Sketch the graph of $y = -\sqrt{x}$.

It begins at the origin and passes through $(1, -1)$.

For $y = -\sqrt{x - 3} + 2$, $h = 3$ and $k = 2$.
Shift the graph of $y = -\sqrt{x}$ right 3 units and up
2 units. The graph begins at $(3, 2)$ and passes
through $(4, 1)$.

Domain: $\{x \mid x \geq 3\}$ Range: $\{y \mid y \leq 2\}$

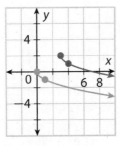

KEY EXAMPLE   *(Lesson 10.3)*

Graph $y = \sqrt[3]{x + 2} - 4$.

Sketch the graph of $y = \sqrt[3]{x}$.

It passes through $(-1, -1)$, $(0, 0)$, and $(1, 1)$.

For $y = \sqrt[3]{x + 2} - 4$, $h = -2$ and $k = -4$.
Shift the graph of $y = \sqrt[3]{x}$ left 2 units and down
4 units. The graph passes through $(-3, -5)$,
$(-2, -4)$, and $(-1, -3)$.

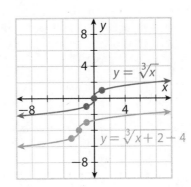

EXERCISES

Find the inverse of each function. Restrict the domain where necessary. *(Lesson 10.1)*

1. $f(x) = 16x^2$

2. $f(x) = x^3 - 20$

Identify the transformations of the graph $f(x) = \sqrt{x}$ that produce the graph of the function. *(Lesson 10.2)*

3. $g(x) = -\sqrt{4x}$

4. $h(x) = \dfrac{1}{2}\sqrt{x} + 1$

Identify the transformations of the graph $f(x) = \sqrt[3]{x}$ that produce the graph of the function. *(Lesson 10.3)*

5. $g(x) = 4\sqrt[3]{x}$

6. $h(x) = \sqrt[3]{x - 5} + 3$

MODULE PERFORMANCE TASK

We Have Liftoff!

A rocket scientist is designing a rocket to visit the planets in the solar system. The velocity that is needed to escape a planet's gravitational pull is called the escape velocity. The escape velocity depends on the planet's radius and its mass, according to the equation $V_{escape} = \sqrt{2gR}$, where R is the radius and g is the gravitational constant for the particular planet. The rocket's maximum velocity is exactly double Earth's escape velocity. For which planets will the rocket have enough velocity to escape the planet's gravity?

Planet	Radius (m)	Mass (kg)	g $\left(\text{m/s}^2\right)$
Mercury	2.43×10^6	3.20×10^{23}	3.61
Venus	6.07×10^6	4.88×10^{24}	8.83
Mars	3.38×10^6	6.42×10^{23}	3.75
Jupiter	6.98×10^7	1.90×10^{27}	26.0
Saturn	5.82×10^7	5.68×10^{26}	11.2
Uranus	2.35×10^7	8.68×10^{25}	10.5
Neptune	2.27×10^7	1.03×10^{26}	13.3

Begin by listing in the space below any additional information you will need to solve the problem. Then use your own paper to complete the task. Be sure to write down all your data and assumptions. Then use graphs, numbers, words, or algebra to explain how you reached your conclusions.

(Ready) to Go On?

10.1–10.3 Radical Functions

- Online Homework
- Hints and Help
- Extra Practice

Find the inverse of each function. State any restrictions on the domain.
(Lesson 10.1)

1. $f(x) = x^2 + 9$

2. $f(x) = -7x^3$

3. $f(x) = -2x^3 + 1$

4. $f(x) = 5x^2 + 3$

Identify the transformations of the graph $f(x) = \sqrt{x}$ or $h(x) = \sqrt[3]{x}$ that produce the graph of the function. *(Lessons 10.2, 10.3)*

5. $g(x) = \frac{1}{3}\sqrt{x-5} - 4$

6. $g(x) = \sqrt[3]{4x} + 3$

7. $g(x) = \sqrt{x-4} - 1$

8. $g(x) = \sqrt[3]{7x + 10}$

ESSENTIAL QUESTION

9. How do you use a parent square root or cube root function to graph a transformation of the function? *(Lessons 10.2, 10.3)*

Assessment Readiness

1. Look at each equation. Is it the inverse of $f(x) = x^3 - 16$? Select Yes or No for A–C.

   A. $f^{-1}(x) = \sqrt[3]{x - 16}$ ◯ Yes   ◯ No

   B. $f^{-1}(x) = \sqrt[3]{x + 16}$ ◯ Yes   ◯ No

   C. $f^{-1}(x) = \sqrt[3]{x} + 16$ ◯ Yes   ◯ No

2. Consider the graphed function. Choose True or False for each statement.

   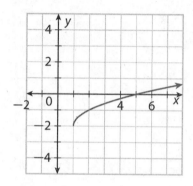

   A. The equation for the function is   ◯ Yes   ◯ No
   $y = \sqrt{x - 1} - 2$.

   B. The function has exactly one y-intercept.   ◯ Yes   ◯ No

   C. The range of the function is $y \leq -2$.   ◯ Yes   ◯ No

3. A plane's average speed when flying from one city to another is 550 mi/h and is 430 mi/h on the return flight. To the nearest mile per hour, what is the plane's average speed for the entire trip? Explain your answer.

4. The kinetic energy E (in joules) of a 1250-kilogram compact car is given by the equation $E = 625s^2$, where s is the speed of the car (in meters per second). Write an inverse model that gives the speed of the car as a function of its kinetic energy. If the kinetic energy doubles, will the speed double? Explain why or why not.

Radical Expressions and Equations

Essential Question: How can you use radical expressions and equations to solve real-world problems?

REAL WORLD VIDEO
A field biologist studying howler monkeys can use radical functions to calculate sound intensity, which decreases faster than linearly with distance.

MODULE PERFORMANCE TASK PREVIEW
Don't Disturb the Neighbors!

The loudness of a sound is subjective and depends on the listener's sensitivity to the frequencies of the sound waves. An objective measure, sound intensity, can be used to measure sounds. Sound intensity decreases the farther you get from the source of a sound. How far away do your neighbors have to be so that a loud band does not bother them? Let's find out!

Bowler/Photo Researchers/Getty Images

Are (YOU) Ready?

Complete these exercises to review skills you will need for this module.

Exponents

- Online Homework
- Hints and Help
- Extra Practice

Example 1 Simplify $\left(x^3\right)^2 + x \cdot x^3 + 3x^4$.

$$\left(x^3\right)^2 + x \cdot x^3 + 3x^4 = \left(x^3\right)\left(x^3\right) + x \cdot x^3 + 3x^4 \qquad \text{Start with the raised power.}$$

$$= x^{3+3} + x^{1+3} + 3x^4 \qquad \text{Add exponents.}$$

$$= x^6 + x^4 + 3x^4 \qquad \text{Simplify.}$$

$$= x^6 + 4x^4 \qquad \text{Add like terms.}$$

Simplify each expression.

1. $\left(-x^5\right)^2$

2. $\left(3x^2\right)^3 - x^4 \cdot x^2$

3. $3x\left(2x\right)^2$

Inverse Linear Functions

Example 2 Write the inverse function of $y = 10x - 4$.

$$y + 4 = 10x \qquad \text{Isolate the } x\text{-term.}$$

$$\frac{y + 4}{10} = \frac{10x}{10} \qquad \text{Divide.}$$

The inverse function of $y = 10x - 4$ is $y = \dfrac{x + 4}{10}$.

Write the inverse function.

4. $y = 3x + 1$

5. $y = 2(x - 9)$

6. $y = \frac{1}{4}(3x + 4)$

Rational and Radical Exponents

Example 3 Write $\sqrt[9]{a^3}$ using a rational exponent.
$$\sqrt[9]{a^3} = a^{\frac{3}{9}} = a^{\frac{1}{3}}$$

Write each radical expression using a rational exponent.

7. $\sqrt[2]{x^5}$

8. $\sqrt[4]{a^2b}$

9. $\sqrt[4]{p^8q^2}$

11.1 Radical Expressions and Rational Exponents

Essential Question: How are rational exponents related to radicals and roots?

Resource
Locker

 Explore **Defining Rational Exponents in Terms of Roots**

Remember that a number a is an nth root of a number b if $a^n = b$. As you know, a square root is indicated by $\sqrt{}$ and a cube root by $\sqrt[3]{}$. In general, the nth root of a real number a is indicated by $\sqrt[n]{a}$, where n is the **index** of the radical and a is the radicand. (Note that when a number has more than one real root, the radical sign indicates only the principal, or positive, root.)

A *rational exponent* is an exponent that can be expressed as $\frac{m}{n}$, where m is an integer and n is a natural number. You can use the definition of a root and properties of equality and exponents to explore how to express roots using rational exponents.

(A) How can you express a square root using an exponent? That is, if $\sqrt{a} = a^m$, what is m?

Given	$\sqrt{a} = a^m$
Square both sides.	$\left(\sqrt{a}\right)^2 = \left(a^m\right)^2$
Definition of square root	$\boxed{} = \left(a^m\right)^2$
Power of a power property	$a = a^{\boxed{}}$
Definition of first power	$a^{\boxed{}} = a^{2m}$
The bases are the same, so equate exponents.	$\boxed{} = \boxed{}$
Solve.	$m = \boxed{}$
So,	$\sqrt{a} = a^{\boxed{}}$.

(B) How can you express a cube root using an exponent? That is, if $\sqrt[3]{a} = a^m$, what is m?

Given	$\sqrt[3]{a} = a^m$
Cube both sides.	$\left(\sqrt{a}\right)^3 = \left(a^m\right)^3$
Definition of cube root	$\boxed{} = \boxed{}$
Power of a power property	$\boxed{} = \boxed{}$

Definition of first power

$\boxed{} = \boxed{}$

The bases are the same,
so equate exponents.

$\boxed{} = \boxed{}$

Solve.

$m = \boxed{}$

So,

$\sqrt[3]{a} = a^{\boxed{}}$.

1. **Discussion** Examine the reasoning in Steps A and B. Can you apply the same reasoning for any nth root, $\sqrt[n]{a}$, where n is a natural number? Explain. What can you conclude?

2. For a positive number a, under what condition on n will there be only one real nth root? two real nth roots? Explain.

3. For a negative number a, under what condition on n will there be no real nth roots? one real nth root? Explain.

Explain 1 Translating Between Radical Expressions and Rational Exponents

In the Explore, you found that a rational exponent $\frac{m}{n}$ with $m = 1$ represents an nth root, or that $a^{\frac{1}{n}} = \sqrt[n]{a}$ for positive values of a. This is also true for negative values of a when the index is odd. When $m \neq 1$, you can think of the numerator m as the power and the denominator n as the root. The following ways of expressing the exponent $\frac{m}{n}$ are equivalent.

Rational Exponents

For any natural number n, integer m, and real number a when the nth root of a is real:

Words	Numbers	Algebra
The exponent $\frac{m}{n}$ indicates the mth power of the nth root of a quantity.	$27^{\frac{2}{3}} = \left(\sqrt[3]{27}\right)^2 = 3^2 = 9$	$a^{\frac{m}{n}} = \left(\sqrt[n]{a}\right)^m$
The exponent $\frac{m}{n}$ indicates the nth root of the mth power of a quantity.	$4^{\frac{3}{2}} = \sqrt{4^3} = \sqrt{64} = 8$	$a^{\frac{m}{n}} = \sqrt[n]{a^m}$

Notice that you can evaluate each example in the "Numbers" column using the equivalent definition.

$$27^{\frac{2}{3}} = \sqrt[3]{27^2} = \sqrt[3]{729} = 9 \qquad 4^{\frac{3}{2}} = \left(\sqrt{4}\right)^3 = 2^3 = 8$$

Example 1 Translate radical expressions into expressions with rational exponents, and vice versa. Simplify numerical expressions when possible. Assume all variables are positive.

Ⓐ a. $(-125)^{\frac{4}{3}}$ b. $x^{\frac{11}{8}}$ c. $\sqrt[5]{6^4}$ d. $\sqrt[4]{x^3}$

a. $(-125)^{\frac{4}{3}} = \left(\sqrt[3]{-125}\right)^4 = (-5)^4 = 625$

b. $x^{11/8} = \sqrt[8]{x^{11}}$ or $\left(\sqrt[8]{x}\right)^{11}$

c. $\sqrt[5]{6^4} = 6^{\frac{4}{5}}$

d. $\sqrt[4]{x^3} = x^{\frac{3}{4}}$

Ⓑ a. $\left(\frac{81}{16}\right)^{\frac{3}{4}}$ b. $(xy)^{\frac{5}{3}}$ c. $\sqrt[3]{11^6}$ d. $\sqrt[3]{\left(\frac{2x}{y}\right)^5}$

a. $\left(\frac{81}{16}\right)^{\frac{3}{4}} = \left(\sqrt[\Box]{\frac{81}{16}}\right)^{\Box} = \left(\Box\right)^3 = \Box$

b. $(xy)^{\frac{5}{3}} = \sqrt[\Box]{(xy)^{\Box}}$ or $\left(\sqrt[\Box]{xy}\right)^{\Box}$

c. $\sqrt[3]{11^6} = 11^{\Box} = 11^{\Box} = \Box$

d. $\sqrt[3]{\left(\frac{2x}{y}\right)^5} = \left(\frac{2x}{y}\right)^{\Box}$

4. How can you use a calculator to show that evaluating $0.001728^{\frac{4}{3}}$ as a power of a root and as a root of a power are equivalent methods?

_____

_____

_____

Your Turn

5. Translate radical expressions into expressions with rational exponents, and vice versa. Simplify numerical expressions when possible. Assume all variables are positive.

a. $\left(-\dfrac{32}{243}\right)^{\frac{2}{5}}$

b. $(3y)^{\frac{b}{c}}$

c. $\sqrt[3]{0.5^9}$

d. $\left(\sqrt[u]{st}\right)^{v}$

🔍 Explain 2 Modeling with Power Functions

The following functions all involve a given power of a variable.

$A = \pi r^2$ (area of a circle)

$V = \frac{4}{3}\pi r^3$ (volume of a sphere)

$T = 1.11 \cdot L^{\frac{1}{2}}$ (the time T in seconds for a pendulum of length L feet to complete one back-and-forth swing)

These are all examples of *power functions*. A power function has the form $y = ax^b$ where a is a real number and b is a rational number.

Example 2   **Solve each problem by modeling with power functions.**

(A) **Biology** The function $R = 73.3\sqrt[4]{M^3}$, known as Kleiber's law, relates the basal metabolic rate R in Calories per day burned and the body mass M of a mammal in kilograms. The table shows typical body masses for some members of the cat family.

Typical Body Mass	
Animal	**Mass (kg)**
House cat	4.5
Cheetah	55
Lion	170

a. Rewrite the formula with a rational exponent.

b. What is the value of R for a cheetah to the nearest 50 Calories?

c. From the table, the mass of the lion is about 38 times that of the house cat. Is the lion's metabolic rate more or less than 38 times the cat's rate? Explain.

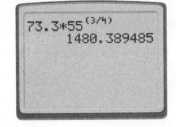

a. Because $\sqrt[n]{a^m} = a^{\frac{m}{n}}$, $\sqrt[4]{M^3} = M^{\frac{3}{4}}$, so the formula is $R = 73.3M^{\frac{3}{4}}$.

b. Substitute 55 for M in the formula and use a calculator.

The cheetah's metabolic rate is about 1500 Calories.

c. Less; find the ratio of R for the lion to R for the house cat.

$$\frac{73.3(170)^{\frac{3}{4}}}{73.3(4.5)^{\frac{3}{4}}} = \frac{170^{\frac{3}{4}}}{4.5^{\frac{3}{4}}} \approx \frac{47.1}{3.1} \approx 15$$

The metabolic rate for the lion is only about 15 times that of the house cat.

B The function $h(m) = 241m^{-\frac{1}{4}}$ models an animal's approximate resting heart rate h in beats per minute given its mass m in kilograms.

a. A common shrew has a mass of only about 0.01 kg. To the nearest 10, what is the model's estimate for this shrew's resting heart rate?

b. What is the model's estimate for the resting heart rate of an American elk with a mass of 300 kg?

c. Two animal species differ in mass by a multiple of 10. According to the model, about what percent of the smaller animal's resting heart rate would you expect the larger animal's resting heart rate to be?

a. Substitute _____ for m in the formula and use a calculator.

$$h(m) = 241\left(\boxed{}\right)^{-\frac{1}{4}} \approx \boxed{}$$

The model estimates the shrew's resting heart rate to be about _____ beats per minute.

b. Substitute _____ for m in the formula and use a calculator.

$$h(m) = 241\left(\boxed{}\right)^{-\frac{1}{4}} \approx \boxed{}$$

The model estimates the elk's resting heart rate to be about _____ beats per minute.

c. Find the ratio of $h(m)$ for the _____ animal to the _____ animal. Let 1 represent the mass of the smaller animal.

$$\frac{241 \cdot \boxed{}^{-\frac{1}{4}}}{241 \cdot 1^{-\frac{1}{4}}} = \boxed{}^{-\frac{1}{4}} = \frac{1}{10^{\boxed{}}} \approx \boxed{}$$

You would expect the larger animal's resting heart rate to be about _____ of the smaller animal's resting heart rate.

6. What is the difference between a power function and an exponential function?

_____

_____

7. In Part B, the exponent is negative. Are the results consistent with the meaning of a negative exponent that you learned for integers? Explain.

_____

_____

_____

Your Turn

8. Use Kleiber's law from Part A.

   a. Find the basal metabolic rate for a 170 kilogram lion to the nearest 50 Calories. Then find the formula's prediction for a 70 kilogram human.

   b. Use your metabolic rate result for the lion to find what the basal metabolic rate for a 70 kilogram human _would_ be _if_ metabolic rate and mass were directly proportional. Compare the result to the result from Part a.

Elaborate

9. Explain how can you use a radical to write and evaluate the power $4^{2.5}$.

_____

10. When $y = kx$ for some constant k, y varies directly as x. When $y = kx^2$, y varies directly as the square of x; and when $y = k\sqrt{x}$, y varies directly as the square root of x. How could you express the relationship $y = kx^{\frac{3}{5}}$ for a constant k?

_____

11. **Essential Question Check-In** Which of the following are true? Explain.

   • To evaluate an expression of the form $a^{\frac{m}{n}}$, first find the nth root of a. Then raise the result to the mth power.

   • To evaluate an expression of the form $a^{\frac{m}{n}}$, first find the mth power of a. Then find the nth root of the result.

_____

_____

Translate expressions with rational exponents into radical expressions. Simplify numerical expressions when possible. Assume all variables are positive.

1. $64^{\frac{5}{3}}$

2. $x^{\frac{p}{q}}$

3. $(-512)^{\frac{2}{3}}$

4. $3^{\frac{2}{7}}$

5. $-\left(\dfrac{729}{64}\right)^{\frac{5}{6}}$

6. $0.125^{\frac{4}{3}}$

7. $vw^{\frac{2}{3}}$

8. $(-32)^{0.6}$

Translate radical expressions into expressions with rational exponents. Simplify numerical expressions when possible. Assume all variables are positive.

9. $\sqrt[7]{y^5}$

10. $\sqrt[7]{(-6)^6}$

11. $\sqrt[3]{3^{15}}$

12. $\sqrt[4]{(\pi z)^3}$

13. $\sqrt[6]{(bcd)^4}$

14. $\sqrt{6^6}$

15. $\sqrt[5]{32^2}$

16. $\sqrt[3]{\left(\dfrac{4}{x}\right)^9}$

17. Music Frets are small metal bars positioned across the neck of a guitar so that the guitar can produce the notes of a specific scale. To find the distance a fret should be placed from the bridge, multiply the length of the string by $2^{-\frac{n}{12}}$, where n is the number of notes higher than the string's root note. Where should a fret be placed to produce a F note on a B string (6 notes higher) given that the length of the string is 64 cm?

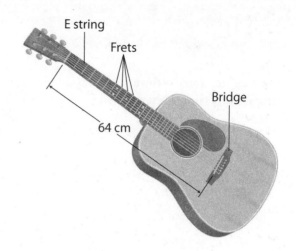

E string

Frets

Bridge

64 cm

18. Meteorology The function $W = 35.74 + 0.6215T - 35.75V^{\frac{4}{25}} + 0.4275TV^{\frac{4}{25}}$ relates the windchill temperature W to the air temperature T in degrees Fahrenheit and the wind speed V in miles per hour. Use a calculator to find the wind chill temperature to the nearest degree when the air temperature is 28 °F and the wind speed is 35 miles per hour.

19. Astronomy New stars can form inside a cloud of interstellar gas when a cloud fragment, or *clump*, has a mass M greater than the *Jean's mass* M_J. The Jean's mass is $M_J = 100n^{-\frac{1}{2}}(T + 273)^{\frac{3}{2}}$ where n is the number of gas molecules per cubic centimeter and T is the gas temperature in degrees Celsius. A gas clump has $M = 137$, $n = 1000$, and $T = -263$. Will the clump form a star? Justify your answer.

20. Urban geography The total wages W in a metropolitan area compared to its total population p can be approximated by a power function of the form $W = a \cdot p^{\frac{9}{8}}$ where a is a constant. About how many times as great does the model predict the total earnings for a metropolitan area with 3,000,000 people will be as compared to a metropolitan area with a population of 750,000?

21. Which statement is true?

A. In the expression $8x^{\frac{3}{4}}$, $8x$ is the radicand.

B. In the expression $(-16)x^{\frac{4}{5}}$, 4 is the index.

C. The expression $1024^{\frac{n}{m}}$ represents the mth root of the nth power of 1024.

D. $50^{-\frac{2}{5}} = -50^{\frac{2}{5}}$

E. $\sqrt{(xy)^3} = xy^{\frac{3}{2}}$

H.O.T. Focus on Higher Order Thinking

22. Explain the Error A teacher asked students to evaluate $10^{-\frac{3}{5}}$ using their graphing calculators. The calculator entries of several students are shown below. Which entry will give the incorrect result? Explain.

$10^{(-3/5)}$ $\sqrt[5]{10^{-3}}$ $10^{-.6}$ $1/10^{5/3}$ $(1/10^{1/5})^3$

23. Critical Thinking The graphs of three functions of the form $y = ax^{\frac{m}{n}}$ are shown for a specific value of a, where m and n are natural numbers. What can you conclude about the relationship of m and n for each graph? Explain.

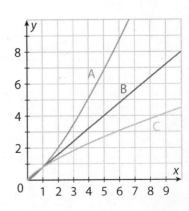

24. Critical Thinking For a negative real number a, under what condition(s) on m and n $(n \neq 0)$ is $a^{\frac{m}{n}}$ a real number? Explain. (Assume $\frac{m}{n}$ is written in simplest form.)

Lesson Performance Task

The formula $W = 35.74 + 0.6215T - 35.75V^{\frac{4}{25}} + 0.4275TV^{\frac{4}{25}}$ relates the wind chill temperature W to the air temperature T in degrees Fahrenheit and the wind speed V in miles per hour. Find the wind chill to the nearest degree when the air temperature is 40 °F and the wind speed is 35 miles per hour. If the wind chill is about 23 °F to the nearest degree when the air temperature is 40 °F, what is the wind speed to the nearest mile per hour?

11.2 Simplifying Radical Expressions

Resource
Locker

Essential Question: How can you simplify expressions containing rational exponents or radicals involving nth roots?

Ⓔ Explore   **Establishing the Properties of Rational Exponents**

In previous courses, you have used properties of integer exponents to simplify and evaluate expressions, as shown here for a few simple examples:

$$4^2 \cdot 4^3 = 4^{2+3} = 4^5 = 1024$$

$$(4^2)^3 = 4^{2 \cdot 3} = 4^6 = 4096$$

$$\left(\frac{4}{x}\right)^3 = \frac{4^3}{x^3} = \frac{64}{x^3}$$

$$(4 \cdot x)^2 = 4^2 \cdot x^2 = 16x^2$$

$$\frac{4^2}{4^3} = 4^{2-3} = 4^{-1} = \frac{1}{4}$$

Now that you have been introduced to expressions involving rational exponents, you can explore the properties that apply to simplifying them.

Ⓐ Let $a = 64$, $b = 4$, $m = \frac{1}{3}$, and $n = \frac{3}{2}$. Evaluate each expression by substituting and applying exponents individually, as shown.

Expression	Substitute	Simplify	Result
$a^m \cdot a^n$	$64^{\frac{1}{3}} \cdot 64^{\frac{3}{2}}$	$4 \cdot 512$	2048
$(a \cdot b)^n$	$(64 \cdot 4)^{\frac{3}{2}}$	$256^{\frac{3}{2}}$	
$(a^m)^n$			
$\dfrac{a^n}{a^m}$			
$\left(\dfrac{a}{b}\right)^n$			

(B) Complete the table again. This time, however, apply the rule of exponents that you would use for integer exponents.

Expression	Apply Rule and Substitute	Simplify	Result
$a^m \cdot a^n$	$64^{\frac{1}{3}+\frac{3}{2}}$	$64^{\frac{11}{6}}$	
$(a \cdot b)^n$			
$(a^m)^n$			
$\dfrac{a^n}{a^m}$			
$\left(\dfrac{a}{b}\right)^n$			

Reflect

1. Compare your results in Steps A and B. What can you conclude?

_____

_____

_____

_____

_____

2. In Steps A and B, you evaluated $\dfrac{a^n}{a^m}$ two ways. Now evaluate $\dfrac{a^m}{a^n}$ two ways, using the definition of negative exponents. Are your results consistent with your previous conclusions about integer and rational exponents?

_____

_____

_____

_____

_____

_____

Simplifying Rational-Exponent Expressions

Rational exponents have the same properties as integer exponents.

Properties of Rational Exponents

For all nonzero real numbers a and b and rational numbers m and n

Words	Numbers	Algebra
Product of Powers Property To multiply powers with the same base, add the exponents.	$12^{\frac{1}{2}} \cdot 12^{\frac{3}{2}} = 12^{\frac{1}{2}+\frac{3}{2}} = 12^2 = 144$	$a^m \cdot a^n = a^{m+n}$
Quotient of Powers Property To divide powers with the same base, subtract the exponents.	$\dfrac{125^{\frac{2}{3}}}{125^{\frac{1}{3}}} = 125^{\frac{2}{3}-\frac{1}{3}} = 125^{\frac{1}{3}} = 5$	$\dfrac{a^m}{a^n} = a^{m-n}$
Power of a Power Property To raise one power to another, multiply the exponents.	$\left(8^{\frac{2}{3}}\right)^3 = 8^{\frac{2}{3} \cdot 3} = 8^2 = 64$	$\left(a^m\right)^n = a^{m \cdot n}$
Power of a Product Property To find a power of a product, distribute the exponent.	$(16 \cdot 25)^{\frac{1}{2}} = 16^{\frac{1}{2}} \cdot 25^{\frac{1}{2}} = 4 \cdot 5 = 20$	$(ab)^m = a^m b^m$
Power of a Quotient Property To find the power of a qoutient, distribute the exponent.	$\left(\dfrac{16}{81}\right)^{\frac{1}{4}} = \dfrac{16^{\frac{1}{4}}}{81^{\frac{1}{4}}} = \dfrac{2}{3}$	$\left(\dfrac{a}{b}\right)^m = \dfrac{a^m}{b^m}$

Example 1 Simplify the expression. Assume that all variables are positive. Exponents in simplified form should all be positive.

Ⓐ **a.** $25^{\frac{3}{5}} \cdot 25^{\frac{7}{5}}$ **b.** $\dfrac{8^{\frac{1}{3}}}{8^{\frac{2}{3}}}$

$= 25^{\frac{3}{5}+\frac{7}{5}}$ Product of Powers Prop. $= 8^{\frac{1}{3}-\frac{2}{3}}$ Quotient of Powes Prop.

$= 25^2$ Simplify. $= 8^{-\frac{1}{3}}$ Simplify.

$= 625$ $= \dfrac{1}{8^{\frac{1}{3}}}$ Definition of neg. power

$= \dfrac{1}{2}$ Simplify.

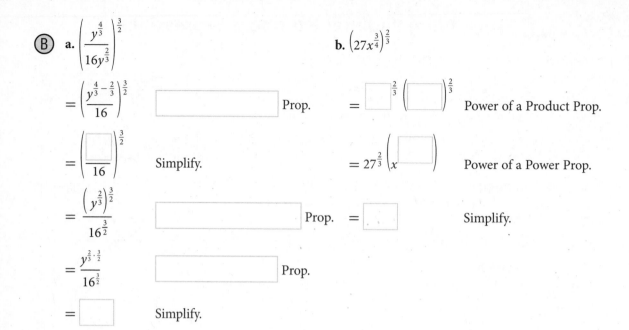

B **a.** $\left(\dfrac{y^{\frac{4}{3}}}{16y^{\frac{2}{3}}}\right)^{\frac{3}{2}}$

$= \left(\dfrac{y^{\frac{4}{3}-\frac{2}{3}}}{16}\right)^{\frac{3}{2}}$ [_____] Prop.

$= \left(\dfrac{\boxed{}}{16}\right)^{\frac{3}{2}}$ Simplify.

$= \dfrac{\left(y^{\frac{2}{3}}\right)^{\frac{3}{2}}}{16^{\frac{3}{2}}}$ [_____] Prop.

$= \dfrac{y^{\frac{2}{3}\cdot\frac{3}{2}}}{16^{\frac{3}{2}}}$ [_____] Prop.

$= \boxed{}$ Simplify.

b. $\left(27x^{\frac{3}{4}}\right)^{\frac{2}{3}}$

$= \boxed{}^{\frac{2}{3}}\left(\boxed{}\right)^{\frac{2}{3}}$ Power of a Product Prop.

$= 27^{\frac{2}{3}}\left(x^{\boxed{}}\right)$ Power of a Power Prop.

$= \boxed{}$ Simplify.

Your Turn

Simplify the expression. Assume that all variables are positive. Exponents in simplified form should all be positive.

3. $\left(12^{\frac{2}{3}}\cdot 12^{\frac{4}{3}}\right)^{\frac{3}{2}}$

4. $\dfrac{\left(6x^{\frac{1}{3}}\right)^{2}}{x^{\frac{5}{3}}y}$

🔎 Explain 2 Simplifying Radical Expressions Using the Properties of Exponents

When you are working with radical expressions involving nth roots, you can rewrite the expressions using rational exponents and then simplify them using the properties of exponents.

Example 2 Simplify the expression by writing it using rational exponents and then using the properties of rational exponents. Assume that all variables are positive. Exponents in simplified form should all be positive.

A $x\left(\sqrt[3]{2y}\right)\left(\sqrt[3]{4x^2y^2}\right)$

$= x(2y)^{\frac{1}{3}}\left(4x^2y^2\right)^{\frac{1}{3}}$ Write using rational exponents.

$= x\left(2y\cdot 4x^2y^2\right)^{\frac{1}{3}}$ Power of a Product Property

$= x\left(8x^2y^3\right)^{\frac{1}{3}}$ Product of Powers Property

$= x\left(2x^{\frac{2}{3}}y\right)$ Power of a Product Property

$= 2x^{\frac{5}{3}}y$ Product of Powers Property

Ⓑ $\dfrac{\sqrt{64y}}{\sqrt[3]{64y}}$

$= \dfrac{(64y)^{\frac{1}{2}}}{(64y)^{\frac{1}{3}}}$ Write using rational exponents.

$= (64y)^{\boxed{}}$ Quotient of Powers Property

$= (64y)^{\boxed{}}$ Simplify.

$= \boxed{}$ Power of a Product Property

$= \boxed{}$ Simplify.

Your Turn

Simplify the expression by writing it using rational exponents and then using the properties of rational exponents.

5. $\dfrac{\sqrt{x^3}}{\sqrt[3]{x^2}}$

6. $\sqrt[6]{16^3} \cdot \sqrt[4]{4^6} \cdot \sqrt[3]{8^2}$

🔑 Explain 3 Simplifying Radical Expressions Using the Properties of nth Roots

From working with square roots, you know, for example, that $\sqrt{8} \cdot \sqrt{2} = \sqrt{8 \cdot 2} = \sqrt{16} = 4$ and $\dfrac{\sqrt{8}}{\sqrt{2}} \cdot = \sqrt{\dfrac{8}{2}} = \sqrt{4} = 2$. The corresponding properties also apply to nth roots.

Properties of nth Roots		
For a > 0 and b > 0		
Words	**Numbers**	**Algebra**
Product Property of Roots The nth root of a product is equal to the product of the nth roots.	$\sqrt[3]{16} = \sqrt[3]{8} \cdot \sqrt[3]{2} = 2\sqrt[3]{2}$	$\sqrt[n]{ab} = \sqrt[n]{a} \cdot \sqrt[n]{b}$
Quotient Property of Roots The nth root of a Quotient is equal to the Quotient of the nth roots.	$\sqrt{\dfrac{25}{16}} = \dfrac{\sqrt{25}}{\sqrt{16}} = \dfrac{5}{4}$	$\sqrt[n]{\dfrac{a}{b}} = \dfrac{\sqrt[n]{a}}{\sqrt[n]{b}}$

Example 3 Simplify the expression using the properties of *n*th roots. Assume that all variables are positive. Rationalize any irrational denominators.

Ⓐ $\sqrt[3]{256x^3y^7}$

$\sqrt[3]{256x^3y^7}$

$= \sqrt[3]{2^8 \cdot x^3y^7}$ Write 256 as a power.

$= \sqrt[3]{2^6 \cdot x^3y^6} \cdot \sqrt[3]{2^2 \cdot y}$ Product Property of Roots

$= \sqrt[3]{2^6} \cdot \sqrt[3]{x^3} \cdot \sqrt[3]{y^6} \cdot \sqrt[3]{4y}$ Factor out perfect cubes.

$= 4xy^2\sqrt[3]{4y}$ Simplify.

Ⓑ

$= \dfrac{\sqrt[4]{81}}{\sqrt[4]{x}}$ ☐

$= \dfrac{\boxed{}}{\sqrt[4]{x}}$ Simplify.

$= \dfrac{3}{\sqrt[4]{x}} \cdot \dfrac{\boxed{}}{\sqrt[4]{x^3}}$ Rationalize the denominator.

$= \dfrac{3\sqrt[4]{x^3}}{\sqrt[4]{x^4}}$ ☐

$= \boxed{}$ Simplify.

Reflect

7. In Part B, why was $\sqrt[4]{x^3}$ used when rationalizing the denominator? What factor would you use to rationalize a denominator of $\sqrt[5]{4y^3}$?

_____

_____

_____

_____

Simplify the expression using the properties of nth roots. Assume that all variables are positive.

8. $\sqrt[3]{216x^{12}y^{15}}$

9. $\sqrt[4]{\dfrac{16}{x^{14}}}$

⚙ Explain 4 Rewriting a Radical-Function Model

When you find or apply a function model involving rational powers or radicals, you can use the properties in this lesson to help you find a simpler expression for the model.

Ⓐ **Manufacturing** A can that is twice as tall as its radius has the minimum surface area for the volume it contains. The formula $S = 6\pi\left(\dfrac{V}{2\pi}\right)^{\frac{2}{3}}$ expresses the surface area of a can with this shape in terms of its volume.

a. Use the properties of rational exponents to simplify the expression for the surface area. Then write the approximate model with the coefficient rounded to the nearest hundredth.

b. Graph the model using a graphing calculator. What is the surface area in square centimeters for a can with a volume of 440 cm³?

a.

$$S = 6\pi\left(\frac{V}{2\pi}\right)^{\frac{2}{3}}$$

Power of a Quotient Property

$$= 6\pi \cdot \frac{V^{\frac{2}{3}}}{(2\pi)^{\frac{2}{3}}}$$

Group Powers of 2π.

$$= \frac{3(2\pi)}{(2\pi)^{\frac{2}{3}}} \cdot V^{\frac{2}{3}}$$

Quotient of Powers Property

$$= 3(2\pi)^{1-\frac{2}{3}} \cdot V^{\frac{2}{3}}$$

Simplify.

$$= 3(2\pi)^{\frac{1}{3}} \cdot V^{\frac{2}{3}}$$

Use a calculator.

$$\approx 5.54 V^{\frac{2}{3}}$$

A simplified model is $S = 3(2\pi)^{\frac{1}{3}} \cdot V^{\frac{2}{3}}$, which gives $S \approx 5.54 V^{\frac{2}{3}}$.

b.

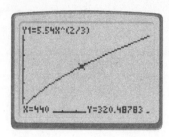

The surface area is about 320 cm².

(B) Commercial fishing The buoyancy of a fishing float in water depends on the volume of air it contains. The radius of a spherical float as a function of its volume is given by $r = \sqrt[3]{\dfrac{3V}{4\pi}}$.

a. Use the properties of roots to rewrite the expression for the radius as the product of a coefficient term and a variable term. Then write the approximate formula with the coefficient rounded to the nearest hundredth.

b. What should the radius be for a float that needs to contain 4.4 ft³ of air to have the proper buoyancy?

a.
$$r = \sqrt[3]{\dfrac{3V}{4\pi}}$$

Rewrite radicand. $\quad = \sqrt[3]{\dfrac{3}{4\pi} \cdot \boxed{}}$

Product Property of Roots $\quad = \sqrt[3]{\dfrac{3}{4\pi}} \cdot \boxed{}$

Use a calculator $\quad \approx \boxed{}$

The rewritten formula is $r = \boxed{}$, which gives $r \approx \boxed{}$.

b. Substitute 4.4 for V.

$$r = 0.62\sqrt[3]{4.4} \approx \boxed{}$$

The radius is about ____ feet.

10. Discussion What are some reasons you might want to rewrite an expression involving radicals into an expression involving rational exponents?

_____

_____

_____

_____

11. The surface area as a function of volume for a box with a square base and a height that is twice the side length of the base is $S = 10\left(\dfrac{V}{2}\right)^{\frac{2}{3}}$. Use the properties of rational exponents to simplify the expression for the surface area so that no fractions are involved. Then write the approximate model with the coefficient rounded to the nearest hundredth.

Elaborate

12. In problems with a radical in the denominator, you rationalized the denominator to remove the radical. What can you do to remove a rational exponent from the denominator? Explain by giving an example.

13. Show why $\sqrt[n]{a^n}$ is equal to a for all natural numbers a and n using the definition of nth roots and using rational exponents.

14. Show that the Product Property of Roots is true using rational exponents.

15. **Essential Question Check-In** Describe the difference between applying the Power of a Power Property and applying the Power of a Product Property for rational exponents using an example that involves both properties.

Simplify the expression. Assume that all variables are positive. Exponents in simplified form should all be positive.

1. $\left(\left(\dfrac{1}{16}\right)^{-\frac{2}{3}}\right)^{\frac{3}{4}}$

2. $\dfrac{x^{\frac{1}{3}} \cdot x^{\frac{5}{6}}}{x^{\frac{1}{6}}}$

3. $\dfrac{9^{\frac{3}{2}} \cdot 9^{\frac{1}{2}}}{9^{-2}}$

4. $\left(\dfrac{16^{\frac{5}{3}}}{16^{\frac{5}{6}}}\right)^{\frac{9}{5}}$

5. $\dfrac{2xy}{\left(x^{\frac{1}{3}}y^{\frac{2}{3}}\right)^{\frac{3}{2}}}$

6. $\dfrac{3y^{\frac{3}{4}}}{2xy^{\frac{3}{2}}}$

Simplify the expression by writing it using rational exponents and then using the properties of rational exponents. Assume that all variables are positive. Exponents in simplified form should all be positive.

7. $\sqrt[4]{25} \cdot \sqrt[3]{5}$

8. $\dfrac{\sqrt[4]{2^{-2}}}{\sqrt[6]{2^{-9}}}$

9. $\dfrac{\sqrt[4]{3^3} \cdot \sqrt[3]{x^2}}{\sqrt{3x}}$

10. $\dfrac{\sqrt[4]{x^4 y^6} \cdot \sqrt{x^6}}{y}$

11. $\dfrac{\sqrt[6]{s^4 t^9}}{\sqrt[3]{st}}$

12. $\sqrt[4]{27} \cdot \sqrt{3} \cdot \sqrt[6]{81^3}$

Simplify the expression using the properties of nth roots. Assume that all variables are positive. Rationalize any irrational denominators.

13. $\dfrac{\sqrt[4]{36} \cdot \sqrt[4]{216}}{\sqrt[4]{6}}$

14. $\sqrt[4]{4096 x^6 y^8}$

15. $\dfrac{\sqrt[3]{x^8 y^4}}{\sqrt[3]{x^2 y}}$

16. $\sqrt[5]{\dfrac{125}{w^6}} \cdot \sqrt[5]{25v}$

17. Weather The volume of a sphere as a function of its surface area is given by $V = \dfrac{4\pi}{3}\left(\dfrac{S}{4\pi}\right)^{\frac{3}{2}}$.

a. Use the properties of roots to rewrite the expression for the volume as the product of a simplified coefficient term (with positive exponents) and a variable term. Then write the approximate formula with the coefficient rounded to the nearest thousandth.

b. A spherical weather balloon has a surface area of 500 ft². What is the approximate volume of the balloon?

18. **Amusement parks** An amusement park has a ride with a free fall of 128 feet. The formula $t = \sqrt{\frac{2d}{g}}$ gives the time t in seconds it takes the ride to fall a distance of d feet. The formula $v = \sqrt{2gd}$ gives the velocity v in feet per second after the ride has fallen d feet. The letter g represents the gravitational constant.

a. Rewrite each formula so that the variable d is isolated. Then simplify each formula using the fact that $g \approx 32 \text{ ft/s}^2$.

b. Find the time it takes the ride to fall halfway and its velocity at that time. Then find the time and velocity for the full drop.

c. What is the ratio of the time it takes for the whole drop to the time it takes for the first half? What is the ratio of the velocity after the second half of the drop to the velocity after the first half? What do you notice?

19. Which choice(s) is/are equivalent to $\sqrt{2}$?

A. $\left(\sqrt[8]{2}\right)^4$

B. $\dfrac{2^3}{2^{-\frac{5}{2}}}$

C. $\left(4^{\frac{2}{3}} \cdot 2^{\frac{2}{3}}\right)^{\frac{1}{4}}$

D. $\dfrac{\sqrt[3]{2^2}}{\sqrt[6]{2}}$

E. $\dfrac{\sqrt{2^{-\frac{3}{4}}}}{\sqrt{2^{-\frac{7}{4}}}}$

20. Home Heating A propane storage tank for a home is shaped like a cylinder with hemispherical ends, and a cylindrical portion length that is 4 times the radius.

The formula $S = 12\pi \left(\frac{3V}{16\pi}\right)^{\frac{2}{3}}$ expresses the surface area of a tank with this shape in terms of its volume.

a. Use the properties of rational exponents to rewrite the expression for the surface area so that the variable V is isolated. Then write the approximate model with the coefficient rounded to the nearest hundredth.

b. Graph the model using a graphing calculator. What is the surface area in square feet for a tank with a volume of 150 ft³ ?

21. Critique Reasoning Aaron's work in simplifying an expression is shown. What mistake(s) did Aaron make? Show the correct simplification.

$$625^{-\frac{1}{3}} \div 625^{-\frac{4}{3}}$$

$$= 625^{-\frac{1}{3} - \left(-\frac{4}{3}\right)}$$

$$= 625^{-\frac{1}{3}\left(-\frac{3}{4}\right)}$$

$$= 625^{\frac{1}{4}}$$

$$= 5$$

22. Critical Thinking Use the definition of nth root to show that the Product Property of Roots is true, that is, that $\sqrt[n]{ab} = \sqrt[n]{a} \cdot \sqrt[n]{b}$. (Hint: Begin by letting x be the nth root of a and letting y be the nth root of b.)

23. Critical Thinking For what real values of a is $\sqrt[4]{a}$ greater than a? For what real values of a is $\sqrt[5]{a}$ greater than a?

Lesson Performance Task

You've been asked to help decorate for a school dance, and the theme chosen is "The Solar System." The plan is to have a bunch of papier-mâché spheres serve as models of the planets, and your job is to paint them. All you're told are the volumes of the individual spheres, but you need to know their surface areas so you can get be sure to get enough paint. How can you write a simplified equation using rational exponents for the surface area of a sphere in terms of its volume?

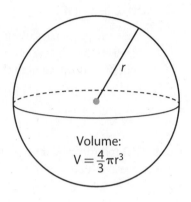

Volume:
$V = \frac{4}{3}\pi r^3$

(The formula for the volume of a sphere is $V = \frac{4}{3}\pi r^3$ and the formula for the surface area of a sphere is $A = 4\pi r^2$.)

11.3 Solving Radical Equations

Essential Question: How can you solve equations involving square roots and cube roots?

Resource
Locker

 Explore Investigating Solutions of Square Root Equations

When solving quadratic equations, you have learned that the number of real solutions depends upon the values in the equation, with different equations having 0, 1, or 2 real solutions. How many real solutions does a square root equation have? In the Explore, you will investigate graphically the numbers of real solutions for different square root equations.

(A) Remember that you can graph the two sides of an equation as separate functions to find solutions of the equation: a solution is any x-value where the two graphs intersect.

The graph of $y = \sqrt{x - 3}$ is shown on a calculator window of $-4 \leq x \leq 16$ and $-2 \leq y \leq 8$. Reproduce the graph on your calculator. Then add the graph of $y = 2$.

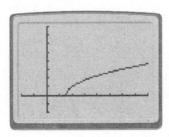

How many solutions does the equation $\sqrt{x - 3} = 2$ have? _____ How do you know?

_____

On your calculator, replace the graph of $y = 2$ with the graph of $y = -1$.

How many solutions does the equation $\sqrt{x - 3} = -1$ have? _____ How do you know?

_____

(B) Graph $y = \sqrt{x - 3} + 2$ on your calculator (you can use the same viewing window as in Step A).

Add the graph of $y = 3$ to the graph of $y = \sqrt{x - 3} + 2$.

How many solutions does $\sqrt{x - 3} + 2 = 3$ have? _____

Replace the graph of $y = 3$ with the graph of $y = 1$.

How many solutions does $\sqrt{x - 3} + 2 = 1$ have? _____

Ⓒ Graph both sides of $\sqrt{4x-4} = x+1$ as separate functions on your calculator.

How many solutions does $\sqrt{4x-4} = x+1$ have? _____

Replace the graph of $y = x+1$ with the graph of $y = \frac{1}{2}x$.

How many solutions does $\sqrt{4x-4} = \frac{1}{2}x$ have? _____

Replace the graph of $y = \frac{1}{2}x$ with the graph of $y = 2x-5$.

How many solutions does $\sqrt{4x-4} = 2x-5$ have? _____

Ⓓ Graph both sides of $\sqrt{2x-3} = \sqrt{x}$ as separate functions on your calculator.

How many solutions does $\sqrt{2x-3} = \sqrt{x}$ have? _____

Replace the graph of $y = \sqrt{x}$ with the graph of $y = \sqrt{2x+3}$.

How many solutions does $\sqrt{2x-3} = \sqrt{2x+3}$ have? _____

Reflect

1. For a square root equation of the form $\sqrt{bx-h} = c$, what can you conclude about the number of solutions based on the sign of c?

    _____

    _____

2. For a square root equation of the form $\sqrt{bx-h} + k = c$, what can you conclude about the number of solutions based on the values of k and c?

    _____

    _____

3. For a cube root equation of the form $\sqrt[3]{bx-h} = c$, will the number of solutions depend on the sign of c? Explain.

    _____

    _____

4. The graphs in the second part of Step D appear to be get closer and closer as x increases. How can you be sure that they never meet, that is, that $\sqrt{2x-3} = \sqrt{2x+3}$ really has no solutions?

    _____

    _____

⊘ Explain 1 Solving Square Root and $\frac{1}{2}$-Power Equations

A *radical equation* contains a variable within a radical or a variable raised to a (non-integer) rational power. To solve a square root equation, or, equivalently, an equation involving the power $\frac{1}{2}$, you can square both sides of the equation and solve the resulting equation.

Because opposite numbers have the same square, squaring both sides of an equation may introduce an apparent solution that is not an actual solution (an extraneous solution). For example, while the only solution of $x = 2$ is 2, the equation that is the square of each side, $x^2 = 4$, has two solutions, -2 and 2. But -2 is not a solution of the original equation.

Example 1 Solve the equation. Check for extraneous solutions.

(A) $2 + \sqrt{x + 10} = x$

$$2 + \sqrt{x + 10} = x$$

Isolate the radical. $\qquad \sqrt{x + 10} = x - 2$

Square both sides. $\qquad \left(\sqrt{x + 10}\right)^2 = (x - 2)^2$

Simplify. $\qquad x + 10 = x^2 - 4x + 4$

Simplify. $\qquad 0 = x^2 - 5x - 6$

Factor. $\qquad 0 = (x - 6)(x + 1)$

Zero Product Property $\qquad x = 6 \text{ or } x = -1$

Check:

$2 + \sqrt{x + 10} = x$ $\qquad\qquad$ $2 + \sqrt{x + 10} = x$

$2 + \sqrt{6 + 10} \overset{?}{=} 6$ $\qquad\qquad$ $2 + \sqrt{-1 + 10} \overset{?}{=} -1$

$2 + \sqrt{16} \overset{?}{=} 6$ $\qquad\qquad$ $2 + \sqrt{9} \overset{?}{=} -1$

$6 = 6 \checkmark$ $\qquad\qquad\qquad$ $5 \neq -1$

$x = 6$ is a solution. $\qquad\qquad$ $x = -1$ is not a solution.

The solution is $x = 6$.

(B) $(x + 6)^{\frac{1}{2}} - (2x - 4)^{\frac{1}{2}} = 0$

Rewrite with radicals. $\qquad \sqrt{x + 6} - \sqrt{2x - 4} = 0$

Isolate radicals on each side. $\qquad \sqrt{x + 6} = \boxed{}$

Square both sides. $\qquad \left(\sqrt{x + 6}\right)^2 = \left(\boxed{}\right)^2$

Simplify. $\qquad \boxed{} = \boxed{}$

Solve. $\qquad \boxed{} = x$

Check:

$$\sqrt{x + 6} - \sqrt{2x - 4} = 0$$

$$\sqrt{10 + 6} - \sqrt{2\left(\boxed{} \cdot\right)} - 4 \overset{?}{=} 0$$

$$\boxed{} - \boxed{} \overset{?}{=} 0$$

$$\boxed{} = 0$$

The solution is  .

5. The graphs of each side of the equation from Part A are shown on the graphing calculator screen below. How can you tell from the graph that one of the two solutions you found algebraically is extraneous?

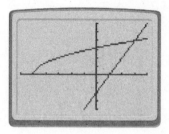

_____

_____

Your Turn

6. Solve $(x + 5)^{\frac{1}{2}} - 2 = 1$.

⊘ Explain 2 Solving Cube Root and $\frac{1}{3}$-Power Equations

You can solve radical equations that involve roots other than square roots by raising both sides to the index of the radical. So, to solve a cube root equation, or, equivalently, an equation involving the power $\frac{1}{3}$, you can cube both sides of the equation and solve the resulting equation.

Example 2 Solve the equation.

(A) $\sqrt[3]{x + 2} + 7 = 5$

$$\sqrt[3]{x + 2} + 7 = 5$$

Isolate the radical. $\qquad \sqrt[3]{x + 2} = -2$

Cube both sides. $\qquad \left(\sqrt[3]{x + 2}\right)^3 = (-2)^3$

Simplify. $\qquad x + 2 = -8$

Solve for x $\qquad x = -10$

The solution is $x = -10$.

Ⓑ $\sqrt[3]{x-5} = x+1$

$$\sqrt[3]{x-5} = x+1$$

Cube both sides. $\left(\sqrt[3]{x-5}\right)^3 = (x+1)^3$

Simplify $\boxed{} = \boxed{}$

Simplify. $0 = \boxed{}$

Begin to factor by grouping. $0 = x^2\left(\boxed{}\right) + 2\left(\boxed{}\right)$

Complete factoring $0 = \left(x^2 + 2\right)\left(\boxed{}\right)$

By the Zero Product Property, $\boxed{} = 0$ or $\boxed{} = 0.$

Because there are no real values of x for which $x^2 = \boxed{}$, the only solution is $\boxed{}$.

Reflect

7. **Discussion** Example 1 shows checking for extraneous solutions, while Example 2 does not. While it is always wise to check your answers, can a cubic equation have an extraneous solution? Explain your answer.

_____

_____

_____

_____

Your Turn

8. Solve $2(x-50)^{\frac{1}{3}} = -10.$

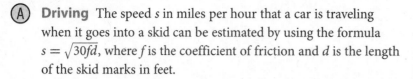
Explain 3 Solving a Real-World Problem

(A) **Driving** The speed s in miles per hour that a car is traveling when it goes into a skid can be estimated by using the formula $s = \sqrt{30fd}$, where f is the coefficient of friction and d is the length of the skid marks in feet.

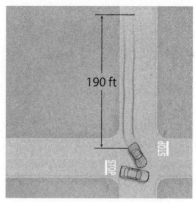

190 ft

After an accident, a driver claims to have been traveling the speed limit of 55 mi/h. The coefficient of friction under the conditions at the time of the accident was 0.6, and the length of the skid marks is 190 feet. Is the driver telling the truth about the car's speed? Explain.

Use the formula to find the length of a skid at a speed of 55 mi/h. Compare this distance to the actual skid length of 190 feet.

$$s = \sqrt{30fd}$$

Substitute 55 for s and 0.6 for f $\quad 55 = \sqrt{30(0.6)d}$

Simplify. $\quad 55 = \sqrt{18d}$

Square both sides. $\quad 55^2 = \left(\sqrt{18d}\right)^2$

Simplify. $\quad 3025 = 18d$

Solve for d. $\quad 168 \approx d$

If the driver had been traveling at 55 mi/h, the skid marks would measure about 168 feet. Because the skid marks actually measure 190 feet, the driver must have been driving faster than 55 mi/h.

(B) **Construction** The diameter d in inches of a rope needed to lift a weight of w tons is given by the formula $d = \dfrac{\sqrt{15w}}{\pi}$. How much weight can be lifted with a rope with a diameter of 1.0 inch?

Use the formula for the diameter as a function of weight, and solve for the weight given the diameter.

$$d = \frac{\sqrt{15w}}{\pi}$$

Substitute. $\quad \boxed{} = \dfrac{\sqrt{15w}}{\pi}$

Square both sides. $\quad \boxed{} = \boxed{}$

Isolate the radical. $\quad \left(\boxed{}\right)^2 = \left(\sqrt{15w}\right)^2$

Simplify. $\quad \boxed{} = 15w$

Solve for w. $\quad \boxed{} \approx w$

A rope with a diameter of 1.0 can hold about _____ ton, or about _____ pounds.

9. **Biology** The trunk length (in inches) of a male elephant can be modeled by $l = 23\sqrt[3]{t} + 17$, where t is the age of the elephant in years. If a male elephant has a trunk length of 100 inches, about what is his age?

💬 Elaborate

10. A student asked to solve the equation $\sqrt{4x + 8} + 9 = 1$ isolated the radical, squared both sides, and solved for x to obtain $x = 14$, only to find out that the apparent solution was extraneous. Why could the student have stopped trying to solve the equation after isolating the radical?

_____

_____

_____

_____

11. When you see a cube root equation with the radical expression isolated on one side and a constant on the other, what should you expect for the number of solutions? Explain. What are some reasons you should check your answer anyway?

_____

_____

_____

12. **Essential Question Check-In** Solving a quadratic equation of the form $x^2 = a$ involves taking the square root of both sides. Solving a square root equation of the form $\sqrt{x} = b$ involves squaring both sides of the equation. Which of these operations can create an equation that is not equivalent to the original equation? Explain how this affects the solution process.

_____

_____

_____

_____

_____

Solve the equation.

1. $\sqrt{x-9} = 5$

2. $\sqrt{3x} = 6$

3. $\sqrt{x+3} = x+1$

4. $\sqrt{(15x+10)} = 2x+3$

5. $(x+4)^{\frac{1}{2}} = 6$

6. $(45-9x)^{\frac{1}{2}} = x - 5$

7. $(x-6)^{\frac{1}{2}} = x - 2$

8. $4(x-2)^{\frac{1}{2}} = (x+13)^{\frac{1}{2}}$

9. $5 - \sqrt[3]{x-4} = 2$

10. $2\sqrt[3]{3x+2} = \sqrt[3]{4x-9}$

11. $\sqrt[3]{69x + 35} = x + 5$

12. $\sqrt[3]{x + 5} = x - 1$

13. $(x + 7)^{\frac{1}{3}} = (4x)^{\frac{1}{3}}$

14. $(5x + 1)^{\frac{1}{4}} = 4$

15. $(-9x - 54)^{\frac{1}{3}} = -2x + 3$

16. $2(x - 1)^{\frac{1}{5}} = (2x - 17)^{\frac{1}{5}}$

17. **Driving** The formula for the speed versus skid length in Example 3A assumes that all 4 wheel brakes are working at top efficiency. If this is not true, another parameter is included in the equation so that the equation becomes $s = \sqrt{30fdn}$ where n is the percent braking efficiency as a decimal. Accident investigators know that the rear brakes failed on a car, reducing its braking efficiency to 60%. On a dry road with a coefficient of friction of 0.7, the car skidded 250 feet. Was the car going above the speed limit of 60 mi/h when the skid began?

18. **Anatomy** The surface area S of a human body in square meters can be approximated by $S = \sqrt{\frac{hm}{36}}$ where h is height in meters and m is mass in kilograms. A basketball player with a height of 2.1 meters has a surface area of about 2.7 m^2. What is the player's mass?

19. Biology The approximate antler length L (in inches) of a deer buck can be modeled by $L = 9\sqrt[3]{t} + 15$ where t is the age in years of the buck. If a buck has an antler length of 36 inches, what is its age?

20. Amusement Parks For a spinning amusement park ride, the velocity v in meters per second of a car moving around a curve with radius r meters is given by $v = \sqrt{ar}$ where a is the car's acceleration in m/s². If the ride has a maximum acceleration of 30 m/s² and the cars on the ride have a maximum velocity of 12 m/s, what is the smallest radius that any curve on the ride may have?

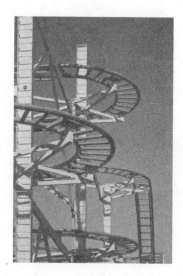

21. For each radical equation, state the number of solutions that exist.

A. $\sqrt{x - 4} = -5$

B. $\sqrt{x - 4} + 6 = 11$

C. $4 = -2\sqrt[3]{x + 2}$

D. $\sqrt{x + 40} = 0$

E. $\sqrt[3]{2x + 5} = -18$

22. **Critical Thinking** For an equation of the form $\sqrt{x + a} = b$ where b is a constant, does the sign of a affect whether or not there is a solution for a given value of b? If so, how? If not, why not?

23. **Explain the Error** Below is a student's work in solving the equation $2\sqrt{3x + 3} = 12$. What mistake did the student make? What is the correct solution?

$$2\sqrt{3x + 3} = 12$$

$$2\left(\sqrt{3x + 3}\right)^2 = 12^2$$

$$2(3x + 3) = 144$$

$$6x + 6 = 144$$

$$x = 23$$

24. **Communicate Mathematical Ideas** Describe the key difference between solving radical equations for which you solve by raising both sides to an even power and those you solve by raising both sides to an odd power.

25. **Critical Thinking** How could you solve an equation for which one side is a rational power expression and the other side is a constant? Give an example. Under what condition would you have to be especially careful to check your solutions?

Lesson Performance Task

For many years scientists have used a scale known as the Fujita Scale to categorize different types of tornados in relation to the velocity of the winds produced. The formula used to generate the scale is given by $V = k(F + 2)^{\frac{3}{2}}$. The scale employs a constant, k, and the tornado's category number to determine wind speed. If you wanted to determine the different category numbers, how could you solve the radical equation for the variable F? (The value for k is about 14.1.) Solve the equation for F then verify the different categories using the minimum wind velocity. Do the values seem reasonable given the value for k?

Fujita Tornado Scale			
Damage Level	Category	Minimum Wind Velocity (mi/h)	Calculations
Moderate	F1	73	
Significant	F2	113	
Severe	F3	158	
Devastating	F4	207	
Incredible	F5	261	

STUDY GUIDE REVIEW
Radical Expressions and Equations

Essential Question: How can you use radical expressions and equations to solve real-world problems?

Key Vocabulary
extraneous solution
   (solución extraña)
radical expression
   (expresión radical)
rational exponent
   (exponente racional)

KEY EXAMPLE   *(Lesson 11.1)*

Evaluate the expression.

$$\left(\sqrt[4]{16}\right)^5 = 2^5 = 32$$
$$27^{\frac{4}{3}} = \left(\sqrt[3]{27}\right)^4 = 3^4 = 81$$

KEY EXAMPLE   *(Lesson 11.2)*

Write the expression in simplest form. Assume all variables are positive.

$$\sqrt[3]{48} = \sqrt[3]{8 \cdot 6}$$ Factor out a perfect cube.

$$= \sqrt[3]{8} \cdot \sqrt[3]{6}$$ Apply the Product Property of Radicals.

$$= 2\sqrt[3]{6}$$ Evaluate.

$$\left(\frac{x^4}{y^8}\right)^{\frac{1}{2}} = \frac{\left(x^4\right)^{\frac{1}{2}}}{\left(y^8\right)^{\frac{1}{2}}}$$ Apply the Power of a Quotient Property.

$$= \frac{x^{4 \cdot \frac{1}{2}}}{y^{8 \cdot \frac{1}{2}}}$$ Apply the Power of a Power Property.

$$= \frac{x^2}{y^4}$$ Simplify.

KEY EXAMPLE   *(Lesson 11.3)*

Solve the equation. $\sqrt{x + 15} = x - 5$

$$\left(\sqrt{x + 15}\right)^2 = (x - 5)^2$$ Square both sides.

$$x + 15 = x^2 - 10x + 25$$

$$x^2 - 11x + 10 = 0$$ Write in standard form.

$$(x - 10)(x - 1) = 0$$ Factor.

$$x = 10 \text{ or } x = 1$$ Solve for x.

$$\sqrt{10 + 15} \overset{?}{=} 10 - 5 \qquad \sqrt{1 + 15} \overset{?}{=} 1 - 5$$ Check.

$$5 = 5 \qquad\qquad\qquad 4 \neq -4$$

The solution $x = 1$ is extraneous. The only solution is $x = 10$.

EXERCISES

Evaluate the expression. *(Lesson 11.1)*

1. $\sqrt[3]{-64}$

2. $81^{\frac{1}{4}}$

3. $256^{\frac{3}{4}}$

Write the expression in simplest form. Assume that all variables are positive. *(Lesson 11.2)*

4. $\sqrt[3]{80}$

5. $\left(3^4 \cdot 5^4\right)^{-\frac{1}{4}}$

6. $\left(25a^{10}b^{16}\right)^{\frac{1}{2}}$

7. $\sqrt[5]{\dfrac{c}{d^8}}$

Solve each equation. *(Lesson 11.3)*

8. $\sqrt[3]{5x - 4} = 2$

9. $\sqrt{x + 6} - 7 = -2$

MODULE PERFORMANCE TASK

Don't Disturb the Neighbors!

The faintest sound an average person can detect has an intensity of 1×10^{-12} watts per square meter, where watts are a unit of power. The intensity of a sound is given by $I = \dfrac{P}{4\pi d^2}$, where P is the power of the sound and d is the distance from the source. Yolanda wants to throw a party at her house and plans to invite a band to perform. The power of the sound from the band's speakers is typically 3.0 watts. Yolanda's neighborhood has a rule that between 7 p.m. and 11 p.m., a sound intensity up to $I = 5.0 \times 10^{-5}$ W/m^2 is acceptable; after 11 p.m., the acceptable intensity is $I = 5.0 \times 10^{-7}$ W/m^2. How far away would Yolanda's closest neighbors need to be for the band to play till 11 p.m.? How far would they need to be for the band to play all night?

Start by listing in the space below the information you will need to solve the problem. Then use your own paper to complete the task. Be sure to write down all your data and assumptions. Then use graphs, numbers, words, or algebra to explain how you reached your conclusion.

(Ready) to Go On?

11.1–11.3 Radical Expressions and Equations

Simplify each expression. Assume that all variables are positive. *(Lessons 11.1, 11.2)*

1. $32^{\frac{1}{5}}$

2. $\left(\sqrt[3]{64}\right)^4$

3. $\sqrt[3]{27x^6}$

4. $\sqrt[4]{2x^6y^8}$

Solve each equation. *(Lesson 11.3)*

5. $\sqrt{10x} = 3\sqrt{x+1}$

6. $\sqrt[3]{2x-2} = 6$

7. $(4x+7)^{\frac{1}{2}} = 3$

8. $(x+3)^{\frac{1}{3}} = -6$

ESSENTIAL QUESTION

9. How do you solve a radical equation and identify any extraneous roots?

Assessment Readiness

1. Look at each expression. Can the expression be simplified to a rational number? Select Yes or No for A–C.

   A. $\sqrt{2} + \sqrt{2}$ ○ Yes   ○ No

   B. $\sqrt{4} \cdot \sqrt{20}$ ○ Yes   ○ No

   C. $\left(\sqrt{12}\right)^2$ ○ Yes   ○ No

2. Consider the function $f(x) = \frac{2x^2 - 5x - 3}{x - 3}$. Choose True or False for each statement.

   A. This function looks like a straight line when graphed.   ○ True   ○ False

   B. There is a hole in this function at $(3, 7)$.   ○ True   ○ False

   C. There is a hole in this function at $(-0.5, 0)$.   ○ True   ○ False

3. Explain how to find the product of $(4 - 3i)(2 - i)$, then state the product.

4. The formula $s = \sqrt{\frac{A}{4.828}}$ can be used to approximate the side length s of a regular octagon with area A. A stop sign is shaped like a regular octagon with a side length of 12.4 in. To the nearest square inch, what is the area of the stop sign? Explain how you got your answer.

1. Consider the graph of $g(x) = \frac{1}{3}\sqrt{x-1}$ as related to the graph of $f(x) = \sqrt{x}$.

   Select True or False for each statement.

   A. $g(x)$ is a vertical stretching by a factor of $\frac{1}{3}$ and a translation of 1 unit up from $f(x)$. ○ True ○ False

   B. $g(x)$ is a vertical compression by a factor of $\frac{1}{3}$ and a translation 1 unit right from $f(x)$. ○ True ○ False

   C. $g(x)$ is a vertical compression by a factor of $\frac{1}{3}$ and a translation 1 unit left from $f(x)$. ○ True ○ False

2. Consider each transformation in relation to $f(x) = \sqrt[3]{x}$.

   Select True or False for each statement.

   A. $g(x) = 5\sqrt[3]{x+1} - 2$ is a transformation of $f(x)$ by a vertical stretch by a factor of 5 and a translation 1 unit left and 2 units down. ○ True ○ False

   B. $g(x) = 5\sqrt[3]{x-1} + 2$ is a transformation of $f(x)$ by a horizontal stretch by a factor of 5 and a translation of 1 unit left and 2 units down. ○ True ○ False

   C. $g(x) = \frac{1}{5}\sqrt[3]{x+1} - 2$ is a transformation of $f(x)$ by a horizontal stretch by a factor of $\frac{1}{5}$ and a translation of 1 unit left and 2 units down. ○ True ○ False

3. Consider each equation. Is the equation the inverse of $f(x) = \frac{1}{2}x^3 + 5$?

   Choose Yes or No for A–C.

   A. $f^{-1}(x) = \sqrt[3]{2(x-5)}$ ○ Yes ○ No

   B. $f^{-1}(x) = \sqrt[3]{2(x+5)}$ ○ Yes ○ No

   C. $f^{-1}(x) = \sqrt[3]{\frac{1}{2}(x-5)}$ ○ Yes ○ No

4. Consider each expression. Can the expression be simplified to 25?

   Choose Yes or No for A–C.

   A. $\left(\sqrt[2]{125}\right)^3$ ○ Yes ○ No

   B. $\left(\sqrt[3]{125}\right)^2$ ○ Yes ○ No

   C. $\left(\sqrt{125}\right)^{\frac{1}{3}}$ ○ Yes ○ No

5. A company produces canned tomatoes. They want the height h of each can to be twice the diameter d. Write an equation for the surface area A of the can in terms of the radius r. If the company wants to use no more than 90 square inches of metal for each can, what is the maximum radius of the can they will produce?

6. The period T of a pendulum in seconds is given by $T = 2\pi\sqrt{\frac{L}{9.81}}$, where L is the length of the pendulum in meters. If you want to use a pendulum as a clock, with a period of 2 seconds, how long should the pendulum be?

7. Tandra says that $\sqrt[3]{\frac{8x^6}{y}}$ can be simplified to $\frac{2x^2}{\sqrt[3]{y}}$. Elizabeth says that $\sqrt[3]{\frac{6x^6}{y}}$ can be simplified to $\frac{2x^2}{\sqrt[3]{y}}$. Who is correct, or are they both correct? Explain.

Performance Tasks

★ **8.** The formula $P = 73.3\sqrt[4]{m^3}$, known as Kleiber's law, relates the metabolism rate P of an organism in Calories per day and the body mass m of the organism in kilograms. The table shows the typical body mass of several members of the cat family.

Typical Body Mass	
Animal	**Mass(kg)**
House cat	4.5
Cheetah	55.0
Lion	170.0

A. What is the metabolism rate of a cheetah to the nearest Calorie per day?

B. Approximately how many more Calories of food does a lion need to consume each day than a house cat does?

★★ **9.** On a clear day, the approximate distance d in miles that a person can see is given by $d = 1.2116\sqrt{h}$, where h is the person's height in feet above the ocean.

A. To the nearest tenth of a mile, how far can the captain on a clipper ship 15 feet above the ocean see?

B. How much farther, to the nearest tenth of a mile, will a sailor at the top of a mast 120 feet above the ocean be able to see than will the captain?

C. A pirate ship is approaching the clipper ship at a relative speed of 10 miles per hour. Approximately how many minutes sooner will the sailor be able to see the pirate ship than will the captain?

★★★ **10.** The time it takes a pendulum to make one complete swing back and forth depends on its string length, as shown in the table.

String Length (m)	2	4	6	8	10
Time (s)	2.8	4.0	4.9	5.7	6.3

A. Graph the relationship between string length and time, and identify the parent function which best describes the data.

B. The function $T(x) = 2\pi\sqrt{\frac{x}{9.8}}$ gives the period in seconds of a pendulum of length x. The period of a pendulum is the time it takes the pendulum to complete one back-and-forth swing. Describe the graph of T as a transformation of $f(x) = \sqrt{x}$.

C. By what factor must the length of a pendulum be increased to double its period?

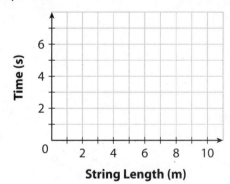

Nutritionist Body mass index (BMI) is a measure used to determine healthy body mass based on a person's height. BMI is calculated by dividing a person's mass in kilograms by the square of his or her height in meters. The median BMI measures for a group of boys, ages 2 to 10 years are given in the chart below.

Age of Boys	2	3	4	5	6	7	8	9	10
Median BMI	16.6	16.0	15.6	15.4	15.4	15.5	15.8	16.2	16.6

a. Create a scatter plot for the data in the table, treating age as the independent variable x and median BMI as the dependent variable y.

b. Use a calculator to find a quadratic regression model for the data. What is your model?

c. Give the domain of $f(x)$ based on the data set. Because $f(x)$ is quadratic, it is not one-to-one and its inverse is not a function. Restrict the domain of $f(x)$ to values of x for which $f(x)$ is increasing so that its inverse will be a function. What is the restricted domain of $f(x)$?

d. Find and graph the inverse of $f(x)$. What does $f^{-1}(x)$ model?

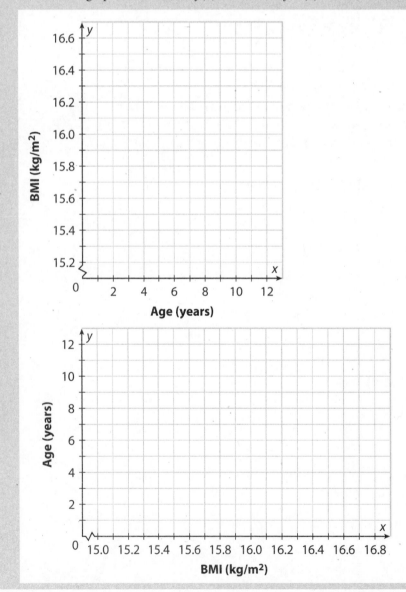

Glossary/Glosario

A

ENGLISH	SPANISH	EXAMPLES
absolute value of a complex number The absolute value of $a + bi$ is the distance from the origin to the point (a, b) in the complex plane and is denoted $\lvert a + bi \rvert = \sqrt{a^2 + b^2}$.	**valor absoluto de un número complejo** El valor absoluto de $a + bi$ es la distancia desde el origen hasta el punto (a, b) en el plano complejo y se expresa $\lvert a + bi \rvert = \sqrt{a^2 + b^2}$.	$\lvert 2 + 3i \rvert = \sqrt{2^2 + 3^2} = \sqrt{13}$
absolute value of a real number The absolute value of x is the distance from zero to x on a number line, denoted $\lvert x \rvert$. $$\lvert x \rvert = \begin{cases} x & \text{if } x \geq 0 \\ -x & \text{if } x < 0 \end{cases}$$	**valor absoluto de un número real** El valor absoluto de x es la distancia desde cero hasta x en una recta numérica y se expresa $\lvert x \rvert$. $$\lvert x \rvert = \begin{cases} x & \text{si } x \geq 0 \\ -x & \text{si } x < 0 \end{cases}$$	$\lvert 3 \rvert = 3$ $\lvert -3 \rvert = 3$
absolute-value function A function whose rule contains absolute-value expressions.	**función de valor absoluto** Función cuya regla contiene expresiones de valor absoluto.	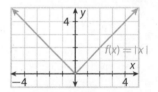
amplitude The amplitude of a periodic function is half the difference of the maximum and minimum values (always positive).	**amplitud** La amplitud de una función periódica es la mitad de la diferencia entre los valores máximo y mínimo (siempre positivos).	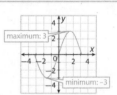 amplitude $= \frac{1}{2}\left[3 - (-3)\right] = 3$
angle of depression The angle formed by a horizontal line and a line of sight to a point below.	**ángulo de depresión** Ángulo formado por una recta horizontal y una línea visual a un punto inferior.	
angle of elevation The angle formed by a horizontal line and a line of sight to a point above.	**ángulo de elevación** Ángulo formado por una recta horizontal y una línea visual a un punto superior.	
angle of rotation An angle formed by a rotating ray, called the terminal side, and a stationary reference ray, called the initial side.	**ángulo de rotación** Ángulo formado por un rayo en rotación, denominado lado terminal, y un rayo de referencia estático, denominado lado inicial.	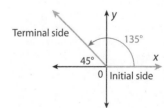

Glossary/Glosario

ENGLISH	SPANISH	EXAMPLES
arithmetic sequence A sequence whose successive terms differ by the same nonzero number d, called the *common difference*.	**sucesión aritmética** Sucesión cuyos términos sucesivos difieren en el mismo número distinto de cero d, denominado *diferencia común*.	4, 7, 10, 13, 16, ... $+ 3 + 3 + 3 + 3$ $d = 3$
arithmetic series The indicated sum of the terms of an arithmetic sequence.	**serie aritmética** Suma indicada de los términos de una sucesión aritmética.	$4 + 7 + 10 + 13 + 16 + ...$
asymptote A line that a graph approaches as the value of a variable becomes extremely large or small.	**asíntota** Línea recta a la cual se aproxima una gráfica a medida que el valor de una variable se hace sumamente grande o pequeño.	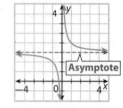
augmented matrix A matrix that consists of the coefficients and the constant terms in a system of linear equations.	**matriz aumentada** Matriz formada por los coeficientes y los términos constantes de un sistema de ecuaciones lineales.	System of equations $\quad$ Augmented matrix $3x + 2y = 5$ $2x - 3y = 1$ $\quad \begin{bmatrix} 3 & 2 & 5 \\ 2 & -3 & 1 \end{bmatrix}$
average rate of change The ratio of the change in the function values, $f(x_2) - f(x_1)$ to the change in the x-values, $x_2 - x_1$.	**tasa de cambio promedio** Razón entre el cambio en los valores de la función, $f(x_2) - f(x_1)$ y el cambio en los valores de x, $x_2 - x_1$.	
axis of symmetry A line that divides a plane figure or a graph into two congruent reflected halves.	**eje de simetría** Línea que divide una figura plana o una gráfica en dos mitades reflejadas congruentes.	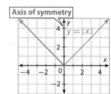

B

base of an exponential function The value of b in a function of the form $f(x) = ab^x$, where a and b are real numbers with $a \neq 0, b > 0$, and $b \neq 1$.	**base de una función exponencial** Valor de b en una función del tipo $f(x) = ab^x$, donde a y b son números reales con $a \neq 0, b > 0, y\ b \neq 1$.	$f(x) = 5(2)^x$ $\uparrow$ base
biased sample A sample that does not fairly represent the population.	**muestra no representativa** Muestra que no representa adecuadamente una población.	
binomial A polynomial with two terms.	**binomio** Polinomio con dos términos.	$x + y$ $2a^2 + 3$ $4m^3n^2 + 6mn^4$

Glossary/Glosario

binomial experiment A probability experiment consists of n identical and independent trials whose outcomes are either successes or failures, with a constant probability of success p and a constant probability of failure q, where $q = 1 - p$ or $p + q = 1$.

experimento binomial Experimento de probabilidades que comprende n pruebas idénticas e independientes cuyos resultados son éxitos o fracasos, con una probabilidad constante de éxito p y una probabilidad constante de fracaso q, donde $q = 1 - p$ o $p + q = 1$.

A multiple-choice quiz has 10 questions with 4 answer choices. The number of trials is 10. If each question is answered randomly, the probability of success for each trial is $\frac{1}{4} = 0.25$ and the probability of failure is $\frac{3}{4} = 0.75$.

---

binomial probability In a binomial experiment, the probability of r successes $(0 \leq r \leq n)$ is $P(r) = {}_nC_r \cdot p^r q^{n-r}$.

probabilidad binomial En un experimento binomial, la probabilidad de r éxitos $(0 \leq r \leq n)$ es $P(r) = {}_nC_r \cdot p^r q^{n-r}$.

In the binomial experiment above, the probability of randomly guessing 6 problems correctly is $P = {}_{10}C_6 (0.25)^6 (0.75)^4 \approx 0.016$.

Binomial Theorem For any positive integer n,
$(x + y)^n = {}_nC_0 x^n y^0 + {}_nC_1 x^{n-1} y^1 + {}_nC_2 x^{n-2} y^2 + ... + {}_nC_{n-1} x^1 y^{n-1} + {}_nC_n x^0 y^n$.

Teorema de los binomios Dado un entero positivo n,
$(x + y)^n = {}_nC_0 x^n y^0 + {}_nC_1 x^{n-1} y^1 + {}_nC_2 x^{n-2} y^2 + ... + {}_nC_{n-1} x^1 y^{n-1} + {}_nC_n x^0 y^n$.

$(x + 2)^4 = {}_4C_0 x^4 2^0 + {}_4C_1 x^3 2^1 + {}_4C_2 x^2 2^2 + {}_4C_3 x^1 2^3 + {}_4C_4 x^0 2^4 = x^4 + 8x^3 + 24x^2 + 32x + 16$

---

branch of a hyperbola One of the two symmetrical parts of the hyperbola.

rama de una hipérbola Una de las dos partes simétricas de la hipérbola.

C

categorical data Data that represent observations or attributes that can be sorted into groups or categories.

datos categóricos Datos que representan observaciones o atributos que pueden ser clasificados en grupos o categorías.

---

census A survey of an entire population.

censo Estudio de una población entera.

---

closure A set of numbers is said to be closed, or to have closure, under a given operation if the result of the operation on any two numbers in the set is also in the set.

cerradura Se dice que un conjunto de números es cerrado, o tiene cerradura, respecto de una operación determinada, si el resultado de la operación entre dos numerous cualesquiera del conjunto también está en el conjunto.

The natural numbers are closed under addition because the sum of two natural numbers is always a natural number.

---

coefficient matrix The matrix of the coefficients of the variables in a linear system of equations.

matriz de coeficientes Matriz de los coeficientes de las variables en un sistema lineal de ecuaciones.

System of equations	Coefficient matrix
$2x + 3y = 11$ $5x - 4y = 16$	$\begin{bmatrix} 2 & 3 \\ 5 & -4 \end{bmatrix}$

Glossary/Glosario

Glossary/Glosario

Glossary/Glosario

ENGLISH	SPANISH	EXAMPLES
combination A selection of a group of objects in which order is *not* important. The number of combinations of r objects chosen from a group of n objects is denoted $_nC_r$.	**combinación** Selección de un grupo de objetos en la cual el orden *no* es importante. El número de combinaciones de r objetos elegidos de un grupo de n objetos se expresa así: $_nC_r$.	For 4 objects A, B, C, and D, there are $_4C_2 = 6$ different combinations of 2 objects: AB, AC, AD, BC, BD, CD.
common difference In an arithmetic sequence, the nonzero constant difference of any term and the previous term.	**diferencia común** En una sucesión aritmética, diferencia constante distinta de cero entre cualquier término y el término anterior.	In the arithmetic sequence 3, 5, 7, 9, 11, …, the common difference is 2.
common logarithm A logarithm whose base is 10, denoted $\log_{10}$ or just log.	**logaritmo común** Logaritmo de base 10, que se expresa $\log_{10}$ o simplemente log.	$\log 100 = \log_{10} 100 = 2$, since $10^2 = 100$.
common ratio In a geometric sequence, the constant ratio of any term and the previous term.	**razón común** En una sucesión geométrica, la razón constante r entre cualquier término y el término anterior.	In the geometric sequence 32, 16,18, 4, 2 …, the common ratio is $\frac{1}{2}$.
complement of an event All outcomes in the sample space that are not in an event E, denoted $\bar{E}$.	**complemento de un suceso** Todos los resultados en el espacio muestral que no están en el suceso E y se expresan $\bar{E}$.	In the experiment of rolling a number cube, the complement of rolling a 3 is rolling a 1, 2, 4, 5, or 6.
completing the square A process used to form a perfect-square trinomial. To complete the square of $x^2 + bx$, add $\left(\frac{b}{2}\right)^2$.	**completar el cuadrado** Proceso utilizado para formar un trinomio cuadrado perfecto. Para completar el cuadrado de $x^2 + bx$, hay que sumar $\left(\frac{b}{2}\right)^2$.	$x^2 + 6x + \blacksquare$ Add $\left(\frac{6}{2}\right)^2 = 9$. $x^2 + 6x + 9$ $(x + 3)^2$ *is a perfect square.*
complex conjugate The complex conjugate of any complex number $a + bi$, denoted $\overline{a + bi}$, is $a - bi$.	**conjugado complejo** El conjugado complejo de cualquier número complejo $a + bi$, expresado como $\overline{a + bi}$, es $a - bi$.	$\overline{4 + 3i} = 4 - 3i$ $\overline{4 - 3i} = 4 + 3i$
complex fraction A fraction that contains one or more fractions in the numerator, the denominator, or both.	**fracción compleja** Fracción que contiene una o más fracciones en el numerador, en el denominador, o en ambos.	$\dfrac{\frac{1}{2}}{1 + \frac{2}{3}}$
complex number Any number that can be written as $a + bi$, where a and b are real numbers and $i = \sqrt{-1}$.	**número complejo** Todo número que se puede expresar como $a + bi$, donde a y b son números reales e $i = \sqrt{-1}$.	$4 + 2i$ $5 + 0i = 5$ $0 - 7i = -7i$
complex plane A set of coordinate axes in which the horizontal axis is the real axis and the vertical axis is the imaginary axis; used to graph complex numbers.	**plano complejo** Conjunto de ejes cartesianos en el cual el eje horizontal es el eje real y el eje vertical es el eje imaginario; se utiliza para representar gráficamente números complejos.	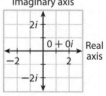

ENGLISH	SPANISH	EXAMPLES
composition of functions The composition of functions f and g, written as $(f \circ g)(x)$ and defined as $f(g(x))$ uses the output of $g(x)$ as the input for $f(x)$.	**composición de funciones** La composición de las funciones f y g, expresada como $(f \circ g)(x)$ y definida como $f(g(x))$ utiliza la salida de $g(x)$ como la entrada para $f(x)$.	If $f(x) = x^2$ and $g(x) = x + 1$, the composite function $(f \circ g)(x) = (x + 1)^2$.
compound event An event made up of two or more simple events.	**suceso compuesto** Suceso formado por dos o más sucesos simples.	In the experiment of tossing a coin and rolling a number cube, the event of the coin landing heads and the number cube landing on 3.
compound interest Interest earned or paid on both the principal and previously earned interest, found using the formula $A(t) = P\left(1 + \frac{r}{n}\right)^{nt}$ where A is the final amount, P is the principal, r is the interest rate given as a decimal, n is the number of times interest is compounded, and t is the time.	**interés compuesto** Interés ganado o pagado tanto sobre el capital inicial como sobre el interés previamente ganado. Se halla usando la fórmula $A(t) = P\left(1 + \frac{r}{n}\right)^{nt}$, donde A es la cantidad final, P es el capital inicial, r es la tasa de interés indicada en forma de número decimal, n es el número de veces que se reinvierte el interés y t es el tiempo.	
compression A transformation that pushes the points of a graph horizontally toward the y-axis or vertically toward the x-axis.	**compresión** Transformación que desplaza los puntos de una gráfica horizontalmente hacia el eje y o verticalmente hacia el eje x.	
conditional probability The probability of event B, given that event A has already occurred or is certain to occur, denoted $P(B \mid A)$; used to find probability of dependent events.	**probabilidad condicional** Probabilidad del suceso B, dado que el suceso A ya ha ocurrido o es seguro que ocurrirá, expresada como $P(B \mid A)$; se utiliza para calcular la probabilidad de sucesos dependientes.	
confidence interval An approximate range of values that is likely to include an unknown population parameter.	**intervalo de confianza** Un rango aproximado de valores que probablemente incluirá un parámetro de población desconocido.	
conic section A plane figure formed by the intersection of a double right cone and a plane. Examples include circles, ellipses, hyperbolas, and parabolas.	**sección cónica** Figura plana formada por la intersección de un cono regular doble y un plano. Algunos ejemplos son círculos, elipses, hipérbolas y parábolas.	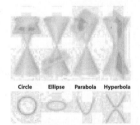 Circle Ellipse Parabola Hyperbola 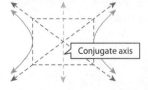
conjugate axis The axis of symmetry of a hyperbola that separates the two branches of the hyperbola.	**eje conjugado** Eje de simetría de una hipérbola que separa las dos ramas de la hipérbola.	Conjugate axis

ENGLISH	SPANISH	EXAMPLES
constraint One of the inequalities that define the feasible region in a linear-programming problem.	**restricción** Una de las desigualdades que definen la región factible en un problema de programación lineal.	Constraints: Feasible region $x > 0$ $y > 0$ $x + y \leq 8$ $3x + 5y \leq 30$ 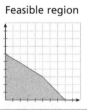
continuous function A function whose graph is an unbroken line or curve with no gaps or breaks.	**función continua** Función cuya gráfica es una línea recta o curva continua, sin espacios ni interrupciones.	
contradiction An equation that has no solutions.	**contradicción** Ecuación que no tiene soluciones.	$x + 1 = x$ $1 = 0 \: x$
correlation A measure of the strength and direction of the relationship between two variables or data sets.	**correlación** Medida de la fuerza y dirección de la relación entre dos variables o conjuntos de datos.	Positive correlation No correlation Negative correlation
correlation coefficient A number r, where $-1 \leq r \leq 1$, that describes how closely the points in a scatter plot cluster around the least–squares line.	**coeficiente de correlación** Número r, donde $-1 \leq r \leq 1$, que describe a qué distancia de la recta de mínimos cuadrados se agrupan los puntos de un diagrama de dispersión.	An r–value close to 1 describes a strong positive correlation. An r–value close to 0 describes a weak correlation or no correlation. An r–value close to -1 describes a strong negative correlation.
cosecant In a right triangle, the cosecant of angle A is the ratio of the length of the hypotenuse to the length of the side opposite A. It is the reciprocal of the sine function.	**cosecante** En un triángulo rectángulo, la cosecante del ángulo A es la razón entre la longitud de la hipotenusa y la longitud del cateto opuesto a A. Es la inversa de la función seno.	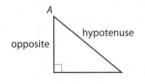 $\csc A = \dfrac{\text{hypotenuse}}{\text{opposite}} = \dfrac{1}{\sin A}$
cosine In a right triangle, the cosine of angle A is the ratio of the length of the side adjacent to angle A to the length of the hypotenuse. It is the reciprocal of the secant function.	**coseno** En un triángulo rectángulo, el coseno del ángulo A es la razón entre la longitud del cateto adyacente al ángulo A y la longitud de la hipotenusa. Es la inversa de la función secante.	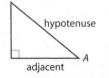 $\cos A = \dfrac{\text{adjacent}}{\text{hypotenuse}} = \dfrac{1}{\sec A}$

Glossary/Glosario

ENGLISH	SPANISH	EXAMPLES

cotangent In a right triangle, the cotangent of angle A is the ratio of the length of the side adjacent to A to the length of the side opposite A. It is the reciprocal of the tangent function.

cotangente En un triángulo rectángulo, la cotangente del ángulo A es la razón entre la longitud del cateto adyacente a A y la longitud del cateto opuesto a A. Es la inversa de la función tangente.

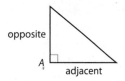

$$\cot A = \frac{\text{adjacent}}{\text{opposite}} = \frac{1}{\tan A}$$

---

coterminal angles Two angles in standard position with the same terminal side.

ángulos coterminales Dos ángulos en posición estándar con el mismo lado terminal.

---

critical values Values that separate the number line into intervals that either contain solutions or do not contain solutions.

valores críticos Valores que separan la recta numérica en intervalos que contienen o no contienen soluciones.

---

cube-root function The function $f(x) = \sqrt[3]{x}$.

función de raíz cúbica La función $f(x) = \sqrt[3]{x}$.

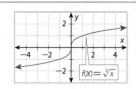

---

cubic function A polynomial function of degree 3.

función cúbica Función polinomial de grado 3.

---

cumulative probability The probability that a random variable is less than or equal to a given value.

probabilidad acumulada La probabilidad de que una variable aleatoria sea menor o igual que un valor determinado.

---

cycle of a periodic function The shortest repeating part of a periodic graph or function.

ciclo de una función periódica La parte repetida más corta de una gráfica o función periódica.

D

---

decay factor The base $1 - r$ in an exponential expression.

factor decremental Base $1 - r$ en una expresión exponencial.

$$2(0.93)^t$$

decay factor (representing $1 - 0.07$)

---

decay rate The constant percent decrease, in decimal form, in an exponential decay function.

tasa de disminución Disminución porcentual constante, en forma decimal, en una función de disminución exponencial.

In the function $f(t) = a(1 - 0.2)^t$, 0.2 is the decay rate.

Glossary/Glosario

ENGLISH	SPANISH	EXAMPLES
decreasing A function is decreasing on an interval if $f(x_1) > f(x_2)$ when $x_1 > x_2$ for any x-values x_1 and x_2 from the interval.	**decreciente** Una función es decreciente en un intervalo si $f(x_1) > f(x_2)$ cuando $x_1 > x_2$ dados los valores de x, x_1 y x_2, pertenecientes al intervalo.	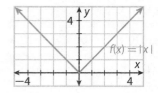 $f(x)$ is decreasing on the interval $x < 0$.
degree of a monomial The sum of the exponents of the variables in the monomial.	**grado de un monomio** Suma de los exponentes de las variables del monomio.	$4x^2y^5z^3$ Degree: $2 + 5 + 3 = 10$ 5 Degree: $0 \ (5 = 5x^0)$
degree of a polynomial The degree of the term of the polynomial with the greatest degree.	**grado de un polinomio** Grado del término del polinomio con el grado máximo.	$3x^2y^2 + 4xy^5 - 12x^3y^2$ Degree 6 Degree 4 Degree 6 Degree 5
dependent events Events for which the occurrence or nonoccurrence of one event affects the probability of the other event.	**sucesos dependientes** Dos sucesos son dependientes si el hecho de que uno de ellos se cumpla o no afecta la probabilidad del otro.	From a bag containing 3 red marbles and 2 blue marbles, drawing a red marble, and then drawing a blue marble without replacing the first marble.
dependent system A system of equations that has infinitely many solutions.	**sistema dependiente** Sistema de ecuaciones que tiene infinitamente muchas soluciones.	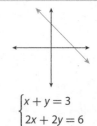 $\begin{cases} x + y = 3 \\ 2x + 2y = 6 \end{cases}$
difference of two squares A polynomial of the form $a^2 - b^2$, which may be written as the product $(a + b)(a - b)$.	**diferencia de dos cuadrados** Polinomio del tipo $a^2 - b^2$, que se puede expresar como el producto $(a + b)(a - b)$.	$x^2 - 4 = (x + 2)(x - 2)$
directrix A fixed line used to define a *parabola*. Every point on the parabola is equidistant from the directrix and a fixed point called the *focus*.	**directriz** Línea fija utilizada para definir una *parábola*. Cada punto de la parábola es equidistante de la directriz y de un punto fijo denominado *foco*.	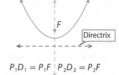 $P_1D_1 = P_1F$ $P_2D_2 = P_2F$
discontinuous function A function whose graph has one or more jumps, breaks, or holes.	**función discontinua** Función cuya gráfica tiene uno o más saltos, interrupciones u hoyos.	
discriminant The discriminant of the quadratic equation $ax^2 + bx + c = 0$ is $b^2 - 4ac$.	**discriminante** El discriminante de la ecuación cuadrática $ax^2 + bx + c = 0$ es $b^2 - 4ac$.	The discriminant of $2x^2 - 5x - 3 = 0$ is $(-5)^2 - 4(2)(-3) = 25 + 24 = 49$.
distribution A set of numerical data that you can graph using a data display that involves a number line, such as a line plot, histogram, or box plot.	**distribución** Un conjunto de datos numéricos que se pueden representar gráficamente mediante una representación de datos que incluye una recta numérica, como un diagrama de puntos, un histograma o un diagrama de cajas.	

Glossary/Glosario

E

ENGLISH	SPANISH	EXAMPLES
elementary row operations *See* row operations.	**operaciones elementales de fila** *Véase* operaciones de fila.	
elimination A method used to solve systems of equations in which one variable is eliminated by adding or subtracting two equations of the system.	**eliminación** Método utilizado para resolver sistemas de ecuaciones por el cual se elimina una variable sumando o restando dos ecuaciones del sistema.	
empty set A set with no elements.	**conjunto vacío** Conjunto sin elementos.	The solution set of $|x| < 0$ is the empty set, $\{\ \}$, or $\varnothing$.
end behavior The trends in the y-values of a function as the x-values approach positive and negative infinity.	**comportamiento extremo** Tendencia de los valores de y de una función a medida que los valores de x se aproximan al infinito positivo y negativo.	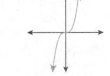 End behavior: $f(x) \rightarrow \infty$ as $x \rightarrow \infty$ $f(x) \rightarrow -\infty$ as $x \rightarrow -\infty$
even function A function in which $f(-x) = f(x)$ for all x in the domain of the function.	**función par** Función en la que para todos los valores de x dentro del dominio de la función.	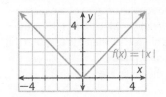 $f(x) = |x|$ is an even function.
event An outcome or set of outcomes in a probability experiment.	**suceso** Resultado o conjunto de resultados en un experimento de probabilidad.	In the experiment of rolling a number cube, the event "an odd number" consists of the outcomes 1, 3, and 5.
expected value The weighted average of the numerical outcomes of a probability experiment.	**valor esperado** Promedio ponderado de los resultados numéricos de un experimento de probabilidad.	The table shows the probability of getting a given score by guessing on a three-question quiz. | Score	0	1	2	3 | | --- | --- | --- | --- | --- | | Probability | 0.42 | 0.42 | 0.14 | 0.02 | The expected value is a score of $0\,(0.42) + 1\,(0.42) + 2\,(0.14) + 3\,(0.02) = 0.76.$
experiment An operation, process, or activity in which outcomes can be used to estimate probability.	**experimento** Una operación, proceso o actividad cuyo resultado se puede usar para estimar la probabilidad.	Tossing a coin 10 times and noting the number of heads.
experimental probability The ratio of the number of times an event occurs to the number of trials, or times, that an activity is performed.	**probabilidad experimental** Razón entre la cantidad de veces que ocurre un suceso y la cantidad de pruebas, o veces, que se realiza una actividad.	Kendra made 6 of 10 free throws. The experimental probability that she will make her next free throw is $P(\text{free throw}) = \dfrac{\text{number made}}{\text{number attempted}} = \dfrac{6}{10}.$

Glossary/Glosario

ENGLISH	SPANISH	EXAMPLES
explicit formula A formula that defines the nth term a_n, or general term, of a sequence as a function of n.	**fórmula explícita** Fórmula que define el enésimo término a_n, o término general, de una sucesión como una función de n.	Sequence: 4, 7, 10, 13, 16, 19, … Explicit formula: $a_n = 1 + 3n$
exponential decay An exponential function of the form $f(x) = ab^x$ in which $0 < b < 1$. If r is the rate of decay, then the function can be written $y = a(1 - r)^t$, where a is the initial amount and t is the time.	**decremento exponencial** Función exponencial del tipo $f(x) = ab^x$ en la cual $0 < b < 1$. Si r es la tasa decremental, entonces la función se puede expresar como $y = a(1 - r)^t$, donde a es la cantidad inicial y t es el tiempo.	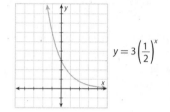 $y = 3\left(\frac{1}{2}\right)^x$
exponential equation An equation that contains one or more exponential expressions.	**ecuación exponencial** Ecuación que contiene una o más expresiones exponenciales.	$2^{x+1} = 8$
exponential function A function of the form $f(x) = ab^x$, where a and b are real numbers with $a \neq 0, b > 0$, and $b \neq 1$.	**función exponencial** Función del tipo $f(x) = ab^x$, donde a y b son números reales con $a \neq 0, b > 0$ y $b \neq 1$.	
exponential growth An exponential function of the form $f(x) = ab^x$ in which $b > 1$. If r is the rate of growth, then the function can be written $y = a(1 + r)^t$, where a is the initial amount and t is the time.	**crecimiento exponencial** Función exponencial del tipo $f(x) = ab^x$ en la que $b > 1$. Si r es la tasa de crecimiento, entonces la función se puede expresar como $y = a(1 + r)^t$, donde a es la cantidad inicial y t es el tiempo.	
exponential regression A statistical method used to fit an exponential model to a given data set.	**regresión exponencial** Método estadístico utilizado para ajustar un modelo exponencial a un conjunto de datos determinado.	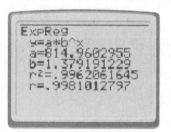
extraneous solution A solution of a derived equation that is not a solution of the original equation.	**solución extraña** Solución de una ecuación derivada que no es una solución de la ecuación original.	To solve $\sqrt{x} = -2$, square both sides; $x = 4$. **Check** $\sqrt{4} = -2$ is false; so 4 is an extraneous solution.

F

Factor Theorem For any polynomial $P(x)$, $(x - a)$ is a factor of $P(x)$ if and only if $P(a) = 0$.	**Teorema del factor** Dado el polinomio $P(x)$, $(x - a)$ es un factor de $P(x)$ si y sólo si $P(a) = 0$.	$(x - 1)$ is a factor of $P(x) = x^2 - 1$ because $P(1) = 1^2 - 1 = 0$.

Glossary/Glosario (sidebar)

ENGLISH	SPANISH	EXAMPLES
factorial If n is a positive integer, then n factorial, written $n!$, is $n \cdot (n-1) \cdot (n-2) \cdot \ldots \cdot 2 \cdot 1$. The factorial of 0 is defined to be 1.	**factorial** Si n es un entero positivo, entonces el factorial de n, expresado como $n!$, es $n \cdot (n-1) \cdot (n-2) \cdot \ldots \cdot 2 \cdot 1$ Por definición, el factorial de 0 será 1.	$7! = 7 \cdot 6 \cdot 5 \cdot 4 \cdot 3 \cdot 2 \cdot 1 = 5040$ $0! = 1$
Fibonacci sequence The infinite sequence of numbers beginning with 1, 1 such that each term is the sum of the two previous terms.	**sucesión de Fibonacci** Sucesión infinita de números que comienza con 1, 1 de forma tal que cada término es la suma de los dos términos anteriores.	1, 1, 2, 3, 5, 8, 13, 21, …
finite geometric series A geometric series in which the sum of a finite number of terms of a geometric sequence is found.	**serie geométrica finita** Una serie geométrica en la que se halla la suma de un número finito de términos de una secuencia geométrica.	
finite sequence A sequence with a finite number of terms.	**sucesión finita** Sucesión con un número finito de términos.	1, 2, 3, 4, 5
finite set A set with a definite, or finite, number of elements.	**conjunto finito** Conjunto con un número de elementos definido o finito.	$\{2, 4, 6, 8, 10\}$
first differences The differences between y-values of a function for evenly spaced x-values.	**primeras diferencias** Diferencias entre los valores de y de una función para valores de x espaciados uniformemente.	<table><tr><td>**x**</td><td>0</td><td>1</td><td>2</td><td>3</td></tr><tr><td>**y**</td><td>3</td><td>7</td><td>11</td><td>15</td></tr></table> first differences +4 +4 +4
focus (pl. foci) of a parabola A fixed point F used with a *directrix* to define a *parabola*.	**foco de una parábola** Punto fijo F utilizado con una *directriz* para definir una *parábola*.	
frequency of a data value The number of times the value appears in the data set.	**frecuencia de un valor de datos** Cantidad de veces que aparece el valor en un conjunto de datos.	In the data set 5, 6, 6, 6, 8, 9, the data value 6 has a frequency of 3.
frequency of a periodic function The number of cycles per unit of time. Also the reciprocal of the period.	**frecuencia de una función periódica** Cantidad de ciclos por unidad de tiempo. También es la inversa del periodo.	The function $y = \sin(2x)$ has a period of π and a frequency of $\frac{1}{\pi}$.
function rule An algebraic expression that defines a function.	**regla de función** Expresión algebraica que define una función.	$f(x) = 2x^2 + 3x - 7$ ↑ function rule

Glossary/Glosario

ENGLISH	SPANISH	EXAMPLES
Fundamental Counting Principle For n items, if there are m_1 ways to choose a first item, m_2 ways to choose a second item after the first item has been chosen, and so on, then there are $m_1 \cdot m_2 \cdot \ldots \cdot m_n$ ways to choose n items.	**Principio fundamental de conteo** Dados n elementos, si existen m_1 formas de elegir un primer elemento, m_2 formas de elegir un segundo elemento después de haber elegido el primero, y así sucesivamente, entonces existen $m_1 \cdot m_2 \cdot \ldots \cdot m_n$ formas de elegir n elementos.	If there are 4 colors of shirts, 3 colors of pants, and 2 colors of shoes, then there are $4 \cdot 3 \cdot 2 = 24$ possible outfits.

G

Gaussian Elimination An algorithm for solving systems of equations using matrices and row operations to eliminate variables in each equation in the system.	**Eliminación Gaussiana** Algoritmo para resolver sistemas de ecuaciones mediante matrices y operaciones de fila con el fin de eliminar variables en cada ecuación del sistema.	
general form of a conic section $Ax^2 + Bxy + Cy^2 + Dx + Ey + F = 0$, where A and B are not both 0.	**forma general de una sección cónica** $Ax^2 + Bxy + Cy^2 + Dx + Ey + F = 0$, donde A y B no son los dos 0.	A circle with a vertex at $(1, 2)$ and radius 3 has the general form $x^2 + y^2 - 2x - 4y - 4 = 0$.
geometric mean In a geometric sequence, a term that comes between two given nonconsecutive terms of the sequence. For positive numbers a and b, the geometric mean is $\sqrt{ab}$.	**media geométrica** En una sucesión geométrica, un término que se encuentra entre dos términos no consecutivos dados de la sucesión. Dados los números positivos a y b, la media geométrica es $\sqrt{ab}$.	The geometric mean of 4 and 9 is $\sqrt{4(9)} = \sqrt{36} = 6$.
geometric probability A form of theoretical probability determined by a ratio of geometric measures such as lengths, areas, or volumes.	**probabilidad geométrica** Una forma de la probabilidad teórica determinada por una razón de medidas geométricas, como longitud, área o volumen.	 The probability of the pointer landing the 80° angle is $\frac{2}{9}$.
geometric sequence A sequence in which the ratio of successive terms is a constant r, called the common ratio, where $r \neq 0$ and $r \neq 1$.	**sucesión geométrica** Sucesión en la que la razón de los términos sucesivos es una constante r, denominada razón común, donde $r \neq 0$ y $r \neq 1$.	$1, \quad 2, \quad 4, \quad 8, \quad 16, \quad \ldots$ $\cdot 2 \ \cdot 2 \ \cdot 2 \ \cdot 2 \qquad r = 2$
geometric series The indicated sum of the terms of a geometric sequence.	**serie geométrica** Suma indicada de los términos de una sucesión geométrica.	$1 + 2 + 4 + 8 + 16 + \ldots$

ENGLISH	SPANISH	EXAMPLES

greatest-integer function
A function denoted by $f(x) = [x]$ or $f(x) = \lfloor x \rfloor$ in which the number x is rounded down to the greatest integer that is less than or equal to x.

función de entero mayor
Función expresada como $f(x) = [x]$ o $f(x) = \lfloor x \rfloor$ en la cual el número x se redondea hacia abajo hasta el entero mayor que sea menor que o igual a x.

$\lfloor 4.98 \rfloor = 4$
$\lfloor -2.1 \rfloor = -3$

---

growth factor The base $1 + r$ in an exponential expression.

factor de crecimiento La base $1 + r$ en una expresión exponencial.

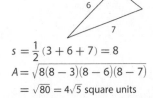
$12{,}000(1 + 0.14)^t$
growth factor

---

growth rate The constant percent increase, in decimal form, in an exponential growth function.

tasa de crecimiento Aumento porcentual constante, en forma decimal, en una función de crecimiento exponencial.

In the function $f(t) = a(1 + 0.3)^t$, 0.3 is the growth rate.

H

Heron's Formula A triangle with side lengths a, b, and c has area $A = \sqrt{s(s-a)(s-b)(s-c)}$, where s is one-half the perimeter, or $s = \frac{1}{2}(a + b + c)$.

fórmula de Herón Un triángulo con longitudes de lado a, b y c tiene un área $A = \sqrt{s(s-a)(s-b)(s-c)}$, donde s es la mitad del perímetro ó $s = \frac{1}{2}(a + b + c)$.

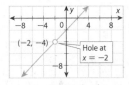
$s = \frac{1}{2}(3 + 6 + 7) = 8$
$A = \sqrt{8(8-3)(8-6)(8-7)}$
$= \sqrt{80} = 4\sqrt{5}$ square units

---

hole (in a graph) An omitted point on a graph. If a rational function has the same factor $x - b$ in both the numerator and the denominator, and the line $x = b$ is not a vertical asymptote, then there is a hole in the graph at the point where $x = b$.

hoyo (en una gráfica) Punto omitido en una gráfica. Si una función racional tiene el mismo factor $x - b$ tanto en el numerador como en el denominador, y la línea $x = b$ no es una asíntota vertical, entonces hay un hoyo en la gráfica en el punto donde $x = b$.

$f(x) = \dfrac{(x-2)(x+2)}{(x+2)}$ has a hole at $x = -2$.

$(-2, -4)$ Hole at $x = -2$

---

hypothesis testing A type of testing used to determine whether the difference in two groups is likely to be caused by chance.

comprobación de hipótesis Tipo de comprobación que sirve para determinar si el azar es la causa probable de la diferencia entre dos grupos.

I

imaginary axis The vertical axis in the complex plane, it graphically represents the purely imaginary part of complex numbers.

eje imaginario Eje vertical de un plano complejo. Representa gráficamente la parte puramente imaginaria de los números complejos.

Glossary/Glosario

ENGLISH	SPANISH	EXAMPLES

imaginary number The square root of a negative number, written in the form bi, where b is a real number and i is the imaginary unit, $\sqrt{-1}$. Also called a *pure imaginary number*.

número imaginario Raíz cuadrada de un número negativo, expresado como bi, donde b es un número real e i es la unidad imaginaria, $\sqrt{-1}$. También se denomina *número imaginario puro*.

$$\sqrt{-16} = \sqrt{16} \cdot \sqrt{-1} = 4i$$

---

imaginary unit The unit in the imaginary number system, $\sqrt{-1}$.

unidad imaginaria Unidad del sistema de números imaginarios, $\sqrt{-1}$.

$$\sqrt{-1} = i$$

---

inconsistent system A system of equations or inequalities that has no solution.

sistema inconsistente Sistema de ecuaciones o desigualdades que no tiene solución.

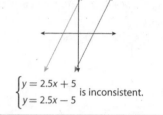

$\begin{cases} y = 2.5x + 5 \\ y = 2.5x - 5 \end{cases}$ is inconsistent.

Increasing A function is increasing on an interval if $f(x_1) < f(x_2)$ when $x_1 < x_2$ for any x-values x_1 and x_2 from the interval.

creciente Una función es creciente en un intervalo si $f(x_1) < f(x_2)$ cuando $x_1 < x_2$ dados los valores de x, x_1 y x_2, pertenecienlos al intervalo.

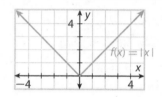

$f(x)$ is increasing on the interval $x > 0$.

---

independent events Events for which the occurrence or non-occurrence of one event does not affect the probability of the other event.

sucesos independientes Dos sucesos son independientes si el hecho de que se produzca o no uno de ellos no afecta la probabilidad del otro suceso.

From a bag containing 3 red marbles and 2 blue marbles, drawing a red marble, replacing it, and then drawing a blue marble.

---

independent system A system of equations that has exactly one solution.

sistema independiente Sistema de ecuaciones que tiene exactamente una solución.

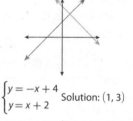

$\begin{cases} y = -x + 4 \\ y = x + 2 \end{cases}$ Solution: $(1, 3)$

---

independent variable The input of a function; a variable whose value determines the value of the output, or dependent variable.

variable independiente Entrada de una función; variable cuyo valor determina el valor de la salida, o variable dependiente.

$y = 2x + 1$

independent variable

---

initial side The ray that lies on the positive x-axis when an angle is drawn in standard position.

lado inicial El rayo que se encuentra en el eje positivo x cuando se traza un ángulo en la posición estándar.

Terminal side 135° 45° x 0 Initial side

Glossary/Glosario

GL14

Glossary/Glosario

ENGLISH	SPANISH	EXAMPLES

interval notation A way of writing the set of all real numbers between two endpoints. The symbols [and] are used to include an endpoint in an interval, and the symbols (and) are used to exclude an endpoint from an interval.

notación de intervalo Forma de expresar el conjunto de todos los números reales entre dos extremos. Los símbolos [y] se utilizan para incluir un extremo en un intervalo y los símbolos (y) se utilizan para excluir un extremo de un intervalo.

Interval notation	Set-builder notation
(a, b)	$\{x \mid a < x < b\}$
$(a, b]$	$\{x \mid a < x \leq b\}$
$[a, b)$	$\{x \mid a \leq x < b\}$
$[a, b]$	$\{x \mid a \leq x \leq b\}$

inverse function The function that results from exchanging the input and output values of a one-to-one function. The inverse of $f(x)$ is denoted $f^{-1}(x)$.

función inversa Función que resulta de intercambiar los valores de entrada y salida de una función uno a uno. La función inversa de $f(x)$ se expresa $f^{-1}(x)$

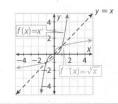

inverse relation The inverse of the relation consisting of all ordered pairs (x, y) is the set of all ordered pairs (y, x). The graph of an inverse relation is the reflection of the graph of the relation across the line $y = x$.

relación inversa La inversa de la relación que consta de todos los pares ordenados (x, y) es el conjunto de todos los pares ordenados (y, x). La gráfica de una relación inversa es el reflejo de la gráfica de la relación sobre la línea $y = x$.

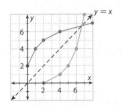

irreducible factor A factor of degree 2 or greater that cannot be factored further.

factor irreducible Factor de grado 2 o mayor que no se puede seguir factorizando.

$x^2 + 7x + 1$

J

joint relative frequency The ratio of the frequency in a particular category divided by the total number of data values.

frecuencia relativa conjunta La razón de la frecuencia en una determinada categoría dividida entre el número total de valores.

L

Law of Cosines For $\triangle ABC$ with side lengths a, b, and c,
$a^2 = b^2 + c^2 - 2bc \cos A$
$b^2 = a^2 + c^2 - 2ac \cos B$
$c^2 = a^2 + b^2 - 2ab \cos C$.

Ley de cosenos Dado $\triangle ABC$ con longitudes de lado a, b y c,
$a^2 = b^2 + c^2 - 2bc \cos A$
$b^2 = a^2 + c^2 - 2ac \cos B$
$c^2 = a^2 + b^2 - 2ab \cos C$

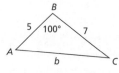

$b^2 = 7^2 + 5^2 - 2(7)(5)\cos 100°$
$b^2 \approx 86.2$
$b \approx 9.3$

Law of Sines For $\triangle ABC$ with side lengths a, b, and c,
$\frac{\sin A}{a} = \frac{\sin B}{b} = \frac{\sin C}{c}$.

Ley de senos Dado $\triangle ABC$ con longitudes de lado a, b y c,
$\frac{sen A}{a} = \frac{sen B}{b} = \frac{sen C}{c}$.

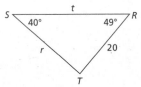

$\frac{\sin 49°}{r} = \frac{\sin 40°}{20}$
$r = \frac{20 \sin 49°}{\sin 40°} \approx 23.5$

ENGLISH	SPANISH	EXAMPLES
leading coefficient The coefficient of the first term of a polynomial in standard form.	**coeficiente principal** Coeficiente del primer termino de un polinomio en forma estandar	$3x^2 + 7x - 2$ ↑ Leading coefficient
limit For an infinite arithmetic series that converges, the number that the partial sums approach.	**límite** Para un serie que coverge, el número que se aproximan las sumas.	The series $\frac{1}{2} + \frac{1}{4} + \frac{1}{8} + \frac{1}{16} + \ldots$ has a limit of 1.
line of best fit The line that comes closest to all of the points in a data set.	**línea de mejor ajuste** Línea que más se acerca a todos los puntos de un conjunto de datos.	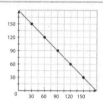
linear equation in three variables An equation with three distinct variables, each of which is either first degree or has a coefficient of zero.	**ecuación lineal en tres variables** Ecuación con tres variables diferentes, sean de primer grado o tengan un coeficiente de cero.	$5 = 3x + 2y + 6z$
linear regression A statistical method used to fit a linear model to a given data set.	**regresión lineal** Método estadístico utilizado para ajustar un modelo lineal a un conjunto de datos determinado.	
linear system A system of equations containing only linear equations.	**sistema lineal** Sistema de ecuaciones que contiene sólo ecuaciones lineales.	$\begin{cases} y = 2x + 1 \\ x + y = 8 \end{cases}$
local maximum For a function f, $f(a)$ is a local maximum if there is an interval around a such that $f(x) < f(a)$ for every x-value in the interval except a.	**máximo local** Dada una función f, $f(a)$ es el máximo local si hay un intervalo en a tal que $f(x) < f(a)$ para cada valor de x en el intervalo excepto a.	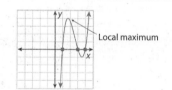
local minimum For a function f, $f(a)$ is a local minimum if there is an interval around a such that $f(x) > f(a)$ for every x-value in the interval except a.	**mínimo local** Dada una función f, $f(a)$ es el mínimo local si hay un intervalo en a tal que $f(x) > f(a)$ para cada valor de x en el intervalo excepto a.	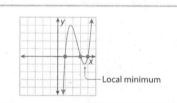
logarithm The exponent that a specified base must be raised to in order to get a certain value.	**logaritmo** Exponente al cual debe elevarse una base determinada a fin de obtener cierto valor.	$\log_2 8 = 3$, because 3 is the power that 2 is raised to in order to get 8; or $2^3 = 8$.
logarithmic equation An equation that contains a logarithm of a variable.	**ecuación logarítmica** Ecuación que contiene un logaritmo de una variable.	$\log x + 3 = 7$

ENGLISH	SPANISH	EXAMPLES

logarithmic function A function of the form $f(x) = \log_b x$, where $b \neq 1$ and $b > 0$, which is the inverse of the exponential function $f(x) = b^x$.

función logarítmica Función del tipo $f(x) = \log_b x$, donde $b \neq 1$ y $b > 0$, que es la inversa de la función exponencial $f(x) = b^x$.

$f(x) = \log_4 x$

logarithmic regression A statistical method used to fit a logarithmic model to a given data set.

regresión logarítmica Método estadístico utilizado para ajustar un modelo logarítmico a un conjunto de datos determinado.

M

margin of error In a random sample, it defines an interval, centered on the sample percent, in which the population percent is most likely to lie.

margen de error En una muestra aleatoria, define un intervalo, centrado en el porcentaje de muestra, en el que es más probable que se encuentre el porcentaje de población.

matrix A rectangular array of numbers.

matriz Arreglo rectangular de números.

$$\begin{bmatrix} 1 & 0 & 3 \\ -2 & 2 & -5 \\ 7 & -6 & 3 \end{bmatrix}$$

maximum value of a function The y-value of the highest point on the graph of the function.

máximo de una función Valor de y del punto más alto en la gráfica de la función.

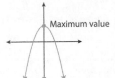

midline For the graph of a sine or cosine function, the horizontal line halfway between the maximum and minimum values of the curve; for the graph of a tangent function, the horizontal line through the point of each cycle that is midway between the asymptotes.

línea media En la gráfica de una función seno o coseno, la línea horizontal a medio camino entre los valores máximo y mínimo de la curva; en la gráfica de una función tangente, la línea horizontal que atraviesa el punto de cada ciclo que está a medio camino entre las asíntotas.

minimum value of a function The y-value of the lowest point on the graph of the function.

mínimo de una función Valor de y del punto más bajo en la gráfica de la función.

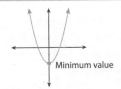

monomial A number or a product of numbers and variables with whole-number exponents, or a polynomial with one term.

monomio Número o producto de números y variables con exponentes de números cabales, o polinomio con un término.

$8x$, 9, $3x^2y^4$

Glossary/Glosario

Glossary/Glosario

ENGLISH	SPANISH	EXAMPLES
multiple root A root r is a multiple root when the factor $(x - r)$ appears in the equation more than once.	**raíz múltiple** Una raíz r es una raíz múltiple cuando el factor $(x - r)$ aparece en la ecuación más de una vez.	3 is a multiple root of $P(x) = (x - 3)^2$.
multiplicity If a polynomial $P(x)$ has a multiple root at r, the multiplicity of r is the number of times $(x - r)$ appears as a factor in $P(x)$.	**multiplicidad** Si un polinomio $P(x)$ tiene una raíz múltiple en r, la multiplicidad de r es la cantidad de veces que $(x - r)$ aparece como factor en $P(x)$.	For $P(x) = (x - 3)^2$, the root 3 has a multiplicity of 2.
mutually exclusive events Two events are mutually exclusive if they cannot both occur in the same trial of an experiment.	**sucesos mutuamente excluyentes** Dos sucesos son mutuamente excluyentes si ambos no pueden ocurrir en la misma prueba de un experimento.	In the experiment of rolling a number cube, rolling a 3 and rolling an even number are mutually exclusive events.

N

ENGLISH	SPANISH	EXAMPLES
natural logarithm A logarithm with base e, written as ln.	**logaritmo natural** Logaritmo con base e, que se escribe ln.	$\ln 5 = \log_e 5 \approx 1.6$
natural logarithmic function The function $f(x) = \ln x$, which is the inverse of the natural exponential function $f(x) = e^x$. Domain is $\{x \mid x > 0\}$; range is all real numbers	**función logarítmica natural** Función $f(x) = \ln x$, que es la inversa de la función exponencial natural $f(x) = e^x$. El dominio es $\{x \mid x > 0\}$; el rango es todos los números reales.	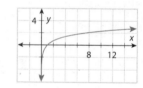
nonlinear system of equations A system in which at least one of the equations is not linear.	**sistema no lineal de ecuaciones** Sistema en el cual por lo menos una de las ecuaciones no es lineal.	$\begin{cases} y = 2x^2 \\ y = -3^2 + 5 \end{cases}$
normal distribution A distribution that is mounded in the middle with symmetric "tails" at each end, forming a bell shape.	**distribución normal** Una distribución que está elevada en el centro con "colas" simétricas en los extremos, lo que forma la figura de una campana.	
nth root The nth root of a number a, written as $\sqrt[n]{a}$ or $a^{\frac{1}{n}}$, is a number that is equal to a when it is raised to the nth power.	**enésima raíz** La enésima raíz de un número a, que se escribe como $\sqrt[n]{a}$ o $a^{\frac{1}{n}}$, es un número igual a a cuando se eleva a la enésima potencia.	$\sqrt[5]{32} = 2$, because $2^5 = 32$.
null hypothesis The assumption made that any difference between the control group and the treatment group in an experiment is due to chance, and not to the treatment.	**hipótesis nula** La suposición de que cualquier diferencia entre el grupo de control y el grupo de tratamiento en un experimento se debe al azar, no al tratamiento.	

ENGLISH	SPANISH	EXAMPLES

numerical data Data that represent quantities or observations that can be measured.

datos numéricos Datos que representan cantidades u observaciones que pueden medirse.

O

observational study A study that observes individuals and measures variables without controlling the individuals or their environment in any way.

estudio de observación Estudio que permite observar a individuos y medir variables sin controlar a los individuos ni su ambiente.

odd function A function in which $f(-x) = -f(x)$ for all x in the domain of the function.

función impar Función en la que $f(-x) = -f(x)$ para todos los valores de x dentro del dominio de la función

$f(x) = x^3$

$f(x) = x^3$ is an odd function.

one-to-one function A function in which each y-value corresponds to only one x-value. The inverse of a one-to-one function is also a function.

función uno a uno Función en la que cada valor de y corresponde a sólo un valor de x. La inversa de una función uno a uno es también una función.

ordered triple A set of three numbers that can be used to locate a point (x, y, z) in a three-dimensional coordinate system.

tripleta ordenada Conjunto de tres números que se pueden utilizar para ubicar un punto (x, y, z) en un sistema de coordenadas tridimensional.

$(2, -1, 3)$

overlapping events Events in the sample space of a probability experiment that have one or more outcomes in common.

eventos solapados Eventos en el espacio muestral de un experimento de probabilidad que tienen uno o más resultados en común.

P

parabola The shape of the graph of a quadratic function. Also, the set of points equidistant from a point F, called the focus, and a line d, called the *directrix*.

parábola Forma de la gráfica de una función cuadrática. También, conjunto de puntos equidistantes de un punto F, denominado *foco*, y una línea d, denominada *directriz*.

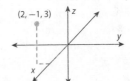
Focus
Directrix

parameter One of the constants in a function or equation that may be changed. Also the third variable in a set of parametric equations.

parámetro Una de las constantes en una función o ecuación que se puede cambiar. También es la tercera variable en un conjunto de ecuaciones paramétricas.

$y = (x - h)^2 + k$
parameters

parent cube root function The function $f(x) = \sqrt[3]{x}$.

función madre de la raíz cúbica Función del tipo $f(x) = \sqrt[3]{x}$.

$f(x) = \sqrt[3]{x}$

parent function The simplest function with the defining characteristics of the family. Functions in the same family are transformations of their parent function.

función madre La función más básica con las características de la familia. Las funciones de la misma familia son transformaciones de su función madre.

$f(x) = x^2$ is the parent function for $g(x) = x^2 + 4$ and $h(x) = 5(x + 2)^2 - 3$.

---

parent square root function The function $f(x) = \sqrt{x}$, where $x \geq 0$.

función madre de la raíz cuadrada Función del tipo $f(x) = \sqrt{x}$, donde $x \geq 0$.

$f(x) = \sqrt{x}$

---

partial sum Indicated by $S_n = \sum_{i=1}^{n} a_i$, the sum of a specified number of terms n of a sequence whose total number of terms is greater than n.

suma parcial Expresada por $S_n = \sum_{i=1}^{n} a_i$, la suma de un número específico n de términos de una sucesión cuyo número total de términos es mayor que n.

For the sequence $a_n = n^2$, the fourth partial sum of the infinite series $\sum_{k=1}^{\infty} k^2$ is

$$\sum_{k=1}^{4} k^2 = 1^2 + 2^2 + 3^2 + 4^2 = 30.$$

Pascal's triangle A triangular arrangement of numbers in which every row starts and ends with 1 and each other number is the sum of the two numbers above it.

triángulo de Pascal Arreglo triangular de números en el cual cada fila comienza y termina con 1 y cada uno de los demás números es la suma de los dos números que están encima de él.

```
        1
      1   1
    1   2   1
  1   3   3   1
1   4   6   4   1
```

---

perfect-square trinomial A trinomial whose factored form is the square of a binomial. A perfect-square trinomial has the form $a^2 - 2ab + b^2 = (a - b)^2$ or $a^2 + 2ab + b^2 = (a + b)^2$.

trinomio cuadrado perfecto Trinomio cuya forma factorizada es el cuadrado de un binomio. Un trinomio cuadrado perfecto tiene la forma $a^2 - 2ab + b^2 = (a - b)^2$ o $a^2 + 2ab + b^2 = (a + b)^2$.

$x^2 + 6x + 9$ is a perfect square trinomial, because $x^2 + 6x + 9 = (x + 3)^2$.

---

period of a periodic function The length of a cycle measured in units of the independent variable (usually time in seconds). Also the reciprocal of the frequency.

periodo de una función periódica Longitud de un ciclo medido en unidades de la variable independiente (generalmente el tiempo en segundos). También es la inversa de la frecuencia.

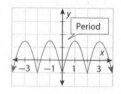

---

periodic function A function that repeats exactly in regular intervals, called *periods*.

función periódica Función que se repite exactamente a intervalos regulares denominados *periodos*.

---

permutation An arrangement of a group of objects in which order is important. The number of permutations of r objects from a group of n objects is denoted $_nP_r$.

permutación Arreglo de un grupo de objetos en el cual el orden es importante. El número de permutaciones de r objetos de un grupo de n objetos se expresa $_nP_r$.

For 4 objects A, B, C, and D, there are $_4P_2 = 12$ different permutations of 2 objects: AB, AC, AD, BC, BD, CD, BA, CA, DA, CB, DB, and DC.

ENGLISH	SPANISH	EXAMPLES

permutation test A significance test performed on the results of an experiment by forming every possible regrouping of all the data values taken from the control and treatment groups into two new groups, finding the distribution of the differences of the means for all of the new group pairings, and then finding the likelihood, given that the null hypothesis is true, of getting a difference of means at least as great as the original experimental difference.

prueba de permutación Una prueba de significancia realizada sobre los resultados de un experimento al formar todos los reagrupamientos posibles de todos los valores de datos tomados de los grupos de control y de tratamiento en dos nuevos grupos, hallar la distribución de las diferencias de las medias para todos los emparejamientos nuevos, y luego hallar la probabilidad, suponiendo que la hipótesis nula es verdadera, de obtener una diferencia de medias al menos tan grande como la diferencia experimental original.

---

phase shift A horizontal translation of a periodic function.

cambio de fase Traslación horizontal de una función periódica.

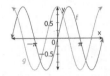

g is a phase shift of f $\frac{\pi}{2}$ units left.

---

piecewise function A function that is a combination of one or more functions.

función a trozos Función que es una combinación de una o más funciones.

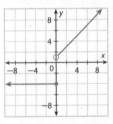

$$f(x) = \begin{cases} -4 & \text{if } x \le 0 \\ x+1 & \text{if } x > 0 \end{cases}$$

---

polynomial A monomial or a sum or difference of monomials.

polinomio Monomio o suma o diferencia de monomios.

$2x^2 + 3x - 7$

---

polynomial function A function whose rule is a polynomial.

función polinomial Función cuya regla es un polinomio.

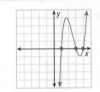

$f(x) = x^3 - 8x^2 + 19x - 12$

---

polynomial identity A mathematical relationship equating one polynomial quantity to another.

identidad de polinomios Relación matemática que iguala una cantidad polinomial con otra.

$(x^4 - y^4) = (x^2 + y^2)(x^2 - y^2)$

---

population The entire group of objects or individuals considered for a survey.

población Grupo completo de objetos o individuos que se desea estudiar.

In a survey about the study habits of high school students, the population is all high school students.

---

probability A number from 0 to 1 (or 0% to 100%) that is the measure of how likely an event is to occur.

probabilidad Número entre 0 y 1 (o entre 0% y 100%) que describe cuán probable es que ocurra un suceso.

A bag contains 3 red marbles and 4 blue marbles. The probability of choosing a red marble is $\frac{3}{7}$.

ENGLISH	SPANISH	EXAMPLES

probability distribution for an experiment The function that pairs each outcome with its probability.

distribución de probabilidad para un experimento Función que asigna a cada resultado su probabilidad.

A number cube is rolled 10 times. The results are shown in the table.

Outcome	1	2	3	4	5	6
Probability	$\frac{1}{10}$	$\frac{1}{5}$	$\frac{1}{5}$	0	$\frac{3}{10}$	$\frac{1}{5}$

probability sample A sample in which every member of the population being sampled has a nonzero probability of being selected.

muestra de probabilidad Muestra en la que cada miembro de la población que se estudia tiene una probabilidad distinta de cero de ser elegido.

pure imaginary number *See* imaginary number.

número imaginario puro Ver número imaginario.

$3i$

Q

quadratic equation An equation that can be written in the form $ax^2 + bx + c = 0$, where a, b, and c are real numbers and $a \neq 0$.

ecuación cuadrática Ecuación que se puede expresar como $ax^2 + bx + c = 0$, donde a, b y c son números reales y $a \neq 0$.

$x^2 + 3x - 4 = 0$
$x^2 - 9 = 0$

Quadratic Formula The formula $x = \frac{-b \pm \sqrt{b^2 - 4ac}}{2a}$, which gives solutions, or roots, of equations in the form $ax^2 + bx + c = 0$, where $a \neq 0$.

fórmula cuadrática La fórmula $x = \frac{-b \pm \sqrt{b^2 - 4ac}}{2a}$, que da soluciones, o raíces, para las ecuaciones del tipo $ax^2 + bx + c = 0$, donde $a \neq 0$.

The solutions of $2x^2 - 5x - 3 = 0$ are given by
$$x = \frac{-(-5) \pm \sqrt{(-5)^2 - 4(2)(-3)}}{2(2)}$$
$$= \frac{5 \pm \sqrt{25 + 24}}{4} = \frac{5 \pm 7}{4};$$
$x = 3$ or $x = -\frac{1}{2}$.

quadratic function A function that can be written in the form $f(x) = ax^2 + bx + c$, where a, b, and c are real numbers and $a \neq 0$, or in the form $f(x) = a(x - h)^2 + k$, where a, h, and k are real numbers and $a \neq 0$.

función cuadrática Función que se puede expresar como $f(x) = ax^2 + bx + c$, donde a, b y c son números reales y $a \neq 0$, o como $f(x) = a(x - h)^2 + k$, donde a, h y k son números reales y $a \neq 0$.

$f(x) = x^2 - 6x + 8$

quadratic model A quadratic function used to represent a set of data.

modelo cuadrático Función cuadrática que se utiliza para representar un conjunto de datos.

x	4	6	8	10
$f(x)$	27	52	89	130

A quadratic model for the data is $f(x) = x^2 + 3.3x - 2.6$.

quadratic regression A statistical method used to fit a quadratic model to a given data set.

regresión cuadrática Método estadístico utilizado para ajustar un modelo cuadrático a un conjunto de datos determinado.

R

radian A unit of angle measure based on arc length. In a circle of radius r, if a central angle has a measure of 1 radian, then the length of the intercepted arc is r units.

2π radians $= 360°$
1 radian $\approx 57°$

radián Unidad de medida de un ángulo basada en la longitud del arco. En un círculo de radio r, si un ángulo central mide 1 radián, entonces la longitud del arco abarcado es r unidades.

2π radianes $= 360°$
1 radián $\approx 57°$

radical An indicated root of a quantity.

radical Raíz indicada de una cantidad.

$\sqrt{36} = 6,\ \sqrt[3]{27} = 3$

radical equation An equation that contains a variable within a radical.

ecuación radical Ecuación que contiene una variable dentro de un radical.

$\sqrt{x+3} + 4 = 7$

radical function A function whose rule contains a variable within a radical.

función radical Función cuya regla contiene una variable dentro de un radical.

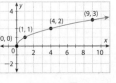

$f(x) = \sqrt{x}$

radicand The expression under a radical sign.

radicando Número o expresión debajo del signo de radical.

$\underset{\text{Radicand}}{\sqrt{x+3}} - 2$

random variable A variable whose value is determined by the outcome of a probability experiment.

variable aleatoria Una variable cuyo valor viene determinado por el resultado de un experimento de probabilidad.

randomized comparative experiment An experiment in which the individuals are assigned to the control group or the treatment group at random, in order to minimize bias.

experimento comparativo aleatorizado Experimento en el que se elige al azar a los individuos para el grupo de control o para el grupo experimental, a fin de minimizar el sesgo.

range of a function or relation The set of output values of a function or relation.

rango de una función o relación Conjunto de los valores desalida de una función o relación.

The range of $y = x^2$ is $\left\{ y \mid y \geq 0 \right\}$.

rational equation An equation that contains one or more rational expressions.

ecuación racional Ecuación que contiene una o más expresiones racionales.

$\dfrac{x+2}{x^2 + 3x - 1} = 6$

rational exponent An exponent that can be expressed as $\frac{m}{n}$ such that if m and n are integers, then $b^{\frac{m}{n}} = \sqrt[n]{b^m} = \left(\sqrt[n]{b}\right)^m$.

exponente racional Exponente quese puede expresar como $\frac{m}{n}$ tal que, si m y n son números enteros, entonces
$b^{\frac{m}{n}} = \sqrt[n]{b^m} = \left(\sqrt[n]{b}\right)^m$

$4^{\frac{2}{2}} = \sqrt{4^3} = \sqrt{64} = 8$
$4^{\frac{2}{2}} = \left(\sqrt{4}\right)^3 = 2^3 = 8$

Glossary/Glosario

Glossary/Glosario

ENGLISH	SPANISH	EXAMPLES
rational expression An algebraic expression whose numerator and denominator are polynomials and whose denominator has a degree ≥ 1.	**expresión racional** Expresión algebraica cuyo numerador y denominador son polinomios y cuyo denominador tiene un grado ≥ 1.	$\dfrac{x+2}{x^2+3x-1}$
rational function A function whose rule can be written as a rational expression.	**función racional** Función cuya regla se puede expresar como una expresión racional.	$f(x) = \dfrac{x+2}{x^2+3x-1}$
real axis The horizontal axis in the complex plane; it graphically represents the real part of complex numbers.	**eje real** Eje horizontal de un plano complejo. Representa gráficamente la parte real de los números complejos.	
recursive rule A rule for a sequence in which one or more previous terms are used to generate the next term.	**Regla recurrente** Regla para una sucesión en la cual uno o más términos anteriores se utilizan para generar el término siguiente.	For the sequence 5, 7, 9, 11, ..., a recursive rule is $a_1 = 5$ and $a_n = a_{n-1} + 2$.
reduced row-echelon form A form of an augmented matrix in which the coefficient columns form an identity matrix.	**forma escalonada reducida por filas** Forma de matriz aumentada en la que las columnas de coeficientes forman una matriz de identidad.	$\begin{bmatrix} 1 & 0 & \vdots & -1 \\ 0 & 1 & \vdots & 3 \end{bmatrix}$
reference angle For an angle in standard position, the reference angle is the positive acute angle formed by the terminal side of the angle and the x-axis.	**ángulo de referencia** Dado un ángulo en posición estándar, el ángulo de referencia es el ángulo agudo positivo formado por el lado terminal del ángulo y el eje x.	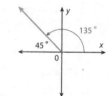
reflection A transformation that reflects, or "flips," a graph or figure across a line, called the line of reflection, such that each reflected point is the same distance from the line of reflection but is on the opposite side of the line.	**reflexión** Transformación que refleja, o invierte, una gráfica o figura sobre una línea, llamada la línea de reflexión, de manera tal que cada punto reflejado esté a la misma distancia de la línea de reflexión pero que se encuentre en el lado opuesto de la línea.	
regression The statistical study of the relationship between variables.	**regresión** Estudio estadístico de la relación entre variables.	
Remainder Theorem If the polynomial function $P(x)$ is divided by $x - a$, then the remainder r is $P(a)$.	**Teorema del resto** Si la función polinomial $P(x)$ se divide entre $x - a$, entonces, el residuo r será $P(a)$.	
representative sample A sample that is a good estimator for its corresponding population parameter.	**muestra representativa** Una muestra que es un buen estimador para su parámetro de población correspondiente.	

Glossary/Glosario

ENGLISH	SPANISH	EXAMPLES
rotation A transformation that rotates or turns a figure about a point called the center of rotation.	**rotación** Transformación que hace rotar o girar una figura sobre un punto llamado centro de rotación.	

row operation An operation performed on a row of an augmented matrix that creates an equivalent matrix.

operación por filas Operación realizada en una fila de una matriz aumentada que crea una matriz equivalente.

$$\begin{bmatrix} 2 & 0 & \vdots & -2 \\ 0 & 1 & \vdots & 3 \end{bmatrix} = \begin{bmatrix} \frac{1}{2}(2) & \frac{1}{2}(0) & \vdots & \frac{1}{2}(-2) \\ 0 & 1 & \vdots & 3 \end{bmatrix}$$
$$= \begin{bmatrix} 1 & 0 & \vdots & -1 \\ 0 & 1 & \vdots & 3 \end{bmatrix}$$

row-reduction method The process of performing elementary row operations on an augmented matrix to transform the matrix to reduced row echelon form.

método de reducción por filas Proceso por el cual se realizan operaciones elementales de filas en una matriz aumentada para transformar la matriz en una forma reducida de filas escalonadas.

$$\begin{bmatrix} 2 & 0 & \vdots & -2 \\ 0 & 1 & \vdots & 3 \end{bmatrix} = \begin{bmatrix} \frac{1}{2}(2) & \frac{1}{2}(0) & \vdots & \frac{1}{2}(-2) \\ 0 & 1 & \vdots & 3 \end{bmatrix}$$
$$= \begin{bmatrix} 1 & 0 & \vdots & -1 \\ 0 & 1 & \vdots & 3 \end{bmatrix}$$

S

ENGLISH	SPANISH	EXAMPLES
sample A part of the population.	**muestra** Una parte de la población.	In a survey about the study habits of high school students, a sample is a survey of 100 students.
sample space The set of all possible outcomes of a probability experiment.	**espacio muestral** Conjunto de todos los resultados posibles en un experimento de probabilidades.	In the experiment of rolling a number cube, the sample space is 1, 2, 3, 4, 5, 6.
sampling distribution A distribution that shows how a particular statistic varies across all samples of n individuals from the same population.	**distribución de muestreo** Una distribución que muestra de qué manera una determinada estadística varía a lo largo de todas las muestras de n individuos de la misma población.	
second-degree equation in two variables An equation constructed by adding terms in two variables with powers no higher than 2.	**ecuación de segundo grado en dos variables** Ecuación compuesta por la suma de términos en dos variables con potencias no mayores a 2.	$ax^2 + by^2 + cx + dy + e = 0$

second differences Differences between first differences of a function.

segundas diferencias Diferencias entre las primeras diferencias de una función.

x	0	1	2	3
y	1	4	9	16

first differences   +3   +5   +7
second differences   +2   +2

ENGLISH	SPANISH	EXAMPLES
self-selected sample A sample in which members volunteer to participate.	**muestra de voluntarios** Muestra en la que los miembros se ofrecen voluntariamente para participar.	
sequence A list of numbers that often form a pattern.	**sucesión** Lista de números que generalmente forman un patrón.	1, 2, 4, 8, 16, ...

ENGLISH	SPANISH	EXAMPLES
series The indicated sum of the terms of a sequence.	**serie** Suma indicada de los términos de una sucesión.	$1 + 2 + 4 + 8 + 16 + \dots$
set A collection of items called elements.	**conjunto** Grupo de componentes denominados elementos.	$\{1, 2, 3\}$
set-builder notation A notation for a set that uses a rule to describe the properties of the elements of the set.	**notación de conjuntos** Notación para un conjunto que se vale de una regla para describir las propiedades de los elementos del conjunto.	$\{x \mid x > 3\}$ read, "The set of all x such that x is greater than 3."
simple event An event consisting of only one outcome.	**suceso simple** Suceso que contiene sólo un resultado.	In the experiment of rolling a number cube, the event consisting of the outcome 3 is a simple event.
simulation A model of an experiment, often one that would be too difficult or time-consuming to actually perform.	**simulación** Modelo de un experimento; generalmente se recurre a la simulación cuando realizar dicho experimento sería demasiado difícil o llevaría mucho tiempo.	A random number generator is used to simulate the roll of a number cube.
sine In a right triangle, the ratio of the length of the side opposite $\angle A$ to the length of the hypotenuse.	**seno** En un triángulo rectángulo, razón entre la longitud del cateto opuesto a $\angle A$ y la longitud de la hipotenusa.	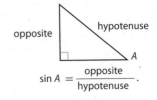 $\sin A = \dfrac{\text{opposite}}{\text{hypotenuse}}.$
skewed distribution A distribution that is mounded but not symmetric because one "tail" is much longer than the other.	**distribución sesgada** Una distribución que está elevada pero no es simétrica porque una de las "colas" es mucho más larga que la otra.	
square-root function A function whose rule contains a variable under a square-root sign.	**función de raíz cuadrada** Función cuya regla contiene una variable bajo un signo de raíz cuadrada.	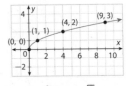 $f(x) = \sqrt{x}$
standard deviation A measure of dispersion of a data set. The standard deviation σ is the square root of the variance.	**desviación estándar** Medida de dispersión de un conjunto de datos. La desviación estándar σ es la raíz cuadrada de la varianza.	Data set: $\{6, 7, 7, 9, 11\}$ Mean: $\dfrac{6 + 7 + 7 + 9 + 11}{5} = 8$ Variance: $\frac{1}{5}(4 + 1 + 1 + 1 + 9) = 3.2$ Standard deviation: $\sigma = \sqrt{3.2} \approx 1.8$
standard error of the mean The standard deviation of the sampling distribution of the sample mean, denoted $\sigma_{\bar{x}}$.	**error estándar de la media** La desviación estándar de la distribución de muestreo de la media de la muestra, que se indica así: $\sigma_{\bar{x}}$.	

ENGLISH	SPANISH	EXAMPLES
standard error of the proportion The standard deviation of the sampling distribution of the sample proportion, denoted $\sigma_{\hat{p}}$.	**error estándar de la proporción** La desviación estándar de la distribución de muestreo de la proporción de la muestra, que se indica así: $\sigma_{\hat{p}}$.	
standard form of a polynomial A polynomial in one variable is written in standard form when the terms are in order from greatest degree to least degree.	**forma estándar de un polinomio** Un polinomio de una variable se expresa en forma estándar cuando los términos se ordenan de mayor a menor grado.	$3x^3 - 5x^2 + 6x - 7$
standard form of a quadratic equation $ax^2 + bx + c = 0$, where a, b, and c are real numbers and $a \neq 0$.	**forma estándar de una ecuación** cuadrática $ax^2 + bx + c = 0$, donde a, b y c son números reales y $a \neq 0$.	$2x^2 + 3x - 1 = 0$
standard normal distribution A normal distribution that has a mean of 0 and a standard deviation of 1.	**distribución normal estándar** Una distribución normal que tiene una media de 0 y una desviación estándar de 1.	
standard normal value A value that indicates how many standard deviations above or below the mean a particular value falls, given by the formula $z = \frac{x - \mu}{\sigma}$, where z is the standard normal value, x is the given value, μ is the mean, and σ is the standard deviation of a standard normal distribution.	**valor normal estándar** Valor que indica a cuántas desviaciones estándar por encima o por debajo de la media se encuentra un determinado valor, dado por la fórmula $z = \frac{x - \mu}{\sigma}$, donde z es el valor normal estándar, x es el valor dado, μ es la media y σ es la desviación estándar de una distribución normal estándar.	
standard position An angle in standard position has its vertex at the origin and its initial side on the positive x-axis.	**osición estándar** Ángulo cuyo vértice se encuentra en el origen y cuyo lado inicial se encuentra sobre el eje x.	
statistic A number that describes a sample.	**estadística** Número que describe una muestra.	
statistical significance A determination that the likelihood that an experimental result occurred by chance is so low that a conclusion in favor of rejecting the null hypothesis is justified.	**significación estadística** Una determinación de que la probabilidad de que un resultado experimental ocurriera por azar es tan reducida que está justificada una conclusión a favor de rechazar la hipótesis nula.	
step function A piecewise function that is constant over each interval in its domain.	**función escalón** Función a trozos que es constante en cada intervalo en su dominio.	

Glossary/Glosario

Glossary/Glosario

Glossary/Glosario

stretch A transformation that pulls the points of a graph horizontally away from the y–axis or vertically away from the x–axis.

estiramiento Transformación que desplaza los puntos de una gráfica en forma horizontal alejándolos del eje y o en forma vertical alejándolos del eje x.

---

summation notation A method of notating the sum of a series using the Greek letter $\sum$ (capital *sigma*).

notación de sumatoria Método de notación de la suma de una serie que utiliza la letra griega $\sum$ (SIGMA mayúscula).

$$\sum_{n=1}^{5} 3k = 3 + 6 + 9 + 12 + 15 = 45$$

---

survey A data collection tool that uses questions to measure characteristics of interest about a population using a sample selected from the population.

encuesta Una herramienta para recopilar datos que usa preguntas para medir las características de interés sobre una población mediante una muestra seleccionada de entre la población.

---

synthetic division A shorthand method of dividing by a linear binomial of the form $(x - a)$ by writing only the coefficients of the polynomials.

división sintética Método abreviado de división que consiste en dividir por un binomio lineal del tipo $(x - a)$ escribiendo sólo los coeficientes de los polinomios.

$$(x^3 - 7x + 6) \div (x - 2)$$

$$\begin{array}{r|rrrr} 2 & 1 & 0 & -7 & 6 \\ & & 2 & 4 & 6 \\ \hline & 1 & 2 & -3 & \underline{0} \end{array}$$

$$(x^3 - 7x + 6) \div (x - 2) = x^2 + 2x - 3$$

---

synthetic substitution The process of using synthetic division to evaluate a polynomial $p(x)$ when $x = c$.

sustitución sintética Proceso que consiste en usar la división sintética para evaluar un polinomio $p(x)$ cuando $x = c$.

---

system of equations A set of two or more equations that have two or more variables.

sistema de ecuaciones Conjunto de dos o más ecuaciones que contienen dos o más variables.

$$\begin{cases} 2x + 3y = -1 \\ x^2 = 4 \end{cases}$$

---

system of linear inequalities A system of inequalities in two or more variables in which all of the inequalities are linear.

sistema de desigualdades lineales Sistema de desigualdades en dos o más variables en el que todas las desigualdades son lineales.

$$\begin{cases} 2x + 3y \geq -1 \\ x - 3y < 4 \end{cases}$$

T

term of a sequence An element or number in the sequence.

término de una sucesión Elemento o número de una sucesión.

5 is the third term in the sequence 1, 3, 5, 7, ...

---

terminal side For an angle in standard position, the ray that is rotated relative to the positive x–axis.

lado terminal Dado un ángulo en una posición estándar, el rayo que rota en relación con el eje positivo x.

ENGLISH	SPANISH	EXAMPLES
theoretical probability The ratio of the number of equally likely outcomes in an event to the total number of possible outcomes.	**probabilidad teórica** Razón entre el número de resultados igualmente probables de un suceso y el número total de resultados posibles.	The theoretical probability of rolling an odd number on a number cube is $\frac{3}{6} = \frac{1}{2}$.
three-dimensional coordinate system A space that is divided into eight regions by an x–axis, a y–axis, and a z-axis. The locations, or coordinates, of points are given by ordered triples.	**sistema de coordenadas tridimensional** Espacio dividido en ocho regiones por un eje x, un eje y y un eje z. Las ubicaciones, o coordenadas, de los puntos son dadas por tripletas ordenadas.	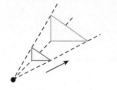
transformation A change in the position, size, or shape of a figure or graph.	**transformación** Cambio en la posición, tamaño o forma de una figura o gráfica.	
translation A transformation that shifts or slides every point of a figure or graph the same distance in the same direction.	**traslación** Transformación en la que todos los puntos de una figura se mueven la misma distancia en la misma dirección.	
trial In probability, a single repetition or observation of an experiment.	**prueba** En probabilidad, una sola repetición u observación de un experimento.	In the experiment of rolling a number cube, each roll is one trial.
trigonometric function A function whose rule is given by a trigonometric ratio.	**función trigonométrica** Función cuya regla es dada por una razón trigonométrica.	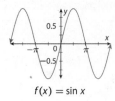 $f(x) = \sin x$
trigonometric ratio Ratio of the lengths of two sides of a right triangle.	**razón trigonométrica** Razón entre dos lados de un triángulo rectángulo.	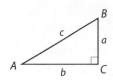 $\sin A = \frac{a}{c}$, $\cos A = \frac{b}{c}$, $\tan A = \frac{a}{b}$
trigonometry The study of the measurement of triangles and of trigonometric functions and their applications.	**trigonometría** Estudio de la medición de los triángulos y de las funciones trigonométricas y sus aplicaciones.	
trinomial A polynomial with three terms.	**trinomio** Polinomio con tres términos.	$4x^2 + 3xy - 5y^2$

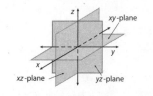

Glossary/Glosario

Glossary/Glosario

ENGLISH	SPANISH	EXAMPLES

turning point A point on the graph of a function that corresponds to a local maximum (or minimum) where the graph changes from increasing to decreasing (or vice versa).

punto de inflexión Punto de la gráfica de una función que corresponde a un máximo (o mínimo) local donde la gráfica pasa de ser creciente a decreciente (o viceversa).

U

uniform distribution A distribution that is basically level, forming a shape that looks like a rectangle.

distribución uniforme Una distribución que es básicamente llana, formando una figura similar a un rectángulo.

unit circle A circle with a radius of 1, centered at the origin.

círculo unitario Círculo con un radio de 1, centrado en el origen.

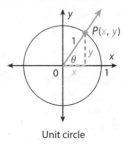

Unit circle

V

variance The average of squared differences from the mean. The square root of the variance is called the *standard deviation*.

varianza Promedio de las diferencias cuadráticas en relación con la media. La raíz cuadrada de la varianza se denomina *desviación estándar*.

Data set: is {6, 7, 7, 9, 11}

Mean: $\dfrac{6 + 7 + 7 + 9 + 11}{5} = 8$

Variance: $\frac{1}{5}(4 + 1 + 1 + 1 + 9) = 3.2$

vertex form of a quadratic function A quadratic function written in the form $f(x) = a(x - h)^2 + k$, where a, h, and k are constants and (h, k) is the vertex.

forma en vértice de una función cuadrática Una función cuadrática expresada en la forma $f(x) = a(x - h)^2 + k$, donde a, h y k son constantes y (h, k) es el vértice.

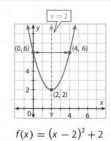

$f(x) = (x - 2)^2 + 2$

vertex of an absolute-value graph The point where the axis of symmetry intersects the graph.

vértice de una gráfica de valor absoluto Punto donde en el eje de simetría interseca la gráfica.

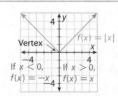

vertex of a parabola The highest or lowest point on the parabola.

vértice de una parábola Punto más alto o más bajo de una parábola.

Z

z-axis The third axis in a three-dimensional coordinate system.

eje z Tercer eje en un sistema de coordenadas tridimensional.

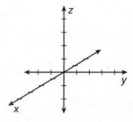

z-score A standardized data value from a normal distribution with mean μ and standard deviation σ found by using the formula $z = \frac{x-\mu}{\sigma}$ where x is the original data value.

puntaje z Un valor de datos estandarizado de una distribución normal con una media μ y una desviación estándar σ que se halla usando la fórmula $z = \frac{x-\mu}{\sigma}$, donde x es el valor de datos original.

zero of a function For the function f, any number x such that $f(x) = 0$.

cero de una función Dada la función f, todo número x tal que $f(x) = 0$.

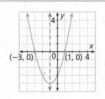

The zeros of $f(x) = x^2 + 2x - 3$ are -3 and 1.

Glossary/Glosario

Index

Index locator numbers are in Module. Lesson form. For example, 2.1 indicates Module 2, Lesson 1 as listed in the Table of Contents.

Index

Index

Table of Measures

LENGTH

1 inch = 2.54 centimeters

1 meter = 39.37 inches

1 mile = 5,280 feet

1 mile = 1760 yards

1 mile = 1.609 kilometers

1 kilometer = 0.62 mile

MASS/WEIGHT

1 pound = 16 ounces

1 pound = 0.454 kilograms

1 kilogram = 2.2 pounds

1 ton = 2000 pounds

CAPACITY

1 cup = 8 fluid ounces

1 pint = 2 cups

1 quart = 2 pints

1 gallon = 4 quarts

1 gallon = 3.785 liters

1 liter = 0.264 gallons

1 liter = 1000 cubic centimeters

Symbols

$\neq$	is not equal to	π	pi: (about 3.14)
$\approx$	is approximately equal to	$\perp$	is perpendicular to
10^2	ten squared; ten to the second power	$\parallel$	is parallel to
$2.\overline{6}$	repeating decimal 2.66666...	$\overleftrightarrow{AB}$	line AB
$|-4|$	the absolute value of negative 4	$\overrightarrow{AB}$	ray AB
$\sqrt{\ }$	square root	$\overline{AB}$	line segment AB
		$m\angle A$	measure of $\angle A$

Formulas

Triangle	$A = \frac{1}{2}bh$	Pythagorean Theorem	$a^2 + b^2 = c^2$
Parallelogram	$A = bh$	Quadratic Formula	$x = \dfrac{-b \pm \sqrt{b^2 - 4ac}}{2a}$
Circle	$A = \pi r^2$	Arithmetic Sequence	$a_n = a_1 + (n - 1)d$
Circle	$C = \pi d$ or $C = 2\pi r$	Geometric Sequence	$a_n = a_1 r^{n-1}$
General Prisms	$V = Bh$	Geometric Series	$S_n = \dfrac{a_1 - a_1 r^n}{1 - r}$ where $r \neq 1$
Cylinder	$V = \pi r^2 h$	Radians	$1 \ radian = \frac{180}{\pi} \ degrees$
Sphere	$V = \frac{4}{3}\pi r^3$	Degrees	$1 \ degree = \frac{\pi}{180} \ radians$
Cone	$V = \frac{1}{3}\pi r^2 h$	Exponential Growth/Decay	$A = A_0 \, e^{k(t - t_0)} + B_0$
Pyramid	$V = \frac{1}{3}Bh$		